Ethical Issues in Engineering

D1401561

DEBORAH G. JOHNSON

Rensselaer Polytechnic Institute

 PRENTICE HALL,   Englewood Cliffs, New Jersey   07632

Library of Congress Cataloging-in-Publication Data

Johnson, Deborah G. [date]
    Ethical issues in engineering / Deborah G. Johnson.
        p.   cm.
    Includes bibliographical references.
    ISBN 0-13-290578-7
    1. Engineering ethics.   2. Engineers.   I. Title.
TA157.J58   1991
174'.962—dc20   90–30973
                                                              CIP

Editorial/production supervision
        and interior design: Louise B. Capuano
Cover design: Patricia Kelly
Pre-press buyer: Herb Klein
Manufacturing buyer: Dave Dickey

For Sam, my partner in many of life's adventures

 © 1991 by Prentice-Hall, Inc.
A Division of Simon & Schuster
Englewood Cliffs, New Jersey 07632

Printed in the United States of America

10   9   8   7   6   5   4   3   2   1

ISBN 0-13-290578-7

Prentice-Hall International (UK) Limited, *London*
Prentice-Hall of Australia Pty. Limited, *Sydney*
Prentice-Hall Canada Inc., *Toronto*
Prentice-Hall Hispanoamericana, S.A., *Mexico*
Prentice-Hall of India Private Limited, *New Delhi*
Prentice-Hall of Japan, Inc., *Tokyo*
Simon & Schuster Asia Pte. Ltd., *Singapore*
Editora Prentice-Hall do Brasil, Ltda., *Rio de Janeiro*

Contents

C.   **The Corporate Context**

3   The Role of Professional Codes of Ethics   93

4   The Engineer's Responsibilities to Society   155

Preface

When I first came to Rensselaer in 1977, Robert J. Baum and Albert Flores were directing the National Project on Philosophy and Engineering Ethics, funded by the National Endowment for the Humanities (NEH). I watched this project from a distance, and became involved only indirectly when a year or so later I became an associate editor of the *Business & Professional Ethics Newsletter*. A few years later, as co-editor of the *Business & Professional Ethics Journal*, I reviewed several of the articles that had been initially developed as part of that project. (Several of those articles are included in this book.) Much has happened since those years, but I owe a debt to Robert J. Baum and Albert Flores, as well as to NEH, for starting me out on the path that has led to this anthology.

In 1982 I moved from the Department of Philosophy to the Department of Science and Technology Studies at Rensselaer and, among other things, took over responsibility for teaching a course on engineering ethics. I was surprised at how little material was available for teaching what were fascinating ethical issues of great importance to my students and the profession of engineering. During the next few years, several helpful books appeared, especially Michael W. Martin and Roland Schinzinger's *Ethics in Engineering* (New York: McGraw-Hill Book Company, 1983) and Stephen H. Unger's *Controlling Technology: Ethics and the Responsible Engineer* (New York: Holt, Rinehart and Winston, 1982). Both of these books were valuable to me, but neither quite did what I wanted to do in the classroom. I kept gathering articles that made various points that I wanted to make, and soon it occurred to me that they might all be put together in an anthology.

I received a Paul Beer Trust Minigrant Award for the 1987–88 academic year, which allowed me to make a concerted effort to put the anthology together and write the chapter introductions.

Although I thought at first that I could produce an anthology quickly and easily, I soon found more and more that might be done to make it better. Hence, this book was in process for several years. During those years, many people gave me generous and useful comments. In addition to those who reviewed the book for Prentice Hall, I am grateful to Albert Flores, Vivian Weil, and Rachelle Hollander for their suggestions.

Students who took my course on engineering ethics at Rensselaer have been a most invaluable resource. They were boldly honest in telling me which readings they could relate to best, which they could not understand, which order would be best, and so forth. I was inspired by their response to the material and can safely say that this book would not have been possible without their guidance.

I am fortunate in several ways that contribute immeasurably to my work. I have wonderful colleagues in the Department of Science and Technology at Rensselaer. They continue to create, and re-create, an intellectually rich and exciting environment in which to write and teach. I especially appreciate the support of my department chair and friend, Shirley Gorenstein.

Sam Johnson helped out in this project, as in others, in ways that only he knows. Jesse and Rose Johnson kept me smiling.

D.G.J.

1

Introduction

Falsifying Data

Jay's boss is an acknowledged expert in the field of catalysis. Jay is the leader of a group that has been charged with developing a new catalyst system and the search has narrowed to two possibilities, Catalyst A and Catalyst B.

The boss is certain that the best choice is A, but he directs that tests be run on both, "just for the record." Owing to inexperienced help, the tests take longer than expected, and the results show that B is the preferred material. The engineers question the validity of the tests, but because of the project's timetable, there is no time to repeat the series. So the boss directs Jay to work the math backwards and come up with phony data to substantiate the choice of Catalyst A, a choice that all the engineers in the group, including Jay, fully agree with. Jay writes the report.

In the case above, Jay has written the report to suit his boss, and the company has gone ahead with an ambitious commercialization program for Catalyst A. Jay has been put in charge of the pilot plant where development work is being done on the project. To allay his doubts, he personally runs some clandestine tests on the two catalysts. To his astonishment and dismay, the tests determine that while Catalyst A works better under most conditions (as everyone had expected), at the operating conditions specified in the firm's process design, Catalyst B is indeed considerably superior.

What, if anything, should Jay do now?

Reprinted from Philip M. Kohn and Roy V. Hughson, "Perplexing Problems in Engineering Ethics," Chemical Engineering, *May 5, 1980, pp. 96–107, with permission.*

Conflict of Interest

A government employee has a responsible position with a government engineering bureau. The government bureau is to let an engineering design contract in the near future to one of three firms whichever appears to be most capable of performing the work. At a social gathering one night, the government employee is approached by the head of one of the firms and told that if his firm receives the contract, the government employee could come to work for him at a considerable increase in salary. The government employee has been thinking of leaving government service because the office location is a long commuting distance from his home. He could leave and withdraw his retirement pay and purchase a small orchard which he had been looking at for several months. The orchard is only a short distance from the offices of the consulting firm, located in a suburban area.

The government employee makes no commitment to the head of the consulting firm but keeps thinking about the advantages of the change in employment. A couple of weeks later he is in a meeting with the government engineers responsible for the decision on which firm to select for the design work. The choice is narrowed down to two firms, one of which is the firm that made the covert approach. No decision is reached that day. They are all told to study the two proposals and then reach a decision within three days. The government engineer is sure he can swing the decision to the firm which approached him by using mild persuasion on one or two members of the selection committee. He feels that both firms are capable of performing the design; in fact, it may be true that the firm from which he received the offer was in a slightly superior position.

He wonders if he should make a contact before the selection committee meets to see that the offer still holds and, if so, to have a firm commitment on salary and position within the company and to be sure the company would wait six months so that no one would be suspicious.

What would you do if you were the government engineer?

Reprinted from D. Allan Firmage, Modern Engineering Practice: Ethical Professional and Legal Aspects *(New York: Garland STPM Press, 1980), pp. 64–65, with permission.*

Gifts to Foreign Officials

Richard Roe, P.E., is president and chief executive officer of an engineering firm which has done overseas assignments in various parts of the world. The firm is negotiating for a contract in a foreign country in which it has not worked previously. Roe is advised by a high-ranking government official of that country that it is established practice for those awarded contracts to make personal gifts to the government officials who are authorized to award the contracts, and that such practice is legal in that country. Roe is further advised that while the condition is not to be included in the contract, his failure to make the gifts will result in no further work being awarded to the firm and to expect poor cooperation in performing the first contract. He is further told that other firms have adhered to the local practice in regard to such gifts.

Would it be ethical for Roe to accept the contract and make the gifts as described?

Reprinted from the National Society of Professional Engineers, Opinions of the Board of Ethical Review, *Case No. 76-6 (Washington, D.C.: National Society of Professional Engineers, 1981), V, 11, with permission.*

INTRODUCTION

As the role of technology in our society has become more important, so has the role of engineers. In the preceding scenarios we see just a few of the important positions that engineers hold in our society. They serve as educators, consultants, managers, public servants, designers, producers, and sellers. In each of these roles, engineers may find themselves facing tough ethical choices, choices in which their integrity is pitted against their personal security, and their employer's interests are in conflict with social good. With these choices engineers make statements about who they are and the nature of engineering.

The twentieth century is often characterized as an era of rapid technological growth. Similarly, contemporary American society is often called "a highly technological society." Although it is probably true to say that throughout the ages, societies have always been affected by the technologies they have adopted, contemporary American society seems unique because of the complexity of its technological systems, and the speed at which we create new and better technologies. Most analysis of technology and its impact on our society focuses on economic and political impacts, but engineers and the system of engineering play a critical role in how technologies are developed and ultimately used in our society. This text focuses directly on engineers and engineering.

Critics have raised serious questions about the impact of technology on our society, and, in so doing, have raised questions about the role of engineers and engineering in creating risky technologies that have unforeseen and unforeseeable consequences. It is not far-fetched to say that the bottom line in engineering ethics is the idea that engineering ought to be aimed at the good of humanity, and that individual engineers ought to be using their skills to improve the lot of humanity. Yet recently we have been confronted with several technological disasters—the Challenger disaster, Bhopal, O-zone depletion—and these raise questions about what it is that engineers are, and should be, doing. One cannot help but ask: Is it good to be an engineer? What can engineers do to make the world a better place? Is something wrong with the system of engineering in our society?

The question at the heart of this anthology is: What are the social responsibilities of engineers? A second and more practical question is: How can we get engineers to behave in socially responsible ways? These are not easy questions to answer, and we will look at many different issues in trying to answer them. In the process, our attention will be focused in two rather different ways: We will focus on individuals and look at what individual engineers can and should do when confronted with tough ethical choices; and we will focus on engineering as a system (a set of practices created by laws, rules, and conventions) that encourages and constrains various kinds of behavior. The system includes engineering education, professional societies, the culture of corporations, laws regulating the work of engineers, and so forth. The readings in this anthology have been selected to ensure that both approaches are represented—that is, the problem(s) focused on in each chapter or section are considered both as they arise for individual engineers, and in terms of the relevant rules or practices constituting the profession.

The subject of engineering ethics is rarely discussed during the education of engineers. Yet many engineers experience ethical dilemmas while practicing engineering. This anthology of readings was assembled with the idea that engineers will be better able to deal with ethical questions that arise in their practice if they have an opportunity to reflect on these issues long before they face them, and if they have an opportunity to hear what others faced with similar situations have thought and done.

Organization of the Book

Most of the chapters in this anthology begin with scenarios describing situations involving an engineer and requiring that the engineer make a decision. Although these may give the false impression that engineering ethics is all a matter of personal choice, they are included here as the most concrete way to raise complicated and often systemic issues. The hope here is that the scenarios will stimulate the reader's interests and continue to serve as a focus throughout the chapter.

The scenarios are followed by chapter introductions that discuss the issues more abstractly and introduce the readings. The readings are meant to be the substance of the book and are intended to provide both a variety of perspectives on each issue, and deeper and more theoretical analyses than might occur simply from a discussion of the scenarios alone.

Some will be surprised at the lack of readings devoted specifically to ethics or ethical theory. Indeed, some grounding in ethical theory will be useful to the reader. The readings have been selected, however, for accessibility without that background. Those who desire more background reading on ethics or ethical theory should supplement this book with a short introductory text on ethics.

Note on Gender-Neutral Language

In selecting articles and chapters of books to be included in this anthology, an effort was made to choose pieces with gender-neutral language. I regret that this was not always possible.

Readings in Chapter 1

The three readings gathered in this first chapter are intended to familiarize the reader quickly with real cases that have given rise to contemporary concerns about engineering ethics. The first two readings are by an engineer and a computer scientist, so it should be clear that the issues are not fanciful. They are of concern to those who are in the business of developing technology.

The fact that these readings come first is not meant to give the reader a negative view of engineering, though one might get that impression because all three pieces describe problems created by engineering endeavors. Instead, these readings are offered to "set the scene" for the rest of the book as a problem that needs to be addressed.

The first two readings are personal statements by Roger Boisjoly and David Parnas. Each of their accounts serves as a dramatic illustration of the difficult issues that sometimes face engineers and scientists who are involved in the creation of technologies. They illustrate the personal turmoil and struggle that engineers in important roles may feel about the work they do.

The final reading in this chapter is by John Ladd, a philosopher. He surveys the ethical issues in engineering, most of which will be explored in detail in the next chapters. Ladd provides a realistic account of what moral philosophy can and cannot do by way of helping to resolve the ethical issues in engineering.

1 The Challenger Disaster: Moral Responsibility and the Working Engineer

Roger M. Boisjoly

Distinguished faculty of MIT, students, ladies and gentlemen. I am very honored to be invited to speak to you today [January 7, 1987]. I will present a background summary of important events from January 1985 through the evening before the Challenger launch then continue with the post-disaster chronology of my working relationship with Morton Thiokol management.

The significance of January 1985 as the starting point results from the observations made during the post flight hardware inspection of Flight 51C. During this inspection I found evidence that hot combustion gases had compromised the primary seals on two field joints. My concern heightened as a result of the large amount of blackened grease I observed between the two seals. Subsequent to reporting the findings to my superiors, I was asked to proceed to the Marshall Space Flight Center (MSFC) in Huntsville, Alabama to brief them with a preliminary viewgraph presentation which included my observations and an explanation of the scenarios that cause the seal erosion and hot gas blow-by.

Morton Thiokol was then asked to prepare a detailed presentation as part of the Flight Readiness Review (FRR) for Flight 51E which was scheduled for launch in April 1985. This presentation was given in February at three successively higher-level review boards with refinements in contents made at each level. I presented my belief that the lower than usual launch temperature was responsible for such a large witness of hot gas blow-by, but NASA management insisted that this position be softened for the final review board. The final flight readiness assessment chart read as follows:

Conclusions:
STS-51C consistent with erosion data base

Low temperature enhanced probability of blow-by—
STS-51C experienced worst case temperature change in Florida history
STS-51E could exhibit same behavior
Condition is acceptable
STS-51E field joints are acceptable for flight

These conclusions were accepted and the flight was certified ready for launch.

Later, I met with Arnie Thompson to discuss the blow-by scenario and the affect of cold temperature on O-ring resiliency which is the ability of the seal to restore itself to a round shape when the squeeze on the seal is removed. Arnie proposed that subscale lab tests be conducted which would provide us with assessment data. The resiliency testing was performed in March and showed that low temperature was a problem. The results indicated that the seals would lift off their sealing surfaces for several seconds at 75 degrees farenheit and in excess of 10 minutes at 50 degrees farenheit. This data was discussed with Morton Thiokol engineering management but was thought to be too sensitive by them to release.

Another post flight inspection occurred in June 1985 at Morton Thiokol in Utah. This time a nozzle joint from Flight 51B, which flew on April 29, 1985, was found to have a primary seal eroded in three places over a 1.3 inch length up to a maximum depth of 0.120 inches and the secondary seal in the same joint was eroded 0.032 inches. It was postulated that this primary seal had never sealed during the full two minutes of flight.

My former concerns now escalated because if this same scenario happened in a field joint, the secondary seal could also be compromised especially during a low temperature launch. A Flight Readiness Review presentation was prepared for Flight 51F which was scheduled for launch on July 29, 1985. The presentation was given to NASA at MSFC on July 1, 1985 with an additional presentation on the overall status of the booster seal given the next day. The preliminary results of the O-ring resiliency testing in March were presented for the first time during this meeting. All O-ring test samples were 0.280 inch diameter and compressed to 0.040 inches with a decompression distance of 0.030 inches at a 2 inch per minute rate as compared with a flight rate of approximately 3.2 inches per minute. The results showed that the seals did not lose contact at 100 degrees farenheit; lost contact for 2.4 seconds at 75 degrees and lost contact in excess of 10 minutes at 50 degrees. Test results also indicated that a 0.295 inch diameter seal lost contact for 2 to 3 seconds at 50 degrees which meant that the 0.295 inch diameter seal performance at 50 degrees was similar to the performance of a 0.28 inch diameter seal at 75 degrees. Everyone on the program for the first time was now aware of the influence of low temperature on the joint seals.

My concern increased once again due to lack of attention being given to this problem. My notebook entry on August 15, 1985 reads as follows: "An attempt to form the team (referring to the Solid Rocket Motor seal erosion team) was made on 19 July 1985. This attempt virtually failed and resulted in my writing memo 2870:FY86:073. This memo finally got some response and a team was formed officially. The first meeting was held on August 15, 1985 at 2:30 pm." The memo referred to is the one I read to the Presidential Commission on February 25, 1986, which was written to the vice president of engineering at Morton Thiokol on July 31, 1985. The memo ended by saying, "It is my honest and very real fear that if we do not take immediate action to dedicate a team to solve the problem, with the field joint having the number one priority, then we stand in jeopardy of losing a flight along with all the launch pad and facilities."

During this July period, NASA headquarters in Washington D.C. asked Morton Thiokol to prepare a presentation on the problems with all the booster seals. The presentation was prepared by MSFC on August 19, 1985 with Morton Thiokol personnel in attendance.

Morton Thiokol was then asked by MSFC in September to send a representative to the SAE conference in October to discuss the seals and solicit help from the experts. I prepared and presented a six page overview of the joints and the seal configuration to approximately 130 technical experts on October 7, 1985. However, I was given strict instructions, which came from NASA, not to express the critical urgency of fixing the joint but to only emphasize the joint improvement aspect during my presentation. After my presentation I asked for help in the form of design improvement suggestions but no one said a word so Bob Ebeling and I spent the remainder of the convention time meeting with seal vendors whom we had previously contacted for help.

The Seal Task Team was frustrated from the beginning from lack of management support to provide the resources necessary for us to accomplish our task. Accordingly, I wrote a series of very damning activity reports in which I left no room for error about how I felt concerning the lack of management support. Unfortunately, I never received any comments back and never knew if they had been incorporated into reports up through the management structure.

The evening meeting of January 27, 1986 was the concluding event preceding the launch disaster. The major activity that day focused upon the predicted 18 degrees farenheit overnight temperature and meeting with engineering management to per-suade them not to launch. The day concluded with the hurried preparation of fourteen viewgraphs which detailed our concerns about launching at such a low temperature. The teleconference with KSC (Kennedy Space Center) and MSFC started with a history of O-ring damage in field joints. Data was presented showing a major concern with seal resiliency and the change to the sealing timing function and the criticality of this on the ability to seal. I was asked several times during my portion of the presen-tation to quantify my concerns but I said I could not since the only data I had was what I had presented and that I had been trying to get more data since last October. At this comment, the general manager of Morton Thiokol gave me a scolding look as if to say, "Why are you telling that to them?" The presentation ended with the recommendation not to launch below 53 degrees which was not well received by NASA. The Vice President of Space Booster Programs, Joe Kilminster, was then asked by NASA for his launch decision. He said he did not recommend launching based upon the engi-neering position just presented. Then Larry Mulloy of NASA who was at KSC asked George Hardy of NASA who was at MSFC for his launch decision. George responded that he was appalled at Thiokol's recommendation but said he would not launch over the contractor's objection. Then Larry Mulloy spent some time giving his interpreta-tion of the data with his conclusion that the data presented was inconclusive.

Just as he finished his conclusion, Joe Kilminster asked for a five minute off-line caucus to re-evaluate the data and as soon as the mute button was pushed our general manager, Jerry Mason, said in a soft voice "We have to make a management decision." I became furious when I heard this because I knew that an attempt would be made by management to reverse our recommendation not to launch.

Some discussion had started between the managers when Arnie Thompson moved from his position down the table to a position in front of the managers and once again tried to explain our position by sketching the joint and discussing the problem with the seals at low temperature. Arnie stopped when he saw the unfriendly look in Mason's eyes and also realized that no one was listening to him. I then grabbed the photographic evidence showing the hot gas blow-by and placed it on the table and, somewhat angered, admonished them to look and not ignore what the photos were telling us, namely, that low temperature indeed caused more hot gas blow-by in the joints. I too received the same cold stares as Arnie with looks as if to say "Go away and don't bother us with the facts." At that moment I felt totally helpless and that further argument was fruitless so I, too, stopped pressing my case.

What followed made me both sad and angry. The managers were struggling to make a pro-launch list of supporting data but unfortunately for them the data actually supported a decision not to launch. During the closed manager's discussion, Jerry Mason asked in a low voice if he was the only one who wanted to fly. The discussion continued, then Mason turned to Bob Lund, the vice-president of engineering, and told him to take off his engineering hat and put on his management hat. The decision to launch resulted from the yes vote of only the four senior executives since the rest of us were excluded from both the final decision and the vote poll. The telecon resumed and Joe Kilminster read the launch support rationale from a handwritten list and recommended that the launch proceed. NASA promptly accepted the recommendation to launch without any probing discussion and asked Joe to send a signed copy of the chart.

The change in decision so upset me that I do not remember Stanley Reinhartz of NASA asking if anyone had anything else to say over the telecon. The telecon was then disconnected so I immediately left the room feeling badly defeated. I wrote the following entry in my notebook after returning to my office. "I sincerely hope that this launch does not result in a catastrophe. I personally do not agree with some of the statements made in Joe Kilminster's written summary stating that SRM-25 is okay to fly."

As it turned out I didn't agree with any of his statements after I had a chance to review a copy of the chart. A review of the chart will produce the following conclusions from anyone having normal powers of reason. The chart lists nine separate statements, seven of which are actually reasons against launch, while one is actually a neutral statement of engineering fact. The remaining statement concerning a factor of safety of three on soil erosion is not even applicable to the discussion which had ensued for over an hour. Therefore, Morton Thiokol senior management reversed a sound technical decision without one shred of supporting data and without any re-evaluation of the data they had promised when they requested the caucus.

The next morning I paused outside Arnie Thompson's office and told him and the manager of applied mechanics, who was my boss, that I hoped the launch was safe, but

I also hoped that when we inspected the booster joints we would find all the seals burned almost through the joint, then maybe we could get someone with authority to stand up and stop the flights until we fixed the joints.

It was approximately five minutes prior to launch as I was walking past the room used to view launches when Bob Ebeling stepped out to encourage me to enter and watch the launch. At first I refused but he finally persuaded me to watch the launch. The room was filled so I seated myself on the floor closest to the screen and leaned against Bob's legs as he was seated in a chair. The boosters ignited and as the vehicle cleared the tower, Bob whispered to me that we had just dodged a bullet. At approximately T + 60 seconds Bob told me that he had just completed a prayer of thanks to the Lord for a successful launch. Just 13 seconds later we both saw the horror of destruction as the vehicle exploded. We all sat in stunned silence for a short time then I got up and left the room and went directly to my office where I remained the rest of the day. Two of my seal task-team colleagues inquired at my office to see if I was okay but I was unable to speak to them and hold back my emotions so I just nodded yes to them and they left after a short silent stay.

Within a day of the launch one of my colleagues, after reviewing the video tape, told me that he thought he saw a plume of flame coming from one of the boosters as it exited the explosion. My first thought was that one of the joints had failed and I postulated several scenarios to fit the observed failure. A failure investigation team was formed at Morton Thiokol on January 31, 1986, which included Arnie Thompson and me. The team was immediately sent to MSFC in Huntsville, Alabama.

The following is a description of my post-disaster experiences with Morton Thiokol management. The first indication that there was a division between me and management came when I was informed on February 13th that a Presidential Commission hearing would be held the next day. I was waiting at the Huntsville Airport when the company jet landed and Bob Lund asked each person who was at the telecon if he wanted to testify. When he came to me he simply stated that he didn't need to ask me because he knew that I wanted to testify. I replied that he was absolutely correct in his assumption. Apparently Morton Thiokol management had plenty of notice concerning this meeting since they had the publications group prepare a formal set of viewgraphs for their version of the events leading to the launch decision, but they didn't inform me so I could make similar preparations. Meanwhile, I had approximately two hours total by myself and was struggling to organize a set of notes to aid me during my testimony. After the testimony there were obvious tense feelings between Morton Thiokol management and those who testified, namely, myself, Al McDonald and Arnie Thompson.

Approximately five days later at MSFC, two Commission members requested a closed interview session with Arnie Thompson, Joe Kilminster and me. During this meeting, I handed a packet of memos and activity reports to a Commission member and this upset our company attorney. I sensed quite clearly from this time on that I had not endeared myself with management since my memos would clarify the true circumstances leading to the disaster and would also counteract both NASA and Morton Thiokol management attempts to discredit our testimony up to this point. My senses proved quite accurate because Joe Kilminster had a heated discussion with Arnie and me in the presence of our company attorney after our meeting with the two Presidential Commission members. Joe strenuously objected to Arnie and me constantly correcting his technical version of what the data meant. Joe said we were welcome to express our opinions but that he also was entitled to express his. We agreed with him but said that we would continue to correct his version if his input was technically incorrect as it had been up to this point. We also expressed very clearly that we didn't give a hoot for his interpretation of the data. He became angry with us but we didn't let him intimidate us.

I suspect I fell into further disfavor with Morton Thiokol management after my February 25th testimony which was a public hearing open to the whole country. Again, management had prepared beautiful color graphic viewgraphs, while I struggled with my notes. However, this time management did not get the opportunity to speak from their viewgraphs but only to hand the written material to the Commission and answer their questions. During my testimony I rebutted our general manager's testimony concerning our supposed non-unanimous engineering position. My rebuttal was based on the fact that I remembered only Arnie and me as the principals involved in the continuing discussion during the whole telecon. Brian Russell and Bob Ebeling were the only other ones that spoke and they only said a few sentences. No one else said anything, either pro or con, so I therefore consider all those people as non-entities and it matters not what they may say after the fact since they did not have the conviction or the courage to speak during the telecon. Mason and others in management apparently talked to some of these people after the disaster who said that they supported the management decision to fly, and so Mason decided that he had received sufficient knowledge for him to state in testimony that the engineering position was not unanimous. I submit that this is an example of management's deceit and half truth at its best.

After the testimony on the 25th of February, we all gathered at our Washington, D.C., resident office where feelings were very tense once again. The feelings were so tense that someone in management suggested that the company jet take us back to Huntsville as soon as we gathered our belongings from the motel. Eventually cooler heads prevailed and we stayed overnight and took a commercial flight the next morning. Al McDonald then asked if he and I could stay and listen to NASA's testimony since they had heard ours and because Chairman Rogers had said that we would have the opportunity to rebut or clarify any testimony given. We were told in no uncertain terms that we would be leaving Washington and going back to work the next morning. Subsequent to this decision we found out that both Joe Kilminster and Jerry Mason stayed to hear NASA's testimony. Later that same evening management decided to send me back to Utah and keep Arnie at MSFC until the failure investigation was completed.

I was happy to return home because I was not pleased with the direction of the failure investigation. I had observed NASA management diligently attempting to find a condition other than low temperature which caused the disaster. This was being accomplished with the full knowledge and, I assume, approval of Morton Thiokol management who were extremely supportive of every NASA move.

In Utah I began to sense the first signs of isolation, but I didn't fully recognize the situation while it was happening to me. I continued to argue for full truthful disclosure while factions of Morton Thiokol and NASA management were fully content to tell only half truths about the history of the development and production of the solid rocket boosters.

Sometime in April I realized that from mid-March on I was being used only for public relations purposes so the company could say if asked, yes, Roger Boisjoly still works here and in fact he is the new seal coordinator for the re-design effort. Actually, I was being carefully isolated from NASA and the re-design effort with great subtlety by management while they were telling me of my great importance in contributing to the re-design. I was being asked to furnish technical design information for the new design which was sometimes changed without my knowledge and was being presented by someone else with no copies of the final version of the presentation given to me for feedback. I was in effect actually isolated from the main re-design effort. Previous to my testimony, I always prepared and presented my own material and often my supervision gave me total freedom because of the confidence that they had in my ability. During this same time period, Al McDonald was re-assigned and no longer had any people reporting to him.

Conditions kept deteriorating for us who had testified until we were called once again to testify before the Presidential Commission in closed session on May 2, 1986. On the evening of May 1st we met with the president of aerospace operations for Morton Thiokol, Ed Garrison, at our Washington, D.C., resident office. Mr. Garrison opened the meeting with a few general remarks about the upcoming session with the Commission the following day. He then addressed me and chastised me for airing the company's dirty laundry via my memos which I had given to the Commission. He also stated that Morton Thiokol had suffered enough as a result of public disclosure, but that we should continue to tell the truth, but we should consider the best way to state it before speaking. I quickly took exception to his remarks about me and said that I had simply tried to restore the truth in all the testimony and that I did not consider my actions as airing dirty laundry. Just then Bob Ebeling spoke up with support for my remarks but Garrison told him to stop and to quit telling him how to run the company.

We went into the session with the Commission the next day with conditions as tense as they had ever been and Chairman Rogers asked Al and I about our current job assignments. We answered him and he was visibly upset because we were being punished for our honesty in our testimony. The commission decided to release the closed session testimony and Morton Thiokol received tremendous criticism from the Congress, the Presidential Commission and the news media.

A few days later Al and I were invited back to Washington by the Presidential Commission to review and comment on the final SRM accident analysis team report which was submitted to them by MSFC. The Commission had somehow found out that neither Al or I had seen the final report version. I submitted 12 pages of comments on the report and then Al and I gave verbal testimony about the report to a group of four Commission members. I testified that the report findings were biased towards an attempt to downplay the affect of low temperature on the joint failure by trying to first focus blame on such things as assembly problems and other areas. The Commission agreed with my comments and thanked us for our willingness to review and comment on the report on such short notice.

Those of us who had been testifying now sensed a major division developing within the company as some of our colleagues perceived that our testimony was damaging the company, but we didn't agree with this assessment and decided to correct it by requesting a meeting with the three top executives who could do something about the company's internal strife.

A private meeting was held on May 16th with the CEO, the president of aerospace operations and the vice-president now heading the shuttle program. The meeting produced a very candid discussion from our side, but it was essentially one-sided with management telling us nothing. The CEO even made it sound like we were on probation and if we worked hard and proved ourselves during the re-design, then everything would be forgiven. His attitude was certainly consistent with his criticism of Al and me in his previous statements to *The Wall Street Journal*. I believe it was at this meeting that the CEO made the statement that the company was doing just fine until Al and I testified about our job re-assignments on May 2nd. He said that those statements caused the company more harm than all the previous releases up to that time.

Al McDonald and I were supposedly restored to our former positions after the company was scolded by some very angry U.S. Senators, but it was actually only a superficial restoration which the company skillfully reported by inference as a promotion for Al McDonald who was now heading the re-design effort while my interface with NASA was restored. Apparently, the press release was taken as Gospel by the news media because they all reported that Al was given a promotion and I was given my former job. Actually Al got his old job back without a promotion while some people who remained silent got promotions and the same people who wouldn't face up to the original bad joint design were directing the joint re-design effort. Simply put, the joint is being re-designed by top management with direction down to the working level engineer who is trying to engineer the details to make it work.

I have been ignored, chastised before my colleagues and criticized for not getting approval of my design proposals prior to presenting them to NASA in informal telecons. The best example is management's refusal to support the best design as the primary re-design candidate. The best design in my opinion, and others agreed, was submitted by Gray Tool Company of Houston, Texas, but it was simply carried as a back-up design in case the company's primary design fails to meet the testing requirements. I was the only one who responded to the Gray Tool design proposal and I fought hard to secure them a chance to present their design to our management, but the decision had already been made on the primary design, so Gray Tool has only a back-up position.

Al McDonald, Arnie Thompson, and I along with Morton Thiokol management were asked to testify at the House of Representatives Committee on Science and Technology hearing on June 17 and 18, 1986. The preparation and testimony for these hearings was almost more than I could withstand but fortunately I was on medication which allowed me to get through each day. Unfortunately, the medication also slowed me down, and I didn't realize it until I saw myself on video tape. My testimony on February 25th versus my testimony before the House Committee in June is from two different people. I now realize why one of Morton Thiokol's managers complimented me on my testimony after the first day of House hearings. Friends who have seen both video tapes have expressed similar comments.

Within a month after the House Committee testimony, I could no longer endure the hostile environment so I have been on extended sick leave since July 21, 1986. This is why my current detailed knowledge about the joint re-design is sketchy at best. I cannot comment further on any re-design effort, but I surely can state with certainty that all of you who are young aspiring engineers must prepare to leave this university with the knowledge and conviction that you have a professional and moral responsibility to yourselves and your fellow man to defend the truth and expose any questionable practice that may lead to an unsafe product. This is accomplished by diligent application of your learned skills and by continuing to seek after knowledge in your chosen field of employment so you can rise to the top of your field.

Don't just sit passively in meetings when you know in your heart that you can make a constructive contribution and also be prepared to share your design ideas and to compliment others for their ideas, especially when their idea is better and may even replace yours. This is the best way to cultivate colleague respect and friendship which always results in a positive long-term benefit for you, the company and its product line.

I wish the shuttle disaster had never happened, and since I cannot turn the clock back, I hope that if anything good can result from this tragedy, then I desire that all universities like this great one will recognize the importance of teaching ethical behavior by using actual case histories like this one so you are aware of what to expect when you commence your careers.

I have been asked by some if I would testify again if I knew in advance of the potential consequences to me and my career. My answer is always an immediate yes. I couldn't live with any self respect if I tailored my actions based upon potential personal consequences as a result of my honorable actions. As a result of this and other exposures to real case histories, I hope that your answer will also be yes if and when you are confronted with a similar decision.

I thank you again for inviting me to share my experience with you.

2 SDI: A Violation of Professional Responsibility

David Lorge Parnas

In May of 1985 I was asked by the Strategic Defense Initiative Organization, the group within the Office of the U.S. Secretary of Defense that is responsible for the "Star Wars" program, to serve on a $1000/day advisory panel, the SDIO Panel on Computing in Support of Battle Management. The panel was to make recommendations about a research and development program to solve the computational problems inherent in space-based defense systems.

Like President Reagan, I consider the use of nuclear weapons as a deterrent to be dangerous and immoral. If there is a way to make nuclear weapons "impotent and obsolete" and end the fear of such weapons, there is nothing I would rather work on. However, two months later I had resigned from the panel. I have since become an active opponent of the SDI. This article explains why I am opposed to the program.

My View of Professional Responsibility. My decision to resign from the panel was consistent with long-held views about the individual responsibility of a professional. I believe this responsibility goes beyond an obligation to satisfy the short-term demands of the immediate employer.

As a professional:

· I am responsible for my own actions and cannot rely on any external authority to make my decisions for me.
· I cannot ignore ethical and moral issues. I must devote some of my energy to deciding whether the task that I have been given is of benefit to society.
· I must make sure that I am solving the real problem, not simply providing short-term satisfaction to my supervisor.

Reprinted from *Abacus*, vol. 4, no. 2 (1987): 46–52, © Springer-Verlag, with permission.

Some have held that a professional is a "team player" and should never "blow the whistle" on his colleagues and employer. I disagree. As the Challenger incident demonstrates, such action is sometimes necessary. One's obligations as a professional precede other obligations. One must not enter into contracts that conflict with one's professional obligations.

My Views on Defense Work.   Many opponents of the SDI oppose all military development. I am not one of them. I have been a consultant to the Department of Defense and other components of the defense industry since 1971. I am considered an expert on the organization of large software systems, and I lead the U.S. Navy's Software Cost Reduction Project at the Naval Research Laboratory. Although I have friends who argue that "people of conscience" should not work on weapons, I consider it vital that people with a strong sense of social responsibility continue to work within the military/industrial complex. I do not want to see that power completely in the hands of people who are *not* conscious of social responsibility.

My own views on military work are close to those of Albert Einstein. Einstein, who called himself a militant pacifist, at one time held the view that scientists should refuse to contribute to arms development. Later in his life he concluded that to hold to a "no arms" policy would be to place the world at the mercy of its worst enemies. Each country has a right to be protected from those who use force, or the threat of force, to impose their will on others. Force can morally be used only against those persons who are themselves using force. Weapons development should be limited to weapons that are suitable for that use. Neither the present arms spiral nor nuclear weapons are consistent with Einstein's principles. One of our greatest scientists, he knew that international security requires progress in political education, not weapons technology.

SDI BACKGROUND

The Strategic Defense Initiative, popularly known as "Star Wars," was initiated by a 1983 presidential speech calling on scientists to free us from the fear of nuclear weapons. President Reagan directed the Pentagon to search for a way to make nuclear strategic missiles impotent and obsolete. In response, the SDIO has embarked upon a project to develop a network of satellites carrying sensors, weapons, and computers to detect intercontinental ballistic missiles (ICMBs) and intercept them before they can do much damage. In addition to sponsoring work on the basic technologies of sensors and weapons, SDI has funded a number of Phase I "architecture studies," each of which proposes a basic design for the system. The best of these have been selected, and the contractors are now proceeding to "Phase II," a more detailed design.

My Early Doubts.   As a scientist, I wondered whether technology offered us a way to meet these goals. My own research has centered on computer software, and I have used military software in some of my research. My experience with computer-controlled weapon systems led me to wonder whether any such system could meet the requirements set forth by President Reagan.

I also had doubts about a possible conflict of interest. I have a project within the U.S. Navy that could benefit from SDI funding. I suggested to the panel organizer that this conflict might disqualify me. He assured me that if I did not have such a conflict, they would not want me on the panel. He pointed out that the other panelists—employees of defense contractors and university professors dependent on DoD funds for their research—had similar conflicts. Readers should think about such conflicts the next time they hear of a panel of "distinguished experts."

My Work for the Panel.   The first meeting increased my doubts. In spite of the high rate of pay, the meeting was poorly prepared; presentations were at a disturbingly unprofessional level. Technical terms were used without definition; numbers were used without supporting evidence. The participants appeared predisposed to discuss many of the interesting but tractable technical problems in space-based missile defense, while ignoring the basic problems and "big picture." Everyone seemed to have a pet project of their own that they thought should be funded.

At the end of the meeting we were asked to prepare position papers describing research problems that must be solved in order to build an effective and trustworthy shield against nuclear missiles. I spent the weeks after the meeting writing up those problems and trying to convince myself that SDIO-supported research could solve them. I failed. I could not convince myself that it would be possible to build a system that we could trust, nor that it would be useful to build a system we did not trust.

Why Trustworthiness Is Essential.   If the U.S. does not trust SDI, it will not abandon deterrence and nuclear missiles. Even so, the U.S.S.R. could not assume that SDI would be completely ineffective. Seeing both a "shield" and missiles, it would feel impelled to improve its offensive forces in an effort to compensate for SDI. The U.S., not trusting its defense, would feel a need to build still more nuclear missiles to compensate for the increased Soviet strength. The arms race would speed up. Further, because NATO would be wasting an immense amount of effort on a system it couldn't trust, we would see a weakening of our relative strength. Instead of the safer world that President Reagan envisions, we would have a far more dangerous situation. Thus, the issue of our trust in the system is critical. Unless the shield is trustworthy, it will not benefit any country.

THE ROLE OF COMPUTERS

SDI discussions often ignore computers, focusing on new developments in sensors and weapons. However, the sensors will produce vast amounts of raw data that computers must process and analyze. Computers must detect missile firings, determine the source of the attack, and compute the attacking trajectories. Computers must discriminate between threatening warheads and mere decoys designed to confuse our defensive system. Computers will aim and fire the weapons. All the weapons and sensors will be useless if the computers do not function properly. Software is the glue that holds such systems together. If the software is not trustworthy, the system is not trustworthy.

The Limits of Software Technology.   Computer specialists know that software is always the most troublesome component in systems that depend on computer control. Traditional engineering products can be verified by a combination of mathematical analysis, case analysis, and prolonged testing of the complete product under realistic operating conditions. Without such validation, we cannot trust the product. None of these validation methods works well for software. Mathematical proofs verify only abstractions of small programs in restricted languages. Testing and case analysis sufficient to ensure trustworthiness take too much time. As E. W. Dijkstra has said, "Testing can show the presence of bugs, never their absence."

The lack of validation methods explains why we cannot expect a real program to work properly the first time it is really used. This is confirmed by practical experience. We can build adequately reliable software systems, but they become reliable only after extensive use in the field. Although responsible developers perform many tests, including simulations, before releasing their software, serious problems always remain when the first customers use the product. The test designers overlook the same problems the software designers overlook. No experienced person trusts a software system before it has seen extensive use under actual operating conditions.

Why Software for SDI Is Especially Difficult.   SDI is far more difficult than any software system we have ever attempted. Some of the reasons are listed here; a more complete discussion can be found in an article published in *American Scientist* (see reference list).

SDI software must be based on assumptions about target and decoy characteristics, and those characteristics are controlled by the attacker. We cannot rely upon our information about them. The dependence of any program on local assumptions is a rich source of effective countermeasures. Espionage could render the whole multi-billion-dollar system worthless without our knowledge. It could show an attacker how to exploit the inevitable differences between the computer model on which the program is based and the real world.

The techniques used to provide high reliability in other systems are hard to apply for SDI. In space, the redundancy required for high reliability is unusually expensive. The dependence of SDI on communicating computers in satellites makes it unusually vulnerable. High reliability can be achieved only if the failures of individual components are statistically independent; for a system subject to coordinated attacks, that is not the case.

Overloading the system will always be a potent countermeasure, because any computer system will have a limited capacity, and even crude decoys would consume computer capacity. An overloaded system must either ignore some of the objects it should track, or fail completely. For SDI, either option is catastrophic.

Satellites will be in fixed orbits that will not allow the same one to track a missile from its launch and to destroy it. The responsibility for tracking a missile will transfer from one satellite to another. Because of noise caused by the battle and enemy interference, a satellite will require data from other satellites to assist in tracking and discrimination. The results is a distributed real-time database. For the shield to be effective, the data will have to be kept up-to-date and consistent in real time. This means that satellite clocks will have to be accurately synchronized. None of this can be done when the network's components and communication links are unreliable, and unreliability must be expected during a real battle in which an enemy would attack the network. Damaged stations are likely to inject inaccurate or false data into the database.

Realistic testing of the integrated hardware and software is impossible. Thorough testing would require "practice" nuclear wars, including attacks that partially damage the satellites. Our experience tells us that many potential problems would not be revealed by lesser measures such as component testing, simulations, or small-scale field tests.

Unlike other weapon systems, this one will offer us no opportunity to modify the software during or after its first battle. It must work the first time. These properties are inherent in the problem, not some particular system design. As we will see below, they cannot be evaded by proposing a new system structure.

MY DECISION TO ACT

After reaching the conclusion described above, I solicited comments from other scientists and found none that disagreed with my technical conclusions. Instead, they told me that the program should be continued, not because it would free us from the fear of nuclear weapons, but because the research money would advance the state of computer science! I disagree with that statement, but I also consider it irrelevant. Taking money allocated for developing a shield against nuclear missiles, while knowing that such a shield was impossible, seemed like fraud to me. I did not want to participate, and submitted my resignation. Feeling that it would be unprofessional to resign without explanation, I submitted position papers to support my letter. I sent copies to a number of government officials and friends, but did not send them to the press until after they had been sent to reporters by others. They have since been widely published.

SDIO's Reaction.   The SDIO's response to my resignation transformed my stand on SDI from a passive refusal to participate to an active opposition. Neither the SDIO nor the other panelists reacted with a serious and scientific discussion of the technical problems that I raised.

The first reaction came from one of the panel organizers. He asked me to reconsider, but not because he disagreed with my technical conclusions. He accepted my view that an effective shield was unlikely, but argued that the money was going to be spent and I should help to see it well spent. There was no further reaction from the SDIO until a *New York Times* reporter made some inquiries. Then, the only reaction I received was a telephone call demanding to know who had sent the material to the *Times*.

After the story broke, the statements made to the press seemed, to me, designed to mislead rather than inform the public. Examples are given below. When I observed that the SDIO was engaged in "damage control," rather than a serious consideration of my arguments, I felt that I should inform the public and its representatives of my own view. I want the public to understand that no trustworthy shield will result from the SDIO-sponsored work. I want them to understand that technology offers no magic that will eliminate the fear of nuclear weapons. I consider this part of my personal professional responsibility as a scientist and an educator.

CRITICAL ISSUES

Democracy can only work if the public is accurately informed. Again, most of the statements made by SDIO supporters seem designed to mislead the public. For example, one SDIO scientist told the public that there could be 100,000 errors in the software and it would still work properly. Strictly speaking, this statement is true. If one picks one's errors very carefully, they won't matter much. However, a single error caused the complete failure of a Venus probe many years ago. I find it hard to believe that the SDIO spokesman was not aware of that.

Another panelist repeatedly told the press that there was no fundamental law of computer science that said the problem could not be solved. Again, strictly speaking, the statement is true, but it does not counter my arguments. I did not say that a correct program was impossible; I said that it was impossible that we could trust the program. It is not impossible that such a program would work the first time it was used; it is also not impossible that 10,000 monkeys would reproduce the works of Shakespeare if allowed to type for five years. Both are highly unlikely. However, we could tell when the monkeys had succeeded; there is no way that we could verify that the SDI software was adequate.

Another form of disinformation was the statement that I—and other SDI critics—were demanding perfection. Nowhere have I demanded perfection. To trust the software we merely need to know that the software is free of catastrophic flaws, flaws that could cause massive failure or that could be exploited by a sophisticated enemy. That is certainly easier to achieve than perfection, but there is no way to know when we have achieved it.

A common characteristic of all these statements is that they argue with statements other than the ones I published in my papers. In fact, in some cases SDIO officials dispute statements made by earlier panels or by other SDIO officials, rather than debating the points I made.

The "90%" Distraction.   One of the most prevalent arguments in support of SDI suggests that if there are three layers, each 90% effective, the overall "leakage" would be less than 1% because the effectiveness multiplies. This argument is accepted by many people who do not have scientific training. However,

- There is no basis for the 90% figure; an SDI official told me it was picked for purpose of illustration.
- The argument assumes that the performance of each layer is independent of the others, when it is clear that there are actually many links.

- It is not valid to rate the effectiveness of such systems by a single "percentage." Such statistics are only useful for describing a random process. Any space battle would be a battle between two skilled opponents. A simple percentage figure is no more valid for such systems than it is as a way of rating chess players. The performance of defensive systems depends on the opponent's tactics. Many defensive systems have been completely defeated by a sophisticated opponent who found an effective countermeasure.

The "Loose Coordination" Distraction.   The most sophisticated response was made by the remaining members of SDIO's Panel on Computing in Support of Battle Management, which named itself the Eastport group, in December 1985. This group of SDI proponents wrote that the system structures proposed by the best Phase I contractors, those being elaborated in Phase II, would not work because the software could not be built or tested. They said that these "architectures" called for excessively tight coordination between the "battle stations"—excessive communication—and they proposed that new Phase I studies be started. However, they disputed my conclusions, arguing that the software difficulties could be overcome using "loose coordination."

The Eastport Report neither defines its terms nor describes the structure that it had in mind. Parts of the report imply that "loose coordination" can be achieved by reducing the communication between the stations. Later sections of the report discuss the need for extensive communication in the battle-station network, contradicting some statements in the earlier section. However, the essence of their argument is that SDI could be trustworthy if each battle station functioned autonomously, without relying on help from others.

Three claims can be made for such a design:

- It decomposes an excessively large program to a set of smaller ones, each one of which can be built and tested.
- Because the battle stations would be autonomous, a failure of some would allow the others to continue to function.
- Because of the independence, one could infer the behavior of the whole system from tests on individual battle stations.

The Eastport group's argument is based on four unstated assumptions:

1. Battle stations do not need data from other satellites to perform their basic functions.
2. An individual battle station is a small software project that will not run into the software difficulties described above.
3. The only interaction between the stations is by explicit communication. This assumption is needed to conclude that test results about a single station allow one to infer the behavior of the complete system.
4. A collection of communicating systems differs in fundamental ways from a single system.

All of these assumptions are false!

1. The data from other satellites is essential for accurate tracking, and for discriminating between warheads and decoys in the presence of noise.
2. Each battle station has to perform all of the functions of the whole system. The original arguments apply to it. Each one is unlikely to work, impossible to test in actual operating conditions, and consequently impossible to trust. Far easier projects have failed.
3. Battle stations interact through weapons and sensors as well as through their shared targets. The weapons might affect the data produced by the sensors. For example, destruction of a single warhead or decoy might produce noise that makes tracking of other objectives impossible. If we got a single station working perfectly in isolation, it might fail completely when operating near others. The failure of one station might cause others to fail because of overload. Only a real battle would give us confidence that such interactions would not occur.
4. A collection of communicating programs is mathematically equivalent to a single program. In practice, distribution makes the problem harder, not easier.

Restricting the communication between the satellites does not solve the problem. There is still no way to know the effectiveness of the system, and it would not be trusted. Further, restrictions on communication are likely to reduce the effectiveness of the system. I assume that this is why none of the Phase I contractors chose such an approach.

The first claim in the list is appealing, and reminiscent of arguments made in the '60s and '70s about modular programming. Unfortunately, experience has shown that modular programming is an effective technique for making errors easier to correct, not for eliminating errors. Modular programming does not solve the problems described earlier in this paper. None of my arguments was based on an assumption of tight coupling; some of the arguments do assume that there will be data passed from one satellite to another. The Eastport Report, like earlier reports, supports that assumption.

The Eastport group is correct when it says that designs calling for extensive data communication between the battle stations are unlikely to work. However, the Phase I contractors were also right when they assumed that without such communication the system could not be effective.

Redefining the Problem.   The issue of SDI software was debated in March 1986 at an IEEE computer conference. While two of us argued that SDI could not be trusted, the two SDI supporters argued that it did not matter. Rather than argue the computer-science issues, they tried to use strategic arguments to say that a shield need not be considered trustworthy. One of them argued, most eloquently, that the president's "impotent and obsolete" terminology was technical nonsense. He suggested that we ignore what "the President's speechwriters" had to say and look at what was actually feasible. Others argue that increased uncertainty is a good thing—quite a contrast to President Reagan's promise of increased security.

In fact, the ultimate response of the computer scientists working on SDI is to redefine the problem in such a way that there is a trivial solution and improvement is always possible. Such a problem is the ideal project for government sponsorship. The contractor can always show both progress and the need for further work. Contracts will be renewed indefinitely!

Those working on the project often disparage statements made by the president and his most vocal supporters, stating that SDIO scientists and officials are not responsible for such statements. However, the general public remains unaware of their position, and believes that the president's goals are the goals of those who are doing the scientific work.

BROADER QUESTIONS

Is SDIO-Sponsored Work of Good Quality?   Although the Eastport panel were unequivocally supportive of continuing SDI, their criticisms of the Phase I studies were quite harsh. They assert that those studies, costing a million dollars each, overlooked elementary problems that were discussed in earlier studies. If the Eastport group is correct, the SDIO contractors and the SDIO evaluators must be considered incompetent. If the Eastport group's criticisms were unjustified, or if their alternative is unworkable, *their* competence must be questioned.

Although I do not have access to much of the SDIO-sponsored work in my field, I have had a chance to study some of it. What I have seen makes big promises, but is of low quality. Because it has bypassed the usual scientific review processes, it overstates its accomplishments and makes no real scientific contribution.

Do Those Who Take SDIO Funds Really Disagree with Me?   I have discussed my views with many who work on SDIO-funded projects. Few of them disagree with my technical conclusions. In fact, since the story became public, two SDIO contractors and two DoD agencies have sought my advice. My position on this subject has not made them doubt my competence.

Those who accept SDIO money give a variety of excuses. "The money is going to be spent anyway; shouldn't we use it well?" "We can use the money to solve other problems." "The money will be good for computer science."

I have also discussed the problem with scientists at the Los Alamos and Sandia National Laboratories. Here, too, I found no substantive disagreement with my analysis. Instead, I was told that the project offered lots of challenging problems for physicists.

In November 1985, I read in *Der Speigel* an interview with the leading German supporter of Star Wars. He made it clear that he thought of SDI as a way of injecting funds into high technology and not as a military project. He even said that he would probably be opposed to participation in any deployment should the project come to fruition.

The Blind Led by Those with Their Eyes Shut.   My years as a consultant in the defense field have shown me that unprofessional behavior is common. When consulting, I often find people doing something foolish. Knowing that the person involved is quite competent, I may say something like, "You know that's not the right way to do that." "Of course," is the response, "but this is what the customer asked for." "Is your customer a computer scientist? Does he know what he is asking?" ask I. "No" is the simple reply. "Why don't you tell him?" elicits the response: "At XYZ Corporation, we don't tell our customers that what they want is wrong. We get contracts."

This may be a businesslike attitude, but it is not a professional one. It misleads the government into wasting taxpayer's money.

The Role of Academic Institutions. Traditionally, universities provide tenure and academic freedom so that faculty members can speak out on issues such as these. Many have done just that. Unfortunately, at U.S. universities there are institutional pressures in favor of accepting research funds from any source. A researcher's ability to attract funds is taken as a measure of his ability.

The president of a major university in the U.S. recently explained his acceptance of a DoD institute on campus by saying, "As a practical matter, it is important to realize that the Department of Defense is a major administrator of research funds. In fact, the department has more research funds at its disposal than any other organization in the country. . . . Increases in research funding in significant amounts can be received only on the basis of defense-related appropriations."

Should We Pursue SDI for Other Reasons? I consider such rationalizations to be both unprofessional and dangerous. SDI endangers the safety of the world. By working on SDI, these scientists allow themselves to be counted among those who believe that the program can succeed. If they are truly professionals, they must make it very clear that an effective shield is unlikely, and a trustworthy one impossible. The issue of more money for high technology should be debated without the smoke screen of SDI. I can think of no research that is so important as to justify pretending that an ABM system can bring security to populations. Good research stands on its own merits; poor research must masquerade as something else.

I believe in research; I believe that technology can improve our world in many ways. I also agree with Professor Janusz Makowski of the Technion Institute, who wrote in the *Jerusalem Post*, "Overfunded research is like heroin, it leads to addiction, weakens the mind, and leads to prostitution." Many research fields in the U.S. are now clearly overfunded, largely because of DoD agencies. I believe we are witnessing the proof of Professor Makowski's statement.

My Advice on Participation in Defense Projects. I believe that it's quite appropriate for professionals to devote their energies to making the people of their land more secure. In contrast, it is not professional to accept employment doing "military" things that do not advance the legitimate defense interests of that country. If the project would not be effective, or if, in one's opinion, it goes beyond the legitimate defense needs of the country, a professional should not participate. Too many do not ask such questions. They ask only how they can get another contract.

It is a truism that if each of us lives as though what we do does matter, the world will be a far better place than it is now is. The cause of many serious problems in our world is that many of us act as if our actions do not matter. Our streets are littered, our environment polluted, and children neglected because we underestimate our individual responsibility.

The arguments given to me for continuation of the SDI program are examples of such thinking. "The government has decided; we cannot change it." "The money will be spent; all you can do is make good use of it." "The system will be built; you cannot change that." "Your resignation will not stop the program."

It is true, my decision not to toss trash on the ground will not eliminate litter. However, if we are to eliminate litter, I must decide not to toss trash on the ground. We all make a difference.

Similarly, my decision not to participate in SDI will not stop this misguided program. However, if everyone who knows that the program will not lead to a trustworthy shield against nuclear weapons refuses to participate, there will be no program. Every individual's decision is important.

It is not necessary for computer scientists to take a political position; they need only be true to their professional responsibilities. If the public were aware of the technical facts, if they knew how unlikely it is that such a shield would be effective, public support would evaporate. We do not need to tell the public not to build SDI. We only need to help them understand why it will never be an effective and trustworthy shield.

REFERENCES

EASTPORT GROUP. 1985. "Summer Study 1985." A Report to the Director—Strategic Defense Initiative Organization, December.

EINSTEIN, ALBERT, and SIGMUND FREUD. 1972. *Warum Krieg?* Zürich: Diogenes Verlag.

PARNAS, D. L. 1972. "On the Criteria to Be Used in Decomposing Systems into Modules." *Communications of the ACM* 15, 12:1053–8.

———. 1985. "Software Aspects of Strategic Defense Systems." *American Scientist*, September–October:432–40. Also published in German in Kursbuch 83, *Krieg und Frieden—Streit um SDI*, by Kursbuch/Rotbuch Verlag, March 1986; and in Dutch in *Informatie*, Nr. 3, March 1986: 175–86.

"Wer kuscht, hat keine Chance." 1985. *Der Spiegel*, Nr. 47, 18 November.

3 Collective and Individual Moral Responsibility in Engineering: Some Questions

John Ladd

In this essay, I shall examine in a rather general way a number of commonly discussed questions of engineering ethics pertaining to the special ethical obligations and responsibilities of engineers as engineers. However, I shall not attempt to provide specific answers to these questions; instead, I shall raise further questions about the questions themselves. For I believe that it is absurd to try to answer questions about obligations and responsibilities before we are clear about the kinds of questions that we are asking, the context in which they arise and the presuppositions underlying them. It is often taken for granted that philosophers are especially qualified to answer ethical questions, including questions of engineering ethics, and philosophers themselves sometimes welcome the opportunity to play the role of preacher or of ethical guidance counselor. This is a view of the practical value of philosophy that is shared by utilitarians and rights theorists, Rawlsians and Nozickians, and by many others, all of whom are only too ready to handout answers telling people, in this case engineers, how they ought to act. My own view of the role of philosophy is entirely different; I believe that the most useful contribution that a philosopher can make is to identify, clarify and sort out problems, and in that connection to unmask superstition, bigotry and illegitimate presuppositions. In this last regard, one of my principal objectives in this essay will be to *demythologize* some current notions in engineering ethics![1]

My purpose, then, is *zetetic*, which means questioning, inquiring, doubting.[2] Approaching the problems of engineering ethics zetetically means moving to a second or meta-level and, as I have already indicated, asking questions about the problems themselves. As a propaedeutic to engineering ethics we need to ask questions like the following: What are the ethical problems of engineering? Why are they ethical rather than simply legal, institutional, organizational, economic, or personal problems facing individual engineers? What is added by saying that they are ethical? Into which of these categories do problems connected with whistle-blowing fall? How should the distinctively ethical problems be formulated? How do they arise? What do they presuppose? What methodology and what concepts are the best tools for analyzing the ethical issues that are involved in engineering? What is the moral status of a corporation? What is the meaning of "responsibility" and of "collective responsibility?" and so on.

ENGINEERING ETHICS AND PROFESSIONALISM

Many of the ethical problems associated with engineering are connected with the professional status of engineering, and so I shall start off with a few remarks about professionalism in general as a way of providing a background for the problems I shall discuss. We must begin with the fact that it is generally felt that there is something honorable about being a member of a profession and it is often supposed that professionals are idealistic. For this reason, members of a profession are considered to have special duties and responsibilities towards society over and above those of ordinary people. Society has high expectations that professional persons, by virtue of being members of a profession, will be honest, dedicated and responsible, more so than laymen or persons in other occupations. On that account, it is thought quite seemly that professionals be better paid, treated with more respect and accorded a higher status in society than others. All of this most likely applies to engineers considered as professionals.

Many professions have adopted codes of ethics in imitation of the original code of ethics of the Royal Society of Physicians. Indeed, it is often assumed that in order to become a full-fledged profession an occupation must adopt a code of ethics. On the other hand, it has been said about such codes that if a person is really honest and responsible, then he does not need a code of ethics and if he needs one then it will not do him any good. I mention this matter simply to warn against the assumption that a code of ethics can be consulted for answers to questions of engineering ethics.[3]

One frequently overlooked aspect of ethics of professionalism is that professionals tend to believe that their professional "obligations," e.g. to clients, outweigh their obligations to others, e. g., to the public. In other words, their professional obligations are given priority. The most obvious example of this sense of priorities is to be found in legal ethics, where lawyers are expected to treat their obligations to clients as having precedence over their obligations to society, e.g., a lawyer's obligation to a client who is guilty of a heinous crime is thought to outweigh any obligation that he might have to the general public whose interest it is to have criminals convicted.[4] Although this assumption about priorities is not always stated explicitly, it is important to remember that it is often there by implication. Indeed, I sense that engineers, like other professionals, frequently take for granted that their obligations to their clients, i.e., their employers, rightfully take precedence over their obligations to society at large. Whether or not this is or ought to be the case is one of the questions that should be examined in engineering ethics. Another typical feature of professionalism that might be mentioned here is what Parsons calls "affective neutrality," that is, the generally felt requirement that a professional ought to adopt an attitude of neutrality towards the ultimate objectives of his client and ought not to allow his personal judgments about their intrinsic value or disvalue to play any role in determining the services he provides.

In general, it should be observed that the elitism of professionalism and its willingness to sacrifice the public interest to other professional responsibilities attest to the profoundly anti-democratic tendencies of professionalism, which have so often been the target of attack by social critics.[5] In any event, an ethics of professionalism in general, and of engineering in particular, needs to cope with the implications of this charge of elitism, which supposes that we are dealing with the best, brightest and wisest members of society when we discuss professionalism.

I mention all of these points about professionalism here, because it is my impression as an outsider that they play a considerable role in an engineer's perception of himself as a professional and of his professional obligations and responsibilities.

DIFFERENTIAL ATTRIBUTES OF ENGINEERING AS A PROFESSION

The profession of engineering differs from other professions such as medicine and law in two respects that are basic for understanding the particular problems of engineering ethics.

First, unlike medicine and law, whose services are ordinarily directed to the needs of individual persons, the services provided by engineers relate to things, e.g., machines, buildings, equipment, products, etc.[6] Insofar as an engineer has a relationship to persons, it is indirect. For example, he relates to persons as clients who purchase or use his services or as persons who are affected by what he makes (or designs), e.g., workers, consumers or the general public. As a result of not being directly structured around interpersonal relationships, as are medicine and law, the engineer–client relationship is not as central a concept for the ethical problems of engineering as the physician–patient relationship is for medical ethics or the lawyer–client relationship is for legal ethics. Thus, for example, paternalism is not a burning issue in engineering ethics as it is in medical or legal ethics.[7]

A second important difference between engineering and the other two professions mentioned is that almost all of a modern engineer's activity takes place in the context of a formal organization of some kind or other, for example, in bureaucratically organized industrial corporations. Solo practice, which provides the traditional background for medical and legal ethics, is uncommon in engineering. Being part of an industrial organization, the ethical problems confront the engineer take on another dimension, because many of them are a direct result of this status as an employee in an organization. Thus, the usual supposition that a professional is an independent operator does not hold for most engineers. This facet of engineering as a profession makes it both simpler and more complicated to frame and to deal with the ethical problems associated with the profession.

It is also easy to see that the ethical problems of engineers are more closely bound up with the particularities of the economic system in which they operate than are those, say, of physicians, who, in many respects, face the same sorts of ethical problems in Russia as they do in the USA. These considerations suggest that we really ought to ask: is there (or should there be) a different kind of engineering ethics for engineers working under a capitalist system from an ethics that would be appropriate for engineers working under a communist or socialist system?

One important aspect of having organizations rather than individuals as clients is that, for engineers, their being part of a system or an organization such as a large corporation often encourages a sense of futility and helplessness as far as being ethical is concerned. It is obviously difficult to be ethical when one is powerless. If, and to the extent that being moral requires self-determination and being able to operate independently, engineers, more than physicians or lawyers, may be inclined to think that they can do nothing about a situation which they deplore. They are caught up in a maelstrom and are powerless to influence the outcome.[8] Unlike other professionals, engineers do not live a sheltered existence where one is accountable to no one but oneself. As members of the organization, they are subject to lines of accountability like all the other employees. (Compare in this regard a company physician, who has a degree of "autonomy" in what he does, with a company engineer, who has almost none.) For these reasons, engineering ethics involve wider issues of responsibility of the sort that are encountered in politics and in organizational ethics in general. In this respect, some of the moral dilemmas that trouble ethically sensitive engineers could be compared to situations experienced by persons living under a totalitarian regime, where responsible action involving remonstrance or resistance leads to extermination. I shall return to this problem later.

THE ETHICS OF LOYALTY

Another quite different ethical aspect of the relationship of engineers to formal organizations of which they are members, whether they be public or private, relates to the issue of loyalty. It is often alleged that, as members of a particular organization, engineers have a special duty of loyalty towards that organization and therefore, having that duty, it would be wrong for them to do anything that might harm the organization, i.e., be against its interest. For example, it would be disloyal of an engineer to reveal the secrets of his organization to an outsider, even secrets about unsafe features of products.

In view of the great emphasis on loyalty in discussions of engineering ethics, we need to ask whether or not there is any validity or merit in the concept of loyalty to an organization. We should note right away that the loyalty in question here is not at all like the loyalty that physicians and lawyers are expected to have towards their patients and clients, for the latter kind of loyalty simply amounts to observing the duties of devotion, dedication, zealousness and avoidance of conflicts of interest that are owed to their patients and clients as individuals as a result of their relationship. The loyalty involved in the physician–patient or lawyer–client relationship has often been compared to loyalty between friends.[9] Loyalty to an organization, on the other hand, seems to be quite different from the loyalty that one individual gives to another and that can exist between friends.[10]

In order to see whether and how the concept of loyalty can be applied to an organization, we need to ask a number of other questions: Is loyalty always a virtue? Does loyalty ever permit or require doing something that would otherwise be wrong? What kinds of things can be the objects of loyalty? Do members of organizations, e.g., engineers, have a duty to loyalty to their organizations? If so, could the claims of an organization to loyalty ever justify wrongdoing of some sort?

If we assume that loyalty, as distinguished from blind obedience or servile compliance, is a virtue, then we must inquire into what we mean by "loyalty" in this sense.[11] When regarded as a virtue, that is, as something morally desirable, loyalty is founded on moral relationships of one sort or other between persons, e.g., originally between lord and vassal, but now also between family members, between friends, between colleagues and between comrades. Loyalty to a nation, to a college, or to a family is simply loyalty to the people in them, including perhaps to past and future generations within these communities. As a virtue, it derives its moral value from these interpersonal relationships and consists in thoroughgoing dedication and devotion of a person to what is owed another by virtue of a relationship of this kind. It is odd therefore to speak of loyalty where there is no prior personal relationship, for example, loyalty to a perfect stranger or to someone one admires at a distance but does not have any personal relationship to, such as a movie star. It is even more odd to speak of loyalty to a non-person.[12] Furthermore, if loyalty is a moral virtue, then it cannot be conceived as requiring something that is not due, or even less, something that is not right. There is no virtue in being a "loyal Nazi" or a "loyal member of the Mafia." Such notions, according to my analysis, would in fact be contradictions in terms.[13]

If this analysis of loyalty is correct, and I think that any analysis that takes loyalty to be a virtue would have to be developed along these lines, there are obvious difficulties with the idea of loyalty to a corporation, in the sense of loyalty that implies that it is morally good to be loyal. First, before we speak meaningfully of loyalty in the context of a corporation, we need to ask: who in the corporation is the object of this loyalty? Is it the managers? the stockholders? one's fellow employees? or all of these? Obviously, loyalty to these different groups requires quite different kinds of conduct, some of which may be inconsistent. If, on the other hand, we choose to say that the object of loyalty is the corporation itself, the corporate entity, we face another paradox. For, quite apart from the issue of corporations being non-persons, something else important for loyalty seems to be missing that might be called "reciprocity." What I mean is that loyalty is thought to be a two-way thing: A is loyal to B and B is loyal to A. Friends are loyal to each other. In this sense, loyalty is a bond tying people to each other reciprocally. Corporate "loyalty" is, in contrast, by its very nature one-way; dedication and devotion can only be in one direction—from the employee to the corporation. A corporation cannot be loyal to employees in the same sense as they are supposed to be loyal to it, not only because it is not a person but also because the actions of a corporation must be conceptually linked to the benefits they bring to the corporation. A corporation can be good to employees only because it is good for business, that is, because it is in its own self-interest. All this is a consequence of the fact that a corporation is logically incapable of having moral attitudes and its conduct can only be understood in relation to the aims of the corporation. As an ethical notion, however, loyalty cannot be founded solely on utility or self-interest.

As I have already indicated a number of times, corporations are not persons in the moral sense. The fact that in law, corporations have the status of persons as far as the Fourteenth Amendment is concerned, does not make them moral persons: law and morality should not be confused. My arguments against the position that corporations are moral persons are based on a particular analysis of the logic of organizational decision-making, according to which organizations are logically incapable of moral decision-making and of moral conduct generally. If, as I contend, rational corporate acts must and can only be logically tied to corporate goals, e.g., profit-making, then such acts cannot be based on moral considerations. Essential to my analysis, it should be observed, is a clear-cut distinction and separation of a corporation as an "abstract" entity from the people within a corporation, who, as individuals, are, of course, persons with the moral responsibilities and rights pertaining to persons.[14]

WHISTLE-BLOWING

If, as I have argued, the issue of loyalty to a corporation is a red herring, then we need not discuss the ethics of whistle-blowing in that connection. However, there are other issues connected with whistle-blowing that we need to examine. The cases of whistle-blowing that have received wide attention are spectacular. They typically involve preventable disasters, errors and mistakes, and usually some hanky-panky.[15] As has been pointed out, whistle-blowing represents a particular kind of solution to a general problem that may have other and better solutions.[16] So we immediately have two issues: the rights and wrongs of whistle-blowing and the problem that whistle-blowing is supposed to solve. As far as whistle-blowing itself is concerned, it is obvious that it is not always good or bad and that it is not always successful or necessary. As De George and others point out, it seems on the face of it undesirable from an ethical point of view to have to solve the kind of a problem that leads to whistle-blowing by demanding that individuals be moral heroes. In any event, there are obvious ethical as well as practical objections to solutions of social problems that depend so heavily on individual self-sacrifice.

Turning to the second issue, let us take a closer look at the problems for which whistle-blowing is supposed to be the solution, that is, the evils that it is supposed to correct. They include such things as faulty design leading to fatal accidents, as in the Hyatt Regency Hotel and the DC-10 crash. What is the underlying problem? If we assume that in general terms it is how to prevent undesirable states of affairs (evils) of some sort, what particular states of affairs are the ones in question? Is the problem simply: how to prevent preventable disasters? Or, to put it positively, is it simply how to promote safety in engineering? If so, is it the same problem that is addressed in the Engineer's Code of Ethics, when it says that "Engineers shall hold paramount the safety, health and welfare of the public in the performance of their professional duties?" One answer to our question, then, might be that the ethical problem behind whistle-blowing is simply how to maximize safety or at least how to reduce unsafety to a decent minimum.

There are two things to say about the problem as I have just defined it. First, it involves a reference to safety. Safety, it should be noted, is the kind of thing that is looked on as a value by everyone. It is like motherhood: no one is against it—in principle. So we start off the discussion of this problem with something that is uncontroversial, for safety is an incontrovertible good, or, if you wish, something whose absence is an incontrovertible evil. It is easy, of course, to see why safety is valued by everyone, for an unsafe bit of machinery, like an airplane or an automobile, might result in one's own death or the death of others who are close. The first point, then, is that our starting place is more solid, so to speak, than the starting place of most ethical problems.

To admit safety as an incontrovertible good is not to say that there are no disagreements about safety. There are disagreements, for example, over the definition of safety, how much safety should be built into a machine, what safety measures are necessary in design, structure, operating procedures, etc.[17] There are also lively disagreements over the costs of safety, over who has responsibility for safety, and over what kind of controls there should be over safety.

The second question about the problem behind whistle-blowing is this: granted that the prevention of preventable disasters is a problem, even a pressing or urgent problem, we must determine what kind of problem it is. Is it a moral or ethical problem? Or is it a social problem? a legal, a political, an institutional (organizational) or an economic problem? Or is it simply a practical human problem concerning means and ends, that is, concerning what measures should be undertaken to avoid the evils in question? In any case, why call it an *ethical problem*, unless we are ready to say that any problem whatsoever of means and ends is automatically an ethical problem.

One way that one might answer these questions is to say that safety is an ethical problem simply because it is an important matter that we need to do something about, i.e., we ought to do what we can to prevent preventable accidents. In that case, it becomes the problem of how to prevent accidents, and that surely is an engineering problem. Of course, we might want to broaden the scope of the problem so defined and amend it by including questions about how to get those in power to do something to prevent preventable accidents, that is, to take problems of safety more seriously. In order to solve it, then, we might need to tackle some political, organizational or perhaps even social problems. It is still unclear, however, why we should call the basic problem an *ethical* problem rather than some other kind of problem and why we should call it a "problem" rather than a "task." Are we faced here with something that is in any sense a moral issue and a perplexity? The only thing that we can say for sure is that whistle-blowing by isolated individuals is not the answer to the problem of preventing preventable accidents.

On the other hand, we might wish to say that the problem in question is ethical because if everyone in a position to do something about safety were aware of their moral responsibilities in that regard and also were moral (i.e., conscientious), then the problem of preventable accidents would be solved. So construed, the "bottom line" becomes the question of how to get people to do what they ought to do, i.e., to be moral. In the final analysis, however, the way we conceive the problem depends on what our basic concern is: is it with the evil of the disaster or is it with the evil of people, that is, their failure to act to prevent disasters. If it is the latter, then the ethical problem turns into a problem of, say, how to raise moral consciousness about safety. It is solved by overcoming insensitivity or callousness on the part of those who are in a position to do something about safety. (This might, of course, include management.) On this view, being moral (ethical) in these senses is valued as a means of preventing accidents, etc. The problem behind whistle-blowing (e.g., concerning faulty engineering) is solved by people becoming more moral, say, through moral education. Accordingly, we have a utilitarian interpretation of the problem itself and a utilitarian answer to it, including a utilitarian view of the value of moral consciousness and moral education. Ethics has been reduced to a means for preventing accidents!

Now, all of this seems to me to be an odd way of thinking about ethics. I want to ask: *whatever became of ethics?* Ethics is treated as if it were a kind of behavior control, an internal behavior control comparable in important respects to external behavior control through law, institutional regulations, social practices, rewards and punishments. As distinct from the latter, ethics is internalized control. But is this what ethics is: internal behavior control? Must we accept the utilitarian answer? Is the problem of how to eliminate preventable accidents simply one of securing moral behavior or one of ethical behavior control?

It might be observed, incidentally, that the assumption that ethics is essentially a kind of behavior control is probably what lies behind the attempts by various professions to codify the rules of their professional ethics. It seems to be taken for granted that if what is ethical is prescribed by a code, then members of the profession will comply and a socially acceptable and desirable outcome will result. Whatever the explicit intent, the underlying purpose of the codes is to create some kind of behavior control analogous to control through law.[18] At this point, I need to make some comments on the use of formal mechanisms of behavior control in the service of ethics.

MECHANISMS OF BEHAVIOR CONTROL: LAW VS. ETHICS

A great deal of confusion in discussions of ethical problems results from the assimilation of ethics to law, institutions, organizational regulations, and other mechanisms of social control. I hardly need mention here the other common fallacy of identifying ethics with the "value-system" of some group or other, that is, with what John Austin called "positive morality,"—the body of moral beliefs and conventions actually accepted by a person, a group, or a society. Ethics, sometimes called "critical morality," is logically prior to all of these institutions and social mechanisms of control. It is used to criticize, evaluate and weigh the validity and desirability of the norms, rules and principles embodied in such institutions as law and positive morality. Consequently, ethics is prior to or superior to these other systems of norms in that it is used to determine what in them is morally acceptable and unacceptable.

There are a number of other important differences between ethics and formal systems of control such as law and management regulations. By a "formal system of control" I mean a system consisting of formally adopted rules, regulations, procedures and sanctions that are and can be used to control behavior. Usually the rules in question are written down and published for the guidance of those subject to them. For our purposes, perhaps the chief difference between these systems of control and ethics is that in formal systems of control such as law and management regulations some person or body of persons is authorized to create, change and rescind the rules—at will, so to speak. The authority to do this is vested in legislatures, courts, commissions, boards, managers and other officials. The principles of ethics (or morals), in contrast, are not the kind of thing that can be arbitrarily created, changed or rescinded. Ethics cannot be dictated. In old fashioned terminology, the principles of ethics are "discovered" rather than created by fiat. They are established through argument and persuasion, not through imposition by an external social authority.

Another critical difference between the formal systems of control that I have been discussing and ethics is their purpose, for law, corporate regulations, institutional requirements, and other formal systems of control are designed and used to control behavior for various and sundry purposes, which may be good, evil, or indifferent. From an ethical point of view, it is our job to weigh the validity and desirability of these purposes. But just as important from the ethical point of view are the ways and means selected to achieve these purposes. Here we need to ask: which ways and means are legitimate and ethically justifiable and which are not. In particular, we need to ask which sorts of social control are ethically permissible and which are not? In connection with the last question, there is one important means of control that has received insufficient attention in the literature on engineering ethics, namely, the use of secrecy as a means of control. When is secrecy justified and when not? are the current self-serving norms regarding secrecy, e.g., within a corporation and regarding engineering projects, tolerable from the ethical point of view? Is it not possible that the best way to avoid political and organizational corruption in the long run is to make public the plans, projects and purposes behind the operations of our public institutions, government and private corporations?[19]

SOCIAL CONTROL AND THEORIES OF HUMAN NATURE

Ethical theories about proper and improper social control always presuppose, either explicitly or implicitly, a theory of human nature of some kind or other. Theories of human nature in this sense are about what motivates human beings and what ought to motivate them, that is, what would be rational for them to want and to do. Although it is generally assumed that theories of human nature and motivation are descriptive and empirical, in actuality they are always inescapably value-laden, both in regard to how individuals ought to act (if they are rational) and in regard to what are the proper means to get them to act in ways that one wants, i.e., to control them. Different theories of human nature come up with quite different answers to these questions. Thus, according to a Hobbesian self-interest model of human nature, it is reasonable for a person to act for his own self-interest and unreasonable for him to act against it, and for that reason the best and proper way to control others is to manipulate their self-interest, to make it in their self-interest to act in certain ways. This is the typical bourgeois economic view of man and it provides the rationale for many of our institutional arrangements that are designed to control behavior, e.g., of employees.[20] Whatever is in a person's self-interest is, other things being equal, permissible, nay, rational for him to do.

For reasons that I cannot give here, the Hobbesian model does not fit individual human beings very well; it ignores not only the "irrational" and emotional side of human nature but also its moral aspect. On the other hand, the model does apply very nicely to corporations, at least to the commonly accepted notion of private corporations as propelled by self-regarding drives for profit, power and glory. The whole Hobbesian apparatus can be usefully applied to an ethical analysis of corporations. Like Hobbesian men, corporations are, in theory at least, in constant competition with each other—as in Hobbes's state of nature—and the only effective control over their "rational" voracity is through the manipulation of their self-interest. Accordingly, if we really want to cut down unsafe practices and to reduce the incidence of industrially caused accidents (evils) we have to make it in a corporation's self-interest to take measures to prevent them. It is absurd to appeal to ethics, because corporations are not moral beings. Profits are what count, and so unsafety should be made unprofitable.

I have argued that underlying most thinking about ethics in corporations is a certain mythology, which holds that corporations are persons and that therefore the same theories of human nature, of motivation and of morality apply to them as apply to individual human beings. This mythology leads us either to anthropomorphize corporations and treat them like "nice people" or else to reduce individual human beings to miniature corporations, each in pursuit of his self-interest and in perpetual strife with others for profit, power and glory. Once we rid ourselves of this mythology, we will be able to sort out more clearly and coherently our mutual rights, duties and responsibilities in society in relation to each other.

MORAL RESPONSIBILITY AND OTHER KINDS OF RESPONSIBILITY

Nowhere is the fallacious assimilation of corporations to moral persons more apparent than in prevalent conceptions of responsibility; different senses of responsibility are confused with each other almost as if there were a plot to get rid of moral responsibility altogether. Pursuing the same line that I have already taken in this essay, I shall argue that the concept of moral responsibility, as contrasted with other kinds of responsibility, cannot properly or even meaningfully be attributed to corporations, that is, to formal organizations. But first we have to sort out a number of different senses of "responsibility."

The *locus classicus* for any discussion of responsibility is Hart's essay on the subject.[21] In his essay, Hart lists four different senses of responsibility, which he calls: (a) Role-responsibility, (b) Causal-responsibility, (c) Liability-responsibility, and (d) Capacity-responsibility. The names speak for themselves: role-responsibilities are the responsibilities that go with roles, tasks and jobs; causal-responsibility is the responsibility for having caused something to happen; liability-responsibility concerns who is to pay for damages, and capacity-responsibility refers to psychological capacities required for legal competence.

It should be noted right away that Hart does not include on his list the most important sense of "responsibility": moral responsibility, that is, responsibility in the virtue sense.[22] He ignores this kind of responsibility because he is interested only in responsibility as it relates to law. Furthermore, it should be observed that all of Hart's four senses of responsibility can be attributed to corporations, for corporations can (a) fill roles; they can (b) cause things to happen; they can be (c) liable, e.g., for damages, and they have (d) the "capacities" that Hart mentions, namely, the capacities of "understanding, reasoning and control of conduct."[23] It is easy to see why Hart's senses of responsibility apply to corporations, for they are essentially legal entities and as such are subject to law, which, as I have pointed out, should not be confused with ethics.

When we come to moral responsibility we are dealing with something quite different.[24] In order to bring out the difference, let me begin by distinguishing between forward-looking and backward-looking senses of responsibility, that is, between responsibility for something that has already taken place and responsibility for what will or might take place in the future. Clearly, liability-responsibility is backward looking in this sense and so is causal-responsibility: "*Who* and *What* is responsible for the crash of the DC-10?" Role-responsibility may be either past or future: a safety officer's role was, is, or will be to monitor such and such for product safety, etc.[25] Retrospectively, a person can be held responsible (liable) for failure to do what his role required, and prospectively, he is responsible (role) for completing certain tasks and controlling certain kinds of results in the future. It should be noted, however, that role-responsibilities (tasks, jobs) are assigned, e.g. by organizations, and from a moral point of view may be non-moral or immoral, as well as moral. Thus, a public relations official may have the responsibility (job, task) for covering up management's failure to report a hazardous condition.

Now, moral responsibility as I conceive it is forward-looking. It is about what people ought to do to bring about or prevent future states of affairs. It is based on the duty each one of us has to watch out for what may happen to others or to oneself. As such, it implies concern, care, and foresight. To be responsible in this sense is a virtue that cannot be meaningfully predicated of a corporation conceived as a formal organization, that is, as a structure of rules, offices and jobs, etc. Corporations, being nonmoral entities, cannot be virtuous or vicious in the moral sense; only the people in them can be so characterized.

Now, one noteworthy property of responsibility in the moral sense as contrasted with the other senses is that it is *nonexclusive*. In the other four senses, responsibility is exclusive in the sense that to impute responsibility to one thing (X) implies that other things (Y,Z) do not have the responsibility. Thus, if one person has a role-responsibility for something, it follows that other people do not have the responsibility. Similarly, causal- and liability-responsibility are exclusionary. Moral responsibility, on the other hand, is not exclusionary in this sense; for one person to be responsible does not entail, as it does for the other kinds of responsibility, that other persons are not also responsible. A father's responsibility for his children does not exclude (or negate) the mother's responsibility—or, for that matter, anyone else's responsibility, e.g., the responsibility of the state. In the moral sense, there are some things that everyone is responsible for, and one of these things is safety. Concern with safety is not just one person's job, i.e., his role-responsibility, to the exclusion of others. It is everyone's moral responsibility—varying in degrees only to the extent that one person is better able to do something about it than others. The concept of moral responsibility implies that there are some things that are everyone's business!

COLLECTIVE RESPONSIBILITY

A very significant ethical consequence of the nonexclusiveness of moral responsibility is that, if many people can be morally responsible for the same thing, then there can be such a thing as group moral responsibility, or if you wish, collective responsibility, that is, a responsibility that falls on many people at the same time. In as much as one person's being responsible does not relieve others of responsibility, everyone in a group may have moral responsibility for a certain thing. Thus, the whole family is responsible for seeing that the baby does not get hurt. The whole community is responsible for the health and safety of its citizens. And all the engineers, as well as others, working on a project are responsible for its safety.

Now it should be clear that underlying my analysis of collective responsibility is a distinction between a group of people, a collection or association of individuals, and a formal organization, which is a structure defined by rules, offices and jobs, etc., apart from the people who come and go in the organization. Moral responsibilities, moral virtues and other moral qualities can be ascribed to groups insofar as they pertain to the individuals in them. But since organizations are not persons, they are, as such, beyond the pale of morality. We cannot and should not shift our moral responsibilities onto abstract entities like corporations.

One of the deep problems of our time is that people have followed the lead of philosophers, lawyers and managers and have simply reduced moral responsibility to the other four kinds of responsibility already mentioned. The net effect of this move is to render all responsibility exclusionary and to provide thereby theoretical support for a wholesale abdication of moral responsibility: "That's her job, not mine"; "he did it, not I," etc. We are constantly looking for someone to fix responsibility onto, be it liability- or role-responsibility. We construe the question of responsibility for engineering errors as a question of fixing responsibility on some engineer, either holding him liable for it (in the past) or assigning him the task of watching out for it in the future. "Divide and conquer" is the motto: if we divide responsibilities like jobs or liabilities we will avoid any trouble and we will know whom to blame.

Our ideology gives us a way to pass the buck as far as moral responsibility is concerned. Against this, it should be pointed out that if everyone in a non-exclusive group with moral responsibility for safety sets out to prevent a disaster, then the world will be much better off then if we simply try to fix a disaster on a single person or if we assign the job (= role-responsibility) for preventing disasters to a particular person or outfit and then forget about our own responsibilities. According to the conception of moral responsibility that I have in mind here, there is a sense in which all of us, engineers and nonengineers alike, are responsible for things like the Pinto accidents, say, because we accept a way of life, based on the Hobbesian model, that assumes that what is good for business, anyone's business, is good for us, for society, and correlatively, it is good for business to mind one's own business.

On a broader front, we can see what happens to a society when a sizable segment of the population abdicates its moral responsibility for the common good, that is, the good of its members, and opts for the principle of minding one's own business (job-responsibility). In Germany, a result of this kind of abdication was Hitler. In the USA, a result of this kind of abdication was Vietnam. And unless we start caring, a future result of our abdication of responsibility will be World War III and a nuclear holocaust. Some would like to blame the engineers for that. But I argue that nuclear weaponry is not simply an engineering problem, that is, a problem for engineering ethics, although it is also that, just as problems of engineering ethics, e.g., concerning safe products and concerning a safe environment, are not simply problems of engineering ethics, but problems for all of us. All of these things are everybody's business.

In conclusion, I want to reiterate what was said at the beginning of this essay: philosophers cannot be expected to provide ready-made solutions to ethical problems in engineering. Instead, following my conception of the zetetic role of a philosopher, I have simply tried to point out a number of questions that need to be asked and some of the pitfalls in ethical thinking about them that ought to be avoided. As far as the latter are concerned, I have tried to show that serious ethical consequences follow from the blithe acceptance of corporations as persons, from the confounding of moral and legal concepts, and from the failure to recognize moral responsibility as a distinctive kind of responsibility that is nonexclusive and that can be predicated of individuals in groups (i.e., collective responsibility) as well as of persons individually. Thus, despite the disclaimers about the practical value of philosophy that I have mentioned, philosophy in the analytic tradition still has an important and perhaps indispensable function in making clear how best to approach the problems that concern us in engineering ethics, even though in the end it does not provide authoritative answers to them.

NOTES

1. My position on these questions is set forth in a number of writings. See, for example, "The Poverty of Absolutism," in Timothy Stroup, ed. *Essays in Memory of Edward Westermarck.* Acta Philosophica Fennica. Helsinki, 1982. See also, "The Task of Ethics," in Warren Reich, ed. *Encyclopedia of Bioethics.* New York: The Free Press, 1978, vol. 1, pp. 400–407.

2. From the Greek *zetein.* It is a word that was used for an ancient school of philosphers known as the Skeptics—otherwise as Zetetics.

3. For a critical discussion of the notion of a professional code of ethics see "The quest for a code of professional ethics: an intellectual and moral confusion." *AAAS Professional Ethics Project,* eds. Rosemary Chalk, Mark S. Frankel and Sallie B. Chafer. Washington, D.C.: American Association for the Advancement of Science, 1980.

4. For a forceful statement of this position, see Monroe Freedman, *Lawyer's Ethics in an Adversary System.* Indianapolis: Bobbs-Merrill, 1975.

5. See, for example, Ivan Illich, Irving Zola, et al. *Disabling Professions*. Boston: Marion Boyars, 1977.

6. It is often advanced as a criticism of modern medical practice that physicians treat patients as bodies that are like machines needing to be repaired rather than as persons. In this way, medicine becomes a technology and in that respect becomes like engineering.

7. There is an extensive literature on paternalism in medicine and law.

8. In this connection, there is a series of rationalizations that are made by members of a bureaucracy to justify their not doing anything about something they think is wrong. For a critical discussion of such attempts to avoid responsibility, see Dennis Thompson, "Moral responsibility of public officials: the problem of many hands." *American Political Science Review*, vol. 74, no. 4 (December 1980).

9. See Pedro Lain Entralgo, *Doctor and Patient*. Tr. Frances Partridge. New York: McGraw-Hill, 1965; and Charles Fried, "The Lawyer as Friend: The Moral Foundations of the Lawyer-Client Relation." *Yale Law Journal*, 85:1060–89 (1976).

10. Hume says in this connection that virtues like rigid loyalty to persons are "virtues that hold less of reason than of bigotry and superstition." *Treatise*, Book III, Part II, Section X.

11. I discuss this concept in "Loyalty," *Encyclopedia of Philosophy*, ed. Paul Edwards. New York: Macmillan and Free Press, 1967, vol. 5, pp. 97–98.

12. Elsewhere I argue that formal organizations, e.g., corporations, are not persons in the moral sense. See my "Morality and the ideal of rationality in formal organizations." *Monist*, vol. 54, no. 4 (October 1970).

13. See "Loyalty."

14. See "Is 'corporate responsibility' a coherent notion?" In *Proceedings of the Second National Conference on Business Ethics*. Ed. Michael Hoffman. Washington, D.C.: University Press of America, 1979, 9, pp. 102–115.

15. See Alan F. Westin, *Whistle-blowing: Loyalty and Dissent in the Corporation*. New York: McGraw-Hill, 1981.

16. See Richard T. De George, "Ethical responsibilities of engineers in large organizations." *Business and Professional Ethics Journal*, vol. 1, no. 1 (Fall 1981).

17. See Willie Hammer, *Product Safety Management and Engineering*. Englewood Cliffs, N.J. Prentice-Hall, 1980.

18. See my "The quest for a code of professional ethics."

19. I should remind the reader that none of these institutions, according to my analysis, is a person and therefore none has a *moral* right to personal privacy.

20. See C. B. McPherson, *Democratic Theory*. Oxford: Clarendon Press, 1973, esp. pp. 224–37.

21. See H. L. A. Hart, *Punishment and Responsibility*. New York: Oxford University Press, 1968, p. 212 et passim.

22. For an account, see Graham Haydon, "On being responsible." *Philosophical Quarterly*, vol. 28, no. 110 (January, 1978).

23. Op. cit., p. 227.

24. Most of the ideas in the following paragraphs are taken from my "The ethics of participation," in *NOMOS XVI: Participation in Politics*. ed. J. Roland Pennock and John W. Chapman. New York: Atherton-Lieber, 1975.

25. See Hammer, op. cit., chapter 12.

2

Putting the Issues in Context

SCENARIOS

_____ **Knowledge Damaging to Client's Interest** _____

The XYZ Corporation has been advised by a State Pollution Control Authority that it has 60 days to apply for a permit to discharge manufacturing wastes into a receiving body of water. XYZ is also advised of the minimum standard that must be met.

In an effort to convince the authority that the receiving body of water after receiving the manufacturing wastes will still meet established environmental standards, the corporation employs Engineer Doe to perform consulting engineering services and submit a detailed report.

After completion of his studies but before completion of any written report, Doe concludes that the discharge from the plant will lower the quality of the receiving body of water below established standards. He further concludes that corrective action will be very costly. Doe verbally advises the XYZ Corporation of his findings. Subsequently, the corporation terminates the contract with Doe with full payment for services performed, and instructs Doe not to render a written report to the corporation.

Thereafter, Doe learns that the authority has called a public hearing and that the XYZ Corporation has presented data to support its view that the present discharge meets minimum standards.

Does Doe have an ethical obligation to report his findings to the authority upon learning of the hearing?

Reprinted from the National Society of Professional Engineers, Opinions of the Board of Ethical Review, *Case No. 76-4 (Washington, D.C.: National Society of Professional Engineers, 1981), V, 7, with permission.*

_____ **Criticism of Engineering in Products** _____

Engineer A, employed by the XYZ Manufacturing Company, which produces and sells a variety of commercial home-use products, became concerned about what he regards as a trend toward the production of "cheap" products for sale to the public. He feels that this trend toward inferior and shoddy products is due in large part to inadequate engineering, and that an increase in engineering effort could produce products of greater durability and efficiency.

Engineer A joins a group of other engineers, not all of whom work for the same company, who feel the same way. They form a "Citizens Committee for Quality Products." Engineer A becomes a leading spokesman for their cause, including public statements, letters to local newspapers and appearance before legislative bodies in support of laws to impose minimum standards for commercial products.

Engineer B, the supervisor of Engineer A, warned him that if he continued in his activities, he would be discharged because he was putting his employer in an embarrassing position, even though Engineer A had not mentioned the products of his employer or any other specific company in activities on behalf of the Citizens Committee.

Was Engineer A in violation of the Code of Ethics? Was Engineer B in violation of the Code of Ethics?

References

Code of Ethics—Section 1—"The Engineer will be guided in all his professional relations by the highest standards of integrity, and will act in professional matters for each client or employer as a faithful agent or trustee."

Section 2—"The Engineer will have proper regard for the safety, health, and welfare of the public in the performance of his professional duties. If his engineering judgment is overruled by nontechnical authority, he will clearly point out the consequences. He will notify the proper authority of any observed conditions which endanger public safety and health."

Section 2 (a)—"He will regard his duty to the public welfare as paramount."

Section 2 (b)—"He shall seek opportunities to be of constructive service in civic affairs and work for the advancement of the safety, health and well-being of his community."

Discussion

Whether or not the engineer-members of the Citizens Committee were justified in their opinions is not germane to this case. It is sufficient to assume that they were sincere in those opinions and believed they were serving the public interest in their activities.

It is basic to the entire concept of a profession that its members will devote their interests to the public welfare, as is made abundantly clear in Section 2 and Section 2(a) of the Code. What was being done, assuming good faith, was in full accord with the mandate of Section 2(b) of the Code.

The same principles and Code provisions are binding on the engineering supervisor who threatened Engineer A with the possible discharge if he continued his activities on behalf of the Citizens Committee. By so doing, Engineer B may have intended to act in the interests of the employer of both, but at the same time he was subordinating the public welfare requirements of the Code.

What we have said does not conflict with the holding in Case 61-10, in which it was found that engineers assigned to the design of a commercial product of lower quality should not question the company's business decision, but have an obligation to point out any safety hazards in the new design, and may offer their personal opinions and comments to management.

In this case we are not dealing with the product of a particular company or any particular product. What Engineer A and his colleagues are doing is taking upon themselves what they regard to be a public service designed to raise the quality of all products. This we believe they are entitled to do under the Code, recognizing that they may place their own position in jeopardy by going counter to the apparent interests of their employers. If punitive action is taken by one or more employers of the engineers engaged in this activity, the Code will not rescue them because the Code applies only to individual engineers and not to companies.

Engineer B, even though intending to act in the best interests of his employer, is in conflict with the cited sections of the Code because by his threat he intends to preclude other engineers from carrying out what they believe to be motives consonant with the Code.

Conclusions

1. Engineer A was not in violation of the Code of Ethics.
2. Engineer B was in violation of the Code of Ethics.

Reprinted from the National Society of Professional Engineers, Opinions of the Board of Ethical Review, *Case No. 67-10 (Washington, D.C.: National Society of Professional Engineers, 1971), III, 19, with permission.*

INTRODUCTION

Any discussion of engineering ethics is bound to lead to discussion of much broader issues. Beliefs about the role of engineers in society are based on responses to questions including the following: Has technology always benefited humanity (or has it sometimes created worse problems than it solved)? Should engineering be accorded the status of a "profession" and be given the power and privileges that are granted to professions like medicine and law? Are engineers different because of their role in large bureaucracies? In this chapter the reader is given an opportunity to delve more deeply into these broad issues before launching into a more narrowly focused discussion on the responsibilities of engineers and the changes that might be made in the practice of engineering.

Perhaps the most important theme of this chapter is the tension in engineering between the engineer's need for autonomy *and* the expectation of loyalty to employers. Engineers see themselves as having responsibility for the safety and welfare of society. Indeed, many engineering professional codes state that this responsibility is paramount. If engineers are to take this responsibility seriously, however, they must have some control of the work they do. Yet most engineers work in large corporations where they have little say in what goes on. They are expected to take orders and act for the interests of their employers. So, on the one hand, they have a professional role that calls for certain kinds of judgment and behavior, and, on the other hand, they work in environments in which their autonomy is highly constrained. This tension is at the heart of the profession and underlies many of the issues that are subsequently addressed in this book.

In the first section of this chapter, engineering is placed in a historical perspective. Edwin T. Layton's account is not just a chronicle of the history of engineering; this excerpt from *The Revolt of the Engineers: Social Responsibility and the American Engineering Profession* suggests that the tension just described goes back to the beginnings of engineering. Layton explains how the need for autonomy and professional independence arises from the special knowledge that engineers possess; he describes how the career paths of engineers, and other factors, have pressured engineers into believing that loyalty to employer is of utmost importance. Layton seems to believe that engineers in this country have not been able to acquire the status they would like precisely because of their deep-rooted ties with business.

Layton's historical analysis suggests several questions that might be pursued in a nonhistorical way. Two such issues are taken up in subsequent sections of this chapter. The first has to do with whether engineering is, or can be considered, a "profession." What makes an occupation a profession? Does hope exist for engineering ever to become more of a "profession" than it is now? The readings by D. Allan Firmage and Ernest Greenwood highlight several features that are ordinarily associated with "professions." These include mastery of an organized body of knowledge, fulfilling a social function, and social sanctioning. Firmage derives his criteria from thinking about engineering, but the reader will have to see how engineering measures up when using the criteria provided by Greenwood. In the process, it is useful to compare engineering to the classic professions (such as law and medicine) as well as to occupational areas not generally thought to be professions, (such as auto mechanics and sales).

Although Greenwood's criteria may not be exhaustive, his idea that a continuum exists of occupations with various degrees of "professionalism," depending on which characteristics they possess and to what degree, seems useful. Whether or not an occupation is a profession or not seems less important than identifying which characteristics it possesses and which it lacks, and figuring out which features are detrimental to the profession's well-being or which characteristics it should strive to adopt. An analysis of this kind focusing on engineering will, no doubt, hark back to Layton's discussion of engineering and the factors that prevent engineering from becoming more of what he considers a profession.

A second issue arising from the historical perspective comes to the fore if we simply accept the strong ties to business that are part of engineering. Many engineers work in business, but how does or should this fact affect their responsibilities to society or their abilities to fulfill such obligations? Is morality out of place in business? Don't businesses have social responsibilities? Can individuals who work for companies be absolved of responsibility for their actions when they act for the company? Some have argued that individual engineers are rarely at fault. It is usually their supervisors or employers who make the important decisions.

To begin to answer this set of questions we read two different opinions on the social responsibilities of business and on the obligations of individuals who are executives in corporations. Milton Friedman argues that the only social responsibility of business is to maximize profit while staying within the requirements of the law. In fact, Friedman argues that it is wrong for corporate officials to take a portion of the profits of a company and give them to charitable causes. To do so is, in effect, to tax the stockholders without their consent. Friedman believes that the profits of a corporation belong to the stockholders. When executives reduce profits by giving to charity or doing more for society than they have to, they deprive the stockholders of the opportunity to decide how those profits are spent, whether it be which charitable causes to give to or something else.

A strong attack on Friedman's argument might be made by asking why capitalists believe in capitalism. Capitalism is often justified by an appeal to the good consequences it achieves. Competition, at least, is often justified on grounds that it leads to better products, produced more cheaply. In other words, it could be argued that members of a society adopt a capitalistic system because they believe it will have good results leading to more improvement in the lot of humanity in the long run. Similarly, a society allows corporations to come into being (through law) because it believes that a system of competing corporations will have good results. In a sense, then, the end is human betterment, and corporations seeking profit are the means. This is just the opposite of what Friedman argues when he claims that the end of a corporation is to seek profit. (Paul F. Caminisch makes this point in "Business Ethics: On Getting to the Heart of the Matter," *Business & Professional Ethics Journal*, I, 1 (1981), 59–69.)

Robert V. Hannaford takes a somewhat different line of attack on Friedman. He tries to point out all the flaws in Friedman's analysis. Hannaford's general point is that corporations and individuals are all suppose to direct their behavior at social good, and nothing is wrong with doing more than the minimal that is expected of us by the law. Hannaford also points out flaws in some specific arguments made by Friedman. For example, he argues that it is a misconception to suppose that corporate executives must simply act out the wishes of the stockholders. They, after all, know much more than stockholders about what is good for the company and the effects of the company's activities on society. He also argues that we must hold corporations responsible because they are such a powerful force in our society.

4 The Engineer and Business

Edwin T. Layton

The engineer is both a scientist and a businessman. Engineering is a scientific profession, yet the test of the engineer's work lies not in the laboratory, but in the marketplace. The claims of science and business have pulled the engineer, at times, in opposing directions. Indeed, one outside observer, Thorstein Veblen, assumed that an irrepressible conflict between science and business would thrust the engineer into the role of social revolutionary.[1]

While nothing like a soviet of engineers has appeared, the tensions between science and business have been among the most important forces shaping the engineer's role on the job, in his professional relations, and in the community at large. Veblen assumed that science and business made mutually exclusive demands on the engineer: in fact, however, they often complement one another. Both, for example, may benefit from technological progress. Nor is the existence of tensions necessarily detrimental to engineering work: attempting to resolve them may account for some of the engineer's drive and creativity.

Despite his mordant irony, Veblen was, in one sense, an optimist: he assumed that the tensions between business and science were resolvable, if only through a cataclysmic destruction of the former by the latter. In this he missed the essence of the engineer's dilemma which is, at base, bureaucracy, not capitalism. The engineer's problem has centered on a conflict between professional independence and bureaucratic loyalty, rather than between workmanlike and predatory instincts. Engineers are unlikely to become revolutionaries because such a role would violate the elitist premises of professionalism and because revolution would not eliminate the underlying source of difficulty. The engineer would still be a bureaucrat. Tensions with

Reprinted from Edwin T. Layton, *The Revolt of the Engineers: Social Responsibility and the American Engineering Profession* (Baltimore: Johns Hopkins University Press, 1986), pp. 1–24, with permission.

business have been dominant because in the American context economic development has been carried out principally through the agencies of private capitalism. But engineers in government have experienced quite analogous conflicts, if anything more severe than those of privately employed engineers; and it can be argued that the market system, in providing a final test acceptable to both the engineer and his employer, has served to buffer discord between the two. Perhaps the engineer's problem ultimately is marginality: he is expected to be both a scientist and a businessman, but he is neither. A social revolution would merely alter the terms of his marginality without ending it.

The engineer's relation to bureaucracy is not new; he is the original organization man. The scientifically trained, professional engineer has characteristically appeared on the technical scene at the point of transition from small to large organizations. Economically, it makes little sense for small enterprises to employ engineers; the gains are not worth the costs. Large corporations, on the other hand, can more readily support engineers and research establishments, since they represent a small percentage of their total costs. Large corporations can get substantial net returns from rather small percentage gains in efficiency. Where large investments are at stake, the engineer can serve a useful function in eliminating guesswork and minimizing risks. Technically, large works are more likely to involve complexities than are small ones; and the larger the project, the more likely it is that such difficulties will transcend the capabilities of artisans and businessmen.

In the eighteenth and through much of the nineteenth century, America developed quite diverse and advanced technologies without requiring a corps of scientifically trained experts. The Mississippi River steamboat, for example, was developed in an area of relatively small, highly competitive enterprise by the cut-and-try methods of the practical mechanic, rather than by the rational analysis of scientists. It was large-scale organizations, such as the navy and private corporations, that supported experts who could approach the steam engineer through the laws of thermodynamics. Similarly, it was not the small ironmasters who first called on the aid of science, but the corporate giants of the post-Civil War era. From the start, engineers have been associated with large-scale enterprises.[2]

There were two stages in the emergence of the engineering profession in America in the nineteenth century. The first demand for engineers came from the construction of large public works, such as canals and railroads, particularly in the period 1816 to 1850. The organizations that undertook these works were pioneers in technology and were also among the largest enterprises in America, representing aggregations of capital that were huge for their day. The civil engineering profession was called into being to meet the technical needs of these organizations.

In 1816, the engineering profession scarcely existed in America. It has been estimated that there were only about thirty engineers or quasi-engineers then available; but by 1850, when the census first took note of this new profession, there were 2,000 civil engineers. Canal and railroad construction generated not only the demand for engineers but, in large measure, the supply as well. From an early stage, organizations employing engineers found it convenient to group their technical staffs into a hierarchy of chief engineer, resident engineers, assistant engineers, and the like. Within this bureaucratic context, regular patterns of recruitment and training emerged on the job, and early engineering projects like the Erie Canal and the Baltimore and Ohio Railroad became famous as training schools for engineers.[3]

The rising demand for engineers by industry began the second stage in the emergence of the engineering profession. The golden age for the application of science to American industry came from 1880 to 1920, a period which also witnessed the rise of large industrial corporations. In these forty years, the engineering profession increased by almost 2,000 percent, from 7,000 to 136,000 members. The civil engineer was overshadowed by the new technical specialists who emerged to meet the needs of industry: by the mining, metallurgical, mechanical, electrical, and chemical engineers. The astonishing growth of engineering continued, though at a less rapid rate, after 1920. In 1930, there were 226,000 engineers when the depression put a brake on expansion, by 1940, the number was but little higher—260,000. Postwar prosperity increased the size of the profession past the half-million mark in 1950, and to over 800,000 by 1960. Engineering is by far the largest of the new professions called forth by the industrial revolution.[4]

The rise of the engineering profession was accompanied by a scientific revolution in technology. The change was not a sudden one; in most cases engineering built upon and extended traditional techniques. But professionalism was associated with a slow incorporation of scientific methods and theory into technology and the accumulation of an esoteric body of technical knowledge. Professionalism was a means of preserving, transmitting, and increasing this knowledge. The transition from traditional rule-of-thumb methods to scientific rationality constitutes a change as momentous in its long-term implications as the industrial revolution itself.

The development of engineering education constitutes a sensitive indicator of the shift from art to science in technology. The early civil engineers were educated by self-study and on-the-job training. Only a minority received a college degree. By 1870, there were twenty-one engineering colleges, but only 866 degrees had been conferred. College education became increasingly common after 1870. By 1896, there were 110 engineering colleges. The number of students increased rapidly, from 1,000 in 1890 to 10,000 in 1900. Only with the twentieth century, however, did the college diploma become the normal means of admission to engineering practice.[5]

College training was a sign of a greater emphasis on science. But even here the change was evolutionary. The engineering curriculum of the latter nineteenth century placed as much or more emphasis on craft skills as upon scientific training. In 1875, Alexander L. Holley, a prominent mechanical engineer, argued that all the great engineering triumphs of his day owed more to art than to science. The aim of college education, Holley maintained, was to train "not *men* of good general education, but *artisans* of good general education," for as Holley emphasized, "the art must precede the science."[6] Despite an increasing emphasis on science, engineering educators down to 1920 seriously debated whether engineering students ought to learn the calculus. Some of them thought such courses were "cultural" embellishments to the curriculum. Only since the end of the Second World War has the balance in engineering education shifted unequivocally toward science.[7]

The origin of engineers carries with it built-in tensions between the bureaucratic loyalty demanded by employers and the independence implicit in professionalism. It is important to note, however, that these tensions are not, as Veblen thought, the outgrowth of a clash between the rationality of science and the irrationality of capitalism. The scientific knowledge possessed by the engineer is highly rational, but his professionalism derives from the mere possession of esoteric knowledge, not its specific content. Incomprehensibility to laymen, rather than rationality, is the foundation of professionalism. In essence, the professional values adopted by American engineers are the same as those of other professions. They may be summarized under the headings of autonomy, colleagual control of professional work, and social responsibility.[8]

Perhaps the most invariant demand by all professions is for autonomy. The classic argument is that outsiders are unable to judge or control professional work, since it involves esoteric knowledge they do not understand. Autonomy operates on at least two distinct levels: it applies to engineers in their corporate sense as an organized profession and to the individual engineer in relation to his employer. In both cases, conflicts have appeared between business demands and the ideal of professional independence. Businessmen usually concede that engineering societies should be free of external control, but in practice business domination is not uncommon. Employers have been unwilling to grant autonomy to their employees, even in principle. They have assumed that the engineer, like any other employee, should take orders. Some engineers, however, have maintained that the engineer, like the doctor, should prescribe the course to be followed and that the very essence of professionalism lies in not taking orders from an employer.[9] The employer, of course, has the power to reward and punish. But the value of the engineer generally hinges on his being a professional in the sense of being both a master of an ever-growing body of knowledge and a creative contributor to that knowledge. Such men are the ones most likely to be inspired by professional ideals. As a result, the role of the engineer represents a patchwork of compromises, between professional ideals and business demands.

The argument for colleagual control of professional work is closely related to that for autonomy. Since professional work cannot be understood fully by outsiders, the person in charge of such work should be a member of the profession. In this manner, doctors have insisted that the heads of hospitals and medical schools should be members of the medical profession. In the same vein, engineers have maintained that engineers should be in charge of engineering work.[10] In practice, engineering departments are usually headed by engineers. But in the case of engineering, this principle can be extended much further. Engineering is intimately related to fundamental choices of policy made by the organizations employing engineers. This can lead to the assertion that engineers ought to be placed in command of the large organizations, public and private, which direct engineering. This is tantamount to saying that society should be ruled by engineers. A more representative manifestation of the ideal of colleagual control has been the repeated demand by the profession for reform of governmental public-works policy. Engineers have advocated the creation of a cabinet-level department of engineering to be headed by a civilian engineer.[11]

Although the arguments for autonomy and colleagual control are fundamentally similar, one of the basic dilemmas of modern engineers has been that these two goals are not completely compatible. Organizations like the federal government or a modern corporation have other ends in view than the best and most efficient engineering. Doctors are in a more fortunate position, since it may be assumed that the professional aim—health—is identical to the ends of the large organizations employing doctors, such as hospitals and medical schools. But, unlike medicine, engineering serves purposes ulterior to itself. Colleagual control of engineering implies, in the extreme, a change in basic social values, to make those of engineering supreme. Such aspirations open up the possibility that outside organizations might reciprocally seek to control engineering, as something potentially dangerous to their purposes.

Professional freedom implies social responsibility. The professional man has a special responsibility to see that his knowledge is used for the benefit of the community. Social responsibility points in two directions: inwardly, at self-policing to prevent abuses by colleagues, and outwardly, to the making of public policy. In either case, it is with social responsibility that professionalism comes most clearly into conflict with bureaucracy. This may be seen in two possible meanings of the term "responsibility." On the one hand, there is the bureaucratic sense implied in the phrase "responsible public official." This denotes responsibility in executing policies, but not necessarily in formulating them. On the other hand, the term "professional responsibility" entails an independent determination of policy by the professional man, based on esoteric knowledge and guided by a sense of public duty. An assertion of professional responsibility, therefore, may signify a rejection of bureaucratic authority. In this manner, the scientists' crusade against the May-Johnson Bill for postwar control of atomic energy was both an assertion of a professional responsibility and a rebellion against General Groves and the formal hierarchy of the Manhattan Project.

For engineers, the most overt element of professionalism has been an obsessive concern for social status. Although the income and the power of engineers would of course be enhanced by professionalism, these ends have been given second place, at least verbally. Professionalism has induced engineers to seek greater deference, in particular, to gain the same social recognition accorded to the traditional learned professions, law and medicine. Spokesmen for the engineering profession have, in fact, frequently made status the fundamental aim, and other professional values means to this end. Thus, engineers have argued that in order to gain more status their profession should show a greater sense of social responsibility.[12]

Although engineers emphasize the importance of status, it is not clear that this distinguishes their goals from those of other interest groups. Engineers differ from nonprofessional groups chiefly in that they are more likely to rationalize their ambitions in terms of protecting the public. Following the cue of the older professions, engineers have secured the enactment of licensing laws, and they have endeavored to raise standards in education and practice. Such measures enable professions to limit competition and alter supply-and-demand relationships in their favor. Engineers have hoped to achieve in this way many of the same goals sought by labor unions through such devices as the closed shop and strike. Professional autonomy and control of the profession's work by colleagues, if fully realized, would lead to control of the conditions of work, an end pursued equally, if by other means, by labor unions. As an interest-group strategy, professionalism offers several advantages. It is "dignified," since the professional abjures "selfish" behavior, at least verbally, and gains group advantage on the pretext of protecting the public. Professionals emphasize the intimacy of the personal relationship with clients, rather than the cash nexus between buyer and seller, employer and employee.

Professionalism for engineers is not exclusively a matter of esoteric knowledge. Engineers do not seek autonomy simply because they are professionals; to some extent they have adopted professionalism as a way of gaining autonomy. Professionalism was, in part, a reaction against organization and bureaucracy. It was a way to prevent engineers from becoming mere cogs in a vast industrial machine. Thus, in 1939, Vannevar Bush made an eloquent plea for a professional spirit in engineering. Without this spirit, Bush thought,

> we may as well resign ourselves to a general absorption as controlled employees, and to the disappearance of our independence. We may as well conclude that we are merely one more group of the population . . . forced in this direction and that by the conflict between the great forces of a civilized community, with no higher ideals than to serve as directed.[13]

Professionalism carries overtones of elitism that grate against the egalitarian assumptions of American democracy. Professionalism stresses hierarchy and the importance of the expert; its emphasis is on the creative few, rather than on the many. But professionalism, not itself democratic, may serve democratic ends. It is one means of preserving the ideal of the autonomous individual, without which democracy could scarcely exist. Democracy requires not only freedom, but an informed public opinion. One of the problems of the modern age is that many issues of public policy involve technical matters. Independent and informed judgments of these questions are badly needed by the public. Professionalism, because of its stress on social responsibility, offers one way of meeting this need by establishing a legitimate role for private judgment by engineers, protected and encouraged by an organized profession.

Whether the emphasis be on esoteric knowledge, public service, or selfish interest, professionalism requires that engineers identify themselves with their profession. Engineers must think of themselves as engineers before they can constitute a profession. There are several factors that link engineers together as a group and encourage self-consciousness. As with all professions, the fundamental tie is a common body of knowledge. Self-interest is another powerful cohesive force. Both find a natural focus in the professional society, which brings engineers together and gives them a sense of corporate identity. These factors have helped to produce a steady push toward professionalism among engineers.

Professionalism, however, has met powerful resistance from business. Business has been reluctant to grant independence to employees. The claims of professionals rest fundamentally on esoteric knowledge; to reduce the importance of this knowledge is to weaken the engineers' aspirations for autonomy. To some extent this may take the form of a depreciation of "theory" and an emphasis on practicality. But if businessmen tend to depreciate esoteric knowledge, they cannot wish it away. Experts have been of increasing, not diminishing importance. A more pervasive and effective argument is the priority of business needs over technical considerations.[14] This contention is not without force. The transition from art to science in engineering has been slow and partial. Even where technical knowledge has achieved a high state of perfection, its importance is limited by the exigencies of business. Engineers work in complex organizations. Engineering is only one factor among many that contribute to their success.

In the long run, the most effective check on professionalism by business has been a career line that carries most engineers eventually into management. The promise of a lucrative career in business does much to ensure the loyalty of the engineering staff. Conversely, it undermines engineers' identification with their profession. Social mobility carries with it an alternative set of values associated with the businessman's ideology of individualism. These values compete with, and to some degree conflict with, those of professionalism. Thus, professionals stress the importance of expert knowledge, but businessmen stress the role of personal characteristics, such as loyalty, drive, initiative, and hard work. Professions value lifetime dedication. But business makes engineering a phase in a successful career rather than a career in itself. Insofar as business treats engineering merely as a stepping stone to management, it represents a denial of much that professions stand for.

It is possible to distinguish several stages in the typical engineering career. The most important source for understanding the engineer's background is a study conducted by the Society for the Promotion of Engineering Education in 1924, as part of a large survey of engineering education. It was based on a questionnaire administered to 20 percent of all engineering freshmen admitted in the fall of that year, 4,079 students selected from thirty-two engineering schools so as to constitute a representative cross section. A very large proportion of the parents of these students were members of the old middle class: 42.5 percent were owners or proprietors of businesses. Of the remainder, more than one-quarter were members of the new middle class: 28.2 percent were employed in executive or supervisory positions and 5.6 percent were engineers or teachers. Another 13 percent of the total were skilled workers, but only 2.7 percent were unskilled workmen and 3.5 percent were clerks.[15]

The engineering students surveyed by the 1924 study were drawn from the poorer and less well-educated segments of the middle class. Almost all of the parents who were owners or proprietors were engaged in small mercantile enterprises or farming. Only 13 percent of the fathers had a college degree. Forty percent had graduated from high school, and the same number had a grammar school education or less. Sixteen percent had started but not finished high school. That the parents were not especially well-off is further suggested by the fact that 90 percent of the freshmen had to work a year before starting college.[16]

The parents of these students were overwhelmingly of Anglo-Saxon or northwestern European stock. Of the students, 96.2 percent were native-born, as were 73.6 percent of their parents and 60.7 percent of their grandparents. Of the grandparents not born in the United States or Canada, two out of three were from northwestern European countries.

More than three out of five of the students' families lived in small towns, villages, or on farms. Only 38.7 percent came from cities with a population of over 25,000.[17] A recent study of similar scope indicates that the proportion of engineers drawn from families of blue-collar workers has significantly increased. Presumably this has affected the ethnic background of the engineers concerned. But the large city continues to be underrepresented in the profession.[18]

The selectivity in recruitment of engineering students from middle-class, small-town, and old-stock families goes far to account for the profession's strong commitment to traditional individualism. One engineer, in tracing his own faith in rugged individualism to the self-reliance of his father, suggested that his own experience was typical of his generation.[19] Another engineer, commenting on the frontier individualism of his home community, noted that "no one growing up in such an environment could escape being influenced by it."[20] A frequent theme in discussions of success in engineering is the importance of an "inner drive," or an "inner urge," or more simply of initiative.[21] It is perhaps no accident that the term "rugged individualism" was given currency by an engineer, Herbert Hoover. But predisposition to individualism also provides the foundations for the development of a commitment to business.

Engineering education is susceptible to business influence in a number of ways. Businessmen serve as trustees of colleges, on alumni boards, and on committees of technical societies concerned with technical education.[22] Engineering educators suffer from the same divided loyalties as other engineers, and some of them have been important spokesmen for a business point of view. Many businessmen, and some engineering educators, have assumed that the buyer, business, has the right to determine both the technical skills to be taught and the ideas to be implanted in students' minds. Business demands on this score have ranged from training in "sound economics" to concern for international responsibilities.[23] In 1932, a group of engineering educators at Ohio State Universivty became interested in training engineering students in social responsibilities; but before undertaking anything definite, they prudently sampled the opinions of business leaders on major issues of the day. One of the educators noted that the "industrial system" was not then working well. He reflected:

> What would happen if these socially awakened young men should come to the conclusion that its very fundamentals are wrong. . . . Manifestly such young reformers might find a cold reception in industry. . . . It is therefore well to ascertain what leading executives think about such matters.[24]

Despite strong business influence, however, the feeling of professional independence is probably stronger in engineering schools than elsewhere. Educators tend to think of themselves as independent practitioners. Shielded by traditions of academic freedom and in contact with other professions, engineering educators have been in a position to assert a professional commitment. It is not surprising that educators have been prominent in movements to uphold and advance professionalism. Perhaps the educators' most important impact has been on their students whom they inculcate with professional ideals.

The next stage in the engineer's development is that of professional engineering proper. The transition is quite marked geographically and environmentally, since most engineers leave their home states on completion of college—59 percent, as against an average of only 38 percent for all other college graduates.[25] The young graduate does not qualify immediately as a full-fledged professional. Four years at college are barely sufficient to lay the foundations upon which the young man must continue to build for a lengthy period thereafter. This process is not simply one of absorbing more knowledge; managerial and personal skills come into play also. The final judge of the young man's gradual advance is as much or more his employer as his professional colleagues. Major engineering societies recognize four stages in the engineer's development, which they embody in their grades of membership: from student to junior, to associate, and finally to full member. But most such societies place as one of their requirements for the higher grades of membership that the candidate be in "responsible charge" of engineering work, a test as much of his bureaucratic status and business success as of his engineering knowledge. Success in business overlaps and may eclipse success in the engineer's profession.

Most engineers work in industrial bureaucracies, which are capable of exerting a considerable amount of pressure on the individual. The effectiveness of this influence is heightened when the individual seeks not only to keep his job, but to rise in the hierarchy. The price of success, in at least some cases, is total and undivided loyalty. An engineering educator made this point in 1935 when he asked a group of young engineers:

> Are you truly loyal to your employer's interests?
> Do you try to advance these on every opportunity?
> Do you have a fighting spirit for the reputation of "our company" and "our products"? The merging of your employer's interests into your own is one of the surest signs of real progress in business life.[26]

Conformist pressures on the job are not limited to company loyalty; they extend to all sorts of social and political norms. As one engineering society president, J. F. Coleman, noted, the employed engineer cannot be as open in expressing his opinion on socio-economic subjects as one who is a free agent.[27] One young engineer complained, in 1942, that on the job "everything possible was done to make alert youth conform to routine. Ideas were discouraged, social and political interests frowned upon."[28] Pressure appears to be especially great against heterodox ideas. A young mechanical engineer wrote, in 1941, that many engineers favored joining unions, but that they were "under the terror of jeopardizing their connections by coming out into the open with their opinions."[29] Another engineer wrote to a leading engineering journal, in 1940, "to my mind for individual engineers themselves to have published in *Mechanical Engineering* their own views of what they would like is very likely to bring about some action which may put us all on the spot."[30] A distinguished civil engineer, Daniel W. Mead, in 1929 advised young engineers to avoid unorthodox dress, since "conspicuous dress usually shows unfortunate idiosyncrasies which need to be eliminated."[31]

Employers have occasionally urged engineers to show more social responsibility. But by this they generally have in mind the defense of business, rather than independent action by the profession. Engineering support for business is often taken for granted. As one mining engineer told a group of young engineers in 1931:

> We as employees owe the company our best efforts not only while at work but at all times, promoting always the company's interests by representing them favorably. This we can best do by active, harmonious participation in the community social, civil, and spiritual activity.[32]

He thought the engineer could best serve his employer by being a "booster imbued with the spirit of boosting at all times."[33] H. B. Gear, an engineer who became the vice-president of the Commonwealth Edison Company of Chicago, in 1942 maintained that engineering best served society as an "implement of management."[34] It is not clear whether Gear had in mind the sort of social service provided by Samuel Insull, the founder of Commonwealth Edison, but in any case Gear's idea of the preeminence of business considerations left little room for an assertion of social responsibility by an independent profession.

The coercive element within bureaucracies should not be exaggerated, however. Pressures internalized within the individual are far more effective. One of the most acute observers of the profession, William E. Wickenden, noted that engineers seeking social premises look to "the presuppositions of the man higher up who sets the engineer at his problem and reserves final judgment on his recommendations."[35] An ardent advocate of professional values, Arthur E. Morgan, sadly noted that "the engineer tends to reflect, somewhat uncritically, the social attitude of his employer."[36] He implored engineers to abandon their "moral servitude" and develop an independent philosophy."[37]

The final phase of the engineer's development, not achieved by all, is the transition from professional engineering to business management. A survey of the six largest American engineering societies, in 1946, revealed that over one-third of their membership was engaged in management.[38] A study of 5,000 engineering graduates by the Society for the Promotion of Engineering Education, in the 1920s, suggested that, on the basis of their sample, over 60 percent of all engineers made this shift eventually. There was a secondary drift from technical to nontechnical management and administration. Half had made this change by forty years of age, and the proportion increased to three-quarters after fifty-five.[39] No doubt monetary rewards have played an important role in encouraging engineers to move into management. Several studies of engineers have stressed the large premiums paid for managerial work as against purely technical engineering.[40] One result of this trend has been that engineers constitute a large and increasing segment of the upper echelons of business. Mabel Newcomer found that the proportion of engineers in the managerial elite of presidents and board chairmen grew from one in eight in 1900 to almost one in five in 1950.[41]

It is not uncommon for engineers who have risen into managerial positions to think of themselves as businessmen. John Mills, a discerning observer of his profession, noted that as engineers climb into supervisory positions, they tend to be blinded by visions of future promotions and to lose sight of colleagues lower down.[42] Although many such men no longer think of themselves as engineers, they may retain professional-society membership for business reasons. But professional commitment is clearly diminished. Others sever their ties with engineering completely. The 1960 census, which relied on the self-identifications of respondents for occupations, counted 541,000 engineers and scientists in manufacturing, the bulk of whom were engineers. A follow-up survey by the National Science Foundation discovered an additional 73,000 technically qualified persons who had been missed because they had identified themselves with nontechnical occupations, presumably managerial.[43]

A number of engineers have looked to the major professional associations to offset the power of business. Arthur E. Morgan, the first head of the Tennessee Valley Authority, was deeply concerned by the fact that the engineer employed in a bureaucracy "tends to be not a free agent, but a technical implement of other men's purposes." But he pessimistically concluded that "the lone individual is largely helpless."[44] Morgan, however, hoped that engineering societies might enable their members collectively to gain the freedom they lacked as individuals. He was aware this would not be easy; he pointed out:

> For engineering associations to be a democratic force in the public interest, they must be more than the summing up of the selfish interests of their members, and more than the reflections of the views of their several employers. . . . Otherwise an engineering organization may be only a more powerful means of regimenting the members along lines of policy which their employers happen to be following.[45]

The professional ideal expressed by Morgan was difficult to attain because business influence had penetrated the very citadel of professionalism, the engineering society. The most important agents of business influence within the organized profession are engineers who have moved into management; they constitute a large and powerful minority of senior and successful men. As the editor of *Mining and Metallurgy* observed: "naturally such men are highly influential in establishing the policies of engineering societies."[46]

Engineers who have risen into top management present a dilemma for engineering societies. Although it has been generally conceded that engineers engaged in technical management are still engineers, this is far from clear in the case of those who have gone up the corporate hierarchy to positions involving general management and administration. Some engineers have argued that such men are no more practicing their profession than a lawyer in a similar position is practicing his.[47] This argument implies that such men should be excluded from the higher grades of membership of engineering societies and, hence, from effective control of their profession. Other engineers have taken a contrary position. They have maintained that the engineer in top management has fulfilled the engineer's cherished ideal of success and that even those who have lost any active interest in technical matters should be encouraged to join engineering societies and participate in their government. In 1953, Frederick S. Blackall, Jr., the president of the American Society of Mechanical Engineers, maintained that

> if ASME . . . is one of the most important factors in molding the character and competence of the technical staff, then too, most certainly the men of top management should make it their business to have a voice in its affairs. Here will be found a splendid sounding board for their view and platforms for their leadership.[48]

However, the fact that engineers in management tend to lose their identification as engineers presents a further difficulty. In 1927, for example, Blackall's society elected Charles M. Schwab as its president; yet in his *Who's Who* autobiography, Schwab listed himself as a "capitalist," down to 1934, and as a "steel manufacturer" thereafter; he did not mention his presidency of the American Society of Mechanical Engineers or even his membership in that organization.[49]

To some extent business influence is checked by the power of majority rule. But engineering societies are not perfectly functioning democracies, and there are serious limitations to the control that rank-and-file members can exercise. Some societies long denied younger members the right to vote; even without formal restrictions on voting, the idea of a hierarchy of professional excellence implicit in membership grades tends to give power to the senior full members and to deny significant influence to junior members. In certain specific instances, employers have canvassed their technical staffs to line-up votes on particular issues. But more commonly, widespread ignorance and apathy give inordinate power to comparatively small minorities. Most members live in remote parts of the country and are little interested in society affairs. Nominations are controlled by committees whose actions are usually shrouded in secrecy; the election presents a mere formality.[50]

It is considered bad form to publicize the inner workings of engineering societies. Even in those rare cases where elections have been contested, both parties have usually taken precautions to keep the real issues secret. In 1914, Morris L. Cooke led a revolt against excessive dominance of the American Society of Mechanical Engineers by the utilities. His election to the society's governing board was opposed by a rival candidate put up by the utility interests. Not only did no mention of this appear in the ASME's official publications, but it was deliberately obscured in the informal circulars distributed by both sides. The opposition based its position on a technicality in the manner of Cooke's nomination. Cooke, though a foremost advocate of publicity in engineering-society affairs, also avoided the real issue for tactical reasons. In writing to a close friend concerning his circulars, Cooke noted that "the utility matter is kept in the background and can be used with telling effect, but we do not draw on ourselves the charge of washing the society's soiled linen in the public."[51]

Given the secrecy surrounding engineering-society affairs and the indifference of most members, the machinery of society government offers many opportunities for small but active groups to exercise control. Three committees have been particularly important as sources of business influence. They are those concerned with nominations, new members, and publications. By controlling nominations, a group can make sure that engineers sympathetic with its interests are in strategic positions in the society's government. Control of membership, in the long run, is the most important power of all, since this committee does much to determine the future composition of the society. Control of membership committees can also be employed to keep out of a particular society individuals not acceptable to particular business interests. Edward W. Bemis, who often took the public side in utilities-valuation cases, was advised not to apply for membership in the American Society of Mechanical Engineers because of the power of the utilities in the committees concerned with passing on new membership applications.[52]

Perhaps the most influential committees of engineering societies are those concerned with publications. Such committees can control the publication of technical papers, censor heretical opinions, or silence proposals that might embarrass particular business interests. The electric utilities have been especially active and successful in this respect. Their power in the American Institute of Electrical Engineers led to a prohibition of papers dealing with costs and rate making. According to Governor Pinchot of Pennsylvania, this practice seriously hampered the efforts of public agencies to regulate utilities.[53] Other societies, lacking such a prohibition, have been prevented from publishing papers opposed by utilities interests. In May of 1938, for example, Gregory M. Dexter submitted a paper to the American Society of Mechanical Engineers that dealt with electric rates of a subsidiary of Consolidated Edison in Scarsdale, New York. A long series of delays and rewritings ensued. Dexter claimed he would be asked to write it one way, and then he would find the "rules" had been changed and he would have to write it another way. Not until January, 1942, was the paper finally rejected. On the committee that ruled the paper unacceptable were several engineers connected in various ways with utilities interests, among whom was an advisory member who held the position of assistant engineer for Consolidated Edison.[54]

Virtually all of the major engineering societies in America have had more or less celebrated cases of censorship, involving a broad spectrum of business interests. Within the American Institute of Mining Engineers, for example, the representatives of the coal and oil industries have been accused of censorship. In 1916, W. H. Shockley claimed that a paper of his was suppressed at the instance of the anthracite section because it presented government statistics showing the wages of coal miners were inadequate.[55] In 1922, another member, Robert B. Brinsmade, complained that a paper of his was censored because of certain comments about oil policy. He sarcastically suggested that his letters would enable members to avoid opinions "which have been put on the prohibited index by the august Committee of Publications."[56]

This sort of censorship is made more effective by the codes of ethics adopted by some societies. These codes may prohibit criticism of fellow engineers and the discussion of engineering subjects in the general press. The codes of ethics of the American Institute of Electrical Engineers and the American Society of Mechanical Engineers both provided that "technical discussions and criticisms of engineering subjects should not be conducted in the public press, but before engineering societies, or in the technical press."[57] These codes of ethics are seldom enforced, so the sanction is perhaps limited. But it is not trivial, either. In order to circumvent the restriction on publication outside the society, Frederick W. Taylor had one of his works privately printed and gave a free copy to each member of the American Society of Mechanical Engineers prior to general circulation.[58] This expedient, however, was available only to those with considerable means.

Censorship, though not absolute, is a significant deterrent to free publication by engineers. In 1932, it led to the expulsion of Bernhard F. Jakobsen and James H. Payne from the American Society of Civil Engineers. Payne and Jakobsen, in 1930, had exposed certain malpractices in connection with the construction of a dam for Los Angeles County. They published their critical findings in the pages of a local newspaper, and they were critical of the chief engineer, among others. The two engineers who made the exposure were then expelled from the American Society of Civil Engineers for unprofessional conduct. It was later established that the contractor had bribed the chairman of the Board of Supervisors, who was sent to jail. The contractor was forced to return over $700,000 to the county. Despite a plea from the Los Angeles County Board of Supervisors to reconsider, the ASCE refused to reinstate Jakobsen and Payne.[59]

In many matters, such as censorship, engineers who hold managerial positions have been the principal agents of business influence in engineering societies. But they are by no means the only source of business power within the profession. Even if such men were excluded from the higher grades of membership—a favorite remedy for some reformers—business influence would remain substantial. Virtually all American engineering societies are financially dependent on business. This is clearest in those smaller societies that have company members; here the subsidy is direct.[60] Other engineering societies are nominally supported solely by the dues of members. But in fact, they receive indirect financial support from business. A substantial number of members have their dues paid by their employers. A survey in 1947 revealed that, in the sample studied, some 30 percent of the employers regularly paid the dues of some of their employees in certain societies.[61] In 1940, a spokesman for the membership committee of the American Institute of Mining Engineers complained that qualified men were not joining the institute because they were waiting for their employers to pay their dues; he found it necessary to remind them that membership in the institute was a personal matter.[62]

A second form of indirect business subsidy is that of employers paying traveling expenses and allowing time off for employees to attend engineering-society meetings, especially when presenting a paper, serving on a committee, or participating in a discussion. The official journal of the American Society of Mechanical Engineers, *Mechanical Engineering*, commented editorially that engineering societies must accept such aid, since without it they "would have to shut up shop, as a majority of the work of engineering societies is done by its members who are encouraged by their employers to do this work."[63]

Business subsidies pose a delicate problem for engineers. Some societies have openly admitted the practice and defended it. *Mechanical Engineering* urged employers to look on engineering-society activities of an employee as an "assignment" and suggested that the employer "send him to a meeting, or encourage his participation in some other form of society activity, with the feeling that he is representing his company's as well as his own interests."[64] Other engineers, concerned with professional independence, have argued that such practices are harmful. One engineer maintained that subsidies from business made their recipients unfit to represent the engineering profession, and he urged support of the National Society of Professional Engineers since it was "for the benefit of the engineering profession primarily and not for the advancement of corporation interests."[65] A further problem here is that "pure" professional organizations, such as the NSPE, do not publish technical papers. It would be financially impossible for them to do so, even if employers would permit publication of papers by their employees by an organization outside their influence.

Although there are significant areas of conflict between business and professionalism, the dimensions of the clash should not be exaggerated. Neither could exist under present circumstances without the other. Modern business needs highly esoteric technical knowledge, and only professionals can supply it. Technologists need organizations in order to apply their knowledge; unlike science, technology cannot exist for its own sake. The problem has been to find suitable mechanisms of balance and accommodation. One of the basic problems of American engineers is that the balance has tended to shift too far in the direction of business, and accommodation has taken place largely on terms laid down by employers. The professional independence of engineers has been drastically curtailed. The losers are not just engineers. The public would benefit greatly from the unbiased evaluations of technical matters that an independent profession could provide. American business too might profit in the long run from the presence of a loyal opposition.

NOTES

1. Thorstein Veblen, *The Engineers and the Price System* (New York, 1933), 70–76.

2. Louis C. Hunter, *Steamboats on Western Waters* (Cambridge, 1949), 175–180, 307–309; William F. Durand, *Robert Henry Thurston* (New York, 1929), 201, *passim*; W. Paul Strassman, *Risk and Technological Innovation: American Manufacturing Methods During the 19th Century* (Ithaca, 1956), 28–46.

3. Daniel Hovey Calhoun, *The American Civil Engineer, Origins and Conflict* (Cambridge, 1960), 22, 27–29, 48–50.

4. U.S. Bureau of Census, *Sixteenth Census, Population, Comparative Occupational Statistics for the United States, 1870–1940* (Washington, 1943), p. 111, table 8; Jay M. Gould, *Technical Elite* (New York, 1966), 172. Here and elsewhere I have rounded off figures for total number of engineers to the nearest thousand.

5. Society for the Promotion of Engineering Education, *Report of the Investigation of Engineering Education, 1923–1929*, 2 vols. (Pittsburgh, 1934), I, 541–547 (hereafter cited as SPEE, *Report of Investigation*), and David L. Fiske, "Are the Professions Overcrowded?" *Civil Engineering*, IV (June, 1934), p 16, table I.

6. Alexander L. Holley, "The Inadequate Union of Engineering Science and Art," *Trans AIME*, IV (1875–1876), 191–192, 201.

7. C. R. Mann, "Report of the Joint Committee on Engineering Education," *Engineering Education*, IX (September, 1918), 19–26; H. D. Gaylord, "The Relation of Mathematical Training to the Engineering Profession," *Engineering Education*, VII (October, 1916), 54–55; Frank McKibben, "The Colleges and the War," *Engineering Education*, IX (May, 1919), 363; and George F. Swain, "The Liberal Element in Engineering Education," *Engineering Education*, IX (December, 1918), 97–107.

8. The literature on professions is vast, but I have been particularly influenced by the writings of Everett C. Hughes. See Everett C. Hughes, "Professions," in Kenneth S. Lynn, ed, *The Professions in America* (Boston, 1965), 1–14, and Everett C. Hughes, *Men and Their Work* (Glencoe, Illinois, 1958). For a discussion of professionalism by an engineer, see William E. Wickenden, "Toward the Making of a Profession," *Electrical Engineering*, LIII, pt. 2 (August, 1934), 1146–48.

9. Frederick H. Newell, "A Practical Plan of Engineering Cooperation," *Journal of the Cleveland Engineering Society*, IX (March, 1917), 311.

10. For an example, see Hunter McDonald, "Address at the Annual Conventions." *Trans ASCE*, LXXVII (December, 1914), 1755.

11. For examples, see Clemens Herschel, "Address at the Annual Convention," *Trans ASCE*, LXXX (1916), 1307–14, and "News of the Federated American Engineering Societies," *Mechanical Engineering*, XLIII (June, 1921), 421–422.

12. C. O. Mailloux, "The Evolution of the Institute and of Its Members," *Trans AIEE*, XXXIII, pt. 1 (January–June, 1914), 827–834.

13. Vannevar Bush, "The Professional Spirit in Engineering," *Mechanical Engineering*, LXI (March, 1939), 198.

14. For one engineering educator's reaction to demands for "practicality," see Abraham Press, "Education Versus Engineering," *Engineering Education*, VIII (September, 1917), 28–30. For an example of the stress on business needs, see H. B. Gear, "The Engineer as an Implement of Management," *Electrical Engineering*, LXI (August, 1942), 426–427.

15. SPEE, *Report of Investigation*, I, 161–164, 188.

16. *Ibid.*, 164–166, 189.

17. *Ibid.*, 162–163, 188–189.

18. Robert Perrucci, William K. Le Bold, and Warren E. Howland, "The Engineer in Industry and Government," *Journal of Engineering Education*, LVI (March, 1966), 239–240.

19. A. W. Robertson, "Industry's New Responsibilities," *Electrical Engineering*, I (September, 1931), 719.

20. Frank B. Jewett, "An Exciting and Pleasant Forty Years," *Electrical Engineering*, LVIII (April, 1939), 161.

21. William E. Wickenden, "The Young Engineer Facing Tomorrow," *Mechanical Engineering*, LXI (May, 1939), 347, 348, and John C. Parker, "Responsibilities in the AIEE," *Electrical Engineering*. LVIII (August, 1939), 331–332.

22. "Industry's Influence," *Mechanical Engineering*. LXVII (August, 1945), 499–500.

23. Thorndike Saville, "Engineering Education in a Changing World," *Journal of Engineering Education*, XLI (September, 1950), 5. See also L. W. W. Morrow, "Industry Demands and Engineering Education," *Electrical Engineering*, LIII, pt. 1 (April, 1934), 518–522.

24. A. Norman, "Industrial Fundamentals," *Journal of Engineering Education*, XXII (March, 1932), 537.

25. Ernest Havemann and Patricia Salter West, *They Went to College* (New York, 1952), 235.

26. A. G. Christie, "Engineers' Business Contacts," *Mechanical Engineering*, LVII (February, 1935), 88.

27. J. F. Coleman, "Reflections on the Status of the Engineer," *Trans ASCE*, XCIV (1930), 1346.

28. Walter J. Gray, "Present-Day Responsibilities of the Engineer" (letter to the editors), *Civil Engineering*, XII (December, 1942), 687.

29. Andrew A. Bato, "Unionization of Engineers" (letter to the editors), *Mechanical Engineering*, LXIII (June, 1941), 476.

30. James M. Sherilla (letter to the editors), *Mechanical Engineering*, LXII (May, 1940), 412.

31. Daniel W. Mead, "The Engineer and His Education," in Dugald C. Jackson and W. Paul Jones, eds. *The Profession of Engineering* (New York, 1929), 28.

32. Henry Coleman, "Loyalty," *Mining and Metallurgy*, XII (August, 1931), 374–375.

33. *Ibid.*

34. H. B. Gear, "Engineering as an Implement of Management," *Electrical Engineering*, LXI (August, 1942), 426–427.

35. William E. Wickenden, "The Social Sciences and Engineering Education," *Mechanical Engineering*, LX (February, 1938), 149.

36. Arthur E. Morgan, "The Faith of the Engineer," *Civil Engineering*, XII (August, 1942), 421.

37. Arthur E. Morgan, "Engineer's Share in Democracy," *Civil Engineering*, IX (November, 1939), 638.

38. Andrew Fraser, *The Engineering Profession in Transition* (New York, 1947), p. 45, table 3.5g. The societies were the American Society of Civil Engineers, the American Institute of Mining Engineers, the American Society of Mechanical Engineers, the American Institute of Electrical Engineers, the American Institute of Chemical Engineers, and the National Society of Professional Engineers.

39. SPEE, *Report of Investigation*, I, 231–232. See also William E. Wickenden and Eliot Dunlap Smith, "Engineers, Managers, and Engineering Education," *Journal of Engineering Education*, XXII (June, 1932), 846–847.

40. Fraser, *Engineering Profession in Transition*, p. 28, table 1.9a. See also "1930 Earnings of Mechanical Engineers," *Mechanical Engineering*, LIII (September, 1931), 655.

41. Mabel Newcomer, *The Big Business Executive* (New York, 1955), 90. In absolute terms, this increase has been still larger since the group of top executives grew from 284 in 1900 to 319 in 1925, and to 868 in 1950. Jay M. Gould has recently extended Newcomer's figures to 1964. He found that the proportion of engineers and scientists had increased from about one in five in 1950 to about one in three in 1964 (see his *Technical Elite*, 82–84).

42. John Mills, *The Engineer in Society* (New York, 1946), 116, 138–139.

43. Gould, *Technical Elite*, 130.

44. Arthur E. Morgan, "Engineer's Share in Democracy." *Civil Engineering*, IX (November, 1939), 638.

45. *Ibid.*

46. A. B. Parsons, "Superorganizing Professional Engineers," *Mining and Metallurgy*, XXIV (September, 1943), 392.

47. Robert E. Doherty, "The Engineering Profession Tomorrow," *Journal of Engineering Education*, XXXV (September, 1944), 9.

48. Frederick S. Blackall, Jr., "ASME's Importance to Management," *Mechanical Engineering*, LXXV (September, 1953), 752.

49. *Who's Who in America*, 1930–1931, pp. 194–195.

50. Morris L. Cooke, "On the Organization of an Engineering Society," *Mechanical Engineering*, XLIII (May, 1921), 323, 325. See also Morris L. Cooke, *Professional Ethics and Social Change* (New York, 1946), 10.

51. Morris L. Cooke to Frederick W. Taylor, October 30, 1914, file "Cooke. July–December, 1914," Frederick William Taylor Collection, Stevens Institute of Technology, Hoboken, New Jersey.

52. Charles W. Baker to Edward W. Bemis, September 21, 1916, and Morris L. Cooke to Bemis, September 27, 1916, file "ASME Engineering Ethics—1916," box 168, Papers of Morris L. Cooke, Franklin D. Roosevelt Library, Hyde Park, New York.

53. "President Lee Answers Governor Pinchot," *Electrical Engineering*, L (March, 1931), 215.

54. Gregory M. Dexter, "An Appeal to Members" (letter to the editors), *Mechanical Engineering*, LXIV (October, 1942), 757.

55. W. H. Shockley, "The American Institute of Mining Engineers as Censor—A Protest," *Mining and Scientific Press*, CXIII (October 21, 1916), 589–590.

56. Robert B. Brinsmade, "Freedom of Discussion in the Institute" (letter to the editors), *Engineering and Mining Journal-Press*, CXIV (December 16, 1922), 1063.

57. "Code of Principles of Professional Conduct of the American Institute of Electrical Engineers," *Trans AIEE*, XXXI, pt. 2 (June–December, 1912), 2229, and "Report of Committee on Code of Ethics," *Trans ASME*, XXXVI (1914), 26. The ASME dropped this provision from its code of ethics in 1922.

58. Frank B. Copley, *Frederick W. Taylor*, 2 vols. (New York, 1923), II, 281.

59. Bernhard F. Jakobsen, *Ethics and the American Society of Civil Engineers* (Los Angeles, 1955), 1–13, and "A.S.C.E. Asked to Reinstate Two Los Angeles Engineers," *Engineering News-Record*, CXVII (October 8, 1936), 525.

60. Engineers Joint Council, *Directory of Engineering Societies and Related Organizations* (New York, 1963), 10–49. About a third of the national societies listed have company members; the

amounts they provide are indicated in the individual societies' annual financial statements, which are usually published in their transactions.

61. Engineers Joint Council Subcommittee on Survey of Employer Practices. "Employer Practices Regarding Engineering Graduates," *Mechanical Engineering*, LXIX (April, 1947), 307.

62. Ernest K. Parks, "Membership in the A.I.M.E. is Purely Personal" (letter to the editors), *Mining and Metallurgy*, XXI (August, 1940), 387.

63. "Afraid to Ask?" *Mechanical Engineering*, LXX (January, 1948), 3.

64. *Ibid.*

65. Harry E. Harris, "Unification of Engineering Societies" (letter to the editors), *Mechanical Engineering*, LX (February, 1938), 177.

5 The Definition of a Profession

D. Allan Firmage

People involved and working in a specialized activity which requires special skill, knowledge and mental concentration define this activity as a profession and themselves as professionals. Considering oneself a professional can satisfy vanity and ego or it can be a motivating element in the striving for excellence and service.

The definition of a profession can best be given by the requirements and attributes of professional practice. However, the American Society of Civil Engineers (ASCE), in the printed *Official Register* defines a profession as "The pursuit of a learned art in the spirit of public service." It expands the definition with the following:

> A profession is a calling in which special knowledge and skill are used in a distinctly intellectual plane in the service of mankind, in which the successful expression of creative ability and application of professional knowledge are the primary rewards. There is implied the application of the highest standards of excellence in the educational fields prerequisite to the calling, in the performance of services, and in the ethical conduct of its members. Also implied is the conscious recognition of the profession's obligation to society to advance its standards and to prescribe the conduct of its members.

The Engineers Council for Professional Development (ECPD),* a council with representation from the major engineering societies, has given the attributes of a profession as follows:

1. It must satisfy an indispensable and beneficial social need.

---

* Reorganized as American Association of Engineering Societies (AAES) in January, 1980.

Reprinted from D. Allan Firmage, *Modern Engineering Practice: Ethical, Professional and Legal Aspects* (New York: Garland STPM Press, 1980), pp. 10–14, with permission.

2. Its work must require the exercise of discretion and judgment and not be subject to standardization.

3. It is a type of activity conducted upon a high intellectual plane.
   a. Its knowledge and skills are not common possessions of the general public; they are the results of tested research and experience and are acquired through a special discipline of education and practice.
   b. Engineering requires a body of distinctive knowledge (science) and art (skill).

4. It must have group consciousness for the promotion of technical knowledge and professional ideals and for rendering social services.

5. It should have legal status and must require well formulated standards of admission.

ECPD has also stated what one who claims to practice a profession must do:

1. They must have a service motive, sharing their advances in knowledge, guarding their professional integrity and ideals, and rendering gratuitous public service in addition to that engaged by clients.

2. They must recognize their obligations to society and to other practitioners by living up to established and accepted codes of conduct.

3. They must assume relations of confidence and accept individual responsibility.

4. They should be members of professional groups and they should carry their part of the responsibility of advancing professional knowledge, ideals, and practice.

Although many working groups may classify their activity as a profession, it does not merit such classification unless the activity is conducted on a high intellectual plane and, as such, requires special training and knowledge in which this training and knowledge is applied with care and judgment. A profession must, as a group, promote the dissemination of knowledge learned through the practice of the profession. True professions will be involved in the education process, not only in providing information to one seeking entrance into the profession, but also to the continuing education of persons already within the profession.

Activity to restrain those who are seeking entrance into the profession by legitimate means is not in keeping with a professional. William H. Wisely, emeritus Executive Director of the American Society of Civil Engineers makes a salient point of professionalism when he states, "The obligation to give primacy to the public interest is the very essence of professionalism. Without this commitment, the effort of a group to seek elite status as exponents of a body of specialized knowledge is but a shallow and selfish charade, no matter how sophisticated that body of knowledge may be or how rigorously it may be pursued."[1]

Voluntary groups within our society have sets of "behavior rules" that are formulated to provide a pleasant environment within the association and prevent encroachment upon the well-being of others. Very often the rules also provide protection from outsiders. A most marked example of this defense from encroachment from the outside is the labor unions.

A professional who is especially qualified in a particular field is expected to perform according to a standard of care that would be expected of any other similar professional and under the same circumstances. This has been the basis for judgment in most liability cases involving professionals. If the objective is service of the highest quality and there is adequate training and experience, then the professional should not be found lacking in his performance. Superior performance is a result of adequate preparation and knowing that what one is doing is right and honest. "Coverup" and dishonesty stems from poor performance which is a result of inadequate preparation, inadequate execution, lack of effort, or a combination of all three.

Deviant behavior in today's complex society can be highly disastrous. Non-thorough engineering can result in failure of an engineering work that as a minimum can waste thousands of dollars and as a maximum take human life. David Novick has stated some of the demands felt by a professional engineer when he says, "he must have a good working knowledge of business, finance, and law because survival in today's marketplace is no longer a matter of just common sense."[2]

There are always groups within society that have a desire to tear down other groups which have achieved success in their activities and thus have reaped monetary rewards as well as public recognition. In recent times such action has become more prevalent as directed toward professional groups. Engineers have been accused of destroying the environment, lawyers have been blamed for unethical practices and having little concern for the safety of society. The medical profession has also been subjected to public limelight, being accused of primary concern for financial rewards and not the welfare of the patient.

All professions are moral enterprises that involve concerns beyond the application of technical principles. How well the professionals meet these moral obligations will determine the freedom of the individual professional enterprise. Already the medical profession has lost a great deal of freedom of operation in some European countries and this wind is already blowing in the direction of North America. If the professions do not regulate the moral actions of their members then others will. And as was stated in a newspaper editorial, "and it's down that road that nations go from regulations to regimentation to tyranny."

A viable society must be aware of any shortcomings of its people, but it must also investigate alleged wrongdoings honestly and fairly. In the present day of rapid and total communication via TV, radio, and the printed page, misleading information and wrongful or half-true statements can perpetrate grave injustices. The public cannot be indifferent to the well-being of a profession, whether it be law, medicine, or engineering. A healthy profession is a plus to the health of society.

The engineering profession is not void of those who desire to "make a fast buck," but the laws of nature are hard task masters and stern judges of incompetent behavior. Engineering is considered one of society's activities that has the highest of ethical standards. Personal opinion polls have been conducted in recent years to obtain the public's feelings toward various professional groups. In such polls engineering has rate near the top in public esteem and judgment of ethical standards. In a 1977 Gallup Poll, engineers were rated in the top three, along with clergymen and medical doctors regarding the question of ethics in each profession. In the "very high" category clergymen had 62 percent, doctors 51 percent, and engineers 46 percent. In ratings of low or very low opinion were clergy 6 percent, doctors 10 percent, and engineers 5 percent. The rating for engineers was the lowest of any category.

A professional is one who has to make decisions, possibly many in the course of a day. Those decisions are based upon a set of data that has been gathered. These data may be sketchy, or very extensive and complete, depending upon the circumstances of the project. The professional must apply judgment to these data and then make the necessary decisions. The correctness of this judgment will be the result of the individual's experience and also the experience of others as obtained from the literature.

A professional engineer should be conscious of social problems in his community and should be willing to freely devote a portion of his time to the solution of these problems. The professional engineer is highly qualified to assist in the solution of community problems, but heavy business demands many times serve as an "out" for not being involved. Many social and community programs are attacked by groups from a purely emotional bias. What is needed in most cases is a careful assembling of facts and data and then a comparison of all alternative solutions based upon the facts available. In this action procedure, the engineer is eminently qualified. The high progress of social development in the United States has been the result of people willing to give their time and talents in the service of their community, whether that community is political, professional, religious, or social. Involvement in community programs will enhance the skill of the engineer. The "rubbing of shoulders" with people from other disciplines as well as other walks of life will give him better insight into the nontechnical aspects of his engineering projects and the social responsibilities of engineers and the engineering profession.

One can think of ethics and morals in a limited sphere of the profession only, but in a broader scope technology has brought about political, economic and educational systems that are the result of technological progress. For such institutions to receive the full benefit of such progress they must operate under a system of ethical standards.

Henry J. Taylor, noted news analyst, once said: "Essentially the problem (of society) is one of integrity. In a home, in a business, in a nation, integrity is what upholds all. It is the weakening of integrity that seems to me to be the greatest illness everywhere. The grand corruption of our age in fact is the inability of so many eminent human beings the world over to practice simple honesty and speak the simple truth."

NOTES

1. W. H. Wisely, "Public Obligation and the Ethics System," American Society of Civil Engineers, Preprint No. 3415, October 1978.

2. D. Novick, "Requirements of Professional Practice," *Engineering Issues*, ASCE, April 1976.

6 Attributes of a Profession

Ernest Greenwood

The professions occupy a position of great importance on the American scene (Parsons 1939). In a society such as ours, characterized by minute division of labor based upon technical specialization, many important features of social organization are dependent upon professional functions. Professional activity is coming to play a predominant role in the life patterns of increasing numbers of individuals of both sexes, occupying much of their waking moments, providing life goals, determining behavior, and shaping personality. It is no wonder, therefore, that the phenomenon of professionalism has become an object of observation by sociologists (Caplow 1954). The sociological approach to professionalism is one that views a profession as an organized group which is constantly interacting with the society that forms its matrix, which performs its social functions through a network of formal and informal relationships, and which create its own subculture requiring adjustments to it as a prerequisite for career success (Government Printing Office 1950).

Within the professional category of its occupational classification the United States Census Bureau includes, among others, the following: accountant, architect, artist, attorney, clergyman, college professor, dentist, engineer, journalists, judge, librarian, natural scientist, optometrist, pharmacist, physician, social scientist, social worker, surgeon, and teacher (Hall 1948, 1949, 1951). What common attributes do these professional occupations possess which distinguish them from the nonprofessional ones? After a careful canvass of the sociological literature on occupations, this writer has been able to distill five elements, upon which there appears to be consensus among the students of the subject, as constituting the distinguishing attributes of a profession.[1] Succinctly put, all professions seem to possess: (1) systematic theory,

(2) authority, (3) community sanction, (4) ethical codes, and (5) a culture. The purpose of this article is to describe fully these attributes.

Before launching into our description, a preliminary word of caution is due. With respect to each of the above attributes, the true difference between a professional and a nonprofessional occupation is not a qualitative but a quantitative one. Strictly speaking, these attributes are not the exclusive monopoly of the professions; nonprofessional occupations also possess them, but to a lesser degree. As is true of most social phenomena, the phenomenon of professionalism cannot be structured in terms of clear-cut classes. Rather, we must think of the occupations in a society as distributing themselves along a continuum.[2] At one end of this continuum are bunched the well-recognized and undisputed professions (e.g., physician, attorney, professor, scientist); at the opposite end are bunched the least skilled and least attractive occupations (e.g., watchman, truckloader, farm laborer, scrubwoman, bus boy). The remaining occupations, less skilled and less prestigeful than the former, but more so than the latter, are distributed between these two poles. The occupations bunched at the professional pole of the continuum possess to a maximum degree the attributes about to be described. As we move away from this pole, the occupations possess these attributes to a decreasing degree. Thus, in the less developed professions, social work among them, these attributes appear in moderate degree. When we reach the mid-region of the continuum, among the clerical, sales, and crafts occupations, they occur in still lesser degree; while at the unskilled end of the continuum the occupations possess these attributes so minimally that they are virtually nonexistent. If the reader keeps this concept of the continuum in mind, the presentation will less likely appear as a distortion of reality.

SYSTEMATIC BODY OF THEORY[3]

It is often contended that the chief difference between a professional and a nonprofessional occupation lies in the element of superior skill. The performance of a professional service presumably involves a series of unusually complicated operations, mastery of which requires lengthy training. The models referred to in this connection are the performances of a surgeon, a concert pianist, or a research physicist. However, some nonprofessional occupations actually involve a higher order of skill than many professional ones. For example, tool-and-die making, diamond-cutting, monument-engraving, or cabinetmaking involve more intricate operations than schoolteaching, nursing, or social work. Therefore, to focus on the element of skill per se in describing the professions is to miss the kernel of their uniqueness.

The crucial distinction is this: the skills that characterize a profession flow from and are supported by a fund of knowledge that has been organized into an internally consistent system, called a *body of theory*. A profession's underlying body of theory is a system of abstract propositions that describe in general terms the classes of phenomena comprising the profession's focus of interest. Theory serves as a base in terms of which the professional rationalizes his operations in concrete situations. Acquisition of the professional skill requires a prior or simultaneous mastery of the theory underlying that skill. Preparation for a profession, therefore, involves considerable preoccupation with systematic theory, a feature virtually absent in the training of the nonprofessional. And so treatises are written on legal theory, musical theory, social work theory, the theory of the drama, and so on; but no books appear on the theory of punchpressing or pipe-fitting or brick-laying.

Because understanding of theory is so important to all professional skill, preparation for a profession must be an intellectual as well as a practical experience. On-the-job training through apprenticeship, which suffices for a nonprofessional occupation, becomes inadequate for a profession. Orientation in theory can be achieved best through formal education in an academic setting. Hence the appearance of the professional school, more often than not university affiliated, wherein the milieu is a contrast to that of the trade school. Theoretical knowledge is more difficult to master than operational procedures; it is easier to learn to repair an automobile than to learn the principles of the internal combustion engine. There are, of course, a number of free-lance professional pursuits (e.g., acting, painting, writing, composing, and the like) wherein academic preparation is not mandatory. Nevertheless, even in these fields various "schools" and "institutes" are appearing, although they may not be run along traditional academic lines. We can generalize that as an occupation moves toward professional status, apprenticeship training yields to formalized education, because the function of theory as a groundwork for practice acquires increasing importance.

The importance of theory precipitates a form of activity normally not encountered in a nonprofessional occupation, viz., theory construction via systematic research. To generate valid theory that will provide a solid base for professional techniques requires the application of the scientific method to the service-related problems of the profession. Continued employment of the scientific method is nurtured by and, in turn, reinforces the element of *rationality* (Parsons 1939). As an orientation, rationality is the antithesis of traditionalism. The spirit of rationality in a profession encourages a critical, as opposed to a reverential, attitude toward the theoretical system. It implies a perpetual readiness to discard any portion of that system, no matter how time honored it may be, with a formulation demonstrated to be more valid. The spirit of rationality generates group self-criticism and theoretical controversy. Professional members convene regularly in their associations to learn and to evaluate innovations in theory. This produces an intellectually stimulating milieu that is in marked contrast to the milieu of a nonprofessional occupation.

In the evolution of every profession there emerges the research-theoretician whose role is that of scientific investigation and the theoretical systematization. In technological professions[4] a division of labor evolves, that between the theory-oriented and the practice-oriented person. Witness the physician who prefers to attach himself to a medical research center rather than to enter private practice. This division may also yield to cleavages with repercussions upon intraprofessional relationships. However, if properly integrated, the division of labor produces an accelerated expansion of the body of theory and a sprouting of theoretical branches around which specialities nucleate. The net effect of such developments is to lengthen the preparation deemed desirable for entry into the profession. This accounts for the rise of graduate professional training on top of a basic college education.

PROFESSIONAL AUTHORITY

Extensive education in the systematic theory of his discipline imparts to the professional a type of knowledge that highlights the layman's comparative ignorance. This fact is the basis for the professional's authority, which has some interesting features.

A nonprofessional occupation has customers; a professional occupation has clients. What is the difference? A customer determines what services and/or commodities he wants, and he shops around until he finds them. His freedom of decision rests upon the premise that he has the capacity to appraise his own needs and to judge the potential of the service or of the commodity to satisfy them. The infallibility of his decisions is epitomized in the slogan: "The customer is always right!" In a professional relationship, however, the professional dictates what is good or evil for the client, who has no choice but to accede to professional judgment. Here the premise is that, because he lacks the requisite theoretical background, the client cannot diagnose his own needs or discriminate among the range of possibilities for meeting them. Nor is the client considered able to evaluate the caliber of the professional service he receives. In a nonprofessional occupation the customer can criticize the quality of the commodity he has purchased, and even demand a refund. The client lacks this same prerogative, having surrendered it to professional authority. This element of authority is one, although not the sole, reason why a profession frowns on advertising. If a profession were to advertise, it would, in effect, impute to the potential client the discriminating capacity to select from competing forms of service. The client's subordination to professional authority invests the professional with a monopoly of judgment. When an occupation strives toward professionalization, one of its aspirations is to acquire this monopoly.

The client derives a sense of security from the professional's assumption of authority. The authoritative air of the professional is a principal source of the client's faith that the relationship he is about to enter contains the potentials for meeting his needs. The professional's authority, however, is not limitless; its function is confined to those specific spheres within which the professional has been educated. This quality in professional authority Parsons calls *functional specificity* (Parsons 1939). Functional specificity carries the following implications for the client-professional relationship.

The professional cannot prescribe guides for facets of the client's life where his theoretical competence does not apply. To venture such prescriptions is to invade a province wherein he himself is a layman, and, hence, to violate the authority of another professional group. The professional must not use his position of authority to exploit the client for purposes of personal gratification. In any association of superordination-subordination, of which the professional-client relationship is a perfect specimen, the subordinate member—here, the client—can be maneuvered into a dependent role. The psychological advantage which thereby accrues to the professional could constitute a temptation for him. The professional must inhibit his impulses to use the professional relationship for the satisfaction of the sexual need, the need to manipulate others, or the need to live vicariously. In the case of the therapeutic professions it is ideally preferred that client-professional intercourse not overflow the professional setting. Extraprofessional intercourse could be used by both client and professional in a manner such as to impair professional authority, with a consequent diminution of the professional's effectiveness.

Thus far we have discussed that phase of professional authority which expresses itself in the client-professional relationship. Professional authority, however, has professional-community ramifications. To these we now turn.

SANCTION OF THE COMMUNITY

Every profession strives to persuade the community to sanction its authority within certain spheres by conferring upon the profession a series of powers and privileges. Community approval of these powers and privileges may be either informal or formal; formal approval is that reinforced by the community's policy power.

Among its powers is the profession's control over its training centers. This is achieved through an accrediting process exercised by one of the associations within the profession. By granting or withholding accreditation, a profession can, ideally, regulate its schools as to their number, location, curriculum content, and caliber of instruction. Comparable control is not to be found in a nonprofessional occupation.[5] The profession also acquires control over admission into the profession. This is achieved via two routes. First, the profession convinces the community that no one should be allowed to wear a professional title who has not been conferred it by an accredited professional school. Anyone can call himself a carpenter, locksmith, or metal-plater if he feels so qualified. But a person who assumes the title of physician or attorney without having earned it conventionally becomes an impostor. Secondly, the profession persuades the community to institute in its behalf a licensing system for screening those qualified to practice the professional skill. A *sine qua non* for the receipt of the license is, of course, a duly granted professional title. Another prerequisite may be an examination before a board of inquiry whose personnel have been drawn from the ranks of the profession. Police power enforces the licensing system; persons practicing the professional skill without a license are liable to punishment by public authority.[6]

Among the professional privileges, one of the most important is that of confidentiality. To facilitate efficient performance, the professional encourages the client to volunteer information he otherwise would not divulge. The community regards this as privileged communication, shared solely between client and professional, and protects the latter legally from encroachments upon such confidentiality. To be sure, only a select few of the professions, notably medicine and law, enjoy this immunity. Its very rarity makes it the ultimate in professionalization. Another one of the professional privileges is a relative immunity from community judgment on technical matters. Standards for professional performance are reached by consensus within the profession and are based on the existing body of theory. The lay community is presumed incapable of comprehending these standards and, hence, of using them to identify malpractice. It is generally conceded that a professional's performance can be evaluated only by his peers.

The powers and privileges described above constitute a monopoly granted by the community to the professional group. Therefore, when an occupation strives toward professional status, one of its prime objectives is to acquire this monopoly. But this is difficult to achieve, because counter forces within the community resist strongly the profession's claims to authority. Through its associations the profession wages an organized campaign to persuade the community that it will benefit greatly by granting the monopoly. Specifically the profession seeks to prove: that the performance of the occupational skill requires specialized education;that those who possess this education, in contrast to those who do not, deliver a superior service; and that the human need being served is of sufficient social importance to justify the superior performance.

REGULATIVE CODE OF ETHICS

The monopoly enjoyed by a profession vis-à-vis clients and community is fraught with hazards. A monopoly can be abused; powers and privileges can be used to protect vested interests against the public weal (Flexner 1915, Merton 1950). The professional group could peg the price of its services at an unreasonably high level; it could restrict the numbers entering the occupation to create a scarcity of personnel; it could dilute the caliber of its performance without community awareness; and it could frustrate forces within the occupation pushing for socially beneficial changes in practices (Merton 1950). Were such abuses to become conspicuous, widespread, and permanent, the community would, of course, revoke the profession's monopoly. This extreme measure is normally unnecessary, because every profession has a built-in regulative code which compels ethical behavior on the part of its members.

The profession's ethical code is part formal and part informal. The formal is the written code to which the professional usually swears upon being admitted to practice; this is best exemplified by the Hippocratic Oath of the medical profession. The informal is the unwritten code, which nonetheless carries the weight of formal prescriptions. Through its ethical code the profession's commitment to the social welfare becomes a matter of public record, thereby insuring for itself the continued confidence of the community. Without such confidence the profession could not retain its monopoly. To be sure, self-regulative codes are characteristic of all occupations, nonprofessional as well as professional. However, a professional code is perhaps more explicit, systematic, and binding; it certainly possesses more altruistic overtones and is more public service-oriented (Flexner 1915). These account for the frequent synonymous use of the terms "professional" and "ethical" when applied to occupational behavior.

While the specifics of their ethical codes vary among the professions, the essentials are uniform. These may be described in terms of client-professional and colleague-colleague relations.

Toward the client the professional must assume an emotional neutrality. He must provide service to whoever requests it, irrespective of the requesting client's age, income, kinship, politics, race, religion, sex, and social status. A nonprofessional may withhold his services on such grounds without, or with minor, censure; a professional cannot. Parsons calls this element in professional conduct *universalism*. In other words, only in his extraoccupational contacts can the professional relate to others on particularistic terms, i.e., as particular individuals with concrete personalities attractive or unattractive to him. In his client contacts particularistic considerations are out of place. Parsons also calls attention to the element of *disinterestedness* in the professional-client relationship (Parsons 1939). In contrast to the nonprofessional, the professional is motivated less by self-interest and more by the impulse to perform maximally. The behavior corollaries of this service orientation are many. For one, the professional must, under all circumstances, give maximum caliber service. The nonprofessional can dilute the quality of his commodity or service to fit the size of the client's fee; not so the professional. Again, the professional must be prepared to render his services upon request, even at the sacrifice of personal convenience.

The ethics governing colleague relationships demand behavior that is co-operative, equalitarian, and supportive. Members of a profession share technical knowledge with each other. Any advance in theory and practice made by one professional is quickly disseminated to colleagues through the professional associations (Johnson 1944). The proprietary and quasi-secretive attitudes toward discovery and invention prevalent in the industrial and commercial world are out of place in the professional. Also out of place is the blatant competition for clients which is the norm in so many nonprofessional pursuits. This is not to gainsay the existence of intra-professional competition; but it is a highly regulated competition, diluted with co-operative ingredients which impart to it its characteristically restrained quality. Colleague relations must be equalitarian; intraprofessional recognition should ideally be based solely upon performance in practice and/or contribution to theory (Flexner 1915). Here, too, particularistic considerations must not be allowed to operate. Finally, professional colleagues must support each other vis-à-vis clientele and community. The professional must refrain from acts which jeopardize the authority of colleagues, and must sustain those whose authority is threatened.[7]

The ways and means whereby a profession enforces the observance of its ethical code constitute a case study in social control. Self-discipline is achieved informally and formally.

Informal discipline consists of the subtle and the not-so-subtle pressures that colleagues exert upon one another. An example in this connection is the phenomenon of consultation and referral (Hall 1948, 1949, 1951). Consultation is the practice of inviting a colleague to participate in the appraisal of the client's need and/or in the planning of the service to be rendered. Referral is the practice of affording colleagues access to a client or an appointment. Thus, one colleague may refer his client to another, because lack of time or skill prevents his rendering the needed service; or he may recommend another for appointment by a prospective employer. Since professional ethics precludes aggressive competition and advertising, consultation and referral constitute the principal source of work to a professional. The consultation-referral custom involves professional colleagues in a system of reciprocity which fosters mutual interdependence. Interdependence facilitates social control; chronic violation of professional etiquette arouses colleague resentment, resulting in the cessation of consultation requests and referrals.

A more formal discipline is exercised by the professional associations, which possess the power to criticize or to censure, and in extreme cases to bar recalcitrants.

Since membership in good standing in the professional associations is a sine qua non of the professional success, the prospect of formal disciplinary actions operates as a potent force toward conformity.

THE PROFESSIONAL CULTURE

Every profession operates through a network of formal and informal groups. Among the formal groups, first there are the organizations through which the profession performs its services; these provide the institutionalized setting where professional and client meet. Examples of such organizations are hospital, clinic, university, law office, engineering firm, or social agency. Secondly, there are the organizations whose functions are to replenish the profession's supply of talent and to expand its fund of knowledge. These include the educational and the research centers. Third among the formal groups are the organizations which emerge as an expression of the growing consciousness-of-kind on the part of the profession's members, and which promote so-called group interests and aims. These are the professional associations. Within and around these formal organizations extends a filigree of informal groupings: the multitude of small, closely knit clusters of colleagues. Membership in these cliques is based on a variety of affinities: specialties within the profession; affiliations with select professional societies; residential and work propinquity; family, religious, or ethnic background; and personality attractions.

The interactions of social roles required by these formal and informal groups generate a social configuration unique to the profession, viz., a professional culture. All occupations are characterized by formal and informal groupings; in this respect the professions are not unique. What is unique is the culture thus begotten. If one were to single out the attribute that most effectively differentiates the professions from other occupations, this is it. Thus, we can talk of a professional culture as distinct from a nonprofessional culture. Within the professions as a logical class each profession develops its own subculture, a variant of the professional culture; the engineering subculture, for example, differs from the subcultures of medicine and social work. In the subsequent discussion, however, we will treat the culture of the professions as a generic phenomenon. The culture of a profession consists of its *values*, *norms*, and *symbols*.

The social values of a professional group are its basic and fundamental beliefs, the unquestioned premises upon which its very existence rests. Foremost among these values is the essential worth of the service which the professional group extends to the community. The profession considers that the service is a social good and that community welfare would be immeasurably impaired by its absence. The twin concepts of professional authority and monopoly also possess the force of a group value. Thus, the proposition that in all service-related matters the professional group is infinitely wiser than the laity is regarded as beyond argument. Likewise nonarguable is the proposition that acquisition by the professional group of a service monopoly would inevitably produce social progress. And then there is the value of rationality; that is, the commitment to objectivity in the realm of theory and technique. By virtue of this orientation, nothing of a theoretical or technical nature is regarded as sacred and unchallengeable simply because it has a history of acceptance and use.

The norms of a professional group are the guides to behavior in social situations. Every profession develops an elaborate system of these role definitions. There is a range of appropriate behaviors for seeking admittance into the profession, for gaining entry into its formal and informal groups, and for progressing within the occupation's hierarchy. There are appropriate modes of securing appointments, of conducting referrals, and of handling consultation. There are proper ways of acquiring clients, of receiving and dismissing them, of questioning and treating them, of accepting and rejecting them. There are correct ways of grooming a protégé, of recompensing a sponsor, and of relating to peers, superiors, and subordinates. There are even group-approved ways of challenging an outmoded theory, of introducing a new technique, and of conducting an intra-professional controversy. In short, there is a behavior norm covering every standard interpersonal situation likely to recur in professional life.

The symbols of a profession are its meaning-laden items. These may include such things as: its insignias, emblems, and distinctive dress; its history, folklore, and argot; its heroes and its villains; and its stereotypes of the professional, the client, and the layman.

Comparatively clear and controlling group values, behavior norms, and symbols, which characterize the professions, are not to be encountered in nonprofessional occupations.

Our discussion of the professional culture would be incomplete without brief mention of one of its central concepts, the *career* concept. The term career is, as a rule, employed only in reference to a professional occupation. Thus, we do not talk about the career of a bricklayer or of a mechanic; but we do talk about the career of an architect or of a clergyman. At the heart of the career concept is a certain attitude toward work which is peculiarly professional. A career is essentially a *calling*, a life devoted to "good works."[8] Professional work is never viewed solely as a means to an end; it is the end itself. Curing the ill, educating the young, advancing science are values in themselves. The professional performs his services primarily for the psychic satisfactions and secondarily for the monetary compensations (Johnson 1944). Self-seeking motives feature minimally in the choice of a profession; of maximal importance is affinity for the work. It is this devotion to the work itself which imparts to professional activity the service orientation and the element of disinterestedness. Furthermore, the absorption in the work is not partial, but complete; it results in a total personal involvement. The work life invades the after-work life, and the sharp demarcation between the work hours and the leisure hours disappears. To the professional person his work becomes his life.[9] Hence the act of embarking upon a professional career is similar in some respects to entering a religious order. The same cannot be said of a nonprofessional occupation.

To succeed in his chosen profession, the neophyte must make an effective adjustment to the professional culture (Hall 1948, 1949, 1951). Mastery of the underlying body of theory and acquisition of the technical skills are in themselves insufficient guarantees of professional success. The recruit must also become familiar with and learn to weave his way through the labyrinth of the professional culture. Therefore, the transformation of a neophyte into a professional is essentially an acculturation process wherein he internalizes the social values, the behavior norms, and the symbols of the occupational group (White 1953). In its frustrations and rewards it is fundamentally no different from the acculturation of an immigrant to a relatively strange culture. Every profession entertains a stereotype of the ideal colleague; and, of course, it is always one who is thoroughly adjusted to the professional culture.[10] The poorly acculturated colleague is a deviant; he is regarded as "peculiar," "unorthodox," "annoying," and in extreme cases a "trouble-maker." Whereas the professional group encourages innovation in theory and technique, it tends to discourage deviation from its social values and norms. In this internal contradiction, however, the professional culture is no different from the larger culture of society.

One of the principal functions of the professional schools is to identify and screen individuals who are prospective deviants from the professional culture. That is why the admission of candidates to professional education must be judged on grounds in addition to and other than their academic qualifications (Hall 1951). Psychic factors presaging favorable adjustment to the professional culture are granted an important equivalent to mental abilities. The professional school provides test situations through initial and graduated exposures of the novice to the professional culture. By his behavior in these social situations involving colleagues, clients, and community, the potential deviant soon reveals himself and is immediately weeded out. Comparable preoccupation with the psychic prerequisites of occupational adjustment is not characteristic of nonprofessional occupations.

NOTES

1. The writer acknowledges his debt to his former students at the School of Social Welfare, University of California, Berkeley, who, as members of his research seminars, assisted him in identifying and abstracting the sociological literature on occupations. Their conscientious assistance made possible the formulation presented in this paper.

2. The occupational classification employed by the U.S. Census Bureau is precisely such a continuum. The categories of this classification are: (a) professionals and semiprofessional technical workers; (b) proprietors and managers, both farm and nonfarm, and officials; (c) clerical, sales and kindred workers; (d) craftsmen, skilled workers and foremen; (e) operatives and semiskilled workers; and (e) laborers, unskilled, service and domestic workers (U.S. Bureau of the Census, op. cit.).

3. The sequence in which the five attributes are discussed in this paper does not reflect upon their relative importance. The order selected has been dictated by logical considerations.

4. A technology is a profession whose aim is to achieve controlled charge in natural relationships. convention makes a distinction between technologists who shape nonhuman materials and those who deal with human beings. The former are called engineers; the latter practitioners.

5. To set up and run a school for floral decorating requires no approval from the national florist's association, but no school of social work could operate long without approval of the Council on Social Work Education.

6. Many nonprofessional occupations have also succeeded in obtaining licensing legislation on their behalf. Witness the plumbers, radio operators, and barbers, to mention a few.

However, the sanctions applied against a person practicing a nonprofessional occupation are much less severe than is the case when a professional occupation is similarly involved.

7. This partly explains why physicians do not testify against each other in malpractice suits.

8. The term *calling* literally means a divine summons to undertake a course of action. Originally, it was employed to refer to religious activity. The Protestant Reformation widened its meaning to include economic activity as well. Henceforth divinely inspired "good works" were to be both secular and sacred in nature. Presumably, then, any occupational choice may be a response to a divine summons. In this connection, it is interesting to note that the German world for vocation is *Beruf*, a noun derived from the verb *berufen*, to call.

9. The all-pervading influence of work upon the lives of professionals results in interesting byproducts. The members of a profession tend to associate with each other outside the work setting (see Hall, "The Stages of a Medical Career"). Their families mingle socially; leisure time is spent together; "shop talk" permeates social discourse; and a consensus develops. The profession thus becomes a whole social environment, nurturing characteristic social and political attitudes, patterns of consumption and recreation, and decorum and *Weltanschauung* (see Caplow, also see Form).

10. The laity also entertain a stereotypic image of the professional group. Needless to say, the layman's conception and the professional's self-conception diverge widely, because they are fabricated out of very different experiences. The layman's stereotype is frequently a distortion of reality, being either an idealization or a caricature of the professional type.

REFERENCES

CAPLOW, T. 1954. *The Sociology of Work.* Minneapolis: University of Minneapolis Press.

FLEXNER, A. 1915. Is social work a profession? In *Proceedings of the National Conference of Charities and Corrections*, Chicago: 576–90.

HALL, O. 1948. The stages of a medical career. *American Journal of Sociology*, 53:327–36.

———. 1949. Types of medical careers. *American Journal of Sociology*, 55:243–53.

———. 1951. Sociological research in the field of medicine: progress and prospects. *American Journal of Sociology*, 16:639–44.

JOHNSON, A. 1944. Professional standards and how they are attained. *Journal of American Dental Association*, 31:1181–1189.

MERTON, R. 1950. Bureaucratic structure and personality. In *Studies in Leadership* ed. Gouldner, A. New York: Harper.

PARSONS, T. 1939. The professions and social structure. *Social Forces*, 17:457–67.

WHITE, R. 1953. "Social workers in society": some further evidence. *Social Work Journal*, 34: 161–64.

7 The Social Responsibility of Business Is to Increase Its Profits

Milton Friedman

When I hear businessmen speak eloquently about the "social responsibilities of business in a free enterprise system," I am reminded of the wonderful line about the Frenchman who discovered at the age of 70 that he had been speaking prose all his life. The businessmen believe that they are defending free enterprise when they declaim that business is not concerned "merely" with profit but also with promoting desirable "social" ends; that business has a "social conscience" and takes seriously its responsibilities for providing employment, eliminating discrimination, avoiding pollution and whatever else may be the catchwords of the contemporary crop of reformers. In fact they are—or would be if they or anyone else took them seriously—preaching pure and unadulterated socialism. Businessmen who talk this way are unwitting puppets of the intellectual forces that have been undermining the basis of a free society these past decades.

The discussion of the "social responsibilities of business" are notable for their analytical looseness and lack of rigor. What does it mean to say that "business" has responsibilities? Only people can have responsibilities. A corporation is an artificial person and in this sense may have artificial responsibilities, but "business" as a whole cannot be said to have responsibilities, even in this vague sense. The first step toward clarity to examining the doctrine of the social responsibility of business is to ask precisely what it implies for whom.

Presumably, the individuals who are to be responsible are businessmen, which means individual proprietors or corporate executives. Most of the discussion of social responsibility is directed at corporations, so in what follows I shall mostly neglect the individual proprietors and speak of corporate executives.

In a free-enterprise, private-property system, a corporation executive is an employee of the owners of the business. He has direct responsibility to his employers. That responsibility is to conduct the business in accordance with their desires, which generally will be to make as much money as possible while conforming to the basic rules of the society, both those embodied in law and those embodied in ethical custom. Of course, in some cases his employers may have a different objective. A group of persons might establish a corporation for an eleemosynary purpose—for example, a hospital or a school. The manager of such a corporation will not have money profit as his objectives but the rendering of certain services.

In either case, the key point is that, in his capacity as a corporate executive, the manager is the agent of the individuals who own the corporation or establish the eleemosynary institution, and his primary responsibility is to them.

Needless to say, this does not mean that it is easy to judge how well he is performing his task. But at least the criterion of performance is straightforward, and the persons among whom a voluntary contractual arrangement exists are clearly defined.

Of course, the corporate executive is also a person in his own right. As a person, he may have many other responsibilities that he recognizes or assumes voluntarily—to his family, his conscience, his feelings of charity, his church, his clubs, his city, his country. He may feel impelled by these responsibilities to devote part of his income to causes he regards as worthy, to refuse to work for particular corporations, even to leave his job, for example, to join his country's armed forces. If we wish, we may refer to some of these responsibilities as "social responsibilities." But in these respects he is acting as a principal, not an agent; he is spending his own money or time or energy, not the money of his employers or the time or energy he has contracted to devote to their purposes. If these are "social responsibilities," they are the social responsibilities of individuals, not of business.

What does it mean to say that the corporate executive has a "social responsibility" in his capacity as businessman? If this statement is not pure rhetoric, it must mean that he is to act in some way that is not in the interest of his employers. For example, that he is to refrain from increasing the price of the product in order to contribute to the social objective of preventing inflation, even though a price increase would be in the best interests of the corporation. Or that he is to make expenditures on reducing pollution beyond the amount that is in the best interest of the corporation or that is required by law in order to contribute to the social objective of improving the environment. Or that, at the expense of corporate profits, he is to hire "hardcore" unemployed instead of better qualified available workmen to contribute to the social objective of reducing poverty.

In each of these cases, the corporate executive would be spending someone else's money for a general social interest. Insofar as his actions in accord with his "social responsibility" reduce returns to stockholders, he is spending their money. Insofar as his actions raise the price to customers, he is spending the customers' money. Insofar as his actions lower the wages of some employees, he is spending their money.

The stockholders or the customers or the employees could separately spend their own money on the particular action if they wished to do so. The executive is exercising a distinct "social responsibility," rather than serving as an agent of the stockholders or the customers or the employees, only if he spends the money in a different way than they would have spent it.

But if he does this, he is in effect imposing taxes, on the one hand, and deciding how the tax proceeds shall be spent, on the other.

This process raises political questions on two levels: principle and consequences. On the level of political principle, the imposition of taxes and the expenditure of tax proceeds are governmental functions. We have established elaborate constitutional, parliamentary and judicial provisions to control these functions, to assure that taxes are imposed so far as possible in accordance with the preferences and desires of the public—after all, "taxation without representation" was one of the battle cries of the American Revolution. We have a system of checks and balances to separate the legislative function of imposing taxes and enacting expenditures from the executive function of collecting taxes and administering expenditure programs and from the judicial function of mediating disputes and interpreting the law.

Here the businessman—self-selected or appointed directly or indirectly by stock-holders—is to be simultaneously legislator, executive and jurist. He is to decide whom to tax by how much and for what purpose, and he is to spend the proceeds—all this guided only by general exhortations from on high to restrain inflation, improve the environment, fight poverty and so on and on.

The whole justification for permitting the corporate executive to be selected by the stockholders is that the executive is an agent serving the interests of his principal. This justification disappears when the corporate executive imposes taxes and spends the proceeds for "social" purposes. He becomes in effect a public employee, a civil servant, even though he remains in name an employee of a private enterprise. On grounds of political principle, it is intolerable that such civil servants—insofar as their action in the name of social responsibility are real and not just window-dressing—should be selected as they are now. If they are to be civil servants, then they must be elected through a political process. If they are to impose taxes and make expenditures to foster "social" objectives, then political machinery must be set up to make the assessment of taxes and to determine through a political process the objectives to be served.

This is the basic reason why the doctrine of "social responsibility" involves the acceptance of the socialist view that political mechanisms, not market mechanisms, are the appropriate way to determine the allocation of scarce resources to alternative uses.

On the grounds of consequences, can the corporate executive in fact discharge his alleged "social responsibilities"? On the one hand, suppose he could get away with spending the stockholders' or customers' or employees' money. How is he to know how to spend it? He is told that he must contribute to fighting inflation. How is he to know what action of his will contribute to that end? He is presumably an expert in running his company—in producing a product or selling it or financing it. But nothing about his selection makes him an expert on inflation. Will his holding down the price of his product reduce inflationary pressure? Or, by leaving more spending power in the hands of his customers, simply divert it elsewhere? Or, by forcing him to produce less because of the lower price, will it simply contribute to shortages? Even if he could answer these questions, how much cost is he justified in imposing on his stockholders, customers and employees for this social purpose? What is his appropriate share and what is the appropriate share of others?

And, whether he wants to or not, can he get away with spending his stockholders', customers' or employees' money? Will not the stockholders fire him? (Either the present ones or those who take over when his action in the name of social responsibility have reduced the corporation's profits and the price of its stock.) His customers and his employees can desert him for other producers and employers less scrupulous in exercising their social responsibilities.

This facet of "social responsibility" doctrine is brought into sharp relief when the doctrine is used to justify wage restraint by trade unions. The conflict of interest is naked and clear when union officials are asked to subordinate the interest of their members to some more general purpose. If the union officials try to enforce wage restraint, the consequence is likely to be wildcat strikes, rank-and-file revolts and the emergence of strong competitors for their jobs. We thus have the ironic phenomenon that union leaders—at least in the U.S.—have objected to Government interference with the market far more consistently and courageously than have business leaders.

The difficulty of exercising "social responsibility" illustrates, of course, the great virtue of private competitive enterprise—it forces people to be responsible for their own actions and makes it difficult for them to "exploit" other people for either selfish or unselfish purposes. They can do good—but only at their own expense.

Many a reader who has followed the argument this far may be tempted to remonstrate that it is all well and good to speak of Government's having the responsibility to impose taxes and determine expenditures for such "social" purposes as controlling pollution or training the hard-core unemployed, but that the problems are too urgent to wait on the slow course of political processes, that the exercise of social responsibility by businessmen is a quicker and surer way to solve pressing current problems.

Aside from the question of fact—I share Adam Smith's skepticism about the benefits that can be expected from "those who affected to trade for the public good"— this argument must be rejected on grounds of principle. What it amounts to is an assertion that those who favor the taxes and expenditures in question have failed to persuade a majority of their fellow citizens to be of like mind and that they are seeking to attain by undemocratic procedures what they cannot attain by democratic procedures. In a free society, it is hard for "evil" people to do "evil," especially since one man's good is another's evil.

I have, for simplicity, concentrated on the special case of the corporate executive, except only for the brief digression on trade unions. But precisely the same argument applies to the newer phenomenon of calling upon stockholders to require corporations to exercise social responsibility (the recent G. M. crusade for example). In most of these cases, what is in effect involved is some stockholders trying to get other stockholders (or customers or employees) to contribute against their will to "social" causes favored by the activists. Insofar as they succeed, they are again imposing taxes and spending the proceeds.

The situation of the individual proprietor is somewhat different. If he acts to reduce the returns of his enterprise in order to exercise his "social responsibility," he is spending his own money, not someone else's. If he wishes to spend his money on such purposes, that is his right, and I cannot see that there is any objection to his doing so. In the process, he, too, may impose costs on employees and customers. However, because he is far less likely than a large corporation or union to have monopolistic power, any such side effects will tend to be minor.

Of course, in practice the doctrine of social responsibility is frequently a cloak for actions that are justified on other grounds rather than a reason for those actions.

To illustrate, it may well be in the long-run interest of a corporation that is a major employer in a small community to devote resources to providing amenities to that community or to improving its government. That may make it easier to attract desirable employees, it may reduce the wage bill or lessen losses from pilferage and sabotage or have other worthwhile effects. Or it may be that, given the laws about the deductibility of corporate charitable contributions, the stockholders can contribute more to charities they favor by having the corporation make the gift than by doing it themselves, since they can in that way contribute an amount that would otherwise have been paid as corporate taxes.

In each of these—and many similar—cases, there is a strong temptation to rationalize these actions as an exercise of "social responsibility." In the present climate of opinion, with its widespread aversion to "capitalism," "profits," the "soulless corporation" and so on, this is one way for a corporation to generate goodwill as a by-product of expenditures that are entirely justified in its own self-interest.

It would be inconsistent of me to call on corporate executives to refrain from this hypocritical window-dressing because it harms the foundations of a free society. That would be to call on them to exercise a "social responsibility"! If our institutions, and the attitudes of the public make it in their self-interest to cloak their actions in this way, I cannot summon much indignation to denounce them. At the same time, I can express admiration for those individual proprietors or owners of closely held corporations or stockholders of more broadly held corporations who disdain such tactics as approaching fraud.

Whether blameworthy or not, the use of the cloak of social responsibility, and the nonsense spoken in its name by influential and prestigious businessmen, does clearly harm the foundations of a free society. I have been impressed time and again by the schizophrenic character of many businessmen. They are capable of being extremely far-sighted and clear-headed in matters that are internal to their businesses. They are incredibly short-sighted and muddle-headed in matters that are outside their businesses but affect the possible survival of business in general. This short-sightedness is strikingly exemplified in the calls from many businessmen for wage and price guidelines or controls or income policies. There is nothing that could do more in a brief period to destroy a market system and replace it by a centrally controlled system than effective governmental control of prices and wages.

The short-sightedness is also exemplified in speeches by businessmen on social responsibility. This may gain them kudos in the short run. But it helps to strengthen the already too prevalent view that the pursuit of profits is wicked and immoral and must be curbed and controlled by external forces. Once this view is adopted, the external forces that curb the market will not be the social consciences, however highly developed, of the pontificating executives; it will be the iron fist of Government bureaucrats. Here, as with price and wage controls, businessmen seem to me to reveal a suicidal impulse.

The political principle that underlies the market mechanism is unanimity. In an ideal free market resting on private property, no individual can coerce any other, all cooperation is voluntary, all parties to such cooperation benefit or they need not participate. There are no values, no "social" responsibilities in any sense other than the shared values and responsibilities of individuals. Society is a collection of individuals and of the various groups they voluntarily form.

The political principle that underlies the political mechanism is conformity. The individual must serve a more general social interest—whether that be determined by a church or a dictator or a majority. The individual may have a vote and a say in what is to be done, but if he is overruled, he must conform. It is appropriate for some to require others to contribute to a general social purpose whether they wish to or not.

Unfortunately, unanimity is not always feasible. There are some respects in which conformity appears unavoidable, so I do not see how one can avoid the use of the political mechanism altogether.

But the doctrine of "social responsibility" taken seriously would extend the scope of the political mechanism to every human activity. It does not differ in philosophy from the most explicitly collectivist doctrine. It differs only by professing to believe that collectivist ends can be attained without collectivist means. That is why, in my book "Capitalism and Freedom," I have called it a "fundamentally subversive doctrine" in a free society, and have said that in such a society, "there is one and only one social responsibility of business—to use its resources and engage in activities designed to increase its profits so long as it stays within the rules of the game, which is to say, engages in open and free competition without deception or fraud."

8 The Theoretical Twist
to Irresponsibility in Business

Robert V. Hannaford

In 1970 the Nobel Laureate economist Milton Friedman wrote an article entitled "The Social Responsibility of Business is to Increase Its Profits." He began his article with this paragraph:

> When I hear businessmen speak eloquently about the "social responsibilities in a free-enterprise system," I am reminded of the wonderful line about the Frenchman who discovered at the age of 70 that he had been speaking prose all his life. The businessmen believe that they are defending free enterprise when they declaim that business is not concerned "merely" with profit but also with promoting desirable "social" ends; that business has a "social conscience" and takes seriously its responsibilities for providing employment, eliminating discrimination, avoiding pollution and whatever else may be the catchwords of the contemporary crop of reformers. In fact, they are—or would be if they or anyone else took them seriously—preaching pure and unadulterated socialism. Businessmen who talk in this way are unwitting puppets of the intellectual forces that have been undermining the basis of a free society these past decades.[1]

Thus, Friedman lends his personal prestige to a deliberate abdication of responsibility. He and other economists have invoked the authority and intellectual defense of economic theory to support unethical attitudes and to give a view of the role of the corporation in society that is oversimplified and confusing. These points become clearer as his article progresses, but begin to emerge in the opening paragraph, in his rejection of any notion of special social responsibility for business, in his use of scare quotes, and in his comparison of the businessperson who would be responsible with Moliere's M. Jourdain, who would learn to speak prose. We are asked to share the laugh on the businessperson because we are supposed to agree that he or she, as one

Reprinted from Wade Robison, Michael Pritchard, and Joseph Ellen, eds., *Profits and Professions* (Clifton, N.J.: Humana Press, 1983), pp. 101–12, with permission.

who succeeded in business, could no more miss being socially responsible than M. Jourdain could fail to speak prose in his normal activity. References to the social responsibilities of business are put in scare quotes to indicate that we are to avoid using these supposedly mistaken expressions and the word "merely" in the clause "business is not concerned 'merely' with profit" is put in scare quotes to indicate that in the pursuit of profit business already bears all the social responsibility it should be concerned with.

Friedman is not alone in taking such a stance. But I want to show how he is able to foster such unethical attitudes by giving a twist to what is already a vague and ambiguous element in classical economic theory. Once that point is made, it will be clear that Friedman's own account of responsibility is incoherent and, if we follow our standard conceptions of responsibility, we will want to say that businesspeople and particularly those who are executives and directors of large, publicly owned corporations, do have special social responsibilities. Moreover, they are responsibilities whose exercise in no way threatens a free market.

I. CLASSICAL AMBIGUITY AND THE FRIEDMAN TWIST

Classical theory's explanation of the free market turns on the explanation of the motive for economic behavior, an explanation based on the phrases "bettering one's condition" and "pursuing one's own interest" or on some variation of those phrases. The Friedman twist is possible because of the vagueness and ambiguity of this phrase (or its substitutes). The original formulation facilitates, though it does not require, Friedman's view. In Smith's *Wealth of Nations*, he wrote that the basic source of economic activity is found in our individual "desire of *bettering our condition*," a desire that "comes with us from the womb and never leaves us 'til we go to the grave."

He wrote that "every individual is continuously exerting himself to find out the most advantageous employment for whatever capital he can command." This assumption (whether literally true or not) is central to the explanation of the free market; the drive it describes is the fundamental force of the price mechanism. From this assumption we can argue that capitalists who seek what is most advantageous to them (in the form of profits) will become informed about, and therefore produce, what will fetch top price, thereby satisfying the greatest economic demand. Similarly, laborers seeking top price for their services will move to the place where the demand for them is greater. Thus, Smith held, each seeking personal financial advantage is "led by an invisible hand" to contribute to the general welfare. Smith's account makes plain how those who do pursue their own financial gain might thereby contribute something valued by the rest of the community. And, thus, their contribution might be regarded as fulfilling some part of their social responsibility. However, nothing is said nor can be inferred to the effect that this contribution fulfills the *sum* of one's social responsibilities. That is Friedman's twist. However, the looseness of the phrase has been exploited by other economists to twist the theory to the same effect.

The notion of each of us striving to better his or her condition has the same looseness of meaning that the notion of pursuing one's interest has. Some senses of that loose expression are true: no doubt we would agree that each person seeks to better his or her condition *as he or she perceives* what would better it, and that each of us uses personal capital in what is perceived to be the most advantageous fashion. However, it is not clear whether our interest or condition is to be taken to include or exclude the interest of others; it is not clear whether our interest is to be given a purely financial interpretation. If the phrase is taken in its broadest, loosest sense, it says that each person is concerned with his or her own affairs and tries to improve on them to the greatest possible extent. That is a truism, but it has the fatal defect that it will not enable us to predict what different people will take to be included, under "bettering their condition" and so as a consequence, it would not enable us to predict or explain any specific kinds of economic behavior. On the other hand, if we give it a stricter interpretation, so that it has some explanatory significance, and say that each person is continuously seeking to improve his or her financial condition, it turns out to be false. It is not true that we always so seek, or ought to seek, the economically most advantageous use of our capital. Not all do: not the ascetics, not the improvident, not the other-worldly, not those who stuff money in mattresses. Nor should we always: not when our friend is starving, not when our neighbor needs medicine only we can provide. Economists when confronted with this problem have sometimes sought refuge in the notion that all the things a person seeks may be regarded as having a kind of utility; they thus seek to rescue the central selfishness axiom. That notion is true, but the rescue is made at the same cost. To say that all persons will seek what they regard as useful does not tell us anything about what in particular they so regard, nor what they will seek. So some economists have done a kind of shuffling two-step back and forth between the different interpretations of the selfishness axiom: first they say, take it as vague and general (in order to have it accepted as true); then, having established that people *seek their own interest*, they assert: We have a right to say that each person seeks his or her own financial interest continuously. When someone raises a question about that proposition,[2] they say: "But surely you don't mean to say that you think people sometimes don't seek what's in their interest?" Thus they hide behind the broad and vacuous sense of the axiom. What this shuffling on the self-interest axiom has done is to provide a defense of egoism: it tells us that *everyone* is selfish, and, if you will but leave them alone in their selfish pursuits, they will contribute their bit to the economy and we will all be happier and more productive. *Greed* is good for us: it makes every body happy. *Only confused* do-gooders worry about social responsibilities.

Smith's point, of course, was that, whatever people were interested in, they could obtain more easily and produce more efficiently in a free market. He showed how a free market was superior to government control of what was bought and produced. A free market will provide the greatest liberty of choice for the buyer and freedom of work for the producer and the most productive use of whatever capital we have at our disposal.

However, that liberty of choice will still be available even to those socially responsible producers who do not want to get absolutely the greatest financial return on their investment. Suppose that, because of some social responsibility that one recognizes, one is prepared to settle for a lesser return. Let us say that one will thereby avoid polluting one's neighbor's water supply and that one elects to do so. Now clearly this is a move that producers have made and will continue to make without any kind of social control forcing them to do so. Farmers, for example (who compete for their income and are part of a free market), have often taken the extra care and time required to avoid polluting others' water supplies. While doing so, they have spent time and capital that might have been spent in earning a buck. In doing so, they have acted freely, facing a social responsibility other than that provided by their role in the price mechanism. But such a decision does not undermine the freedom in the society or the freedom of the market. To suggest that it will is to give a perverted picture of the price mechanism: farmers can continue to produce what others will want and can make a living; scarcity will continue to increase prices; individuals will still be able to make their own economic choices. So it does not make sense to say (as Friedman does) that such behavior is "undermining the basis of a free society." Liberty is not tied to selfishness. People have remarked upon our responsibility to others since the beginning of time. Those who have remarked on such responsibility can hardly be characterized as "preaching pure and unadulterated socialism"—as Friedman would have it. Such people have seen something that they could do to promote a common good and they have chosen to do it. They have thereby enhanced the stability of free societies. I will later suggest that parallel considerations apply to corporate actions and to the responsibility of corporate officers.

However, of the responsibilities of a corporate executive, Friedman writes:

> In a free-enterprise, private property system, a corporate executive is an employee of the owners of the business. He has direct responsibility to his employers. That responsibility is to conduct the business in accord with their desires which generally will be to make as much money as possible while conforming to the basic rules of the society, both those embodied in law and those embodied in ethical custom.
>
> . . . the key point is that . . . the manager is the agent of the individuals who own the corporation . . . and his primary responsibility is to them.

No doubt an executive officer has a responsibility to make money on an owner's investments. But, in the context, the only point of emphasizing it is to deny social responsibility, to suggest that no consideration of public obligation ordinarily would or should modify a business owner's pursuit of private gain. The chief executive officer is to exploit all financial opportunities available within law and custom. For Friedman, corporate responsibility is vested solely in the hands of individual stockholders. By this account the corporate manager has no special social responsibility that accrues as a result of his or her corporate position; the manager's corporate responsibility (unless the manager is specially charged by the stockholders) is simply to make money for them. Neither economic theory nor the facts of corporate ownership will support such an analysis, though Friedman intimates that they do. He uses this intellectually confusing analysis to promote the bottom line mentality that has become a recurrent feature of contemporary business.

It was the bottom line mentality that lay behind the McDonnell-Douglas executive's decision to rush the DC-10 into production to get ahead of its competitors, even though their own engineers had warned the management about the poor design of the cargo door latch. It was this inadequacy that resulted in the disastrous crash of a DC-10 at the Paris airport in 1975.[3] Nor is this an isolated case. Others have noted that

. . . management's tendency to measure performance on the basis of short-term, objective standards often leads a firm to ignore the social impact of its operations, which is difficult to measure. Environmental pollution most readily comes to mind. The corporate decision maker's interest in achieving results that promote his personal goals under the existing reward system often causes the corporation to generate more harmful pollution in order to reduce measurable costs and increase measurable profits.[4]

Studies have shown that where large firms place great emphasis on making the most money, their chief executive officers are "single-mindedly, almost slavishly, committed to achieving" a showing of maximum short-term profits.[5] Roderick M. Hills was chairman of the Securities and Exchange Commission, he noted the temptation of management to be irresponsible:

When reported profits decline to such an extent as to threaten the serenity of their well-paid isolation, some managers are tempted to change the accounting, the figures or the morals of their company in order to present a more pleasing profit picture.[6]

II. CORPORATE OFFICERS DECIDE—RARELY STOCKHOLDERS

It is apparent that Friedman's denial of our social responsibilities turns on the sense of the term "responsible." For our discussion there are two standard relevant senses: one of the senses is that of holding someone responsible who is identified as the agent or cause of some change, a sense found in such questions as "Who's responsible for the broken window?" Another sense is found in our question whether someone is able to respond to a situation in a way that is in accord with the values of others. It is a matter of knowledge and ability and it is used when we ask whether an 18-year-old is mature enough to be responsible. These usages evolved from describing persons and their officers as well. Corporations bring about changes that no single individual could accomplish and corporate executives have power and can recognize possibilities for change that others cannot. As Edward Mason observes:

We are all aware that we live not only in a corporate society but a society of large corporations. The management—that is the control—of these corporations is in the hands of, at most, a few thousand men. Who selected these men, if not to rule over us, at least to exercise vast authority . . .[7]

If we are to give an account of contemporary life, we must be able to speak of the special responsibilities of the corporation and the corporate executive.

However, this will be a suspicious move, as far as Friedman is concerned. In the article cited above, he suggests that one is linguistically confused if one speaks of corporate responsibility and of the responsibility of the corporate executive.

The discussions of the "social responsibilities of business" are notable for their analytical looseness and lack of rigor. What does it mean to say that "business" has responsibilities? Only persons can have responsibilities. A corporation is an artificial person and in this sense may have artificial responsibilities, but "business" as a whole cannot be said to have responsibilities, even in this vague sense.

One should observe that "the responsibilities of business" refers to the responsibilities of *those in* business and note that it is standard to speak of groups that perform a particular job as having a kind of social responsibility because of that job. We speak of education (those in education) as having a kind of responsibility, of (those in) government as having certain responsibilities in a matter, and so on. There is no linguistic confusion here. And there need be no linguistic confusion in speaking of those in business of having special responsibilities that accrue to them as a result of their role in business. Those in business have special responsibility not to misrepresent their product and to see to it that their product does not present any hidden dangers to the consumer. If we deny that businesspeople have special responsibilities, it will not be because our language does not permit it.

However, Friedman also holds that it is not legitimate to speak of one's responsibilities as a corporate executive, except as one's responsibilities to one's stockholders.

> What does it mean to say that the corporate executive has a "social responsibility" in his capacity as businessman? If this statement is not pure rhetoric, it must mean that he is to act in some way that is not in the interest of his employers. For example, that he is to refrain from increasing the price of the product in order to contribute to the social objective of preventing inflation, even though a price increase would be in the best interests of the corporation. Or that he is to make expenditures on reducing pollution beyond that amount that is in the best interests of the corporation. . . .

We note that the argument and Friedman's objections turn on the vague and ambiguous phrase "in the best interest" of the corporation, the phrase that dogs economists' explanations. Here we do not know whether one is using the term to speak of short-term profits, the firm's long-term stability and financial security, prestige in the community, or what. Of course, it will make a material difference which of these senses is being considered by the chief executive officer when choosing what is in the firm's best interest. However, if the officer considers long-term financial interests, stability, or prestige in the community, that officer might well want to consider what might be called the social responsibilities of the firm. Certainly a great many corporations spend a lot of time and money trying to convince us that they are socially responsible. Yet in cases where they are, Friedman finds that:

> . . . the corporate executive would be spending someone else's money for a general social interest. Insofar as his actions in accord with his "social responsibility" (always in scare quotes) reduce returns to stockholders, he is spending their money. Insofar as he is raising the price to customers, he is spending the customer's money.

For Friedman the executive's responsibility is to those hiring him or her, and thus the executive has not right to make decisions in their behalf.

> The stockholders or the customers . . . could separately spend their own money on the particular actions if they wished to do so. The executive is exercising a distinct "social responsibility" rather than serving as an agent of the stockholders or customers . . . only if he spends the money in a different way than they would have spent it.
> But if he does this, he is in effect imposing taxes, on the one hand, and deciding how the tax proceeds shall be spent on the other.

One fulfills one's responsibility as an agent only if one spends the constituents' money in the same way that they would have spent it. But the phrase "that they would have spent it" is not clear. Does it refer to how they would have spent it, given their present knowledge and consequent desires? Or does it refer to how they would have spent it if they were given the knowledge and know-how of one exercising the corporate position? Is it to be supposed that all stockholders and customers would have reached the same conclusion? Would that be before or after they had acquired the understanding?

It may be suggested that we are to have the corporate executive act as the agent of the desires that we as stockholders now have. It may be suggested that all customers will want the commodity at the cheapest possible price and that all stockholders will want the greatest possible return on their investment. But here we run into a difficulty of deciding what we mean by "possible," in "cheapest possible" and "greatest possible return." Possible with what else? We need to know for how long a time period it is to be possible, for what cost to the health of ourselves and others, for what cost to the security of the business and much more. "Greatest possible" and "cheapest possible" will mean very different things depending on which of these many specific conditions is to be preserved. An executive of a publicly owned corporation cannot know what conditions will be considered important for all of the corporation's stockholders, nor for what additional reasons. As a holder of stock in California Edison I might say that its corporate executive acted as the agent of my desires when that executive decided to keep a nuclear power plant in operation because I would thereby be able to obtain an 18% return on my investment for the next quarter. But my desire for an 18% return would change if I discovered that the plant was unsafe and that its continued operation posed a threat similar to that of Three-Mile Island or *The China Syndrome*.

Increased information about such consequences will not bring unanimity of desires on the part of the stockholders. It may be that my aging, misantropic Aunt Ella, now living in London and holding a large block of California Edison stock, will not be concerned to protect either the health of the Los Angeles residents or the long-term viability of the company.

Friedman attempts to answer the question of what conditions are included under the phrase "greatest possible" when he writes:

> . . . (a corporate executive's) responsibility is to conduct the business in accordance with (the owners') desires, which generally will be to make as much money as possible while conforming to the basic rules of the society, both those embodied in law and those embodied in ethical custom.

His answer, then, would be "as much as we can while conforming to the law and ethical custom."

But the answer is unsatisfactory. We cannot appeal to custom, for the judgment of ethical custom about what our corporate responsibilities may be is what we have been unclear about all along. We cannot settle a *dispute* about what our responsibilities are by saying that our responsibilities are what we think them to be. If the nature of responsibilities in individual cases is widely disputed, then ethical custom in such cases cannot resolve the dispute. Nor can we define our responsibility as doing what the law will allow. Fulfilling one's responsibilities involves doing more than avoiding those acts for which one can be legally punished. Harold Williams, chairman of the SEC, remarked that the country's level of social stability and strength is to be measured by the difference between the operative ethical principles and the legal sanctions requiring conformity. The greater the individual responsibility taken without threat of legal sanction, the greater its stability and strength. Friedman cannot preserve a free society by defining our social responsibilities in terms of what the law will allow. All of this disagreement illustrates the possibilities for stockholder disagreement: what they want their company to do will depend in part on what they think it ought to do.

One is led to the conclusion that stockholders in different circumstances will ordinarily differ among themselves as to what policy they think the firm should follow. It will not be possible for the executive officer of a large corporation to avoid spending money (to use Friedman's phrase) in a different way from how they would have spent it. The executive must spend as he or she sees fit.

It does not make sense to speak of the corporate executive as the agent of the stockholders' desires. There could be no construction of Friedman's phrase "how they would have spent the money" according to which large numbers of people of different interests, education, and ability would come to understanding and agreement on a policy to be pursued. Hence, Friedman's notion of the responsibility of a corporation executive as agent of stockholders' desires is unworkable for officers of large, publicly owned corporations.

III. POWERS ENTAIL RESPONSIBILITIES

Corporate decisions must be primarily decisions of corporate officers, not of stockholders. Large, publicly owned corporations have possibilities and resources of such complexity that the stockholders cannot understand them unless they are also involved in management. The Ford Motor Company, e.g., in 1976 had capital assets of over 15 billion dollars and employed 450,000 people. Other corporations have similarly formidable resources, but each is different.

The distinctive features of contemporary society have been created through these corporations. Without them our technology for communication, transportation, and manufacturing could never have come into being. They have transformed our society root and branch. When we give an account of social changes they must be figured in.

These corporations have a kind of life and power of their own, apart from the specific persons who provide them with capital or serve as their officers over any particular time period. But those occupying executive and directorial positions at any time are agents of sweeping social changes affecting us all. For such changes they must be held accountable, if anyone is accountable for anything; such power and capacity carry social responsibilities with them.

Acting to fulfill social obligations is not contrary to a firm's business interests. Business interests include community interests. Corporate decisions should center on what is in the total interest of the corporation. If a corporate decision is well-made, it will be seen to include concern for the community that makes the corporation possible.

If farmers and small businesses can decide to increase their operating costs in order to satisfy social obligations and not thereby threaten their livelihood or the free market, so can publicly owned corporations. The decision process is different in the two cases, but in both cases it turns on the decision-maker's concern for others and ability to do what the common good requires. If either lacks such concern, there is little likelihood that their decision will be responsible and in each case it must be a decision that the decision-maker sees as fit in order for it to be made at all. Corporate decision-makers often have superhuman resources at their disposal for seeing what *is* fit: lawyers, engineers, management consultants, members of the board, and perhaps more. So the decision, often enough, is the result of a sustained inquiry and discussion by the staff rather than the reflection and internal dialog of a single person. By conducting such an inquiry and discussion, the corporate officer does not thereby so increase the cost of production that the firm is removed from competition in the market. That this is so is attested to by the fact that the testing and research divisions are typically used for such purposes and are standard parts of large corporations.

Ordinarily we assign responsibility in accord with one's capacity to understand the implications of his or her actions and to control their outcomes. As Bishop Butler remarks, we hold people responsible for actions to the degree that they are able to foresee and control their consequences. If so, business must not only acknowledge its social responsibility, it must often bear an extra burden of responsibility. Each of us feels more prepared to bear a personal share of responsibility to the extent that others bear theirs. Whoever denies these responsibilities thereby denies any respect for others, and whenever such respect for others is extensively denied, individual rights and freedoms are threatened. Businesspeople who have extolled the single-minded pursuit of profit as the Free-Enterprise Way have engaged in such a denial of respect. The economists who have twisted classical theory to defend such egoism have aggravated their threat to a free society.

NOTES

1. Published in *The New York Times Magazine*, Sept. 13, 1970. All references to Friedman's work will be to this article.

2. If the self-interest axiom is to be of any service for explaining and predicting the operation of the price mechanism, we must take it to refer to what is economically advantageous. Yet it is false that "every individual is continuously exerting himself to find out the (financially) most advantageous employment for whatever capital he has at his command." This makes an assumption about our basic value commitments that is false for many. However, if we are describing economic activity in a materially oriented society, the axiom may be rescued as a basis for making statistical predictions about what *classes* of people will do and about general market trends.

3. Reported by Joseph Iseman, a lawyer for one of the victims of the crash (in a lecture given at Ripon College during the spring 1979 term).

4. From J. Bower's article on "The Amoral Organization" in *The Corporate Society*, Robin Marris, ed. (London: Macmillan, 1974).

5. From C. Argyris's article on "The CEO's Behavior: Key to Organizational Development," *Harvard Business Review* (March-April 1973), 55.

6. Quoted by C. Weiss and B. Schwartz (p. 77) in their "Disclosure Activates Directors" in *Reweaving the Corporate Veil*, a study in Duke University School of Law's series, Law and Contemporary Society (1977).

7. From his Introduction to *The Corporation in Modern Society*, ed. E. Mason (Cambridge, MA: Harvard Univ. Press, 1959).

3

The Role of Professional Codes of Ethics

SCENARIOS

---------------------------- **Use of Engineers' Creed** ----------------------------

Supporters of John Doe, P.E., a candidate for election to the city council (a salaried office), with his knowledge and consent inserted a political advertisement in daily newspapers in his community, containing a reproduction of the Engineers' Creed [see page 97—ED.], his picture, and the following text:

> "John Doe, P.E.*, has followed this creed as an engineer and as a citizen, and we know he will be a credit to our community and profession. We ask your earnest consideration of his candidacy for the city council.
>
> "*P.E. Professional Engineer, Registered in the state of————."

The advertisement listed the names of 20 persons, who were not identified as PE's, or otherwise, but who are, in fact, all registered engineers in the state. The advertisement was clearly identified as a paid political advertisement.

Is it ethical to use a reproduction of the Engineers' Creed in a paid political advertisement on behalf of a professional engineer? Is the text of the advertisement ethical?

Reprinted from the National Society of Professional Engineers, Opinions of the Board of Ethical Review, *Case No. 65-7 (Washington, D.C.: National Society of Professional Engineers, 1967), II, 25, with permission.*

_____ **Supplanting Another Engineer** _____

A local public agency negotiated a contract with a consulting engineering firm for design of an unusual and monumental type structure. The retained firm is located outside the state and has had considerable experience in the type of design involved. In the opinion of the professional engineers on the staff of the public agency there are no consulting firms within the state that are qualified to handle a project of the complexity and magnitude involved.

Several local consulting firms, upon learning of the contract with the out-of-state firm, contacted officials of the public agency and sought to have the contract terminated in favor of a contract with a local firm. The local firm stated that although they did not have direct experience in the type of project involved, they would make arrangements for an adequate staff to handle the design requirements.

Did the local consulting engineers act ethically in attempting to supplant the out-of-state firm which had been retained? Did the professional engineers in the public agency act ethically in recommending retention of an out-of-state firm?

Reference

Code of Ethics—Section 11(a)—"The Engineer will not attempt to supplant another engineer in a particular employment after becoming aware that definite steps have been taken toward the other's employment." [Based on the Code of Ethics adopted by NSPE in July, 1964, as amended through January, 1967—ED.]

Discussion

This case is different from the principles involved in Case 62-18 only in that the obvious effort to supplant an engineering firm which had already been retained involved an out-of-state firm. There is no need to discuss the application of Section 11(a) to the facts because there is clearly a direct conflict with the ethical standard unless it can be excused on the ground that the section does not apply to out-of-state firms.

We can see no implication in the language of Section 11(a) that its application is restricted geographically, or in any other way. The ethical prohibition is applicable to all attempts to supplant another engineer.

Whether it is good policy for a public agency to contract with out-of-state firms is a policy question which may be subject to conflicting points of view. From an ethical standpoint, however, the professional engineers of the agency are justified in seeking the firm deemed best qualified, all factors considered, for a particular project and, in fact, are required to do so. There is no language in the Code which states or implies that this responsibility is subject to geographical limitations.

Conclusions

1. The local consulting engineers acted unethically in attempting to supplant a firm which had been retained for the work.

2. The professional engineers in the public agency acted ethically in recommending the retention of an out-of-state firm which they deemed to be best qualified for the work.

Reprinted from the National Society of Professional Engineers, Opinions of the Board of Ethical Review, *Case No. 65-8 (Washington, D.C.: National Society of Professional Engineers, 1967), II, 27, with permission.*

INTRODUCTION

This chapter begins with the code of ethics of the National Society of Professional Engineers (NSPE). Many engineering organizations have such codes, and it may be interesting for readers to review the code of ethics of the organization representing their specialty within engineering (for example, the code of the American Society of Civil Engineers, American Society of Mechanical Engineers, Institute of Electrical and Electronics Engineers, or Association for Computing Machinery).

The codes of conduct of engineering professional organizations are important for at least two different reasons. First, we can examine them as expressions of the thoughts and feelings of engineers about their ethical or professional responsibilities. As such, we look to the codes to help us to understand how engineers see themselves and to find out what the members of the profession and the profession as a whole have learned over the years. Second, codes are often thought of as a mechanism for controlling the behavior of engineers, in particular for assisting them in behaving in socially responsible ways. In this chapter we will be less concerned with the content of the codes, and more concerned with the purposes that might be served by a code and the limitations of a code. The idea here is to understand the role that a professional code can play in a profession and in the lives of individual practitioners.

It is important to remember that codes have been developed for several different purposes that often conflict. Conflicts aside, one cannot evaluate codes without some sense of what they are supposed to do. The range of goals that engineers might have in putting forth a code is broad. Building on our discussion of what it means to be a profession, we might think of codes simply as statements to the public of a commitment on the part of engineers and a promise to behave in ways that are not harmful to society. Codes might also be seen as genuine attempts to provide guidance to members of the profession. In addition, they might be seen as a sensitizing or socializing device, or as providing protection for engineers against employers. That is, engineers might point to the professional code to support their decisions to refuse to participate in activities that their employers encourage.

The NSPE Code of Ethics is followed in this chapter by a chapter of Stephen H.

Unger's book, *Controlling Technology: Ethics and the Responsible Engineer.* Unger has been active in encouraging professional organizations to support engineers who "blow the whistle" or who perform some other morally worthy action but are perceived as disloyal by their employers. In this chapter of his book, Unger suggests several important functions served by codes and discusses various issues that have to be dealt with in designing a code. One needs, for example, to strike the right balance between generality and specificity. The rules should be general enough to apply to the broad range of situations that different engineers find themselves in, and yet they should be specific enough to have some real meaning. Not all the rules should be negative. The code should be consistent. Unger points out that some codes are contradictory—that is, in some situations if one follows one of the rules, one breaks another. Unger proposes a model code that he thinks superior to some of the codes now in place. Perhaps the most interesting part of this code is his discussion of engineers' responsibility in working on projects with "pernicious ends."

John Ladd in "The Quest for a Code of Professional Ethics" presents a rather cynical view of the role that codes can play in affecting the behavior of engineers. His cynicism seems to arise from the fact that he believes that ethics is a matter of doing things from your own sense of what is right and not because a code says that you have to do it. Bringing in a code, he seems to think, makes the matter legal rather than moral. Ladd considers a host of objectives that a code might aim to achieve, but he finds codes faulty for achieving any one of these. Moreover, he thinks codes produce some negative side effects. Although several of Ladd's criticisms can be refuted, one should come to grips with them to understand fully the proper role for a code in the lives of individual practitioners.

Heinz C. Luegenbiehl, though also critical of the role of codes, provides an insightful discussion of the historical evolution of engineering codes of ethics. He argues that engineering codes have been too much influenced by the codes of physicians and lawyers to the detriment of the engineering codes. His discussion is particularly useful because it ties the discussion of codes back to several issues that came up in chapter 2. He ends by proposing that instead of codes, engineers ought to put forth a set of guides for ethical engineering decision making. The primary job that needs to be done, according to Luegenbiehl, is to provide engineers with aid in the decision-making process in situations that would not usually arise in their everyday lives. These guides would give engineers a sense of the situations that other engineers have found themselves in and the kinds of factors that they found to be relevant to decision making in these situations.

9 Engineers' Creed

National Society of Professional Engineers

As a Professional Engineer, I dedicate my professional knowledge and skill to the advancement and betterment of human welfare.

I pledge:

To give the utmost of performance;
To participate in none but honest enterprise;
To live and work according to the laws of man and the highest standards of professional conduct;
To place service before profit, the honor and standing of the profession before personal advantage, and the public welfare above all other considerations.

In humility and with need for Divine Guidance, I make this pledge.

Adopted by National Society of Professional Engineers, June, 1954.

Reprinted with permission of the National Society of Professional Engineers.

10 Code of Ethics for Engineers

National Society of Professional Engineers

PREAMBLE

Engineering is an important and learned profession. The members of the profession recognize that their work has a direct and vital impact on the quality of life for all people. Accordingly, the services provided by engineers require honesty, impartiality, fairness and equity, and must be dedicated to the protection of the public health, safety and welfare. In the practice of their profession, engineers must perform under a standard of professional behavior which requires adherence to the highest principles of ethical conduct on behalf of the public, clients, employers and the profession.

I. FUNDAMENTAL CANONS

Engineers, in the fulfillment of their professional duties, shall:

1. Hold paramount the safety, health and welfare of the public in the performance of their professional duties.
2. Perform services only in areas of their competence.
3. Issue public statements only in an objective and truthful manner.
4. Act in professional matters for each employer or client as faithful agents or trustees.
5. Avoid deceptive acts in the solicitation of professional employment.

Reprinted with permission of the National Society of Professional Engineers.

II. RULES OF PRACTICE

1. Engineers shall hold paramount the safety, health and welfare of the public in the performance of their professional duties.
    a. Engineers shall at all times recognize that their primary obligation is to protect the safety, health, property and welfare of the public. If their professional judgment is overruled under circumstances where the safety, health, property or welfare of the public are endangered, they shall notify their employer or client and such other authority as may be appropriate.
    b. Engineers shall approve only those engineering documents which are safe for public health, property and welfare in conformity with accepted standards.
    c. Engineers shall not reveal facts, data or information obtained in a professional capacity without the prior consent of the client or employer except as authorized or required by law or this Code.
    d. Engineers shall not permit the use of their name or firm name nor associate in business ventures with any person or firm which they have reason to believe is engaging in fraudulent or dishonest business or professional practices.
    e. Engineers having knowledge of any alleged violation of this Code shall cooperate with the proper authorities in furnishing such information or assistance as may be required.
2. Engineers shall perform services only in the areas of their competence.
    a. Engineers shall undertake assignments only when qualified by education or experience in the specific technical fields involved.
    b. Engineers shall not affix their signatures to any plans or documents dealing with subject matter in which they lack competence, nor to any plan or document not prepared under their direction or control.
    c. Engineers may accept assignments and assume responsibility for coordination of an entire project and sign and seal the engineering documents for the entire project, provided that each technical segment is signed and sealed only by the qualified engineers who prepared the segment.
3. Engineers shall issue public statements only in an objective and truthful manner.
    a. Engineers shall be objective and truthful in professional reports, statements or testimony. They shall include all relevant and pertinent information in such reports, statements or testimony.
    b. Engineers may express publicly a professional opinion on technical subjects only when that opinion is founded upon adequate knowledge of the facts and competence in the subject matter.
    c. Engineers shall issue no statements, criticisms or arguments on technical matters which are inspired or paid for by interested parties, unless they have prefaced their comments by explicitly identifying the interested parties on whose behalf they are speaking, and by revealing the existence of any interest the engineers may have in the matters.
4. Engineers shall act in professional matters for each employer or client as faithful agents or trustees.

a. Engineers shall disclose all known or potential conflicts of interest to their employers or clients by promptly informing them of any business association, interest, or other circumstances which could influence or appear to influence their judgment or the quality of their services.

b. Engineers shall not accept compensation, financial or otherwise, from more than one party for services on the same project, or for services pertaining to the same project, unless the circumstances are fully disclosed to, and agreed to by, all interested parties.

c. Engineers shall not solicit or accept financial or other valuable consideration, directly or indirectly, from contractors, their agents, or other parties in connection with work for employers or clients for which they are responsible.

d. Engineers in public service as members, advisors or employees of a governmental body or department shall not participate in decisions with respect to professional services solicited or provided by them or their organizations in private or public engineering practice.

e. Engineers shall not solicit or accept a professional contract from a governmental body on which a principal or officer of their organization serves as a member.

5. Engineers shall avoid deceptive acts in the solicitation of professional employment.

a. Engineers shall not falsify or permit misrepresentation of their, or their associates', academic or professional qualifications. They shall not misrepresent or exaggerate their degree of responsibility in or for the subject matter of prior assignments. Brochures or other presentations incident to the solicitation of employment shall not misrepresent pertinent facts concerning employers, employees, associates, joint ventures or past accomplishments with the intent and purpose of enhancing their qualifications and their work.

b. Engineers shall not offer, give, solicit or receive, either directly or indirectly, any political contribution in an amount intended to influence the award of a contract by public authority, or which may be reasonably construed by the public of having the effect or intent to influence the award of a contract. They shall not offer any gift, or other valuable consideration in order to secure work. They shall not pay a commission, percentage or brokerage fee in order to secure work except to a bona fide employee or bona fide established commercial or marketing agencies retained by them.

III. PROFESSIONAL OBLIGATIONS

1. Engineers shall be guided in all their professional relations by the highest standards of integrity.

a. Engineers shall admit and accept their own errors when proven wrong and refrain from distorting or altering the facts in an attempt to justify their decisions.

   b. Engineers shall advise their clients or employers when they believe a project will not be successful.

   c. Engineers shall not accept outside employment to the detriment of their regular work or interest. Before accepting any outside employment, they will notify their employers.

   d. Engineers shall not attempt to attract an engineer from another employer by false or misleading pretenses.

   e. Engineers shall not actively participate in strikes, picket lines, or other collective coercive action.

   f. Engineers shall avoid any act tending to promote their own interest at the expense of the dignity and integrity of the profession.

2. Engineers shall at all times strive to serve the public interest.

   a. Engineers shall seek opportunities to be of constructive service in civic affairs and work for the advancement of the safety, health and well-being of their community.

   b. Engineers shall not complete, sign or seal plans and/or specifications that are not of a design safe to the public health and welfare and in conformity with accepted engineering standards. If the client or employer insists on such unprofessional conduct, they shall notify the proper authorities and withdraw from further service on the project.

   c. Engineers shall endeavor to extend public knowledge and appreciation of engineering and its achievements and to protect the engineering profession from misrepresentation and misunderstanding.

3. Engineers shall avoid all conduct or practice which is likely to discredit the profession or deceive the public.

   a. Engineers shall avoid the use of statements containing a material misrepresentation of fact or omitting a material fact necessary to keep statements from being misleading or intended or likely to create an unjustified expectation; statements containing prediction of future success; statements containing an opinion as to the quality of the Engineers' services; or statements intended or likely to attract clients by the use of showmanship, puffery, or self-laudation, including the use of slogans, jingles, or sensational language or format.

   b. Consistent with the foregoing, Engineers may advertise for recruitment of personnel.

   c. Consistent with the foregoing, Engineers may prepare articles for the lay or technical press, but such articles shall not imply credit to the author for work performed by others.

4. Engineers shall not disclose confidential information concerning the business affairs or technical processes of any present or former client or employer without his consent.

   a. Engineers in the employ of others shall not without the consent of all interested parties enter promotional efforts or negotiations for work or make arrangements for other employment as a principal or to practice in connection with a specific project for which the Engineer has gained particular and specialized knowledge.

b. Engineers shall not, without the consent of all interested parties, participate in or represent an adversary interest in connection with a specific project or proceeding in which the Engineer has gained particular specialized knowledge on behalf of a former client or employer.

5. Engineers shall not be influenced in their professional duties by conflicting interests.

   a. Engineers shall not accept financial or other considerations, including free engineering designs, from material or equipment suppliers for specifying their product.

   b. Engineers shall not accept commissions or allowances, directly or indirectly, from contractors or other parties dealing with clients or employers of the Engineer in connection with work for which the Engineer is responsible.

6. Engineers shall uphold the principle of appropriate and adequate compensation for those engaged in engineering work.

   a. Engineers shall not accept remuneration from either an employee or employment agency for giving employment.

   b. Engineers, when employing other engineers, shall offer a salary according to professional qualifications.

7. Engineers shall not attempt to obtain employment or advancement or professional engagements by untruthfully criticizing other engineers, or by other improper or questionable methods.

   a. Engineers shall not request, propose, or accept a professional commission on a contingent basis under circumstances in which their professional judgment may be compromised.

   b. Engineers in salaried positions shall accept part-time engineering work only to the extent consistent with policies of the employer and in accordance with ethical consideration.

   c. Engineers shall not use equipment, supplies, laboratory, or office facilities of an employer to carry on outside private practice without consent.

8. Engineers shall not attempt to injure, maliciously or falsely, directly or indirectly, the professional reputation, prospects, practice or employment of other engineers, nor untruthfully criticize other engineers' work. Engineers who believe others are guilty of unethical or illegal practice shall present such information to the proper authority for action.

   a. Engineers in private practice shall not review the work of another engineer for the same client, except with the knowledge of such engineer, or unless the connection of such engineer with the work has been terminated.

   b. Engineers in governmental, industrial or educational employ are entitled to review and evaluate the work of other engineers when so required by their employment duties.

   c. Engineers in sales or industrial employ are entitled to make engineering comparisons of represented products with products of other suppliers.

9. Engineers shall accept responsibility for their professional activities; provided, however, that Engineers may seek indemnification for professional services arising

out of their practice for other than gross negligence, where the Engineer's interests cannot otherwise be protected.

a. Engineers shall conform with state registration laws in the practice of engineering.

b. Engineers shall not use association with a nonengineer, a corporation, or partnership, as a "cloak" for unethical acts, but must accept personal responsibility for all professional acts.

10. Engineers shall give credit for engineering work to those to whom credit is due, and will recognize the proprietary interests of others.

a. Engineers shall, whenever possible, name the person or persons who may be individually responsible for designs, inventions, writings, or other accomplishments.

b. Engineers using designs supplied by a client recognize that the designs remain the property of the client and may not be duplicated by the Engineer for others without express permission.

c. Engineers, before undertaking work for others in connection with which the Engineer may make improvements, plans, designs, inventions, or other records which may justify copyrights or patents, should enter into a positive agreement regarding ownership.

d. Engineers' designs, data, records, and notes referring exclusively to an employer's work are the employer's property.

11. Engineers shall cooperate in extending the effectiveness of the profession by interchanging information and experience with other engineers and students, and will endeavor to provide opportunity for the professional development and advancement of engineers under their supervision.

a. Engineers shall encourage engineering employees' efforts to improve their education.

b. Engineers shall encourage engineering employees to attend and present papers at professional and technical society meetings.

c. Engineers shall urge engineering employees to become registered at the earliest possible date.

d. Engineers shall assign a professional engineer duties of a nature to utilize full training and experience, insofar as possible, and delegate lesser functions to subprofessionals or to technicians.

e. Engineers shall provide a prospective engineering employee with complete information on working conditions and proposed status of employment, and after employment will keep employees informed of any changes.

"By order of the United States District Court for the District of Columbia, former Section 11(c) of the NSPE Code of Ethics prohibiting competitive bidding, and all policy statements, opinions, rulings or other guidelines interpreting its scope, have been rescinded as unlawfully interfering with the legal right of engineers, protected under the antitrust laws, to provide price information to prospective clients; accordingly, nothing contained in the NSPE Code of Ethics, policy statements, opinions, rulings or other guidelines prohibits the submission of price quotations or competitive bids for engineering services at any time or in any amount."

Statement by NSPE Executive Committee.   In order to correct misunderstandings which have been indicated in some instances since the issuance of the Supreme Court decision and the entry of the Final Judgment, it is noted that in its decision of April 25, 1978, the Supreme Court of the United States declared: "The Sherman Act does not require competitive bidding."

It is further noted that as made clear in the Supreme Court decision:

1. Engineers and firms may individually refuse to bid for engineering services.
2. Clients are not required to seek bids for engineering services.
3. Federal, state, and local laws governing procedures to procure engineering services are not affected, and remain in full force and effect.
4. State societies and local chapters are free to actively and aggressively seek legislation for professional selection and negotiation procedures by public agencies.
5. State registration board rules of professional conduct, including rules prohibiting competitive bidding for engineering services, are not affected and remain in full force and effect. State registration boards with authority to adopt rules of professional conduct may adopt rules governing procedures to obtain engineering services.
6. As noted by the Supreme Court, "nothing in the judgment prevents NSPE and its members from attempting to influence governmental action. . . ."

Note: In regard to the question of application of the Code to corporations vis-à-vis real persons, business form or type should not negate nor influence conformance of individuals to the Code. The Code deals with professional services, which services must be performed by real persons. Real persons in turn establish and implement policies within business structures. The Code is clearly written to apply to the Engineer and it is incumbent on a member of NSPE to endeavor to live up to its provisions. This applies to all pertinent sections of the Code.

NSPE Publication No. 1102 as revised January 1987

11 Codes of Engineering Ethics

Stephen H. Unger

WHY ETHICS CODES?

A code of professional ethics may be thought of as a collective recognition of the responsibilities of the individual practitioners. When specified in a clear, concise form, it can be a major factor in the creation of an ambience in which ethical behavior is a norm. Drafting, debating, and perhaps voting on a code are in themselves valuable exercises, stimulating thought on the subject. The code can serve as a focal point for discussion in classes and at meetings.

Of course, a principal use of an ethics code is as a guide or reminder with respect to behavior in specific situations. This is not to say that it can be used in cookbook fashion to resolve complex problems. But it is valuable in outlining the factors to be considered.

Ethics codes play fundamental roles with respect to other mechanisms such as support or enforcement procedures of professional societies or licensing agencies. They may also be brought into play in lawsuits. Even where no formal processes are involved, a provision of an ethics code can sometimes be pointed to by an engineer to help justify a decision to colleagues or managers when there are countervailing pressures to meet a deadline, cut costs, cover up a blunder, make a sale, and so on. There is thus a sense in which a formally stated rule can provide an "excuse" for ethical behavior.

A secondary value of a good ethics code is to indicate to others a concern within the profession that its members practice in a responsible manner.

SCOPE AND FORM

An ethics code should be designed primarily to inspire, encourage, and support ethical practitioners, rather than to serve as a basis for proceedings against wrongdoers (although it can also be used for this purpose). Unlike a set of laws, which must precisely define prohibited behavior, an ethics code should have a positive emphasis, advocating desirable modes of professional conduct, although there are some important negative provisions that should be included.

Care should be taken to confine the domain of the code to the realm of professional conduct and not to make it into an all-encompassing moral guide. There is great diversity among engineers with respect to religion, politics, and general values. The ethics code must be based on a generally acceptable (and hence necessarily small) set of ethical postulates, leaving ample room for interpretation in the light of the individual's own set of general moral values. People with widely varying political, social, and religious views must feel comfortable with the same set of rules.

But the code must also have genuine content going beyond a few pious admonitions. It must have substantial provisions applicable in real situations. That this is possible, given the constraint of the previous paragraph, is a consequence of the significance of the ethical core acknowledged by virtually everyone. This is discussed in the next section. But first a few words on length and format.

At one extreme an attempt might be made to catalog, for some branch of engineering, all of the detailed situations calling for ethical decisions, supplying rules for each case. Particularly in view of the dynamic nature of modern engineering, it is of course not feasible to do this completely. One problem with overspecific codes is that few will care to read them. Another is that omissions, which are inevitable, become significant "loopholes." For example, suppose the code contains a detailed list of hazards that the public is to be protected against. Then if a question should arise about some hazard *not* on this list, it might be inferred that there is no obligation to protect against it. A more general provision would avoid this problem. An additional drawback of lengthy codes is that important points may be buried in a mass of less significant items, thereby losing much of their impact.

At the other extreme, consider the following comprehensive statement proposed by William H. Wisely as a compact replacement for more conventional ethics codes: "The engineer shall apply his specialized knowledge and skill at all times in the public interest, with honesty, integrity and honor." Virtually every provision that properly belongs in an engineering ethics code is implied by this statement. Furthermore, it does not imply any objectionable rules. Since it is eminently readable and concise, why not stop right here and accept it as our ethics code?

The problem is that, although this statement could serve well as an introduction or summary, it does not specify the principal elements of ethical engineering, does not call attention to those classes of situations calling for ethical judgments, and provides no guidance as to priorities when conflicts occur between different considerations. (Wisely suggests a supplementary listing of the elements of professional responsibility that would tend to serve these functions.) In constructing a good ethics code, a balance must be sought between overspecificity and sweeping generality.

A useful, common practice in the field of ethics codes, and one to be followed here in a fairly conventional manner, is to subdivide the rules into sets corresponding to the objects of concern. Thus, the proposed code . . . presents the engineer's ethical obligations in four parts, directed toward society (including posterity), employers and clients, professional associates (colleagues, co-workers, subordinates), and "the profession" (an abstraction of a somewhat different nature from the others).

BASIC PRINCIPLES

Familiarity with the principal theories of moral philosophy can help clarify one's thinking about the subjects treated here, although it is not essential to an understanding of what follows. . . .

Despite wide variations among the values held by engineers, there are a few that are virtually universal, probably because they are essential to the preservation of society as well as to progress in science and technology. Such a set would include:

1. truth, honesty, trustworthiness
2. respect for human life and welfare, including that of posterity
3. fair play
4. openness
5. competence

Virtually all human achievements depend on an infrastructure that is the result of cooperative efforts extending over substantial periods of time. Even those who work as individuals, such as some painters, writers, and scientists, depend upon the past and present efforts of other people for their subsistence, for their basic tools and materials, and for criticism and appreciation. This necessitates the harmonious coexistence of communities of people. But stable communities can exist only if the members can reasonably assume that their neighbors and associates will, as a general rule, treat them fairly and not knowingly do them harm. Each must be able to rely on others to carry out their assignments in complex enterprises. They must be able to rely on the truth of what others tell them and to depend on others to fulfill agreements. Without a regard for the well-being of posterity, the long-term stability of civilization, which gives meaning to humanity's greatest achievements, would be undermined.

The above considerations justify the first three principles. Note that the cooperative nature of science and technology further amplifies the importance of these principles. Engineers and scientists who could not, for example, rely on the validity of information supplied by colleagues would be unable to function.

Respect for the integrity of the environment is an immediate corollary of principle 2, since both contemporary society and posterity depend upon the environment in many ways, including, but not limited to, obtaining adequate amounts of needed materials. A rich environment, replete with a variety of species of life, tends to be more stable and is also stimulating to the imagination, as well as serving the more mundane purposes of a raw materials warehouse.

Respect for the democratic process follows from principle 3 (fair play) and can also be justified directly by the argument that a social system in which everyone has a voice in the decision-making process is likely to function better in the long run.

In every aspect of society in general, and in science and technology in particular, we require knowledge and data generated by others. Hence the need for principle 4 (openness), which is also closely related to principle 1 (truth, etc.) and is necessary for fair play to prevail.

Since members of a profession are relied upon by others to carry out important tasks requiring special ability and knowledge, it is essential that they should indeed be professionally competent. The results of incompetence and of malice are often indistinguishable.

The above principles pertain to ethical as opposed to other aspects of behavior. Matters such as professional courtesy, public image, and standards of compensation are deliberately excluded, although they have always had an important—if not dominant—place in traditional engineering ethics codes. This exclusion does not necessarily imply opposition to those elements, but simply implies recognition that such admonitions as "uphold the dignity of the engineering profession" or "support the activities of their professional societies" (both of which I heartily endorse) belong elsewhere than in a code of ethics.

There is another dimension to the problem of professional responsibility (or, for that matter, of personal responsibility in general). Although people should be encouraged and urged to do good and prevent harm, it is difficult to specify for any individual how many such acts and which ones specifically should be performed. On the other hand, there is a much stronger and easier-to-delineate duty to refrain from doing harm. (There may, of course, be substantial difficulties and disputes over *whether* a given act is on balance harmful, but that is a different question.) It follows, therefore, that acts in conformity with the positive admonitions of an ethics code tend to draw praise, while the absence of such acts is seldom cause for criticism. Violations of the prohibitions of a code clearly open the way to censure (formal or informal). *Not* committing an act prohibited by a code may be praiseworthy if great pressure to commit it was resisted.

A CODE OF ENGINEERING ETHICS

Presentation of the model code in this section is accompanied by interspersed comments and examples. The text of the code is in italics. . . .

Preamble

In the pursuit of their profession, engineers and scientists should use their skills and knowledge to enhance the quality of life for all people. They should conduct themselves in an honorable and ethical manner so as to merit confidence and respect. This code is a guide to their conduct in the balanced discharge of their responsibilities to society, to employers and clients, to colleagues, co-workers and subordinates, and to the profession.

Article 1. Engineers shall regard their responsibility to society as paramount and shall:
1.1   Inform themselves and others, as appropriate, of the consequences, direct and indirect, immediate and remote, of projects they are involved in

For example, an engineer assigned to the design of a computer terminal ought to have, or acquire, a reasonable knowledge of such matters as how it is likely to be used, who the users are likely to be, whether the possibility of X-ray damage to users has been considered, and what sort of human factor studies have been made (or are contemplated). The word *appropriate* in the text is very important and obviously involves a judgment as to how far it is reasonable to go. Individual engineers cannot generally be expected to undertake deep sociological or environmental studies in the course of each assignment. In the above example, most, if not all, of the questions would probably be answered by relatively brief discussions with those who have made the studies or by perusals of their reports. A greater effort would be called for if the engineer notices that some significant aspect has not been explored. The ethical obligation in that event may overlap the purely technical requirements for doing a good job. The essence here is that true professionals consider the broad contexts of their work and are not satisfied with understanding only the immediate details of their parts of a project.

1.2   Endeavor to direct their professional skills toward conscientiously chosen ends they deem, on balance, to be a positive value to humanity; declining to use those skills for purposes they consider, on balance, to conflict with their moral values

Given the very considerable areas of agreement on general principles, it follows that in most cases there will be little controversy involving the application of this rule. Virtually everyone would consider as desirable safer aircraft landing systems, techniques for reducing the likelihood of methane explosions in coal mines, and devices that would enable blind people to read ordinary printed material. Few would approve of apparatus for torture chambers, a heroin substitute easily made from widely available low-cost materials, or devices for rigging roulette wheels.

There are, nevertheless, exceptional situations. This is the principal area where differing individual values come into play. One engineer, asked to design a piece of apparatus for a whiskey distillery, might decline the assignment on the ground that he considers hard liquor to be a basically harmful product. Another engineer, who sees nothing intrinsically wrong with whiskey, might have no qualms about accepting the job. Both might be acting in this instance as ethical professionals who took into account the social effects of a project before deciding whether to work on it. One may argue as to who came to the right conclusion about the net benefits of alcohol, but this controversy is in a realm outside of engineering ethics.

Even where two people have very similar basic beliefs, they may still legitimately arrive at different conclusions regarding the "on balance" value of a product because of differences in the weights they assign to certain effects or differences in judgment regarding likelihoods of certain events. The decision problem is generally more difficult when the product can be used in widely differing situations.

An improved ultrasonic range-finding device could be of direct use for military submarines, undersea oil exploration, underwater salvage operations, or geologic studies aimed at understanding earthquakes. If one assigns positive weights to the benefits of some of these and negative weights to others, then a judgment must be made as to whether the net effect is positive. One factor would be an estimate of who the actual customers are likely to be. This may in turn be related to the nature of the organization sponsoring the development. For example, in the course of my own career, I have tried, on grounds of conscience, to avoid participation in military applications of technology. One aspect of this effort has been to refrain from working on any project sponsored by a military agency.

Although it is easy to construct hypothetical examples posing difficult dilemmas, and although hard cases really do occur, they are not very common, occurring with no greater relative frequency than other very difficult dilemmas we face in life. The fact that it may be hard in some cases to define a line between acceptable and unacceptable activities is no excuse for not making the effort. It is certainly no excuse for not doing so in the more usual, easy cases.

A Right to Engineering Services?

Two alternative concepts of the engineer's obligations should be mentioned here. First is that enunciated by Samuel C. Florman:

> Should professionals work only on projects that they as citizens approve? . . . If each person is entitled to medical care and legal representation, is it not equally important that each legitimate business entity, government agency, and citizen's group should have access to expert engineering advice? If so then it follows that engineers (within the limits of conscience) will sometimes labor on behalf of causes in which they do not believe.

There are several grounds on which this position may be challenged. First, the entitlement to engineering advice, whether on the part of individuals or groups, is certainly not an established right with the same standing as the right to legal counsel, a basic right stemming from our Constitution, or the right to medical care, which rests on fundamental considerations of humanity.

Suppose, however, that for the sake of argument we assume that such a right does indeed exist. What obligations would this confer on individual engineers? Accepting Florman's analogy to the medical profession, the answer is none. Article VI of the American Medical Association's "Principles of Medical Ethics" (July 1980) reads: "A physician shall, in the provision of appropriate patient care, except in emergencies, be free to choose whom to serve, with whom to associate, and the environment in which to provide medical care." The obligation flowing from the right to medical care rests with the medical profession as a whole, rather than with any particular physician.

Similarly, individual attorneys are not required to accept all cases brought to them. (The most common problem encountered in satisfying the right to counsel is in meeting the needs of the indigent. This is handled through a combination of governmental and private agencies, supplemented by volunteer services provided by individual practitioners. Clearly, Florman is not concerned here with this type of situation.)

The relevant analogy would involve people accused of particularly horrendous crimes. It is sometimes necessary in such cases for judges to appoint attorneys to represent them. This must be done because it is basic to our legal system that every defendant be professionally represented, regardless of how terrible the crime, how overwhelming the case against the accused, or how obnoxious the accused may be to the community at large. Here again the analogy with engineering services fails. Even Samuel Florman admits that there are engineering projects (such as gas chambers in extermination camps) that should not be carried out. . . . If, given the diversity of values and viewpoints among engineers, conscientious objections create serious problems in staffing a project, then there is good reason indeed to pause and reconsider the arguments against that project.

Informed Consent

A second alternative concept of engineers' obligations has been proposed by Robert J. Baum. Based on the notion of informed consent, it can be stated concisely in terms of their responsibilities to:

1. Recognize the right of each individual potentially affected by a project to participate to an appropriate degree in the making of decisions concerning that project.
2. Do everything in their power to provide complete, accurate, and understandable information to all potentially affected parties; and
3. Carry out to the best of their ability assignments which have been appropriately approved by the potentially affected parties, even if the engineers believe that they may (or even will) have harmful consequences.

The basic concept is an appealing one and in certain situations may offer useful guidance as to the proper course of action. But there are serious problems, both theoretical and practical, that severely limit its applicability. Most basic, perhaps, is the admonition in point 3 that engineers must work on projects that they deem pernicious if those affected by it insist. Under the indicated circumstances, this notion casts engineers in the role of tools to be used or misused by others, without regard for their own beliefs. There is a possible loophole if the engineers themselves are included in the sets of people affected by the projects that they work on and are thereby also allowed to participate in the vote. If the voting rules are such that the engineers have a veto power, then the problem disappears. But this, of course, essentially nullifies the third point.

Baum does not suggest what the voting rules should be. If a particular group of people are to be put at risk in order to gain certain benefits (e.g., the risk might be the possibility of a proposed dam collapsing and the benefits a recreational lake, some hydro power, and some irrigation water), what proportion should have to concur before the project can be said to have been "appropriately approved by the potentially affected parties"? Suppose the question is not about whether the dam should be built but about a particular tradeoff between safety and cost. In that case, those who are investing money in the project must also have a say in the decision. But how much in relation to one another and how much in relation to the people in the area? And this is one of the easier problems connected with the concept of letting the informed consent of the affected parties displace completely the role of the conscience of the engineer.

C. Thomas Rogers, commenting on this approach, suggests an example in which identifying the affected parties is much more difficult and where gaining their assent is essentially impossible. This is the situation where the project is to construct a military aircraft. Apart from the population of the country that is commissioning the enterprise, one cannot deny that the people who will be targets of the proposed aircraft may also have an interest in the matter. At the time the plane is being designed, this group may not be known, and, if they are known, it would scarcely be necessary to conduct a poll to determine their views on the issue. Along similar lines is the case where the project is the design of an electric chair. A consequence of the informed consent idea, if pursued to its logical conclusion, may therefore be to require all engineers to be pacifists. Since most people today would not consider this to be an acceptable requirement, some modification of Baum's position would appear necessary on this ground alone.

It is certainly desirable that the people to be affected by a proposed project should be informed about it and that their views should be taken into account. But there are many important situations in which, because of practical limitations or conceptual difficulties, this cannot be accomplished in a satisfactory manner. It then becomes necessary for others to make the decision, in part, perhaps, on the basis of what they think the unrepresented people might have preferred. Certainly the engineers involved are obliged to participate in this decision-making process.

As in the case of the whiskey distillery, there may also be value differences that make a project desired by those directly affected unacceptable to the engineer. It appears difficult to escape the conclusion that engineers should sometimes make conscience-based judgments regarding the acceptability of proposed assignments.

> *1.3   Hold paramount the safety, health, and welfare of the public, speaking out against abuses of the public interest that they may encounter in the course of professional activities in whatever manner is best calculated to lead to a remedy*

As a professional, an engineer is not an ordinary employee and hence cannot simply carry out assignments without giving some thought to the broader consequences. "To hold paramount the public safety, health, and welfare" means that a judgment must be made as to whether the overall effect of a proposed course of action may be harmful to the public interest. Should the engineer conclude that this is indeed the case, then an appropriate response is called for.

Suppose that an engineer involved in the design of the landing gear of a new airliner believes that the mechanism for latching the wheels in the down position is unreliable in that it requires unusually precise adjustments during maintenance.

Clearly he is obligated to call attention to the problem. Now assume that his manager insists on retaining the current design and that his arguments fail to persuade the engineer that it is adequate. Then item 1.3 of the code obligates the engineer to take the matter further—perhaps appealing to the next level of supervision. Depending on the seriousness of the problem, the engineer's degree of confidence in his judgment, and other circumstances, it might ultimately be necessary to go outside the company, for example to the Federal Aviation Agency. Such matters, which must be handled very carefully in a responsible, professional manner, are discussed at some length in Chapter 6. Once again it should be understood that situations calling for drastic action, though of great importance when they do occur, are uncommon. Making them even less common should be a major goal of the engineering profession.

The obligation to act is less pressing when the potentially harmful decision is one that the engineer is aware of but not directly involved in. It is then a matter of *preventing* harm, as opposed to the preceding situation, which entailed refraining from *doing* harm. On the other hand, when engineers have participated in projects that develop in a manner that appears pernicious, they have a particularly strong obligation to take remedial action to prevent the harm and, at a minimum, should be expected to warn those at risk. A good example of such a situation arose in connection with the DC-10 case . . . , where, unfortunately, this responsibility was not met.

In all such matters, the magnitude of the danger and the degree of certainty about it are important factors in determining what should be done. Consideration should be given to the possibility that an alternative intended to reduce the hazards directly associated with some product may result in increasing dangers elsewhere sufficiently to cause a net *increase* in overall risk.

It is sometimes argued that exposing some segment of the public to increased risk may be justified by other considerations, such as economic benefits. A minimal requirement in such cases is to inform, in an effective manner, those to be placed at risk, so that they have an opportunity to influence the decision.

1.4   Help inform the public about technological developments, the alternatives they make feasible, and possible associated problems

An obvious prerequisite for the proper functioning of a democracy is that the public have adequate access to information on matters of concern to it, and certainly a great deal of technological information is in this category. Since there are many channels, activated by a variety of factors, for publicizing such data, this seldom poses serious problems for individual engineers.

1.5   Be encouraged to contribute professional advice to worthy causes

No elaboration seems necessary here.

Article 2. Engineers shall practice their profession in a responsible manner, associating themselves only with honorable enterprises and shall:
2.1   Keep their professional skills up to date and be aware of current events and societal issues pertinent to their work

The pace of modern technology is such that continuous study (formal or informal) is essential for the maintenance of competence, and a well-meaning bungler often does as much harm as a morally blind but competent individual.

An awareness of current events and societal issues is clearly necessary if one is to meet the conditions of items 1.1 and 1.2. Suppose, for example, that a proposed assignment is the development of a communications system for some foreign police force. Before accepting the assignment, the engineer should ascertain whether the police force involved is acting as an instrument of repression on behalf of a totalitarian government. Such an appraisal, based on a reasonable survey of news reports and the like, interpreted in the light of his own background knowledge and values, is an important prerequisite to the decision that must be made in accordance with item 1.2.

2.2   Be honest and realistic in making claims and estimates, never falsifying data

This is a fundamental aspect of professional integrity. Deception in all forms (including the suppression of relevant information as well as explicit falsification) undermines the mutual confidence that is so important in carrying on technology-based enterprises. If, for example, one cannot rely on test data supplied by others, it may be necessary to repeat their work at considerable expense in both time and money.

Overoptimistic estimates of cost and time requirements for portions of a project make it difficult to choose rationally among available alternatives or to predict overall completion dates and costs. Repeated instances of gross errors in engineering estimates can produce distrust on the part of the public, to the extent that sound proposals will be rejected.

In addition to economic costs, that may, in some cases, be tantamount to theft, deception can endanger life and limb or lead to serious environmental damage. The Goodrich brake case . . . is an instance in which falsified data exposed test pilots to an added hazard. . . .

2.3   Accurately describe their qualifications for proposed engineering assignments

Exaggerating one's qualifications is a temptation that all professionals are likely to be exposed to at one time or another. The consequences of this form of dishonesty can obviously be very serious. They include those associated with professional incompetence, with an added element of corruption.

Some explanation is in order as to why the wording here differs somewhat from corresponding provisions of many other codes. In these, engineers are prohibited from accepting assignments for which they are not qualified. Apart from the problem of defining qualifications for particular tasks, there arise situations where no truly qualified person is available for a job. This often occurs in the wake of accidents or disasters but can occur under other circumstances as well. A less than fully qualified engineer might then properly undertake to do the best he can, provided that this does not entail any increased jeopardy to people and that no deception is involved. There are also situations where it may be acceptable to all concerned for the engineer to acquire the necessary qualifications during the course of a project.

Article 3. Engineers shall, in relations with employers and clients:
3.1   Act as faithful agents or trustees in business or professional matters, provided such actions conform with other parts of this code

Normally the expectation is the same for engineers as for others paid to do a job: that they carry out their assignments as best they can. In addition, as professionals, engineers should consider their employers' (or clients') interests from a broader point of view. They should be alert to problems or opportunities not necessarily specific to particular assignments. For example, they might call attention to advances in technology that may render products of their firms obsolete or might be exploited to reduce production costs. As another example, engineers might inform their companys' purchasing departments that particular suppliers are overcharging and that equivalent components are a available elsewhere at lower prices.

The qualifying clause implies that, as professionals, engineers sometimes have overriding obligations. Thus, regardless of explicit or implicit demands by an employer, and regardless of the effects on the employer's business, an engineer may not falsify data (2.2), or endanger the public (1.3) by skimping on the testing of a vital component.

3.2   Keep information on the business affairs or technical processes of an employer or client in confidence while employed and later, until such information is properly released, provided such confidentiality conforms with other parts of this code

Given the key roles played by engineers in many enterprises, it is essential that they can be relied upon to safeguard information they acquire on the job. Difficulties sometimes arise when they change jobs within an industry. It would be unethical to reveal to the new employer such information derived from the previous employer as marketing plans, special manufacturing techniques or as yet unreleased product descriptions. But it is sometimes difficult to differentiate between a proprietary technique developed as a by-product of some project and a technique of general value that an engineer hits upon in the course of an assignment and that he may properly regard as a part of his general professional repertoire.

As in item 3.1, the qualifying clause indicates that this provision cannot be used to inhibit an engineer from revealing information in compliance with other rules such as 1.3. Conflicts between 3.2 and 4.4 can also pose problems; see the discussion of rule 4.4

3.3   Disclose any circumstance that could lead to a conflict of interest

Fair play and openness demand that those relying on one's judgment be informed of any interests one has that they might consider as biasing factors. The application of this provision in purely commercial situations is straightforward. In cases where technical experts are offering their views on controversial issues affecting the public interest, the problem is that experts in any area are virtually always involved with one or more parties to the controversy. Either at present or in the immediate past, they have almost invariably been employed, directly or indirectly, by some organization with a stake in the outcome. This, after all, is how they probably acquired or intend to use their expertise. Even university professors frequently have such ties through consulting (or prospective consulting) relationships, summer jobs, sabbatical employment, or research grants. About the only way to manage such situations is to seek experts with a variety of backgrounds who will then accompany all testimony with clear, honest statements of their interests, as specified in this provision. With respect to this rule, there is generally little to lose and much to gain by openness. (In fact this is not a bad maxim with respect to ethics in general.)

3.4   Neither offer nor accept bribes

The purpose of a bribe is to cause (always surreptitiously) an agent of some organization to favor the interests of an outside party over the interests of the agent's employer. Thus one aspect of bribery is the undermining of loyalty. Where the interest sacrificed is financial (e.g., the opportunity to purchase an item at a lower price), another aspect is indirect theft (for the benefit of both the recipient and offerer of the bribe). Sometimes the interest sacrificed is of a public nature, such as clean air, or safe elevators.

Although nonparticipation in acts of bribery may appear to be a simple, noncontroversial, and obviously necessary admonition, there are circumstances under which otherwise ethical individuals find it exceedingly difficult to follow. These occur in localities where bribery is "a way of life" so that those who refuse to participate are placed at a great disadvantage. . . .

Article 4. Engineers shall, in relations with colleagues, co-workers and subordinates:
4.1   Seek, accept, and offer honest professional criticism, properly credit others for their contributions, never claiming credit for work not done

Mutual criticism is one of the most important ways in which we collectively improve ourselves in every sphere, and it is a vital element in technological progress. Of course, it should be carried out in a civilized, nonhostile manner. ·

It is a common human failing to forget the origins of ideas one uses, so a conscious effort is necessary to adhere to the second part of this rule. Failure to give adequate credit to others often leads to pain, resentment, and embarrassment, whereas erring a bit on the other side costs very little. Thus, in marginal cases, one should opt for generosity. It is particularly important not to neglect the contributions of subordinates.

A corollary to giving proper credit to others is to avoid taking credit where none is due. The classic violation here is when the name of the head of some research group routinely appears as a co-author of all publications by members of that group, even when he had no part in the writing or the work reported on. This also occurs sometimes at universities, with professors similarly taking an excessive share of credit for work done largely by their students.

It is unfortunate that, whereas patentable inventions or contributions to engineering or scientific theory are routinely signed, so that the creators are clearly identified (for better or worse!), this is not usually the case for other forms of engineering work. For example, engineers who develop ingenious production processes or who design clever (but for some reason unpatented) integrated circuits have no way to "sign" their work. Thus they receive recognition only from close associates or possibly from others through word of mouth. It should be a goal of the engineering profession to develop appropriate means for associating the names of individual engineers in all categories with the products of their work.

4.2   Treat them fairly in all respects, regardless of such factors as race, religion, sex, age, ethnic background, or disabilities, and respect their privacy

Fairness is essential, not only for its own sake, but to help foster the cooperative spirit that makes the members of a profession better able to serve society and to prosper individually. With respect to privacy, it is particularly important to avoid misusing personal information acquired about subordinates.

4.3   Help promote their professional growth

For example, in addition to allowing them reasonable time to attend technical meetings and to update their knowledge through formal or informal study, an engineering manager should, when making job assignments, take into account the effects on the careers of his subordinates. Granted that there is always a mixture of routine and more interesting work to be done, care should be taken not to overburden particular individuals with mundane or overspecialized tasks to the point where they may eventually lose their competence for anything else. Failure in this regard is often the root cause of age discrimination problems. When an organization anticipates changes, such as the dropping of a particular product line, engineering managers should to the greatest extent possible, give adequate prior notice to their subordinates who may be affected.

4.4   Report, publish, and disseminate information freely, subject to legal and reasonable proprietary or privacy restraints, provided such actions conform with other parts of this code

This follows directly from the principle of openness, important for the development of both general knowledge and the proficiency of individual engineering colleagues. Acceptable constraints derived from the protection of property rights usually either involve very specialized information or else apply for a relatively short time interval (during which, for example, a patent application is being prepared).

Consider, however, a situation in which an engineer develops a generally useful idea that could lead to a significant improvement in a product produced by his company. Suppose that the company decides that implementing the idea would not be profitable because of a heavy investment in their current product, which is doing well in the market, and therefore that they will neither implement it themselves, nor release it for others to utilize. If the idea is of real social value (e.g., if it is pertinent to an energy-saving device or to an improvement in an important medical instrument), then the engineer ordered to suppress it would be in a serious dilemma. He must make a serious effort to persuade management to change that decision, and should this effort fail, he may, depending on the importance of the matter, have to consider further action, as discussed in subsequent chapters.

Privacy constraints involve information about individuals; respecting them usually does not represent a significant loss to the general fund of knowledge.

An important class of legal constraints is that ostensibly based on national security considerations. The word *ostensibly* is used here to reflect the widely held view that there is little or no legitimate reason for keeping secret the great bulk of information officially restricted on this ground. (Of course, few would deny the existence of *some* very proper national security secrets.) This is a matter of public policy that affects engineers not only as citizens but also in their professional capacities. In recent years, a new threat to the free exchange of technical information has arisen in the form of government efforts to institute a system of prior censorship to restrict publication of information developed by researchers working on unclassified projects.

For example, attempts were made in the late seventies by the National Security Agency to prevent the general dissemination of new results in the field of cryptology. These results were obtained by people doing unclassified research and development work with commercial applicants in mind (e.g., electronic funds transfer systems). Threats were made to invoke obscure provisions of the International Traffic in Arms Regulations against those who were about to present papers at an IEEE symposium. More recently, proposals have been made to restrict information (again generated by unclassified work) in a variety of other fields, including integrated circuit technology.

Are there situations where information should be withheld on public interest grounds not covered above? A possible example might be a simple technique for producing, from widely available materials, some devastating weapon that could be used by criminals. The final clause in rule 4.4 leaves this question to the judgment and conscience of the individual professional.

4.5   Promote health and safety in work situations

Engineers should be concerned not only about the health and safety of the general public but also about the well-being of people at work.

4.6   Encourage and support adherence to this code, never giving directions that would encourage others to compromise their professional responsibilities

On those infrequent occasions when an engineer feels compelled on ethical grounds to take a position that might be unpopular with superiors or even with colleagues, it is particularly important that fellow engineers react in a sympathetic, understanding manner. Even if they disagree with their associate on the basis of differing values or judgments, and even if they feel compelled to oppose his position because of such disagreement, they should show respect for a sincerely held view and support the right to express it and act upon it. They should also back efforts by their professional societies to promote and support the ethical practice of engineering.

Engineers with supervisory responsibilities should be careful not to issue orders that would pressure or unduly tempt subordinates to act unethically.

WHAT SHOULD *NOT* BE IN AN ETHICS CODE

As was mentioned above ["Basic Principles"], a number of features of older ethics codes pertaining to professional courtesy, public relations, income protection, and supporting one's professional society have been deliberately omitted as being, at most, marginally relevant to ethics. (One might, for example, argue that since engineering societies help maintain professional competence and also have a role to play in promulgating professional ethics, their support should hence be an ethical obligation. But the same reasoning would also justify adding to the code a provision calling on engineers to support universities. This does not seem acceptable.)

Also omitted are a considerable number of provisions that pertain to business ethics and that are significant for only a small percentage of engineers, mainly consultants. These are best incorporated in a separate code aimed at this group. In fact, the American Consulting Engineers Council (ACEC) has just such a code.

Constraints on Utterances

Several rules common to many ethics codes have been omitted even though they are relevant. Consider first an admonition against injuring the reputation of or criticizing other engineers (or their work). This is sometimes, but not always, qualified with the words *falsely* and/or *maliciously*. In some cases this statement is in a context dealing with unfair competition. In a similar category is another common provision that engineers should be truthful and objective in public statements.

Certainly the implied objectives of these rules are laudable. Who would deny that engineers who publicly lie about engineering matters or who maliciously malign the reputations of fellow engineers merit contempt? The problem lies not with the basic principles but with the potential for abuse and the difficulty of establishing where a violation has occurred.

When an issue is sufficiently complex and controversial, it is common for emotions to be aroused and for people to charge their opponents with being malicious, subjective, and untruthful. Those who challenge the status quo are particularly vulnerable to such attacks. The road of the dissenter is already sufficiently rough; the addition of a threat of charges filed with an ethics committee would add a further serious impediment. How do we determine if a criticism is malicious? Or if a statement is objective? Or true?

A substantial statement on a complex matter might very well include several false assertions and still be a valuable contribution to a debate. Perhaps honest mistakes were made concerning peripheral points not important to the conclusions. Nevertheless, such errors could be the basis for proceedings against a dissenter that, even if ultimately unsuccessful, could cause considerable hardship and stress.

It is on the basis of such consideration, well buttressed by history, that the United

States Constitution bars legislation making lying a crime (except under very special, precisely defined circumstances). The consensus was, and remains, that even apart from the likelihood of massive abuse, the chilling effect of such legislation on free speech would entail a serious net loss of truth in the public arena. Allowing open combat between truth and falsehood is considered more efficacious than attempting to outlaw lies.

Ethics rules pertaining to the criticism of other engineers and to the nature of public statements can seldom be used to justify positive acts, nor are they of much value in pointing out ethical obligations. They are potentially useful only for inhibiting wrong behavior and, as discussed above, are easily misused. An example of such abuse was the expulsion from the ASCE in 1932 of two engineers who publicly exposed corrupt behavior on the part of another engineer. (Their accusations were subsequently confirmed by the outcome of a criminal trial, but the engineers were not reinstated by the ASCE.)

Disreputable Characters

A rather different set of problems makes me uncomfortable with another common component of ethics codes: that engineers should associate only with reputable people. Here it is not altogether clear that even the direct goal is always a desirable one. Suppose engineer A commits a crime (which may or may not be related to his professional activities), is caught, tried, convicted, and sentenced to prison. After serving his sentence, suppose he resolves henceforth to lead an honest life, and engineer B, an old classmate of A's, hires him as a member of his department in a large company.

By most definitions, A, a convicted felon, is not reputable. Is it really socially desirable that he be barred from ever again practicing his profession? Should B now be considered unethical? What about C, who continues to associate with B?

One might resolve the dilemma by declaring that A, having "paid his debt to society," is no longer disreputable.[1] But if a convicted felon is not disreputable, who is? There are, of course, people with wide and well-deserved reputations as shady characters, who have never been convicted of a crime or censured by a professional society. If, however, the set of people to be shunned is defined by their general reputations, then the next question is, just how is this to be ascertained? Bear in mind that each individual engineer must make such a determination about each potential associate. One who is overly tolerant in his judgment may then himself be judged as unethical. And unless his associates abandon *him*, they too, by recursion, thereby join the set of pariahs. This chain reaction effect, a consequence of the secondary boycott character of this rule, is perhaps the most disturbing aspect, since, in principle, people could be labeled unethical simply because their judgments of the ethical judgments of others are ruled incorrect.

The association rule is another in the "do not" category and hence also a candidate for enforcement. However, perhaps as a result of a tacit agreement to avoid the sort of bizarre scenarios sketched above, it is seldom enforced.

SOME OTHER ETHICS CODES

General Background

No attempt is made here to enumerate the many ethics codes developed by various engineering associations or to detail the history of such codes. Instead, there follows a brief survey of some of the most important engineering codes and an even more cursory sketch of the history involved, confined in both aspects to the United States. The reader may also find it interesting to examine the code of ethics of the Association of Professional Engineers of the Province of Ontario, Canada. . . .

The first engineering ethics code was adopted in 1912 by the American Institute of Electrical Engineers (AIEE; this organization merged with the Institute of Radio Engineers in 1963 to form the Institute of Electrical and Electronics Engineers, or IEEE). As is the case with the code adopted by the American Society of Mechanical Engineers (ASME) in 1914, the AIEE code places as the engineer's first obligation the protection of his client's or employer's interests. A great deal is said about business relationships and the ownership of data. No general concern for the public safety, health, or welfare is included, although a "duty to make every effort to remedy dangerous defects in apparatus or structures or dangerous operation" is mentioned, and these should be brought "to the attention of his client or employer."

No machinery was set up to enforce the code or to educate members about it. In fact, the very existence of the 1912 code was unknown to those who developed the IEEE Code of Ethics in the 1970s. . . .

The Engineers' Council for Professional Development (ECPD)[2] first produced an ethics code in 1947, subsequently revising it in 1963, 1974, and 1977. This series of codes is particularly important because several of the major engineering societies (ASCE, ASME, and American Institute of Mining Engineers or AIME) as well as a number of smaller societies have adopted the Basic Principles and the Canons of this code. (In addition to these parts, there is a third section called "Suggested Guidelines." Some societies substitute their own guidelines for those of the ECPD code.) The evolution of the ECPD code is interesting; only a few threads are traced below. . . .

Increasing Concern for the Public Well-Being

The trend toward increased responsibility to the public is significant. Whereas the 1912 AIEE code mentions the public only in a patronizing manner (e.g., "The engineer should endeavor to assist the public to a fair and correct general understanding of engineering matters."), the 1947 ECPD code mentions in its foreword "fidelity to the public" and the engineer's "duty to interest himself in public welfare, and to be ready to apply his special knowledge for the benefit of mankind." In a subordinate position of the body of the code it is specified that "he will have due regard for the safety. . . ." The 1963 version, which opens with three fundamental principles in place of the foreword, uses stronger language. Principle III reads, "will use his knowledge and skill for the advancement of human welfare." The *first* canon below states that "the engineer" will have proper regard for the safety, health and welfare of the public in the performance of his professional duties." In 1974, what was principle III is promoted to principle I, and the twenty-one canons are reduced to seven, the first of which is further strengthened to "Engineers shall hold *paramount* the safety, health and welfare of the public in the performance of their professional duties" (emphasis added). These remain unchanged in the 1977 revision. The IEEE code refers in its preamble to "the quality of life for all people," and item 1 of Article IV reads, "Protect the safety, health and welfare of the public and speak out against abuses in these areas affecting the public interest."

Associated with this progressive development is an unfortunate, possibly inadvertent regressive step. The weak provision of the AIEE code concerning the effort to remedy hazards covers (implicitly) dangers both to the public and to workers. This is made explicit in the 1947 ECPD code where the canon quoted earlier referring to safety and health mentions "the public and employees." But in the 1963 and subsequent revisions, only the *public* safety is mentioned; no reference at all is made to workers. A similar omission characterizes the IEEE code.

Disreputable Associations, Society Support, Helping Subordinates

With respect to association with disreputable people, no clear pattern is evident. The AIEE and the 1947 ECPD codes proscribe association with enterprises of questionable character, a very different and unobjectionable provision. Nothing at all along these lines is in the 1963 ECPD or IEEE codes. The 1974 ECPD code mandates that "Engineers shall associate only with reputable persons or organizations," whereas the 1977 ECPD code replaces this canon (the *only* changed canon) with "engineers shall act in such a manner as to uphold and enhance the honor, integrity and dignity of the engineering profession": again, an unobjectionable provision (except perhaps for some question as to the ethical relevance of "dignity").

The AIEE code and both the 1947 and 1963 ECPD codes refer to the duty to work through engineering societies as one means of cooperating in the exchange of technical information. In the 1974 and 1977 ECPD codes, "supporting the professional and technical societies of their disciplines" is elevated to the status of one of the four "Fundamental Principles," unqualified by any reference to information exchange. A similar provision, though in a less exalted position, is in the IEEE code. (It is interesting that the American Institute of Chemical Engineers—AIChE—opposes this provision as being outside the realm of ethics.)

All versions of the ECPD code oblige engineers to provide subordinates with opportunities for professional development, and the foreword to the 1947 version requires that "in his dealings with fellow engineers he should be fair and tolerant." The IEEE code is more explicit regarding this latter point, enjoining against bias on the ground of "race, religion, sex or national origin." Its reference to aiding in professional development refers to "colleagues and co-workers."

Specialized Codes and More General Codes

The discussion thus far has centered on codes applicable to engineers in general. Since engineering encompasses so many diverse disciplines and varied functions, it is appropriate that special ethics codes have been devised that focus on the problems unique to these categories. Reference has been made above to one of these, a code focused on consulting engineers. An example of a provision of a code for consulting engineers is as follows: "When they use designs supplied to them by clients, the designs remain the property of the clients and shall not be duplicated for others without express permission" (ACEC code, 4i.3).

As another example, a code for engineers in medicine and biology, promulgated by the IEEE Engineering in Medicine and Biology Society, has this provision (referring to relations between engineers and health professionals): "Promote interdisciplinary communication and understanding while recognizing and maintaining respect for differing cultural values."

The converse of the special code is a universal code for all engineers. Efforts to get agreement on such a code have not yet succeeded, with the ECPD code coming closest to success. Renewed efforts in this direction are now being made through the newly formed American Association of Engineering Societies (AAES), an umbrella group encompassing all of the principal American engineering societies. Success here would give the resulting code a great deal of prestige and would pave the way for unified ethics support and enforcement machinery.

One stimulating and useful proposal for a unified code, by Slowter and Oldenquist, features a core of ethical concepts that captures just those features of existing codes that the authors regard as proper and appropriate. . . . A comparison with the code proposed in ["A Code of Engineering Ethics"] indicates close agreement, with two significant exceptions. The Slowter-Oldenquist core includes a prohibition against working with those who violate the code (I.e), and it does not mention safety in the workplace.

Another code . . . along somewhat similar lines has been developed by an IEEE ethics task force and submitted (November 1981) to AAES for consideration by its constituent societies. This code is noteworthy for the broad range of topics that it covers very compactly.

LIVING UP TO THE ETHICS CODE

An ethics code cannot generally tell people what to do in specific situations. Its function as a guide is more to suggest factors to be considered and to raise questions pertinent to the decision-making process. Ethical dilemmas arise when actions have multiple effects involving different people in different ways, with uncertain results governed by unknown—perhaps unknowable—probabilities. As in any other aspect of real life, it is sometimes very difficult to decide what is the right thing to do, and reasonable people of good will may on occasion disagree. This does not relieve us of the obligation to do the best we can.

In some situations it is easy to see what the right decision is, but a personal penalty may be involved in acting on it. . . . Since most people feel uncomfortable when they act improperly, there is a strong subconscious drive to justify avoidance of the penalty by specious reasoning or even by altering one's values. It is more honest, though painful, to acknowledge (if only to oneself) that one is unwilling to pay the price for doing the right thing in a particular case. An important advantage of such an admission, apart from preserving integrity, is that it is likely to stimulate behavior that, in the long run, will help reduce the cost of ethical behavior, perhaps through the establishment of some of the mechanisms discussed in subsequent chapters.

There are situations in which the success of a clearly ethical course of action is very doubtful, whereas the expected consequences to the actor are severe. Consider, for example, a construction company engineer assigned to help build a dam that he is convinced will serve no useful function adequate to compensate for its cost and the environmental damage it will cause. Refusal of the assignment is very unlikely to stop the project but will probably be damaging to the engineer's career.

It is very natural in such painful situations to resort to some form of what may be called the "futility argument." In the above example this might be "If I don't, someone else will." In other cases it might be "Everyone is doing it" or "You can't fight City Hall." The underlying idea is that individual acts don't count, so why resist the inevitable?

One response to the futility argument is based on the concept that an individual should adhere to his moral principles without direct reference to the consequences. Thus, if the engineer, after mature deliberation, concludes that the dam should not be built, he should refuse the assignment, regardless of his estimate that it will be built in any event. At least *he* will not be guilty of a wrong.

A different (though not inconsistent) refutation of the futility argument is based on the exemplary and long-term effects of principled actions. A well-motivated refusal, especially when it is obviously costly to the refuser, is likely to cause others to reconsider their positions, and some may then change their minds. Quite probably others have privately agreed with the dissident, and his action may inspire them to speak out. In other words, an individual act might trigger a sequence of reactions that could alter what appeared to be inevitable. Even if success is not achieved with respect to the immediate issue, the principled act may significantly affect future events of the same type. There are numerous historical episodes in which a new idea, initially promulgated by a few isolated (and often maligned) individuals, ultimately achieved consensus status. The efforts of such innovators must certainly have appeared futile in the early stages. Thus, while the futility argument poses as a hard-headed statement of reality, it might better be described as a short-sighted excuse for weakness that neglects major factors in human progress.

Engineers have long been a major force in humanity's material progress. Now they must be bolder in defending their work against abuse and directing it toward more beneficial goals. In the next chapter, it is shown that a potentially powerful instrument for this purpose is the engineering society.

SUMMARY

Ethics codes are valuable as general guides to professional conduct, as educational tools, and as a basis for court proceedings and formal support and enforcement procedures. They are useful in justifying ethical behavior to others. An engineering ethics code should be a concise statement of general rules for professional conduct, preferably of a positive nature. It should be based on a widely accepted set of moral precepts such as honesty, fair play, respect for human life and welfare, openness, and competence.

The proposed model code consists of a preamble and four articles. Article 1 treats the engineer's obligations to society. These are: to be informed about the consequences, direct and indirect, of one's work; to direct one's professional efforts toward beneficial ends; to protect the public safety, health, and welfare; to help educate the public about technology; and to contribute professional advice to worthy causes.

Article 2 concerns obligations to the profession. These are: to associate only with honorable enterprises; to maintain one's professional competence; and to be honest in dealing with data and in stating one's professional qualifications.

Obligations to employers and clients are treated in Article 3. Engineers should perform their work with a view toward promoting the goals of their employers in a broader sense than merely carrying out detailed assignments. They should avoid or reveal conflict of interest, should neither offer nor accept bribes, and should not violate confidences.

Article 4 concerns relations with colleagues, co-workers, and subordinates. Honest criticism of work should be freely exchanged. Contributions of others should be acknowledged, and one should not claim credit for the work of others. Engineering managers in particular should be careful about the last point and should also help promote the professional growth of subordinates and not infringe on their privacy. Factors such as race or sex should not influence professional relations. The free dissemination of technical information, subject to reasonable constraints, is another important duty. In addition to having a concern for public health and safety, the engineer should also help reduce workplace hazards. Co-workers and subordinates should be encouraged to follow the ethics code and should be supported when they do so.

Engineering ethics codes should not cover such irrelevant topics as standards of compensation, public image, and courtesy. Other items appearing in some codes, although relevant to ethics and expressing worthy ideas, may cause more trouble than they are worth. For example, rules constraining the public statements of engineers are easily misused to stifle legitimate dissent. Rules prohibiting association with disreputable people entail serious problems of interpretation.

Engineering ethics codes have been evolving for over 60 years. One clear trend is toward more emphasis on responsibility to the public. In other respects there is considerable variation among current codes, and trends are not clear.

A useful idea is the specialized ethics code that adds to the obligations of more general codes those most pertinent in a particular phase of the profession, such as consulting, or a subdiscipline such as bioengineering. There is also a current effort to develop a unified ethics code for all engineers.

Abiding by an ethics code can sometimes be difficult when there are strong pressures to evade one's obligations. One should be wary of distorting one's values in a perhaps unconscious effort to avoid such conflicts. A related phenomenon is the common belief that principled stands by a single person are necessarily futile. On the contrary, these can be effective in a number of ways, both in the short and in the long run.

SOURCES

A major figure in modern thinking about engineering ethics is Victor Paschkis, whose contributions have been through personal contact and organizational work as well as through countless oral presentations and a much smaller body of written works (e.g., 1971, 1975, 1976).

For a good introduction to general ethics, see Taylor (1975). Discussions of general concepts underlying engineering ethics codes are in Unger (1973, 1976). Mario Salvadori (1977), a leader in the field, discusses the value of ethics codes as a tool for making engineers aware of their responsibilities. Arguments against the whole idea of having professional ethics code are presented by philosopher John Ladd (1980). The list of basic principles enunciated in ["Basic Principles"] is an outgrowth of the approach taken by Oldenquist and Slowter (1979) in their very interesting paper. With respect to the importance of openness and mutual criticism in technology, even with respect to such matters as the general acceptance of the validity of mathematical proofs or of the correctness of computer programs, the arguments by De Millo et al. (1979) are very compelling.

A useful classification scheme for ethical statements, listing, in an organized manner, a very comprehensive set of rules from a great many science and engineering ethics codes can be found in Chalk (1980). Elsewhere in the same volume, there are ethics codes of several professional societies. A number of engineering ethics codes, including the 1912 AIEE code, can be found in Baum (1980a).

The quoted statement by William Wisely is from Wisely (1978). Robert Ladenson (1980) presents an illuminating discussion of the philosophical foundations of engineering responsibility, and in particular of the distinction between obligations to do good and to refrain from doing harm.

On the topic of personal responsibility of engineers, I have presented my views earlier (Unger 1972). One who has for many years been a strong advocate of the need for engineers to assume personal responsibility for their work is Adolph J. Ackerman (1969). The "whiskey" example, illustrating how ethical engineers might disagree over the acceptability of a work assignment, was used earlier for that purpose by Paschkis (see Steffens 1975). His comments here are also very pertinent to the futility arguments. The social responsibility of engineers for the consequences of their work is also pointed out by Ashkinazy (1972).

The quotation from Florman is in Florman (1978), and a more extensive presentation of his views can be found in Florman (1976). We engaged in a written debate on this general subject, Florman and Unger (1979). The Baum quotation is from Baum (1980b), and the views of Rogers are expressed in Rogers (1980).

Kipnis (1980) explores the question of the consequences of the "holding paramount the public safety" type of rule, among other things making the argument that, at the very least, the engineer must inform those at risk. The importance of keeping the public informed about technology, and the ways in which governmental secrecy can be used to manipulate public opinion, are graphically illustrated in the important book by Primack and von Hippel (1974). The subject of technology and secrecy is also treated by Brooks (1980), Unger (1977) and DeVolpi (1981).

The idea of associating engineers' names with their work is, among other interesting points, well stated by Robbi (1972). A hypothetical case involving a suppressed invention (resembling that presented in the discussion of item 4.4 of the model ethics code) is in Perry (1981a). Several provisions of Article 4 of the ethics code that pertain to the obligations of an engineering manager to subordinates are based on a proposal by Richard Backe (1981) of the IEEE U.S. Activities Board (USAB). My thinking in the general area of ethics codes has also been influenced by my participation in the activities of the 1981 IEEE USAB Ethics Task Force, chaired by Arthur Rossoff. The wording of item 3.3 and of the preamble of the model code presented here are minor variations of corresponding parts of a draft code . . . produced by the task force, and the wording of a few other provisions was influenced to a lesser extent.

Misuses of engineering ethics codes, including the 1932 ASCE case, are discussed by Layton (1971, 1980). The ACEC ethics code can be found in Baum (1979) and that of the IEEE Engineering in Medicine and Biology Society in EMB (1976). Among other things, I learned about the position of the AIChE on ethics codes in a stimulating conversation with A. Summer West, a former president of that society.

NOTES

1. Indeed, this position is essentially that taken by the NSPE Board of Ethical Review in case no. 78-2 (see Flores 1980, p. 133).

2. The name of this organization was recently changed to the Accreditation Board for Engineering and Technology (ABET).

REFERENCES

ACKERMAN, ADOLPH J. 1969. "Breakdown in Responsibility: Atomic Power—Who Looks after the Public Safety?" In Mock, Jesse (ed.), "The Engineer's Responsibility to Society," Technical Report, ASME, pp. 35–56.
ASHKINAZY, AARON. 1972. "Are Engineers Responsible for the Uses and Effects of Technology?" *Professional Engineer* 42(8):46–47, August.
BACKE, RICHARD. 1981. "Proposed Addition to IEEE Ethics Code." Report to IEEE USAB.
BAUM, ROBERT J., and ALBERT FLORES. 1979. *Ethical Problems in Engineering.* 1st ed. Center for the Study of the Human Dimensions of Science and Technology, Rensselaer Polytechnic Institute, Troy, N.Y. Includes material not in Flores 1980 or Baum 1980a, the second ed.

BAUM, ROBERT J., ed. 1980a. *Ethical Problems in Engineering*. Vol. 2: *Cases*. 2nd ed. Center for the Study of the Human Dimensions of Science and Technology, Rensselaer Polytechnic Institute, Troy, N.Y.

———. 1980b. *Ethics and Engineering Curricula*. Hastings Center, Hastings-on-Hudson, N.Y.

BROOKS, JACK. 1980. "The Government's Classification of Private Ideas." Thirty-fourth Report by the Committee on Government Operations of the U.S. House of Representatives. House Report No. 96-1540. Washington, D.C.: U.S. Government Printing Office.

CHALK, ROSEMARY, MARK S. FRANKEL, and SALLY B. CHAFER. 1980. "AAAS Professional Ethics Project: Professional Ethics Activities in the Scientific and Engineering Societies." AAAS Report on NSF/NEH sponsored project.

DE MILLO, RICHARD A., RICHARD J. LIPTON, and ALAN J. PERLIS. 1979. "Social Processes and Proofs of Theorems and Programs." *Communications of the ACM* 22(5):271–80, May.

DEVOLPI, ALEXANDER, et al. 1981. *Born Secret: The H-Bomb, the Progressive Case and National Security*. Elmsford, N.Y.: Pergamon.

EMB. 1976. "Code of Ethics for Engineers in Medicine and Biology." *IEEE CSIT Newsletter*.

FLORES, ALBERT, ed. 1980. *Ethical Problems in Engineering*. Vol. 1: *Readings*. 2nd ed. Troy, N.Y.: Center for the Study of the Human Dimensions of Science and Technology, Rensselaer Polytechnic Institute.

FLORMAN, SAMUEL C. 1976. *The Existential Pleasures of Engineering*. New York: St. Martin's Press.

———. 1978. "Moral Blueprints." *Harper's* 257:30–33, October. Reprinted in Flores 1980, pp. 235–37.

FLORMAN, SAMUEL C., and STEPHEN H. UNGER. 1979. "Engineering Ethics on the Job: How Far Should an Engineer Go?—A Debate." *IEEE Institute* 3(8):5, August.

KIPNIS, KENNETH. 1980. "Engineers and the Paramountcy of Public Safety." Paper presented Aug. 19 at ASME Pot Pourri Conference, San Francisco. A revised version ["Engineers Who Kill: Professional Ethics and the Paramountcy of Public Safety"] appears in *Business and Professional Ethics Journal*, vol. 1, no. 1 (Fall 1981):77–91.

LADD, JOHN. 1980. "The Quest for a Code of Professional Ethics: An Intellectual and Moral Confusion." In Chalk 1980, pp. 154–59.

LADENSON, ROBERT F., et al. 1980. "A Selected Annotated Bibliography of Professional Ethics and Social Responsibility in Engineering." Technical Report, Center for the Study of Ethics in the Professions, Illinois Institute of Technology.

LADENSON, ROBERT F. 1980. "The Social Responsibilities of Engineers and Scientists: A Philosophical Approach." In Flores 1980.

LAYTON, EDWIN T. JR. 1971. *The Revolt of the Engineers*. Cleveland: Case Western Reserve Press.

———. 1980. "Engineering Ethics and the Public Interest." In Flores 1980, pp. 26–29.

OLDENQUIST, ANDREW G., and EDWARD E. SLOWTER. 1979. "Proposed: A Single Code of Ethics for All Engineers." *Professional Engineer* 49:8–11, May. Reprinted in Flores 1980, pp. 44–47.

PASCHKIS, VICTOR. 1971. "Moving toward Responsible Technology." ASME Winter Annual Meeting, Nov.–Dec., 71-WA/Av-1.

———. 1975. "Ethics in Engineering." ASME Engineering Applications Conference, Baltimore, Md., May, 75-TS-3.

———. 1976. "Engineering Ethics—A New Imperative in Engineering Education." ASME Winter Annual Meeting, New York, December, 76-WA/TS-16.

PERRY, TEKLA. 1981a. "Ethics' Knotty Problems." *IEEE Spectrum* 18(6):53–60, June.

———. 1981b. "Knowing How to Blow the Whistle." *IEEE Spectrum* 18(9):56–61, September.

PRIMACK, JOEL, and FRANK VON HIPPEL. 1974. *Advice and Dissent: Scientists in the Political Arena*. New York: Basic Books.

ROBBI, ANTHONY D. 1972. "Social Ethics and the Modern Engineer." In Fruchtbaum, Harold, ed., The Social Responsibility of Engineers," *Annals of the New York Academy of Sciences*, Vol. 196, Article 10, 1972. pp. 461–64; reprinted in Flores 1980, pp. 60–62.

ROGERS, C. THOMAS. 1980. "The End-Use Problem in Engineering Ethics." *Philosophy of Science Association*, vol. 2, pp. 238–45.

SALVADORI, MARIO G. 1977. "Engineering Ethics and Engineering Education." In ASCE, "Ethics, Professionalism and Maintaining Competence," 1977, pp. 1–5.

STEFFENS, J. H. (chairman). 1975. "Ideas for a Better Code." Panel discussion in ASCE, pp. 97–107; reprinted in Baum 1979, pp. 58–63.

TAYLOR, PAUL W. 1975. *Principles of Ethics: An Introduction*, Encino, CA: Dickenson.

UNGER, STEPHEN H. 1972. "Personal Responsibility of Engineers for Their Work." *IEEE Intercon Digest*, March, pp. 322–23.

———. 1973. "Codes of Engineering Ethics." *IEEE CSIT Newsletter* 2(5):1, 4–5, December. Reprinted in IEEE *Transactions on Industry Applications*, vol. 10, no. 3, May/June 1974, pp. 337–39.

———. 1976. "A Code of Ethics and Its Support." *IEEE CSIT Newsletter* 4(13):24–27, March.

———. 1977. "Privacy, Cryptography and Free Research." *Technology and Society* (20):1–3, December.

WISELY, WILLIAM H. 1978. "Public Obligation and the Ethics System." ASCE Chicago Convention and Exposition, October; reprinted in Flores 1980, pp. 13–16.

12 The Quest for a Code of Professional Ethics: An Intellectual and Moral Confusion

John Ladd

My role as a philosopher is to act as a gadfly. If this were Athens in the fifth century B.C. you would probably throw me in prison for what I shall say, and I would be promptly condemned to death for attacking your idols. But you can't do that in this day and age; you can't even ask for your money back, since I am not being paid. All that you can do is to throw eggs at me or simply walk out!

My theme is stated in the title: it is that the whole notion of an organized professional ethics is an absurdity—intellectual and moral. Furthermore, I shall argue that there are few positive benefits to be derived from having a code and the possibility of mischievous side effects of adopting a code is substantial. Unfortunately, in the time allotted to me I can only summarize what I have to say on this topic.

1.   To begin with, ethics itself is basically an open-ended, reflective and critical intellectual activity. It is essentially problematic and controversial, both as far as its principles are concerned and in its application. Ethics consists of issues to be examined, explored, discussed, deliberated, and argued. Ethical principles can be established only as a result of deliberation and argumentation. These principles are not the kind of thing that can be settled by fiat, by agreement or by authority. To assume that they can be is to confuse ethics with law-making, rule-making, policy-making and other kinds of decision-making. It follows that, ethical principles, as such, cannot be established by associations, organizations, or by a consensus of their members. To speak of codifying ethics, therefore, makes no more sense than to speak of codifying medicine, anthropology or architecture.

2.   Even if substantial agreement could be reached on ethical principles and they could be set out in a code, the attempt to impose such principles on others in the guise

Reprinted from Rosemary Chalk, Mark S. Frankel, and Sallie B. Chafer, eds., *AAAS Professional Ethics Project: Professional Ethics Activities in the Scientific and Engineering Societies* (Washington, D.C.: AAAS, 1980), pp. 154–59, with permission from the American Association for the Advancement of Science.

of ethics contradicts the notion of ethics itself, which presumes that persons are autonomous moral agents. In Kant's terms, such an attempt makes ethics heteronomous; it confuses ethics with some kind of externally imposed set of rules such as a code of law, which, indeed, is heteronomous. To put the point in more popular language: ethics must, by its very nature, be self-directed rather than other-directed.

3.   Thus, in attaching disciplinary procedures, methods of adjudication and sanctions, formal and informal, to the principles that one calls "ethical" one automatically converts them into legal rules or some other kind of authoritative rules of conduct such as the bylaws of an organization, regulations promulgated by an official, club rules, rules of etiquette, or other sorts of social standards of conduct. To label such conventions, rules and standards "ethical" simply reflects an intellectual confusion about the status and function of these conventions, rules and standards. Historically, it should be noted that the term "ethical" was introduced merely to indicate that the code of the Royal College of Physicians was not to be construed as a criminal code (i.e., a legal code). Here "ethical" means simply non-legal.

4.   That is not to say that ethics has no relevance for projects involving the creation, certification and enforcement of rules of conduct for members of certain groups. But logically it has the same kind of relevance that it has for the law. As with law, its role in connection with these projects is to appraise, criticize and perhaps even defend (or condemn) the projects themselves, the rules, regulations and procedures they prescribe, and the social and political goals and institutions they represent. But although ethics can be used to judge or evaluate a disciplinary code, penal code, code of honor or what goes by the name of a "code of ethics," it cannot be identified with any of these, for the reasons that have already been mentioned.

SOME GENERAL COMMENTS ON PROFESSIONALISM AND ETHICS

5.   Being a professional does not automatically make a person an expert in ethics, even in the ethics of that person's own particular profession—unless of course we decide to call the "club rules" of a profession its ethics. The reason for this is that there are no experts in ethics in the sense of expert in which professionals have a special expertise that others do not share. As Plato pointed out long ago in the *Protagoras*, knowledge of virtue is not like the technical knowledge that is possessed by an architect or shipbuilder. In a sense, everyone is, or ought to be, a teacher of virtue; there are no professional qualifications that are necessary for doing ethics.

6.   Moreover, there is no special ethics belonging to professionals. Professionals are not, simply because they are professionals, exempt from the common obligations, duties and responsibilities that are binding on ordinary people. They do not have a special moral status that allows them to do things that no one else can. Doctors have no special right to be rude, to deceive, or to order people around like children, etc. Likewise, lawyers do not have a special right to bend the law to help their clients, to bully witnesses, or to be cruel and brutal—simply because they think that it is in the interests of their client. Professional codes cannot, therefore, confer such rights and immunities; for there is no such thing as professional ethical immunity.

7. We might ask: do professionals, by virtue of their special professional status, have special duties and obligations over and above those they would have as ordinary people? Before we can answer this question, we must first decide what is meant by the terms "profession" and "professional," which are very loose terms that are used as labels for a variety of different occupational categories. The distinctive element in professionalism is generally held to be that professionals have undergone advanced, specialized training and that they exercise control over the nature of their job and the services they provide. In addition, the older professions, lawyers, physicians, professors and ministers typically have clients to whom they provide services as individuals. (I use the term "client" generically so as to include patients, students, and parishioners.) When professionals have individual clients, new moral relationships are created that demand special types of trust and loyalty. Thus, in order to answer the question, we need to examine the context under which special duties and obligations of professionals might arise.

8. In discussing specific ethical issues relating to the professions, it is convenient to divide them into issues of *macro-ethics* and *micro-ethics*. The former comprise what might be called collective or social problems, that is, problems confronting members of a profession as a group in their relation to society; the latter, issues of micro-ethics, are concerned with moral aspects of personal relationships between individual professionals and other individuals who are their clients, their colleagues and their employers. Clearly the particulars in both kinds of ethics vary considerably from one profession to another. I shall make only two general comments.

9. Micro-ethical issues concern the personal relationships between individuals. Many of these issues simply involve the application of ordinary notions of honesty, decency, civility, humanity, considerateness, respect and responsibility. Therefore, it should not be necessary to devise a special code to tell professionals that they ought to refrain from cheating and lying, or to make them treat their clients (and patients) with respect, or to tell them that they ought to ask for informed consent for invasive actions. It is a common mistake to assume that *all* the extra-legal norms and conventions governing professional relationships have a moral status, for every profession has norms and conventions that have as little to do with morality as the ceremonial dress and titles that are customarily associated with the older professions.

10. The macro-ethical problems in professionalism are more problematic and controversial. What are the social responsibilities of professionals as a group? What can and should they do to influence social policy? Here, I submit, the issue is not one of professional roles, but of *professional power*. For professionals as a group have a great deal of power; and power begets responsibility. Physicians as a group can, for instance, exercise a great deal of influence on the quality and cost of health care; and lawyers can have a great deal of influence on how the law is made and administered, etc.

11. So-called "codes of professional ethics" have nothing to contribute either to micro-ethics or to macro-ethics as just outlined. It should also be obvious that they do not fit under either of these two categories. Any association, including a professional association, can, of course, adopt a code of conduct for its members and lay down disciplinary procedures and sanctions to enforce conformity with its rules. But to call such a disciplinary code a code of *ethics* is at once pretentious and sanctimonious. Even worse, it is to make a false and misleading claim, namely, that the profession in question has the authority or special competence to create an ethics, that it is able authoritatively to set forth what the principles of ethics are, and that it has its own brand of ethics that it can impose on its members and on society.

I have briefly stated the case against taking a code of professional ethics to be a serious ethical enterprise. It might be objected, however, that I have neglected to recognize some of the benefits that come from having professional codes of ethics. In order to discuss these possible benefits, I shall first examine what some of the objectives of codes of ethics might be, then I shall consider some possible benefits of having a code, and, finally, I shall point out some of the mischievous aspect of codes.

OBJECTIVES OF CODES OF PROFESSIONAL "ETHICS"

In order to be crystal clear about the purposes and objectives of a code, we must begin by asking: to whom is the code addressed? Although ostensibly codes of ethics are addressed to the members of the profession, their true purposes and objectives are sometimes easier to ascertain if we recognize that codes are in fact often directed at other addressees than members. Accordingly, the real addressees might be any of the following: (a) members of the profession, (b) clients or buyers of the professional services, (c) other agents dealing with professionals, such as government or private institutions like universities or hospitals, or (d) the public at large. With this in mind, let us examine some possible objectives.

First, the objective of a professional code might be "inspirational," that is, it might be used to inspire members to be more "ethical" in their conduct. The assumption on which this objective is premised is that professionals are somehow likely to be amoral or submoral, perhaps, as the result of becoming professionals, and so it is necessary to exhort them to be moral, e.g., to be honest. I suppose there is nothing objectionable to having a code for this reason; it would be something like the Boy Scout's Code of Honor, something to frame and hang in one's office. I have severe reservations, however, about whether a code is really needed for this purpose and whether it will do any good; for those to whom it is addressed and who need it the most will not adhere to it anyway, and the rest of the good people in the profession will not need it because they already know what they ought to do. For this reason, many respectable members of a profession regard its code as a joke and as something not to be taken seriously. (Incidentally, for much the same kind of reasons as those just given, there are no professional codes in the academic or clerical professions.)

A second objective might be to alert professionals to the moral aspects of their work that they might have overlooked. In jargon, it might serve to sensitize them or to raise their consciousness. This, of course, is a worthy goal—it is the goal of moral education. Morality, after all, is not just a matter of doing or not doing, but also a matter of feeling and thinking. But, here again, it is doubtful that it is possible to make people have the right feelings or think rightly through enacting a code. A code is hardly the best means for teaching morality.

Thirdly, a code might, as it was traditionally, be a disciplinary code or a "penal" code used to enforce certain rules of the profession on its members in order to defend the integrity of the professional and to protect its professional standards. This kind of function is often referred to as "self-policing." It is unlikely, however, that the kind of disciplining that is in question here could be handled in a code of ethics, a code that would set forth in detail criteria for determining malpractice. On the contrary, the "ethical" code of a profession is usually used to discipline its members for other sorts of "unethical conduct," such as stealing a client away from a colleague, for making disparaging remarks about a colleague in public, or for departing from some other sort of norm of the profession. (In the original code of the Royal College of Physicians, members who failed to attend the funeral of a colleague were subject to a fine!) It is clear that when we talk of a disciplinary code, as distinguished from an exhortatory code, a lot of new questions arise that cannot be treated here; for a disciplinary code is quasi-legal in nature, it involves adjudicative organs and processes, and it is usually connected with complicated issues relating to such things as licensing.

A fourth objective of a code might be to offer advice in cases of moral perplexity about what to do: e.g., should one report a colleague for malfeasance? Should one let a severely defective newborn die? If such cases present genuine perplexities, then they cannot and should not be solved by reference to a code. To try to solve them through a code is like trying to do surgery with a carving knife! If it is not a genuine perplexity, then the code would be unnecessary.

A fifth objective of a professional code of ethics is to alert prospective clients and employers to what they may and may not expect by way of service from a member of the profession concerned. The official code of an association, say, of engineers, provides as authoritative statement of what is proper and what is improper conduct of the professional. Thus, a code serves to protect a professional from improper demands on the part of employer or client, e.g., that he lie about or cover up defective work that constitutes a public hazard. Codes may thus serve to protect "whistle-blowers." (The real addressee in this case is the employer or client.)

SECONDARY OBJECTIVES OF CODES—NOT ALWAYS SALUTARY

I now come to what I shall call "secondary objectives," that is, objectives that one might hesitate always to call "ethical," especially since they often provide an opportunity for abuse.

The first secondary objective is to enhance the image of the profession in the public eye. The code is supposed to communicate to the general public (the addressee) the idea that the members of the profession concerned are service oriented and that the interests of the client are always given first place over the interests of the professional himself. Because they have a code they may be expected to be trustworthy.

Another secondary objective of a code is to protect the monopoly of the profession in question. Historically, this appears to have been the principal objective of a so-called code of ethics, e.g., Percival's code of medical ethics. Its aim is to exclude from practice those who are outside the professional in-group and to regulate the conduct of the members of the profession so as to protect it from encroachment from outside.

Sometimes this kind of professional monopoly is in the public interest and often it is not.

Another secondary objective of professional codes of ethics, mentioned in some of the literature, is that having a code serves as a status symbol; one of the credentials for an occupation to be considered a profession is that it have a code of ethics. If you want to make your occupation a profession, then you must frame a code of ethics for it: so there are codes for real estate agents, insurance agents, used car dealers, electricians, barbers, etc., and these codes serve, at least in the eyes of some, to raise their members to the social status of lawyers and doctors.

MISCHIEVOUS SIDE-EFFECTS OF CODES OF ETHICS

I now want to call attention to some of the mischievous side-effects of adopting a code of ethics:

The first and most obvious bit of mischief, is that having a code will give a sense of complacency to professionals about their conduct. "We have a code of ethics," they will say, "so everything we do is ethical." Inasmuch as a code, of necessity, prescribes what is minimal, a professional may be encouraged by the code to deliver what is minimal rather than the best that he can do. "I did everything that the code re-quires. . . ."

Even more mischievous than complacency and the consequent self-congratulation, is the fact that a code of ethics can be used as a cover-up for what might be called basically "unethical" or "irresponsible" conduct.

Perhaps the most mischievous side-effect of codes of ethics is that they tend to divert attention from the macro-ethical problems of a profession to its micro-ethical problems. There is a lot of talk about whistle-blowing. But it concerns individuals almost exclusively. What is really needed is a thorough scrutiny of professions as collective bodies, of their role in society and their effect on the public interest. What role should the professions play in determining the use of technology, its development and expansion, and the distribution of the costs (e.g., disposition of toxic wastes) as well as the benefits of technology? What is the significance of professionalism from the moral point of view for democracy, social equality, liberty and justice? There are lots of ethical problems to be dealt with. To concentrate on codes of ethics as if they represented the real ethical problems connected with professionalism is to capitulate to *struthianism* (from the Greek word *struthos*=ostrich).

One final objection to codes that needs to be mentioned is that they inevitably represent what John Stuart Mill called the "tyranny of the majority" or, if not that, the "tyranny of the establishment." They serve to and are designed to discourage if not suppress the dissenter, the innovator, the critic.

By way of conclusion, let me say a few words about what an association of professionals can do about ethics. On theoretical grounds, I have argued that it cannot codify an ethics and it cannot authoritatively establish ethical principles or prescribed guidelines for the conduct of its members—as if it were *creating* an ethics! But there is still much that associations can do to promote further understanding of and sensitivity to ethical issues connected with professional activities. For example, they can fill a very useful educational function by encouraging their members to participate in extended discussions of issues of both micro-ethics and macro-ethics, e.g., questions about responsibility; for these issues obviously need to be examined and discussed much more extensively than they are at present—especially by those who are in a position to do something about them.

13 Codes of Ethics and the Moral Education of Engineers

Heinz C. Luegenbiehl

Codes of ethics have a significant place in the history of the engineering profession, but in their present form they have perhaps outlived their usefulness. A recent survey on hypothetical cases in engineering ethics conducted by the journal *Chemical Engineering* was introduced by the statement that "there are written codes of ethics, but they are often of little value."[1] In light of this preface the survey then revealed: "Although the American Institute of Chemical Engineers, the professional society of many of our U.S. readers, has a code of ethics, this was almost universally ignored in determining the solutions to our survey problems. Fewer than a half-dozen [out of 4,318] respondents even mentioned a code of ethics at all."[2]

The lack of reference to the codes, if it can be assumed to be typical of all engineers, seems to me to be an important piece of information if one is proceeding on the assumption that the codes are meant to be a set of ethical rules that are to govern engineers in their professional lives. In the following, it is my aim to show that the avoidance of the codes by the respondents to the survey is justified because the codes of engineering ethics, in their present form, should not be utilized as a set of ethical rules of behavior and, further, that the attempt to provide such a set of rules is not justifiable. In a more positive vein, I then propose that the codes of ethics be replaced by a set of "guides for ethical engineering decision making."

BACKGROUND

Occupational groups aspiring to professional status have historically made one of their foremost concerns the development of a code of ethics. The American Medical Association (AMA), founded in 1847, adopted its first, very extensive code in the same year.

From *Business and Professional Ethics Journal*, vol. 2, no. 4 (1983), pp. 41–61. Copyright © 1983 by Heinz C. Luegenbiehl. Reprinted by permission of the author.

The adoption of a code is significant for the professionalization of an occupational group, because it becomes one of the external hallmarks testifying to the claim that the group recognizes an obligation to society that transcends mere economic self-interest, an obligation incurred in exchange for the power to regulate itself and to define requirements for membership in the profession. Given either of the two dominant sociological perspectives on the nature of professions, the exchange-structural view or the power-theorist view, a code of ethics thus is a central aspect of the process of becoming recognized as a profession. On the exchange-structural view, a profession is based on a contractual relationship between society and the profession, where the code indicates how the profession will police itself in exchange for the autonomous control of its membership, which is necessary given the specialized knowledge of the profession. On the power-theorist view, the codes are a means to present the proper image to the public so that the profession will be able to attain prestige and monetary rewards.[3] While an understanding of the justification and motivations for the development of a code of ethics, as well as its contents, may thus be influenced by sociological considerations, the existence of a written code seems to be a necessary ingredient of becoming recognized as a profession. As put by one sociologist: "For the newer professions, formation of professional codes may be viewed as part of a defense strategy. The occupation 'proves' that it is a profession by presenting its credentials (i.e., the code of ethics)."[4]

The engineering profession, as well as many other groups aspiring to professional status during the second half of the nineteenth century, recognized the need for a code of ethics. However, for engineering the process was a relatively slow one, and it was not until June 23, 1911, that the American Institute of Consulting Engineers became the first engineering society in the United States to adopt a code of ethics.[5] The American Bar Association (ABA) had adopted its first national code in 1908 and the National Funeral Directors Association, based directly on its professional aspirations, had accepted one as early as 1884.[6] After 1911, however, a number of other major engineering organizations adopted codes of their own in quick succession, including the American Institute of Electrical Engineers (AIEE) in 1912, and the American Society of Mechanical Engineers (ASME) and the American Society of Civil Engineers (ASCE) in 1914.[7]

Once the American engineering profession began formulating codes of ethics, not only did a multiplicity of codes emerge, but a process of seemingly endless revision of existing codes also got under way. While the AMA took about one hundred years to undertake a major revision of its code, in engineering the codes became a source of constant activity, owing in large part to two major issues: the quest for unity in the engineering profession; and the issue of responsibility for the public welfare. As early as 1920, efforts were being made by the Federated American Engineering Societies to produce a common code because "what was forbidden in one code might be tolerated by another."[8] At about the same time the reformer Morris Cooke was arguing that the neglect of the public welfare was a basic flaw in prior codes and that what was needed was "the flatfooted declaration that good engineering must be in the public interest."[9] It is instructive to note that in 1979 the issue of a unified engineering code was still a pressing one,[10] which to this juncture has not yet been resolved, and that the concern of the engineer for the public welfare has still not been completely resolved in the codes when considered in relation to the employed engineer.[11]

Underlying the numerous attempts to develop an adequate code of ethics for the engineering profession, however, has been an idea that has become almost an article of faith, namely, that engineering, in order to be considered a profession, must have a code of ethics very much in line with the format of the early codes. It would thus appear that, in the quest for unification and refinement of the codes, a more fundamental concern is being widely overlooked, that being the issue of whether or not a code of ethics is appropriate for the engineering profession at all. The major purpose of this paper is to suggest that the historical evolution of the engineering codes of ethics has made them inappropriate for fulfilling one of their major, if not the major, functions, that of fostering moral behavior on the part of engineering practitioners.[12] At the same time I want to argue on the positive side that the problems inherent in the codes do not militate against the responsibility of engineering educators to provide training in ethics, and specifically engineering ethics, so that future engineers will become mature and autonomous decision makers in their professional lives. A role for an engineering code of ethics significantly different from the roles currently played by the codes is thus proposed, namely, the replacement of the codes with a set of "guides for ethical engineering decision making."

The conclusions presented in this paper rest on the claim that the codes, as they are currently formulated, potentially create moral conflicts for engineers, such that engineers will be unable to justify univocally their actions if they consider themselves individual autonomous agents as well as professionals governed by a code of ethics. These conflicts can be avoided if the codes are restructured at their very foundation in light of a recognition of what should be their major function—to serve as guides to individual engineers who wish to act ethically in instances where their previous experience proves insufficient to arrive at a rational, autonomous decision. A thrust away from codes of ethics seen as rules of conduct is thus proposed. As Daniel Mead, a former president of ASCE, put it in the 1941 Manual of Engineering Practice:

> It is unlikely that a man of advanced age and long experience would, in his ordinary relations in life, find it necessary to study a code of conduct in order to determine what his own conduct should be; neither would he ponder very deeply concerning the various possible outcomes of his action. His answer would be given at once, based on his established principles, and would probably be correct. If, however, the conduct concerned new conditions entirely beyond and different from his previous experience, then comes the necessity for due consideration; and in such cases the opinion of those who have had similar experiences and have reached definite conclusions cannot safely be ignored.[13]

HISTORICAL CONTEXT

In order to clarify the problems inherent in the engineering codes of ethics, the motivations at work in giving the codes their current form need to be recognized. When engineering was in its infancy as a profession, the models available for emulation were those provided by the traditional professions of law, theology, and medicine.

Each of these professions had a long history of practice to draw on, a firmly established status in society, and a definite focus for its activities, namely, the welfare of individual clients. The 1847 AMA code, for example, treated the public welfare only in passing, and then primarily in the context of "enlightening" the public, while by far the major portions of the code were concerned with the physician/client relationship and the dealings among physicians.[14] Engineers believed that the status granted to the other professions could be theirs through the formation of professional organizations and through the devising of a code of ethics modeled on those of the other professions. As an early commentator put it: "Their [the older, more conservative societies'] concern is mainly for creating and preserving a certain prestige. . . . The reasons for the creation of the 'standards' are those which underlie the ideals of the closed shop which, originated by the medical profession, have been adopted in large part by the lawyers and put into still wider effect by the labor unions."[15] Although the motives of engineers in this regard need not be questioned, it is clear that the engineering leadership was very concerned with strengthening the standing accorded to engineering activities and to engineers by the public. For Schuyler Wheeler, the original driving force behind the first AIEE code, the major interest was in furthering the "importance, dignity, and strength" of the engineering profession.[16] As Edwin Layton has argued in his important history of engineering: "Spokesmen for the engineering profession have, in fact, frequently made status the fundamental aim, and other professional values means to this end. Thus, engineers have argued that in order to gain more status their profession should show a greater sense of social responsibility."[17]

The emphasis on status can be seen, in retrospect, to have been unfortunate in several respects. It meant, first of all, that in utilizing the model of the older, more prestigious professions, the engineering organizations overlooked their unique role in society, a role that could not be expressed simply in terms of the traditional professional/client relationship. The early codes failed to take into account the widespread consequences of engineering work. They instead obligated engineers primarily to their immediate employers. Both the AIEE code and the ASME code, which were almost identical, stressed the engineer's duty to the client. The AIEE code reads: "The engineer should consider the protection of a client's or employer's interests his first professional obligation, and therefore should avoid every act contrary to this duty." Discussion of the relationship of the profession to the public, on the other hand, is limited to extending the knowledge of engineering matters, injunctions against discussions in the public press, and limitation of the types of statements engineers should make in public. In practice this narrow focus on the employer or client meant that the activities of the engineering professional became inextricably tied to the goals and values of the business community, since the vast majority of engineers were (and still are) employees of corporations. As a result the ideals central to the notion of professionalism, such as independence of judgment, became endangered.

Whereas a narrow focus on the welfare of an individual or a group of individuals may be appropriate for the majority of physicians and lawyers, the technological enterprise by its very nature tends to have consequences for a much wider public. When an engineering decision is made it may affect the lives of thousands, or even millions, of people, such as in the instance of the widely publicized DC-10 door lock case or in the Kansas City Hyatt-Regency disaster. Yet in the early codes engineers are asked to look at possibly disastrous consequences of their decisions only in terms of the interests of the client or employer. What is the engineer to do if the employer, such as in the Pinto gas tank case, decides that it is in his or her best interest to endanger the lives of a certain number of people? More recent codes have attempted to shift the focus away from a sole concern with a client or employer but, as will be argued later in the paper, these attempts have done little to improve the situation of the engineer. The early codes set a tone of limited responsibility by engineers that has yet to be overcome. The AIEE position on whistle-blowing can be summed up by the following quotation from the code: "If any other considerations, such as professional obligations or restrictions, interfere with his meeting the legitimate demands of a client or employer, the engineer should inform him of the situation." What else engineers should do is left unsaid, since professional obligations are then defined in terms of the relationships between engineers, rather than between engineers and the public. In fact, the relationship between engineers is the primary focus of most of the early codes.

The second weakness inherited from other professional codes was that the engineering codes were formulated in such a way that the status of the profession became an even more pronounced goal for the engineers than it had been for physicians in the AMA code. The 1914 ASCE code, for example, consists of six short sections, one of which is concerned with the relationship of engineers to clients. The other five deal with injury of another engineer, supplanting another engineer on a job, competing with other engineers, and advertising. These sections are clearly directed at creating a monopolistic business environment. The recent decision by the FCC undercutting restrictions on professional advertising supports this contention. Yet as late as 1969, Milton Lunch, the general counsel of the National Society of Professional Engineers (NSPE), reported the position of the NSPE Board of Ethical Review "that advertising of professional services was not a desirable practice because it tended to commercialize the profession."[18] Much of the content of the early codes was thus directed at improving the financial posture and the standing of engineers in the wider community, rather than at specific ethical issues. Although the trend since the formulation of the first codes has been to give more emphasis to the public welfare, even recent codes still emphasize the fraternalism that Cooke recognized in 1922: "These obsolete codes . . . were drafted under the conception that engineering was a craft and those who practiced it constituted a fraternity and as such owed a higher obligation to fellow-practitioners than to the public."[19]

With additions and revisions to the engineering codes over the last seventy years, the emphases in the codes have changed significantly, especially with regard to public health and safety. However, while the thrust has been away from a sole concern with the client or employer and the professional, the injunctions placed upon engineers by the early codes have largely remained. The unfortunate consequence of the codes' historical evolution has thus been that in the present codes a mixture of duties, without any clear focus, has been established for the practicing engineer. This has become an especially pressing problem with the trend toward societal accountability of professional activity. Questions are now being raised by the public as to why engineers (and others) are not more cognizant of the consequences of their actions, why they are not aware of their societal responsibilities, and why the profession is unable to enforce its codes of ethics.[20] As Jacques Barzun has warned, the professions are "vulnerable institutions." If the public perceives that the professions are more interested in their own welfare than in that of the public, they run the risk of being demoted "to the level of ordinary trades and businesses."[21]

The questioning of the presumed infallibility of the professions has resulted in a considerable amount of soul-searching in the engineering profession. During the last ten years attention to professional ethics has been greatly increased in the engineering organizations. Yet progress, especially in relation to the codes, has been slow. In part this has been the result of the focus given to the initial codes, which concentrated more on fraternal issues than on questions of ethics as that term has usually been understood. More recent codes have emphasized such questions as the safety of the public, the quality of life, and public disclosure and have thereby given the codes a less restrictive scope of concern.[22] However, they have retained their focus on the client or employer and on matters of professional courtesy and etiquette. For instance, they still emphasize issues of competition, advertising, and the reputation of individual engineers and of the profession. The mixture of ethics and fraternal concerns in the current codes links them to their predecessors and necessitates a fundamental reexamination of the codes. This reexamination will ultimately raise questions about the very nature of the codes themselves.

STATUS OF THE CURRENT CODES

Contemporary codes of engineering ethics are generally divided into the following parts: a set of principles that preface the code as a whole; and a number of more explicit rules that are intended to contain more specific interpretations of the principles. The relevant question for us is what implications this form of organization has for the adequacy of a code of ethics.

Let us first look at the principles. As was pointed out earlier, the first codes consisted primarily of specific rules detailing the obligations of engineers to their employers or clients and to the profession. Principles set out as prefaces to the codes, when included at all, usually took the form of vague general statements, such as in the 1914 ASME code, which tells engineers that "all their professional relations should be governed by principles of honor, honesty, strict fidelity to trusts imposed upon them, and courteous behavior toward all." It is only the more recent codes that have provided principles in a context more specifically applicable to engineering. In this regard the adoption in 1947 of the first code of the Engineers' Council for Professional Development (ECPD) was significant, since it included in its rules the injunction that the engineer "will have due regard for the safety of life and health of the public and employees." This rule was reflected in the foreword of the code, where it is enunciated as a principle that "the engineer will discharge his duties with fidelity to the public, his employers, and clients, and with fairness and impartiality to all." Furthermore, it is the engineer's "duty to interest himself in public welfare, and to be ready to apply his special knowledge for the benefit of mankind."[23]

The 1947 code is of great significance because it demonstrated an awareness by the profession of responsibilities beyond those toward the profession and clients or employers. However, the wording in relation to the public remained relatively innocuous, stressing "due regard for" and "interest in" the public. In successive versions of the ECPD code, including revisions in 1963 and 1974, the concern for the pubic became more pressing, so that by the latest version in 1977 human welfare had attained first rank among four explicitly enunciated principles.[24] The principles pertain to the different relationships the engineer has to society, to clients or employers, and to the profession. They reflect a mixture of ethical and fraternal concerns:

1. using their [engineers'] knowledge and skill for the enhancement of human welfare;

2. being honest and impartial, and serving with fidelity the public, their employers and clients;

3. striving to increase the competence and prestige of the engineering profession; and

4. supporting the professional and technical societies of their disciplines.

While it is interesting to note the evolving concern with human welfare in the codes, the issue of concern to us is whether the resulting complex set of principles is consistent insofar as the various principles lead to identical actions in the same circumstances. If they do not, that is, if different principles justify opposing decisions, then the codes are *prima facie* ambiguous and consequently not a useful guide to action. A brief illustration will show that this is the case.[25]

James Doe is employed by a firm that is designing a chemical plant intended to produce a deadly nerve gas to be used in time of war. He discovers what he takes to be a flaw in the design that will make it remotely possible that some of the gas will be released into the surrounding environment of the plant. Upon bringing his discovery to the attention of his superiors, he is informed that his firm considers the risk acceptable and that it is in the interests of his employer that the project go ahead as scheduled. He is further told that the information on which his claim is based is proprietary and he is therefore not to discuss the issue in public.

Given this, perhaps extreme, hypothetical example, two issues arise in relation to the fundamental principles. First, James Doe must ask himself whether he is using his knowledge for "the enhancement of human welfare" in working on the project. Although it might be argued that in the "right hands" the nerve gas may be used to bring about a quicker peace in time of war and thus serve human welfare, he cannot know that the "right hands" will ultimately be in control of the gas.[26] It must at least be conceded that some engineers would decide that the project did not enhance human welfare. If Doe came to that conclusion, the practical solution would be for him to refuse to work on the project or to resign his position. However, if we for the moment use only the principles in the code, we must also notice that he is asked to serve his employer with fidelity, and it is at least questionable whether he would be doing so if he is needed on the project and instead resigns his position. Thus it is at least possible that principles 1 and 2 of the ECPD code would make opposing demands of him.

Further, the second principle by itself can result in inconsistent demands on the engineer. In it the engineer is asked to serve with fidelity both the public and his employer. Given the example, this may not be possible for Doe, for in order to serve the public he would need to inform what is called in the specific rules of the code "other proper authority," whereas the rules related to fidelity to the employer demand that he "will not disclose confidential information concerning the business affairs or technical processes of any . . . employer . . . without his consent." Since he has been told explicitly that the relevant information is confidential, it is not obvious how he could make the proper authorities aware of it without violating the rule of confidentiality.

The basic problem thus is that there appears to be no way of adjudicating between the demand of the separate principles and between the separate demands of each principle. In reply to this point it might be argued that the ECPD code does make an overriding claim which prefaces the individual principles, namely, that "Engineers uphold and advance the integrity, honor and dignity of the engineering profession by. . . ." Perhaps then a duty to the profession is a more fundamental principle designed to resolve conflicts among the other principles, although a more likely explanation is that it is simply intended to be an explanatory device. Assuming for the moment that it is an ethical principle, we can still ask how such a principle could support subprinciples that imply potentially opposing courses of action. Furthermore, in the fundamental canons for engineering practice in the same code, the engineer is told to "hold paramount the safety, health and welfare of the public." Given the standard meaning of "paramount," it would seem that this claim takes precedence over any other, yet it is not given a premier place in the statement of principles. Rather it is placed on the level of concrete injunctions, a level supposedly derivative from the principles. If it were given a premier place, it would at least help James Doe in this particular situation.[27]

At this point rational engineers should be confused. Which injunction should they follow in which cases? The code itself does not provide a way of resolving the conflicts on the level of principles. A second course of action might then be to ignore the general "philosophical" principles and to act on the basis of the specific rules found in the ECPD code. The first difficulty encountered there, however, is that the individual rules are claimed to be explications of the principles and thus moving to this level only solidifies the contradictory nature of the claims, as was shown in the conflict between confidentiality and reporting one's knowledge to the proper authority. More significantly, a number of engineering organizations have adopted only the general principles of the code and not the specific rules associated with them.[28] Thus there is some evidence that these organizations either would reject some of the specific rules or would be opposed to the specific nature of the interpretations in the rules.[29] The more specific the rules become, the more likely they are to be interpreted as having an absolute and exceptionless character.

Although a great deal of detailed work would be necessary (and should be undertaken) to determine all the specific problems associated with the ECPD and other codes, the preceding is enough, given the aim of this paper, to show that the way the codes are currently formulated is inadequate and that the codes therefore need to be restructured. As long as conflicting courses of action seem equally plausible in light of the same code of ethics, a barrier to moral action exists. It might, however, be objected at this point that a number of philosophical ethical theories—Kant's, for instance— have the very same problem in that they generate rules that are potentially in conflict when applied to specific situations. Let us therefore ask ourselves if the current codes can be modified in such a way as to account for the problems raised.

MODIFYING THE CODES

In attempting to revise the codes we might begin with the concrete injunctions laid down for the engineer, because those are seemingly what is required to judge the appropriateness of actions in engineering practice. This approach would in effect be a reversion to the early codes, where the concrete rules of practice were prefaced only by a brief statement of exhortation. If such a set of rules is to serve as a consistent determinant of actions, however, it must include a more fundamental principle that will resolve possible conflicts between the specific rules laid out in the code. If the notion of a foundational principle is objected to, the code would at least need to describe a method for resolving possible conflicts or, alternatively, at least be based on such a method. Thus, in either case, there must be, at least implicitly, a higher court of appeal than the contents of the rules themselves.

An interesting development in this regard can be found in a model code developed by Stephen Unger.[30] Unger adopts the notion from the ECPD code that engineers "shall regard their responsibility to society as paramount," but to sections that are in potential conflict with this claim he adds a subordinating clause. For instance, in the section on employers or clients he writes that engineers shall "act as faithful agents or trustees in business or professional matters, *provided such actions conform with other parts of this code* [emphasis added]." This model code, if "paramount" is interpreted in the strong sense of "overriding," thus at least establishes a hierarchy of rules such that the responsibility of engineers to society could be interpreted as a way of resolving conflicts between rules. Unger's code also addresses a number of other problems I have raised in this paper. It should therefore, in my opinion, be regarded as a significant advance over previous codes. It does not, however, address the basic problem found in the other codes, namely, the coercive nature of the codes. It is this problem that I believe makes it necessary to replace the current codes with a different set of documents.

Whether the final basis of appeal is to a basic principle(s) or to concrete rules, the implications for the engineer are the same. He or she must accept this foundation in order to be considered an ethical engineer by the profession. Yet the previous discussion argues against the fact that all engineers will identify with any given rule or principle provided by the profession. My discussion of the history of the codes has shown that even the basic claim regarding the paramountcy of society's welfare has been a disputed issue. More important, it is doubtful that engineers can legitimately be coerced into acting on the basis of externally imposed moral claims. As John Ladd has argued: "Even if substantial agreement could be reached on ethical principles and they could be set out in a code, the attempt to impose such principles on others in the guise of ethics contradicts the notion of ethics itself, which presumes that persons are autonomous moral agents."[31] But if these principles are to serve as the ethical foundation of the profession, then engineers must be coerced into upholding them.

Now, if we are dealing with somewhat sophisticated engineers, they will have developed, at least implicitly, their own ethical foundations on which they base their actions in everyday life. They will thus see a particular course of action as justified, based on this foundation, in a particular situation. Clearly the foundation advocated by the profession will not necessarily coincide with the one a particular engineer has developed in his or her everyday life, and thus competing courses of action may be advocated. For example, an engineer may believe, based on his or her foundation, that he or she should not harm any human being and may have sufficient justification for that belief. This claim, upon reflection, may well be in conflict with the position of the ECPD code to hold the welfare of the public paramount, for achievement of this end may in a particular situation require harming some individual members of the public.[32] Reasonable engineers can thus find themselves in a quandary. They can act in accordance with their own ethical foundation and thus wrongly by that of their engineering organization, or they can act rightly in terms of the ethical foundation of the organization and thus wrongly in terms of their own. While it is possible that in many instances similar courses of action would be advocated regardless of which foundation is considered, in cases where a conflict arises individual engineers would seem inevitably to come out the losers. Can we in any justified sense, then, ask the engineers to act counter to their own deeply held moral beliefs?

I would claim that we cannot. Given the assumption that one's own ethical foundation is freely and rationally arrived at, it is not clear what source of justification an engineering organization would have for imposing its ethical foundation on the individual. It must be emphasized in this regard that I am here referring specifically to questions of ethics, not to standards of professional behavior in general. It seems to me that such standards can have a nonmoral function and thus can be based on a foundation different from an ethical one. For instance, some standards of professionalism, such as educational requirements, could be founded in a contractual agreement between the profession and the public. Thus it can be argued that certain standards of nonmoral behavior can be demanded as condition of membership in an organization, such as Boy Scouts being required to be neat and cheerful, but the demand for moral behavior on the individual's part should be able to override these standards.[33]

If engineers are to be autonomous moral agents, then the codes of ethics, as they are currently formulated, provide an unacceptable pathway to moral behavior. However, there are in fact good reasons for the existence of such codes. Their primary purpose, although not their sole one, is to help engineers arrive at morally correct decisions. This is what is of ultimate benefit to society and to the profession. The means to accomplishing this goal lie not in setting down a series of hard and fast rules for the engineer, but rather in the process of "educating toward autonomy."

REPLACING THE FUNCTION OF THE CODES

Based on the preceding argument, it seems to me that the role of an engineering "code of ethics" must be rethought. I have indicated some problems with the codes, but I think it would be a mistake to draw from these criticisms the conclusion that the profession should not have a role in the moral development and practice of its membership. We must rather ask ourselves once again what demands can be made of practicing engineers in regards to morality. Is it of primary importance that they obey a given set of rules or adhere to an externally imposed ethical principle, or is it not rather that they behave morally in their professional activities? From society's point of view, at least, it is surely the letter that is more central. In the remainder of this paper I will argue that the interests of society, and therefore indirectly the interests of the profession, can best be met not by forcing engineers into predetermined courses of action in regard to moral issues, but rather by educating them to become autonomous decision-makers in a context specific to engineering.

The reason for the existence of engineering ethics in the first instance is that moral problems are encountered in engineering that do not arise in our everyday lives. Society does not lay out explicit moral rules for us to follow in our everyday lives, but rather expects us to make some decisions based on our own volition. "You should never lie, no matter what the circumstances," might be an acceptable moral rule for some of us, but we would feel unjustifiably restrained if society passed a law imposing such a rule on all of us. We generally recognize that on the moral plane, as opposed to the legal one, we must justify our own decisions.

The justification for engineering ethics is, then, not that it tells engineers what they *must* do in specific circumstances, but rather that it aids in the decision-making process in situations that would not usually arise in their everyday lives. Engineers will encounter *novel* situations in their practice and they deserve guidance in relation to them. Yet they should be able to act on their own, rationally arrived at basis of morality. I thus propose substituting for the current codes of ethics a set of guides for ethical engineering decision making. These "guides" should indicate what novel situations engineers in a particular field of practice might encounter and thereby forewarn and alert them to these situations; they should also point to the kinds of factors typically considered relevant to such situations. Engineers could then use the "guides" in conjunction with their own justified moral foundation in order to evaluate a particular situation from the moral point of view.

For example, if engineer Jane Smith for the first time finds herself in a situation that might involve a conflict of interests, turning to the ECPD code would tell her that "Engineers shall not knowingly undertake any assignment which would knowingly create a potential conflict of interest between themselves and their clients or their employers" and give her some other rules regarding financial matters that do not explicitly mention a conflict of interest. The code, however, neither explicitly specifies what a conflict of interest might be,[34] nor does it require the engineer to take steps to determine whether or not a potential conflict of interest exists.

The proposed "guides" would first define *conflict of interest* in a general way and then would enumerate possible *examples* of conflicts of interest. A limitation of the ECPD code in this regard is that it restricts conflicts of interest to the professional life of the engineer, primarily to different clients, whereas conflicts of interest can also occur between the professional and the personal lives of the engineer.[35] The "guides" would further contain a discussion of: the legal status of conflicts of interest; the likely consequences they could have; the implications of proposed courses of action for the individual, the profession, and society; the distinction between actual and potential conflicts; the distinction between a real conflict and the appearance of one; and the different degrees of seriousness of conflicts of interest.

Weighing this information in conjunction with her own moral rules and/or principles, Jane Smith could then arrive at a decision in regard to a particular situation. Let us say that a supplier to her employer has offered her a Christmas gift that has a value of $50.00. Should she reject or accept the gift? Should she report it to her employer? Should she turn it over to her employer? Should she take any other actions? The answer in this instance depends on a variety of factors. Is she in a position to affect business dealings with her supplier? What are her beliefs in regard to the intentions of the gift? What is considered a gift of nominal value in her industry? How will the gift look to the public? What will her employer's reaction be toward her? These and many other factors will be of importance to her considerations, and the "guides" should make her aware of what type of data would be relevant to the situation.

Let us add, by way of example, that Jane Smith's basic moral principle is that she should try to achieve the maximum beneficial consequences for everyone affected by an action. She would then utilize this principle in conjunction with the specific information in the case to arrive at a decision. If, alternatively, her moral framework consists of a set of general rules, one of which is that she should not knowingly harm anyone, then she would use that rule. In one case she might accept the gift, in the other she might not. In either case, however, she should be able to justify (not just rationalize) her decision in a reasoned manner.

At this point it might be objected that the entire procedure is irrelevant, because Smith's company probably has a specific internal policy regarding gifts. Such a policy would certainly be relevant to her analysis and would in all probability be the major factor. Depending on her moral framework, it might even make an evaluation of the situation unnecessary. However, not all engineers work for corporations with such a policy, and those who do may have to interpret vaguely worded policies, which perhaps employ terminology like *unreasonable* or *nominal*. Nor are all engineers employed engineers. Finally, the example given is only one instance of many possible conflicts of interest.

An attempt to explicate the above example also raises some rather obvious questions that require consideration. First, it might be claimed that the analysis function is already being performed by such groups as the NSPE Board of Ethical Review, by the publication of hypothetical cases in various engineering journals, and by the publication of code decisions by individual engineering organizations such as the ASCE. The purpose of these is to interpret the codes in a more specific way or to decide when a code of ethics has been violated. The procedures used are, however, generally random, after the fact (or, in the case of advisory decisions, take a great deal of time), often relatively inaccessible, and based solely on the existing codes. Thus, a case will generally be dealt with only after it has come to the attention of an appropriate body and the consideration will be limited to that particular instance. Engineers caught up in their day-to-day work are unlikely to spend the time necessary to dig up the one appropriate case out of the library or out of the volumes of the NSPE decisions. The "guides" would need to be made readily available to all engineering students, and this should be feasible if they were made part of an extensive educational program.

Since the "guides" would be intended for application to specific practical problems, a great deal of effort would need to go into their initial formulation as well as into the periodic updating that would be required in a world of innovative technological and social developments. This would require extensive cooperation not only among engineers and among engineering organizations, but also between engineers and philosophers. Second, it might thus be objected that the past lack of success in adopting a unified code of engineering ethics would be multiplied in relation to the "guides." However, since the "guides" would not have regulative force, would not be normative rules, cooperation in their development might be easier to achieve than it has been in the past. But this is an empirical question, and only the carrying out of the attempt would provide an answer.

Third, it is evident that the proposed "guides" would be much more extensive than any existing code of engineering ethics, and it might therefore be claimed that given the scant attention apparently now being paid to the codes, the "guides" will be even less utilized. In order to deal with this objection, it must be remembered that the "guides" are intended, at least in part, to have an educational function, to help the engineer become an autonomous moral decision maker. My suggestion does, in fact, therefore shift a great deal of the burden not only to the individual engineer, but also to the community of engineering educators, both in the academic setting and in the world of practice. A new task for philosophers and engineers must become educating future engineers for moral autonomy. Engineers must not only be educated to make technical decisions on their own, they must also learn how to make decisions regarding morality. The first step in this regard, given my previous analysis, is the formulation of an adequate foundation on which the individual engineer can base his or her actions. Engineering students need to be taught to look beneath their intuitive reactions to situations in order to discover a common basis for their actions. Then they must be asked to examine this foundation critically to see if it can indeed serve as a consistent supporting basis for their actions. This part of the educational process can be undertaken by philosophers, but a second step is required. Not only must the students be shown that they should act on the basis of a well thought out foundation, they must also gain familiarity with the application of their own foundation to practical moral problems. This application will occur, for them as professionals, in specifically engineering contexts. Only practicing engineers can be familiar with the specific details that arise in such contexts, and they must therefore share the burden of preparing future engineers beyond the technical dimension of their work. The "guides for ethical engineering decision making" should be an aid in this respect.[36]

OMITTED FUNCTIONS

In replacing the codes in the way I have suggested, a number of functions that have traditionally been a significant focus of the codes will not be dealt with in the "guides." In the concluding section of this paper I will briefly consider possible dispositions for four major functions: fraternal obligations, ideals of the profession, regulative rules, and fundamental moral beliefs.

Fraternal obligations, or requirements of etiquette toward other members of the profession, constituted a major portion of the early codes, and they still have a significant place in the more recent codes. The 1977 ECPD code, for example, tells engineers that they "shall encourage their engineering employees to further their education," that they "shall uphold the principle of appropriate compensation for those engaged in engineering work," and that they "shall not solicit employment from clients who already have engineers under contract for the same work." Fraternal obligations such as these can be justified under a variety of conceptions of professionalism, perhaps in the strongest sense through a model which requires autonomy for the profession so that it can regulate its own activities.[37] However, it is less clear that they can be justified on an ethical basis, and even if they could be, my previous analysis has shown that this alone would not be enough to make them binding on the engineer. I do, however, believe that an individual engineering organization is entitled to require adherence to some rules as a condition of membership. No engineers are required to join an engineering organization, and those who do so will most likely be motivated by some presumed benefit to themselves.[38] In general, then, fraternal obligations should have the same standing as they would in any other voluntary organization, but they should in no case be able to override the basic moral convictions of an individual member. If the engineering organizations wish to retain such fraternal rules, they should thus remove the misleading heading of "ethics" from them and replace it with a title like "Social Rules for Membership in. . . ".[39]

A major point of discussion in relation to codes of ethics has been the intermixture in them of normative rules of behavior and ideals of the profession. Within the codes themselves the distinction has not always been made clear, and consequently issues of enforcement have been a constant problem, since the striving to meet ideals is not regulatable in the same way as is a minimum adherence to a rule of behavior.[40] Thus, for instance, it would be difficult to determine when a particular engineer has failed to "be committed to improving the environment to enhance the quality of life," whereas it is fairly easy to judge when the following rule has been violated: "Listings in the classified section of telephone directories [shall be] limited to name, address, telephone number and specialities in which the firm is qualified without resorting to special or bold type." If the emphasis in a code is on enforcement, then characterizations such as the latter become preferable. Along with this tactic, however, also comes the danger of trivializing the contents of a code. Yet a set of written ideals for a profession can have a valuable role in the encouragement of the membership of a profession to strive for an ideal of service to society. Thus the publication of a document containing "The Ideals of the Engineer" would be a legitimate contribution by the profession. Again, however, it would need to be made clear to engineers that these do not, and should not, constitute a set of enforceable rules of behavior.

Perhaps the strongest counterargument to my position on the codes of ethics is that their elimination will do away with the possibility of the profession's meeting its obligation to society in relation to basic standards of safety and human well-being. Given either of the two dominant sociological models of the professions mentioned previously, however, this argument strikes me as being specious. In light of the exchange-structural view, it would seem that the professions require a code of ethics in order to demonstrate to society that they are fulfilling their part of the bargain that has given them freedom from societal control. In light of the power theory, codes are primarily a means to further the profession itself and to get society to go along with this self-aggrandizement. As Lisa Newton has pointed out, however, the record of the professions in relation to enforcement of the codes points more to furthering the prestige and power of the professions than it does to meeting obligations to society.[41] In engineering, in particular, the record has been weak in this regard. Stephen Unger, who has for a number of years been involved in the ethics activities of engineering organizations, writes:

> They [the organizations] have largely confined themselves to disciplining members in the consulting field for violations of code provisions pertaining to business practices. In many, if not most, cases that have led to the imposition of sanctions, violations of law as well as ethics codes were involved. An occasional plagiarism case stands out as an exception. I know of no case of an engineer being censured for an act contravening the public safety, health, or welfare, such as involvement in the release of harmful chemicals to the environment.[42]

When it comes to enforcement of issues of public safety and human well-being, it is thus not clear that engineering has earned the privilege of self-enforcement. This may not even be possible, given the legal system in this country, according to which the engineering organizations run the risk of lawsuits by censured engineers, unless normative rules are given statutory authority through a licensing process similar to that of the AMA or the ABA.[43]

Ensurance of adequate standards of safety and health are demands society can make of a profession. Unenforceable or unenforced codes of ethics, however, are not the appropriate instruments of regulating such matters. Perhaps more effort should be expended instead on codifying such requirements in the legal system, as has already been done in numerous instances in such areas as product liability, the ASME boiler code, or professional liability for services rendered. Many engineers will oppose such a suggestion on the grounds that only the profession can set up and regulate such standards. The legal system, however, has not shown itself to be opposed to coordination with the expertise of professionals.

Finally, the "guides to ethical engineering decision making" will not address basic moral issues such as fairness, honesty, and impartiality, which are a significant dimension of the present codes. Furthermore, these issues are not dealt with directly in any of the preceding suggestions for supplementing the "guides." Nor, it is my position, should they be. If truth-telling is a moral obligation, it is a universal one, not just one that applies to engineers. To propose that special mention must be made of it in an engineering code assumes either that engineers have no prior moral education or that the remainder of society fails to adhere to any basic moral beliefs. Even if either of these assumptions were justified, it cannot be the role of the profession to teach engineers to be moral. The profession is justified only in aiding engineers to apply their moral foundation to a specifically engineering context.

A number of functions have been performed by the codes of ethics. The above brief consideration has shown that my suggestion for elimination of the codes does not mean that all of the functions should be eliminated. Some of them are quite valuable in their own right. The discussion, however, points out that the mixture of concerns in the existing codes in part is responsible for much of the confusion surrounding these codes, whereas that discussion should have, as I have argued, been concentrated on more fundamental issues.

SUMMARY

I have attempted to show that morality should not be legislated in the profession of engineering any more than it can be in our everyday lives. Yet this is what the engineering codes of ethics, as they are presently formulated, attempt to do. Given this and other problems with the codes, I have therefore advocated that for the codes of ethics a set of "guides for ethical engineering decision making" should be substituted. Rather than laying out actual rules of normative behavior, these would designate areas of concern for practicing engineers. This suggestion in turn implies that increased emphasis must be given in engineering education to the ability of engineers to apply a rationally chosen ethical foundation to specific engineering situations. An added task is thus proposed for all engineering educators, because moral autonomy is true autonomy only if it is based on sufficient information and reasoned choice.

NOTES

An earlier version of this paper was presented at the Second National Conference on Ethics in Engineering held in Chicago in March 1982. I am grateful to Dr. Vivian Weil for organizing the conference and to Professor John Ladd for his extensive comments on several versions of this paper.

1. Philip M. Kohn and Roy V. Hughson, "Perplexing Problems in Engineering Ethics," *Chemical Engineering*, May 5, 1980, p. 100.

2. Roy V. Hughson and Philip M. Kohn, "Ethics," *Chemical Engineering*, September 22, 1980, p. 132. An earlier survey, with similar results, was carried out by the editors of the journal in 1963.

3. Lisa H. Newton discusses extensively the relationship of codes of ethics to these sociological perspectives in "The Origin of Professionalism: Sociological Conclusions and Ethical Implications," *Business & Professional Ethics Journal* 1, 4 (Summer 1982):33–42.

4. Arlene K. Daniels, "How Free Should the Professions Be?" in *The Professions and Their Prospects*, ed. Eliot Freidson (Beverly Hills: Sage Publications, 1973), p. 46.

5. William H. Wisely, "The Influence of Engineering Societies on Professionalism and Ethics," *Proceedings, Conference on Ethics, Professionalism and Maintaining Competence* (American Society of Civil Engineers, March 1977), pp. 56–57.

6. Burton J. Bledstein, *The Culture of Professionalism* (New York: W. W. Norton, 1976), pp. 34 and 108.

7. The codes are reprinted in the *Annals of the American Academy of Political and Social Science* 101 (May 1922):271–77.

8. A. G. Christic, "A Proposed Code of Ethics for All Engineers," *Annals of the American Academy of Political and Social Science* 101 (May 1922):99.

9. Morris L. Cooke, "Ethics and the Engineering Profession," *Annals of the American Academy of Political and Social Science* 101 (May 1922):70.

10. Andrew G. Oldenquist and Edward E. Slowter, "Proposed: A Single Code of Ethics for All Engineers," *Professional Engineer*, May 1979, pp. 8–11.

11. C. C. Herskind, "The Code of Ethics and the Professional Engineer in Industry," *Professional Engineer*, May 1970, pp. 27–29.

12. Much of the analysis undertaken here could be applied to the codes of ethics of other professions as well. However, the multiplicity of engineering codes, their lack of legal status, and the apparent inability of engineers to develop sufficient enforcement powers makes the situation for engineering somewhat unique.

13. Daniel W. Mead, "Why a Code of Conduct?" *Standards of Professional Relations and Conduct*, Manual of Engineering Practice, no. 21 (American Society of Civil Engineers, 1941), p. 12.

14. The 1847 AMA code is reprinted in the appendix to the *Encyclopedia of Bioethics*, Warren T. Reich, ed.-in-chief (New York: Free Press, 1978).

15. Frederick H. Newell, "Ethics and the Engineering Profession," *Annals of the American Academy of Political and Social Science* 101 (May 1922):81.

16. As cited in Edwin T. Layton, Jr., *The Revolt of the Engineers* (Cleveland: Press of Case Western Reserve University, 1971), p. 84.

17. Ibid., p. 6.

18. Milton F. Lunch, "Engineering Ethics: A Blend of the Ideal and the Practical," *Professional Engineer*, April 1969, p. 33.

19. Cooke, op. cit.

20. See, for example, the discussion by Charles R. Schrader in "Professionalism—And a Relevant Code of Ethics," *Engineering Issues*, October 1974, pp. 337–41.

21. Jacques Barzun, "The Professions under Siege," *Harper's*, October 1978, pp. 61–68.

22. See the discussion on the evolution of a concern for the public welfare in the codes in Stephen H. Unger, *Controlling Technology: Ethics and the Responsible Engineer* (New York: Holt, Rinehart and Winston, 1982), pp. 49–50.

23. The 1947 ECPD and other engineering codes are reprinted in the *Annals of the American Academy of Political and Social Science* 297 (January 1955):53–58.

24. In the following I will be using the 1977 version of the ECPD code as the source for my discussion. In terms of memberships in engineering organizations, more engineers are bound to this code than to any other. Major competing codes are those adopted by the Institute of Electrical and Electronics Engineers and the NSPE, but as Oldenquist and Slowter, op. cit., have pointed out, the codes share much in terms of content. Since 1977 the ECPD has changed its name to Accreditation Board for Engineering and Technology (ABET), which has resulted in some confusion when referring to the code, but it has affected neither the adoption by engineering organizations of the ECPD code nor the contents of the code.

25. For a more complete discussion of this point see my "Society as Engineers' Client," *Liberal Studies Educator* 4 (1981–82):1–10.

26. See the detailed discussion by Robert Baum, "The Limits of Professional Responsibility," in *Engineering Professionalism and Ethics*, ed. James Schaub and Karl Pavlovic (New York: John Wiley, 1983), pp. 287–94, regarding this issue. Baum argues that the knowledge of engineers is limited and that their obligations to obey the teleological principles in the codes are therefore limited. However, he substitutes a doctrine of informed consent for these principles, and therefore his conclusions regarding the basic obligations of engineers differ from my own.

27. Kenneth Kipnis argues that this is actually the case in "Engineers Who Kill: Professional Ethics and the Paramountcy of Public Safety," *Business & Professional Ethics Journal* I, 1 (Fall 1981):77–91.

28. The extent to which different organizations have adopted parts of the ECPD code is discussed in A. S. West, "AIChE's Position on Codes of Ethics," *Chemical Engineering Progress* 77, 2 (February 1981):22–25.

29. An additional political problem in this regard is pointed out by Oldenquist and Slowter, op. cit., p. 10: "perhaps the most obvious stumbling block has been the "NIH" (Not Invented Here) concept. One organization is usually reluctant to endorse or accept a concept produced by another organization; this has led to a number of codes only slightly different in wording."

30. Unger, op. cit., pp. 35–46. He adds a detailed discussion of specific parts of the model code.

31. John Ladd, "The Quest for a Code of Professional Ethics: An Intellectual and Moral Confusion," in *AAAS Professional Ethics Project*, ed. Rosemary Chalk, Mark S. Frankel, and Sallie B. Chafer (Washington, DC: American Association for the Advancement of Science, 1980), p. 154.

32. The vagueness of the words *harming* and *welfare* might be considered a weakness in the example. Clearly, the terms need to be interpreted in a more specific way. Their use, however, being internal to the codes, simply reflects another basic weakness of the codes.

33. I have argued in greater detail for this point in "Engineering: Profession and Professionals," *Proceedings, Frontiers in Education Conference* (Institute of Electrical and Electronics Engineers, 1981), pp. 190–95.

34. The code does, however, prohibit certain actions in other rules that are specific examples of conflicts of interest, such as the issue of compensation from more than one client for the same service, but these rules are not tied explicitly to the conflict-of-interest clause.

35. See the extended discussion of examples of conflicts of interest in Mike W. Martin and Roland Schinzinger, *Ethics in Engineering* (New York: McGraw-Hill, 1983), pp. 169–73.

36. For further discussion of the role of engineering educators in the teaching of ethics see my "Professionalism through Learned Autonomy: Ethics Codes as a Tool," *ASEE Annual Conference Proceedings* (American Society for Engineering Education, June 1983), pp. 420–24.

37. Luegenbiehl, "Engineering: Profession and Professionals," op. cit.

38. The situation is less clear if licensing is required as a condition for employment. I would argue that a code applicable to such situations, e.g., the NSPE code, should have no fraternal content.

39. John Ladd, op. cit., p. 155, has pointed out that the original use of the word *ethical* in codes was intended simply to distinguish them from criminal (legal) codes. This is a broader usage than most would now find acceptable.

40. See Lunch, op. cit., and Kipnis, op. cit.

41. Newton, op. cit.

42. Unger, op. cit., p. 56. The appendix to Chalk et al., op. cit., part of which is devoted to surveying the ethics activities of various engineering organizations, also shows that enforcement activities are quite rare.

43. The issue of required licensing is a hotly debated one in engineering. Many engineers escape licensing requirements through what is known as the "industrial exemption." While it is difficult to determine the actual percentage of engineers who are licensed because of the flexibility in the usage of the term engineer, T. E. Stivers uses the figure 325,000 out of 1,200,000 engineers. He also claims "that less than 10 percent of all engineers in industry are licensed." See "Professional Licensing: The Ancient Rite of Protecting the Public," *Consulting Engineer*, September 1975, pp. 41–44.

4

The Engineer's Responsibilities to Society

_____ **Writing an Environmental Impact Report** _____

Engineer Stan, in the Atlanta office of a large consulting firm, is retained by a neighborhood association to write an environmental impact study on a private oil company's proposed petrochemical complex. Stan concludes that the project, as planned, would harm the habitat of several endangered species. The client has already reviewed draft copies of the report and is planning to hold a press conference when the final version of the report is delivered.

A few days before delivery, the New York office of Stan's firm learns of the study and tells Stan to hold up on it. Engineer Bruce flies down from New York to explain to Stan that the oil company is one of the firm's most valued clients, and that the company's president has threatened to pull all their business if the report is delivered to the neighborhood association. Bruce tells Stan to rewrite the report to show that the project would cause no significant environmental damage.

Reprinted from Elizabeth M. Endy and P. Aarne Vesilind, "Ethics in the Field," Civil Engineering, December 1985, with permission.

_____ **"Natural" May Not Mean "Good"** _____

Ruth works as a group leader for a company that sells large quantities of a major food product that is processed before sale, by heating. Her product-development group has been analyzing the naturally occurring flavor constituents of the product, and she discovers that several of the flavor components (actually pyrolysis products, present in minute quantities) are chemicals that have been found to cause cancer in animals when given in large doses. Yet, the product—in worldwide use literally for centuries—has never been implicated as a cause of cancer.

Although in the United States the Delaney amendment to the Pure Food and Drug Act prohibits adding cancer-causing agents to food, no government regulations exist concerning those that may occur naturally.

Reprinted from Phillip M. Kohn and Roy V. Hughson, "Perplexing Problems in Engineering Ethics," Chemical Engineering, *May 5, 1980, with permission.*

_____ **Inquiring about the Customer Base** _____

Joan, a product engineer, was hired to do continuing technical enhancements to a general-purpose data base management system product. Her co-workers have no interest in learning about the company's customer base and the applications for which the product is ultimately used. Should they?

Joan wants to know whether the product is being sold for uses that she considers morally objectionable—for example, political repression in South Africa. She is unable to get complete information from the company, which regards their customer base as proprietary information that they disclose only to selected sales and marketing personnel. Should Joan do anything else?

Later, she becomes friendly with a salesman in the company and learns that the customer base is well distributed among federal agencies, military agencies, commercial companies, and a few foreign governments (not including South Africa). The salesman says the company knows little about the particular applications for which the product is used after it is sold. Joan is uncomfortable not knowing the purposes for which her work is used. What should she do?

Reprinted from the Annual Meeting of Computer Professionals for Social Responsibility, October 17, 1987, with permission.

INTRODUCTION

It has become clear, from many of the readings in the preceding chapters, that engineers see themselves as having responsibility for the safety and welfare of society. It is now time to explore this responsibility. The most important, and perhaps most difficult, question has to do with what such a responsibility might require of engineers. What does it mean that engineers ought to do? In chapter 5, we will examine the implications of having an obligation of loyalty to one's employer and how this obligation may conflict with an engineer's responsibility for the safety and welfare of society;

however, for now, we want simply to understand the significance of having a responsibility to society. What aspects of engineering practice does or should it affect? How much personal sacrifice must engineers be willing to make to protect society? What changes should be made so that individual engineers or engineers collectively can better fulfill this responsibility? Many of the authors we read try to get a handle on this by exploring the underlying basis for saying that engineers have a social responsibility. The presumption here seems to be that an understanding of *why* engineers have such a responsibility will give us insight into what the responsibility entails.

We begin with a reading by Michael McFarland in which he focuses on nuclear power to understand what should be the proper role of engineers in social decision making about such a technology. MacFarland starts by putting forth a set of conditions that when met would justify our saying that someone has an obligation to come to the aid of another. He derives these conditions from consideration of the nonengineering case of Kitty Genovese, who was murdered while thirty-eight of her neighbors listened or watched. MacFarland uses this case as an analogue for engineers when society is in need of help, when no other sources of help are available, when engineers are close to the problem. He notes that a problem may occur when engineers do not have the ability to help as separate individuals but might have this ability if they acted collectively. Even if we accept the idea that engineers should act collectively to aid society when it is in need, difficult issues emerge about the best form of collective action, which MacFarland considers in depth.

The next readings focus on individual behavior. Richard T. De George explores the Pinto case by asking the hard question: Can we say that the engineers did anything wrong? Engineers working on the Pinto told their superiors that a problem existed with the placement of the gas tank and even recommended installment of a part that would make the car safer, but then they backed off and did nothing when management decided not to install the part. De George argues that these engineers did exactly what they should have, and he offers specific criteria for when an engineer has an obligation to blow the whistle—criteria that were not met in the Pinto case. He emphasizes that engineers have expertise about the amount of risk that a project might present, but they do not have expertise about what amount of risk is acceptable. It may be useful for you to compare your responses to the Pinto case and De George's arguments with your responses to the reading by Roger Boisjoly (in chapter 1) about the Challenger disaster.

Kenneth D. Alpern takes issue with De George. He seems to believe that De George lets engineers off the hook much too easily. Alpern argues that engineers must be willing to make greater sacrifices than others, and he bases his claims on an account of the origins of the social responsibilities of engineers. He proposes that these obligations come from a fundamental principle of ordinary morality that one must do no harm. Because engineers are in a position to do greater harm than are many other people, they have a greater responsibility. He thinks engineers should know this when they enter the profession and should not enter the profession unless they are willing to make sacrifices for social good.

In a different vein, Mike W. Martin and Roland Schinzinger get at the social responsibilities of engineers by proposing a new way of thinking about engineering. They argue that engineering, by its very nature, is experimental. It is experimental because we learn by failure, and because some risk is always involved. They then suggest that we think of the responsibilities of engineers like those of experimenters. This suggestion reveals a set of attitudes and responses appropriate for the tasks of engineers.

This chapter ends with a piece that I wrote for a conference focusing on ethical issues in doing research for the military. In this article I examine several principles that engineers might follow when they select employers and projects. It is important to remember that social responsibility entails more than blowing the whistle on wrong-doing. When engineers choose specialties and problems to research, and when they choose an employer, their choices have an important effect on society. Some problems are solved, but others are ignored. The interests of some industries or companies are furthered, whereas others are not.

14 The Public Health, Safety and Welfare: An Analysis of the Social Responsibilities of Engineers

Michael C. McFarland, S.J.

INTRODUCTION

If you were to observe someone being mugged on the street outside your house, you would certainly have some obligation to try to prevent it, at least to the point of calling the police. Now suppose that you were aware of a group of people being "mugged" by the misuse of a certain type of technology—for example, by having a toxic waste dump placed in their town, or by being put in danger by shoddy design or construction of their automobile. Would there be an obligation to try to prevent that? What if the people were not necessarily being injured, but were being put in danger of suffering a catastrophe—for example, by having a poorly-designed nuclear power plant placed a few miles from them? Is there an obligation in that case to try to make the situation safer for them? Suppose you were partly responsible for the development and use of the technology in question. How might that affect your obligation? Do technologists have any special obligation to protect people from the technologies they create?

The purpose of this paper is to give an account of the social responsibilities of engineers and, more importantly, to explore ways in which they might best fulfill those responsibilities. Most of the writing on engineering ethics in the past has focused on the responsibilities of the individual engineer to employers, clients, and users—responsibilities that could be met adequately by loyalty, competence, and integrity on the job [1]. My thesis, however, is that engineers must be seen in a wider social context. Unless their work is seen in its relation to society, an adequate account of their ethical responsibilities cannot be given, as some of the most recent literature on engineering ethics has recognized [2]. Furthermore, unless individual engineers learn to act in collaboration with others, both inside and outside their profession, they will not be able to meet those responsibilities.

We will investigate the social responsibilities of engineers by looking at their role in the development of a specific technology. The technology I have chosen is nuclear power generation. This is especially well suited to our purposes for a number of reasons. First, nuclear power technology has very serious social implications. On the one hand, it offers the possibility of a long-term, relatively clean and inexpensive power source. On the other hand, it carries great risks with it, especially those connected with the release of radiation into the environment [3]. Second, many in our society have become deeply concerned about the implications of nuclear power, and almost every aspect of the problem has been the subject of intense debate. Third, technical issues have played an important part in the debate, issues that require a great deal of technical training and knowledge to understand. Fourth, nuclear power is a good paradigm for large technological projects, illustrating all the financial, governmental, scientific and social forces that influence such projects. Finally, nuclear power has been an issue for long enough that there is a very large body of literature on all aspects of the problem.

We will analyze the role of engineers in the development, use and criticism of nuclear technology. In particular, we will look at some of the ways in which engineers have tried to fulfill their responsibilities, and analyze the strengths and weaknesses of each response. This will lead to some conclusions about ways in which the society in general and the engineering professions in particular must move so that engineers might better fulfill their social responsibilities.

ETHICAL CONSIDERATIONS

Most engineers would, in theory, recognize the existence of broader obligations, beyond those of doing their jobs well. The difficulty is in discerning those obligations in particular circumstances and understanding how they apply to individual engineers. A study done by John G. Simon, Charles W. Powers and Jon P. Gunneman on the social responsibilities of universities regarding the investment of their funds provides some useful guidelines [4]. The authors begin by analyzing the case of Kitty Genovese, the woman who was stabbed to death outside her Queens apartment while at least thirty-eight of her neighbors looked on. It is generally agreed that the refusal of all the neighbors to help represented a serious failing. But what created the obligation to act when none of the neighbors was responsible for causing the situation? When is there an obligation beyond that of not harming another? From consideration of this case, the authors identify four factors that must be present in order for there to be an obligation to come to the aid of another. They are:

1. Critical need: some fundamental right or good must be threatened.
2. Promixity: this is "largely a function of notice," but it also involves role relationships. "We do expect certain persons and perhaps institutions to look harder for information about critical need. In this sense proximity has to do with the network

of social relations that follow from notions of civic duty, duties to one's family, and so on." [4, p. 24]

3. Ability to help, without damage to self and without interference with important duties owed to others.

4. Absence of other sources of help.

Further consideration of the Genovese case can lead us, I believe, to two other important points. First of all, part of the reason that the neighbors did not help the woman out was their sense of fear, isolation and helplessness. This does not excuse them from at least calling the police, of course. But their options were severely limited by their inability to take common action. If the thirty eight of them had rushed the assailant at once, they certainly could have overcome him, or at least scared him off, without great risk to any one of them. This shows the power, indeed the necessity, of organized social action in meeting social obligations. Secondly, the reason the neighbors did not act together was that they had no history of common action and no institutional basis for it. If there had been a neighborhood association or, better yet, a "crime watch" organization, it is much more likely that the neighbors would have come together and done something [5]. This shows the importance of having adequate social structures to enable and to support common action.

The importance of social structures and their place in our democratic system has been the subject of much recent literature, both secular and religious [6–8]. Consideration of this social dimension of the human person widens our sense of responsibility to include those obligations that we share by reason of the groups to which we belong; but it also presents us with new possibilities for responding to those obligations and thus increases our freedom.

THE SOCIAL RESPONSIBILITIES OF ENGINEERS

It is not difficult to see how conditions (1), (2) and (4) in the analysis of Simon, Powers, and Gunneman, apply to engineers in the nuclear industry.

With regard to (1), there is certainly a *critical need* either to make nuclear power safer or to find alternative energy sources. Nuclear power does offer benefits that make it extremely attractive if it can be produced safely. Nuclear fuel is relatively inexpensive and abundant in the United States, and its use in preference to coal could actually save lives because of reduced air pollution [9]. Yet there are many serious dangers connected with nuclear power. These include health hazards due to radiation encountered during the mining and processing of nuclear fuel [10], the possibility of a catastrophic accident at a nuclear power plant [11], and the long-term effects of nuclear wastes [12].

Regarding point (2), engineers have a special *proximity* to the problem. Their potential contribution to the responsible use of nuclear power is unique and irreplaceable for a number of reasons. One is that engineers, because of their special training and expertise and their involvement in the design and maintenance of nuclear power plants, are best qualified to clarify the technical issues in the nuclear power debate. They can define the risks involved and give the best available estimates of the costs of reducing or eliminating those risks.

Another reason why the contribution of engineers is so important is that they are the first to see and to evaluate the dangers and risks of the technology. They work with and evaluate the systems while they are still in the design stage, before an irreversible commitment has been made to them. Thus the engineers, and they alone, are in a position to recognize potential dangers while something can still be done about them.

The final contribution engineers can make is to propose and explore alternatives to the current technology that might avoid some of its problems. It is a fundamental ethical principle that the best way to handle ethical dilemmas, where a certain amount of evil must be accepted in order to do good, is to find imaginative alternatives that minimize the evil effects or avoid the conflict entirely. If engineers could find alternatives to current nuclear technology that do not have many of the safety problems that it has, they would have made a considerable contribution to the nuclear power debate. In fact, David Freeman, the director of the TVA, a large user of nuclear power, has predicted that the future of nuclear power in the U.S. depends on "our choosing a more 'forgiving' nuclear reactor design and then standardizing it." [13, p. 273]

The fourth condition of Simon, Powers, and Gunneman is the absence of other sources of help. Indeed, engineers do often excuse themselves from responsibility on the assumption that existing institutions, such as government regulation or the discipline of the marketplace, will take care of any problems. In the case of nuclear power, however, these institutions have not performed in a way that inspires great confidence.

From the very beginning, the Atomic Energy Commission, which was given the responsibility of regulating nuclear power, was also deeply involved in its promotion. As a result, substantial questions about safety were not raised, or, if they were, were swept under the rug. While a licensing procedure for nuclear power plants was set up, no specific standards for safety were set, and the main interest seemed to be in expediting the approval process in order to get plants on line as quickly as possible [14]. A study done by Steven Ebbin and Raphael Kasper on the nuclear regulatory process in 1974 found that "the licensing process is one which is geared to the promotion of nuclear power plants. The hearing process was originally designed to provide a mechanism to inform the local citizenry of the benefits of a nuclear power generating plant." [15, p. 5]

It was only after the Three Mile Island accident that the Nuclear Regulatory Commission, the successor to the AEC, began demanding a number of design changes in nuclear power plants, both those already in operation and those being designed and built. These changes have had an effect, making the plants perhaps three to six times safer than before [16]. Yet they have been costly because they have come so late. Certainly they do not make up for the years of neglect of safety issues. Nor have they served to win back public confidence in nuclear power or its regulators.

None of this is to be taken to mean that government regulation is unnecessary, or that it will always perform as badly as it has in the case of nuclear power. But it does show that for commercial power, as for any large-scale technology, it cannot be taken for granted that the government will be able to protect the public adequately from the risks of the technology.

Nor is there any basis for supposing that without government regulation the nuclear industry would have sought solutions to the problems of nuclear safety or that consumers would have demanded that the cost of electricity be raised in order to make nuclear power safer. The history of private industry in the U.S. has shown that both producers and consumers have to be forced to accept responsibility for the long term effects of economic activity. [18, p. 39] The nuclear industry in particular has showed itself quite content to enjoy government protection from such "external" costs as the risks to public health and safety from possible radiation releases, the cost of nuclear fuel processing, and the problems of disposing of nuclear wastes. In fact, such protection was a necessary condition for the involvement of private industry in the development of nuclear power [17].

POSSIBLE RESPONSES

The remaining condition of Simon, Powers, and Gunneman is the third one, the ability to act effectively. This presents a much more difficult problem. It often seems that existing social structures limit seriously the ability of engineers to act on behalf of the public safety without undue risk to themselves. To see how this is so, we will now look at four ways in which engineers have tried to respond to the ethical problems raised by nuclear power. By studying these responses, we hope to learn something about the possibilities for engineers' involvement in social problems and the limitations on it.

Control by the Technical Elite

The first response is what might be called technical paternalism. It springs from the attitude that the issues involved are purely technical and that the public should simply step aside and let the engineers and scientists decide them. In the early years of nuclear power, this took the form of the "technical fix." The assumption was that a well designed nuclear power plant would not pose any danger to the public. If a safety problem arose, it would simply be fixed. "While many of the hazards of radiation were clearly apparent in 1946, no one viewed the potential threat of an evolving nuclear technology as intolerable or something good engineering could not acceptably control." [14, p. 22] In the commercial nuclear power industry, this was based on a reliance on multiple backup safety systems, designed to handle all imaginable contingencies. " 'Defense in depth' bespeaks nuclear engineers' confidence that scientific method, carefully applied, can permanently triumph over human fallibility. The key assumption behind this approach is that nuclear experts can anticipate each and every sequence of events that might lead to serious accidents. Armed with that foreknowledge, they can construct systems that no combination of human error or national catastrophe can compromise." [13, p. 176] The problem was that it never quite worked. Critics kept finding holes in the safety systems, and accidents kept occurring with alarming frequency. Each emergency, of course, was met with more technology. "However, each attempted solution seemed to bring with it further problems, while continued scientific research and experience kept bringing to the surface problems that were either unsuspected or had been considered remote possibilities." [18, p. 45]

Finally, with the greater public awareness of the problems of nuclear safety, the industry had to admit that there were risks. To justify these risks, they attempted to "prove," by a supposedly objective calculus, that the benefits outweighed the risks and therefore made them worth taking. This approach is standard practice for an engineer: As a top manager in the nuclear industry put it, "An engineer is a practical man. He is resigned to using science for the betterment of mankind. And he's used to making tradeoffs. Cost-benefits are put into him from day one of engineering school—if you do this, you'll get that, is it worth it?" [13, p. 180]

A prime example of this type of analysis is a study on reactor safety commissioned by the AEC and conducted by a committee chaired by Professor Norman Rasmussen of MIT. The study used current reliability analysis techniques to estimate the probability of failure of a certain type of reactor and the consequences of such a failure. It had unquestionable value as an engineering tool, pointing out weaknesses in the reactor safety systems and providing a basis for comparing alternative reactor designs [19]. However, the AEC also used its calculated probabilities and consequences as the basis for estimating the absolute risk of human life imposed by the present generation of nuclear reactors [20]. Since this was found to be less than 0.1 percent of the total risk due to all manmade and natural causes, it was assumed to be acceptable.

This paternalistic approach does have certain advantages, of course. For one thing, some problems actually can be solved by applying proper engineering techniques. For example, in the first commercial power plants, the release of radiation during routine operation was a major concern. New standards and the redesign of the existing plants took care of that. "The limits on the allowable release of radioactivity from nuclear power plants have now been reduced to the point where few critics think that the issue is worth their time anymore." [21, p. 38]

Nevertheless technological paternalism brings dangers of its own. First of all, it tends to overlook the uncertainties in technological determinations. It assumes that all the factors are well-defined, well-understood, and quantifiable. "[Nuclear engineers] tend to ignore uncertainty and concentrate only on that part of the knowledge base that is subject to quantifiable manipulation. As a result, a point of view emerges whereby technical analyses are expected to resolve the problem. Because of the wide bands of uncertainty on safety improvements, we need different kinds of decisions that aren't technical." [22, p. 60]

In the case of the Rasmussen Report, for example, later analyses have shown that for various reasons the actual "best estimate" of the risk to human life due to reactor accidents could be higher than the one calculated in the report by several orders of magnitude [11]. This would make the risk more than what the public has found acceptable in similar situations, so that there is no basis for pronouncing the risk acceptable on the basis of Rasmussen's study [23], as the AEC claimed when the report first came out.

The second problem with a cost-benefit analysis is that it is not as "objective" or "value-free" as its proponents claim. Like any utilitarian calculus, it contains hidden assumptions about the value of competing goods and how they are to be compared [24]. For example, there must be some assumption about the economic value of a human life, so that threats to human life can be compared with other "goods." Furthermore, even if cost-benefit analysis were an acceptable way to determine overall whether a certain risk was acceptable, it is not sensitive to inequities in the distribution of risks. It simply finds the course that brings the largest net benefit. A cost-benefit analysis might find it desirable to expose a small and powerless minority to grave danger, so that the rest of the society could benefit. That would be a gross injustice, of course, and totally unacceptable for that reason, but the cost-benefit analysis by itself would not reflect that fact.

The insensitivity of cost-benefit analysis to justice and other nonquantifiable values is one reason why the nuclear debate has become so intractable. Many of those who challenge nuclear power do not take issue with the facts and figures of the engineering analyses but with the underlying assumptions, especially the assumption that human life can be qualified or have a price tag put on it. In other words, the real issues are ethical ones, and they must be decided on the level of ethics, of value judgments, not as a result of technical calculations. "Scientists . . . cannot determine when something is safe or safe enough, because that is a matter of preference or judgment. Does the group want to live with the risks described by the scientist as accompanying the product, pay for reducing the risk, or, instead, forego the product?" [14, p. 3]

The third objection to paternalism is that it violates the right to self-determination of those who are affected by the use of technology. Lurking behind the paternalistic ideal is the assumption that technically trained people should make all the decisions on the use of technology, since they are the ones who best understand it. This has certainly been the attitude of the nuclear industry and its regulators. According to a former legal counsel for Babcock and Wilcox, "The public should rely on the NCR to carry out the task it is charged with: protecting the public. The public must have confidence that these people are doing their jobs, and if they're not, to get new people to do it. But to have housewives coming into these highly sophisticated technical decisions is ridiculous." [13, p. 152] Yet no group of technical experts has the right to impose significant risks on the public without their consent. The risk bearers have the right to decide if the risk is worth bearing.

These and other objections to risk assessment procedures such as those used in the Rasmussen Report are detailed in a recent study by K. S. Shrader-Frechette [25].

Engineers have an obligation to be involved with issues of public safety and welfare; but that does not entitle them to control the decisions to be made. Rather they must help the public decide what they want and whether it is worth assuming the burden required to get it. As the National Academy of Sciences' Panel on Technology Assessment has said, "Decisions affecting the course of technology, and hence the course of history, require the broadest possible public participation and should not, even if they could, be delegated to narrow elites." [3, p. 50]

Going Public

What can engineers do when they are aware of a serious safety problem, or some other misuse of a technology they are involved with, and they are blocked in their attempts to seek remedies through normal channels? One possibility is to speak out publicly in the hope of bringing enough pressure to bear to force action on the problem. This is commonly known as "whistle-blowing." Sometimes this is accompanied by resignation, on the grounds that the protesting engineer can no longer in good conscience be associated with the project. Even if the engineer is willing to stay on, he or she is often fired.

There have been a number of whistle-blowing incidents in the nuclear industry. One involved Peter Faulkner, a systems application engineer with Nuclear Services Corp. In March, 1974, Faulkner presented a paper that raised questions about the adequacy of the design of one of General Electric's reactor containment structures to a Senate subcommittee hearing on energy research and development. The paper also expressed concern about mismanagement and inadequate attention to safety in the nuclear industry. Faulkner did this, he wrote later, because "through my studies of safety, management and reliability problems, I became aware of many engineering deficiencies in nuclear power systems that were already on the market." [26] Three weeks later, Faulkner was fired. He continued to speak out, however, and in 1975 GE began its own investigation of the adequacy of the containment design. The next year, the manager of the study, Dale Bridenbaugh, and two other engineers, Greg Minor and Dick Hubbard, resigned and began speaking out on nuclear risks. They testified before the Joint Committee on Atomic Energy that "the cumulative effect of all design effects and deficiencies in the design, construction and operation of nuclear power plants make a nuclear power plant accident, in our opinion, a certain event." [13, p. 92]

Engineers like Faulkner and the "GE Three" are caught in a tragic conflict between their loyalties to their jobs and their employers, on the one hand, and their "wider loyalties" to the public good, on the other. That they have chosen to honor the wider loyalties, even at great personal expense, is commendable. In doing this, they are being faithful to their responsibilities as engineers. "A determination that a project entails an unjustifiable risk to the public is a matter of engineering judgment and general values. Having made such a judgment, a decision to withdraw from the project clearly falls in the realm of engineering ethics." [27, p. 56]

Sometimes whistle-blowing can be effective. Faulkner, the "GE Three," and other engineers and scientists who have "gone public," have been able to bring their message to the public through Congressional hearings, the electronic and print media, and Nuclear Regulatory Commission licensing hearings. Moreover, they have been able to lend scientific substance and credibility to the protests of activists. Certainly these engineers cannot be dismissed by their opponents as either ignorant of the technical issues or as anti-technology.

Whistle-blowing may be the best available response for an individual under certain tragic circumstances. Nevertheless, it cannot in general be accepted as an adequate way for the engineering profession to meet its social responsibilities. For one thing, it is unjust to the engineer who speaks out and then must accept the consequences. Faulkner, for example, not only was fired, but was never able to get another job in the nuclear industry, even though he applied to 67 corporations for employment. Whether he was blackballed or not, at the very least companies regard with suspicion anyone who might make embarrassing allegations about them, no matter how justified. Harassment and hostility are the standard response to whistle-blowing. As a result, very few are willing to take the chance and speak out. Faulkner's colleagues agreed with him on the substantive issues of his allegations but had "no desire to rock the boat."

Another problem is the polarization that is almost inevitable in a whistle-blowing situation. The organization against which the charges are being made regards the action as a threat and an act of disloyalty and reacts accordingly. It is usually intent on both intimidating and discrediting the whistle-blower. The individual, meanwhile, has taken a big risk in taking a stand and now is enduring unjust harassment because of it. As a result, positions harden and personal animosities enter into the debate. It becomes almost impossible for either side to be objective and fair. This often obscures the original point of the whistle-blower's challenge, so that the important concerns that inspired the challenge become lost amidst the charges and counter-charges.

A number of authors have proposed procedures for whistle blowers that are designed to keep the discussion as fair and rational as possible, prevent overreaction, keep alive the possibility of resolving the dispute, and provide some measure of protection for the whistle-blower [27]. These are not likely, however, to overcome the fundamental limitations of whistle-blowing as a way of responding to social needs. The fact that the whistle-blower acts alone, taking on a large organization without supporting structures and usually without being part of an organized opposition, both puts him or her at great risk and limits the impact of the protest.

Organized Opposition

When Robert Pollard, a project manager with the Nuclear Regulatory Commission, resigned from the NRC because of its "poor attention to safety concerns." He joined the staff of a group called the Union of Concerned Scientists (UCS). Through the auspices of the UCS, he gained much greater access to the press than he might otherwise have had, and he was able to contribute his considerable expertise to a UCS study of the NRC's suppression of information on reactor safety problems. Thus by joining forces with other similarly concerned technical people, Pollard was able both to soften the effects of his loss of a job and to increase the effectiveness of his protest. This illustrates the value of engineers coming together and organizing their efforts to correct the misuse of technology.

The Union of Concerned Scientists is an excellent example of such an organization. It was formed by a group of professors and graduate students at MIT in 1969 "to encourage more humane use of scientific and technical knowledge." The safety of the nuclear power industry has been a major concern of the organization, along with alternative energy sources, and nuclear arms limitation. The UCS has contributed to the nuclear power debate in three ways: through analysis of some of the key technical issues; through public education; and through participation in legislative and administrative hearings and other phases of the regulatory process.

The UCS has done a number of expert studies on the safety of nuclear power, including a study of the many dangers involved in the preparation of nuclear fuel and the disposal of nuclear wastes [10]; an analysis of the fire at the Brown's Ferry nuclear plant, which exposed the laxity of the NRC in enforcing safety standards [28]; and a very careful and detailed critique of the Rasmussen Report on reactor safety [11]. The last, along with the responses of a number of other technical groups, eventually caused the NRC in 1979 to repudiate many of the findings of the Rasmussen Report.

The UCS has participated aggressively in the regulatory process, both on its own behalf and in concert with groups of concerned citizens. It has been an intervener in reactor licensing hearings and has petitioned the NRC to close some plants because of safety problems. These maneuvers have brought some improvements in reactor safety features. The UCS has also intervened in general NRC hearings on the reliability of the Emergency Core Cooling System (ECCS), a key safety system in nuclear reactors, asking for more through testing and an independent evaluation of the system. As a result, some progress has been made toward making the ECCS safer and more reliable [29].

The participation of the UCS in such hearings has been very important because citizens' groups who have tried to challenge the nuclear power industry often have not been able to marshal enough technical expertise to make a credible showing. "The entire proceeding [of an NRC hearing] is reminiscent of David versus Goliath. The intervenor's counsel sitting alone, usually without adequate technical assistance, faces two or three AEC attorneys, two or three attorneys for the applicant, and large teams of experts who support the AEC and applicants' attorneys." [17, p. 134] Therefore a group of scientists and engineers like the UCS, who are committed to working for the responsible use of technology and the protection of the public safety, and who are willing to use the political process to do so, fills a critical need. Not only do they ensure that the important technical issues regarding public safety are raised and adequately debated, but they also help give a voice to the people who are being asked to bear the risk and who therefore have a right to be heard in the debate. "Technical expertise is a crucial political resource in conflicts over science and technology. For access to knowledge and the resulting ability to question the data used to legitimize decisions is an essential basis of power and influence." [30, p. 15]

By organizing themselves and by allying themselves with the public, therefore, engineers can overcome some of the problems inherent in paternalism and whistleblowing. But other problems remain. One of the strengths of a group like the UCS, its independence, can also be a limitation. The fact that the organization is seen as an "intervenor," a group that is outside the normal decision-making process, gives it less credibility and influence than it might otherwise have. The UCS has met many obstructions, and has lost on a number of issues because of unresponsive administrators or judges. This marginalization also means that the outside group must scramble for resources and information, whereas the establishment forces are well-funded and have access to all the data and analyses collected by the nuclear industry and the NRC. The fact that the UCS and similar groups have accomplished as much as they have is a tribute to their determination, persistence and political sophistication. It certainly cannot be attributed to the fairness of the regulatory system.

Questions could also be raised about the wisdom and propriety of trying to settle technical issues in a highly charged political atmosphere. It is true that decisions on the use of technology are necessarily political; yet they should also be well-informed, and sometimes technical clarity is lost in the heat of battle. Scientific objectivity is a fragile thing. "The boundaries of the problem to be studied, the alternatives weighed, and the issues regarded as appropriate—all tend to determine which data are selected as important, which facts emerge." [30, p. 16] This has led one major study of the regulatory process for nuclear power to question the effectiveness of the current adversarial system used to make decisions on reactor design and siting, waste disposal and so on.

> It is the difference in the goals of scientific method and the adversarial system that lead us to the conclusion that for the purpose of determining technical efficacy and identifying the impacts of nuclear power plants on safety and on the environment, adversary science and resolution of scientific issues in a trial type of proceeding must fail to provide an adequate resolution of scientific and technical issues [15, p. 222]

As we have seen, the engineer has a specific contribution to make to problems on the use of technology precisely in his or her role as engineer. But it is not possible to fulfill that role adequately without room for objectivity, cooperation and the free flow of information. if the system does not allow that, it cannot be said to be protecting the rights either of the public or of the engineer, and changes are called for.

Professional Societies

The one institution through which engineers act corporately as members of their profession, and which has a broad base of support, is the professional society. Most of the engineering specialities have such societies. They are generally very involved in technical activities such as the publication of research, and sponsoring of technical conferences, continuing education, and the development of technical standards. They also are involved in lobbying for government action on issues that affect the welfare of their members, such as the improvement of engineering education, increased funding for engineering research, the free flow of scientific information, and more liberal standards for Individual Retirement Accounts. The focus of the societies, then, is more often on the profession itself than on the profession's responsibilities to the public. As Judith Swazey said, in a speech to the AAAS Workshop on Professional Ethics, "Professions tend to operate as fairly narrow self-interest groups when push comes to shove, that in the end are more apt to protect the guild than to protect the public interest when there is a conflict." [31, p. 63]

Most engineering societies have codes of ethics. These tend to concentrate on the responsibilities of individual engineers to serve employers and clients with competence and integrity [31]. Nevertheless, there has been a growing awareness of the profession's wider responsibilities to the public. For instance, while the 1912 code of the

American Institute for Electrical Engineers said that "the engineer should consider the protection of a client's or employer's interests his first professional obligation, and therefore should avoid every act contrary to this duty," the current code of the Institute of Electrical and Electronics Engineers (IEEE) says that the responsibility to employers or clients is limited by the responsibility to "protect the safety, health and welfare of the public." The code of the Engineers' Council for Professional Development is even stronger: "Engineers shall hold paramount the safety, health and welfare of the public." [32, p. 8] These acknowledgments of the broader social responsibilities of engineers are important; but to date little has been done to put them into practice. A study by the American Association for the Advancement of Science on the ethical activities of professional societies found that "the professional scientific and engineering societies have not developed in-depth programs addressing the ethical implications of their members' work." [31, p. 8]

There are two areas where professional societies could take practical measures to "protect the safety, health and welfare of the public." First of all they could lend their technical expertise to those who are questioning the use of certain technologies; or they could act as independent evaluators of controversial technical issues such as those involved in reactor safety or the disposal of radioactive wastes. If the technical expertise were to come from the professional societies, with their broadly based membership, their prestige, and their independence, it might avoid some of the problems of partisanship that have arisen with organizations whose sole purpose is to challenge certain technologies.

The IEEE took one small step in this direction by agreeing to do an independent accreditation of laboratories that test and certify safety equipment used in nuclear power plants. After inviting the IEEE to do this, however, the NRC refused to go ahead with the plan [33]. This indicates that existing institutions and attitudes still must change before any very meaningful involvement is possible.

The other action the professional societies can take on behalf of social responsibility is to protect whistle-blowers from reprisals from their employers. A number of proposals have been made in that regard. For example, Stephen Unger has urged that engineering societies work for an environment where the engineer can "function as a professional rather than a cog in a machine. . . . Where his professional judgment is overruled in serious matters involving the public welfare, and where protests to his management are to no avail, the engineer should be free to take his cases to professional societies, government, or any other appropriate forum." [34] The society could investigate the case and publish its conclusions, identifying the employer if it is found at fault. The society could also perhaps give legal aid.

The IEEE, for one, does have a section in its bylaws in which it pledges support for "any member involved in a matter of ethical principle which stems in whole or in part from such member's adherence to the Code of Ethics, and which can jeopardize the member's livelihood, compromise the discharge of such member's professional responsibilities, or which can be detrimental to the interests of the IEEE or of the engineering profession." This provision has been invoked once in support of a member. The employer was found at fault and was publicly identified. [31, p. 93f] To date, however, the professional societies have hesitated to take strong united action in support of their members, so that they have limited influence in such cases. "Employers may have little incentive to settle disputes with the professional society, which often lacks the motivation, evidence or resources to pursue more serious options such as publicizing the violation and naming the offending employer, or taking legal action." [31, p. 57]

The engineering societies do have the potential for providing an institutional base for engineers to act on social issues. But they are still a long way from realizing that potential. There are various legal and institutional obstacles, to be sure. But the major problem seems to be internal. Because of the pluralism of the engineering profession, engineers' preference to concentrate on technical issues and stay away from "people problems," and the tradition of putting clients' and employers' interests before the public's, engineers have to date been slow to take united action on issues of social responsibility.

NEW DIRECTIONS

As the above study has shown, engineers should not simply act as individuals in meeting their social responsibilities, but should look for ways to foster collaboration, both within the profession and with those outside the profession. Collaboration within the profession is important especially when engineers must challenge the established forces of government and industry, not only to make the protest more effective, but also to provide protection and support for those who might have to endure reprisals because of the challenge. Collaboration with the general public is important because decisions about the use of technology involve value judgments as well as technical knowledge. Therefore the obligation of engineers to protect the public does not mean that they, or any elite group, should decide what risks are worth taking or how they are to be distributed. Engineers should rather help the public make responsible, well-informed decisions on these issues.

One reason that such collaboration has not occurred as much as it should is that existing social structures have not supported it. Certainly the government and the private sector are too committed to the technology to tolerate a really critical view of it. Organizations such as the UCS have accomplished a great deal. But, through no fault of their own, they have been kept out of the decision-making process as much as possible, so that an adversarial situation is almost inevitable. Professional societies have not yet shown themselves capable of sustained, effective action on behalf of the public welfare.

There is a need, then, for new structures, for new ways of making decisions about the development and use of technology. These structures should first of all allow independent technical evaluations as part of the decision-making process. These evaluations should be free both from pressures to bias the results to serve some particular interests and from the distortions of the adversarial process. Without this freedom it is very difficult for engineers to maintain their integrity and to make their unique contribution to the responsible use of technology. Ebbin and Kasper, for example, after studying the present regulatory system for nuclear power, concluded that there was a need for independent "technology assessment teams" of experts who could evaluate the consequences of a technology so that the public debate could at least be well-informed [15].

Second, the structures should be collaborative. They should not only allow interdisciplinary teams of scientists and engineers, but should also bring these technical people together with other interested parties, including representative of government, industry, labor and, of course, the public. This is the only way to ensure that all legitimate interests are represented and that the different sides begin to appreciate one another's point of view. This is crucial for any kind of fair and reasonable resolution of the problems. If the technical people do not understand what the real values at stake are, for example, they are not likely to define the technical issues in a way that is helpful for the discussion. And if the public and other nontechnical interests do not appreciate both the possibilities and the limitations of technical expertise, they will not be able to evaluate the alternatives intelligently.

One way to foster greater collaboration between engineers and other interested parties is to use a consensus model of decision making. In this model, all the relevant interests in effect sit around a table and hammer out a solution that everyone can live with. This is different from an adversarial process, where opposing sides make as strong a case as possible for their chosen alternatives and a supposedly neutral third party decides between them. In a consensus model, many conflicting interests are represented, but all those involved ultimately have the same goal: to find a solution that satisfies all interests. Thus there is a great deal of give and take, with the forming of alliances and the shifting of positions, in an attempt to build a consensus around a particular solution. All interests get a fair hearing, at least, and there is a better chance either to make the necessary compromises and tradeoffs or to find creative alternatives that better satisfy the competing interests. In this type of many-sided discussion, too, engineers and scientists can take part as independent parties not aligned with any one side yet very much in dialogue with everyone.

One example of such a broadly based consensus process was the Kemeny Commission that was convened to investigate the accident at Three Mile Island. The commission included a biochemist, a nuclear engineer, a physicist, a state governor, an ex-presidential aide, an industrialist, a trade unionist, a sociologist, a journalism professor, an environmentalist and a woman not employed outside the home, commonly called a housewife. According to Kemeny, "I think it would be wrong for the Commission to consist of a bunch of engineers. We are sort of a national jury on this issue and would you want the jury to consist of experts? I think it would be a mistake; you want the average American to believe what this Commission says." [35, p. 137]

The Commission did in fact produce a credible report. It was endorsed by groups as diverse as the Union of Concerned Scientists [29] and *Nuclear News*, a publication of the American Nuclear Society, which has always been most supportive of the nuclear industry [36]. Investigating an accident is somewhat different from deciding whether and how to use a certain technology, of course, but the idea of a "national jury," representing a broad range of interests, to assess the technical facts, weigh the value judgments, and recommend a course of action on the use of a particular technology is a promising one.

These are only rough suggestions. Much more investigation, discussion and development will be needed to build the necessary structures. But until the mechanisms and institutions are in place that give engineers the freedom and opportunities for collaboration that they need in order to respond to social needs, the public will be without an important source of protection from the risks of technology, and engineers themselves will not be able to fulfill some of the most important duties of their profession.

REFERENCES

1. Alger, P., N. A. Christensen, and S. Olmsted, *Ethical Problems in Engineering*, New York: John Wiley and Sons, 1965.

2. Fruchtbaum, H., "Engineers and the commonwealth: notes toward a reformation," *Ethical Problems in Engineering*, A. Flores, ed. Troy, N.Y.: Center for the Study of the Human Dimensions of Science and Technology, 1980, p. 253–261.

3. Keating, W., "Politics, energy and the environment: the role of technology assessment," *American Behavioral Scientists*, vol. 19, no. 1, Sept./Oct. 1975, pp. 39–42.

4. Simon, J. G., C. W. Powers, and J. P. Gunneman, *The Ethical Investor: Universities and Corporate Responsibility*, New Haven: Yale University Press, 1972.

5. McMillan, G., "Neighborhood raises a cry and a rape is prevented," *The Boston Globe*, vol. 227, no. 14, Apr. 24, 1985, p. 21.

6. Adams, J. L., *On Being Human Religiously: Selected Essays in Religion and Society*, Max Stackhouse, ed. Boston: Beacon Press, 1976, pp. 57–88.

7. Berger, P. L. and R. J. Neuhaus, *To Empower People: the Role of Mediating Structures in Public Policy*. Washington, D.C.: American Enterprise Institute, 1977.

8. Lodge, G. C., *The New American Ideology*. New York: Alfred A. Knopf, 1975.

9. Jordan, W., "Nuclear energy benefits versus risks," *Physics Today*, May 1970, p. 33.

10. Union of Concerned Scientists, *The Nuclear Fuel Cycle: A Survey of the Public Health Environmental, and National Security Effects of Nuclear Power*. Cambridge, MA: MIT Press, 1975.

11. Kendall, H. W., *The Risks of Nuclear Power Reactors: A Review of the NRC Reactor Safety Study WASH-1400*. Cambridge, MA: Union of Concerned Scientists, 1977.

12. Walker, C. A., L. C. Gould and E. J. Woodhouse, eds., *Too Hot to Handle: Social and Policy Issues in the Management of Radioactive Wastes*. New Haven: Yale University Press, 1983.

13. Hertsgaard, M., *Nuclear, Inc.: The Men and Money Behind Nuclear Energy*. New York: Pantheon Books, 1983.

14. Rolph, E., *Nuclear Power and the Public Safety*. Lexington, MA: D. C. Heath, 1979.

15. Ebbin, S. and R. Kasper, *Citizen Groups and the Nuclear Power Controversy: Uses of Scientific and Technological Information*. Cambridge, MA: MIT Press, 1974.

16. Phung, D. L., "Technical note: LWR safety after TMI," *Nuclear Safety*, vol. 25, no. 3, May/June, 1984, pp. 317–323.

17. Del Sesto, S. L., *Science, Politics and Controversy: Civilian Nuclear Power in the United States, 1946–1974*, Boulder, CO: Westview Press, 1979.

18. Falk, J., *Global Fission: The battle over Nuclear Power*. London: Oxford University Press, 1982.

19. Weatherwax, R. K., "Virtues and limitations of reactor safety," *Bulletin of the Atomic Scientists*, vol. 31, Sept. 1975, pp. 29–32.

20. Rasmussen, N., "The safety study and its feedback," *Bulletin of the Atomic Scientists*, vol. 31, Sept. 1975, pp. 25–28.

21. Von Hippel, F., "A perspective on the debate," *Bulletin of the Atomic Scientists*, vol. 31, Sept. 1975, pp. 37–41.

22. Sugarman, R., "Nuclear power and the public risk," *Spectrum*, vol. 16, no. 11, Nov. 1979, p. 60.

23. Rowe, W., "Risk analyst sees need of vote of confidence on nuclear power," *Spectrum*, vol. 16, no. 11, Nov. 1979, p. 60.

24. MacIntyre, A., "Utilitarianism and cost/benefit analysis," in Donald Scherer and Thomas Attig, eds., *Ethics and the Environment*. Englewood Cliffs, NJ: Prentice-Hall, 1983, p. 139–152.

25. Shrader-Frechette, K. S., "The conceptual risks of risk assessment," *IEEE Technology and Society Magazine*, vol. 5, no. 2, June, 1986, pp. 4–11.

26. Faulkner, P., "Exposing risks of nuclear disaster," in *Whistle Blowing: Loyalty and Dissent in the Corporation*, Alan F. Westin, Ed., New York: McGraw-Hill, 1981, pp. 39–54.

27. Unger, S., "How to be ethical and survive," *Spectrum*, vol. 16, no. 12, Dec. 1979, pp. 56f.

28. Ford, D. F., H. W. Kendall, and L. Stye, *Brown's Ferry: The Regulatory Failure.* Cambridge, MA: Union of Concerned Scientists, 1976.

29. "15 years of UCS," *Nucleus* (a quarterly report of the UCS), vol. 6, no. 1, Spring, 1984.

30. Nelkin, D., ed., *Controversy: Politics of Technical Decision.* Beverly Hills, CA: Sage Publications, 1979.

31. Chalk, R., M. Frankel and S. Chafer, *Professional Ethics Activities in the Scientific and Engineering Societies.* American Association for the Advancement of Science, Washington, D.C., 1980.

32. Baum, R., *Ethics and Engineering Curricula.* Hastings-on-Hudson, NY: The Hastings Center, 1980.

33. "Nuclear laboratory accreditation: IEEE presses NRC for action," in *The Institute*, vol. 7, no. 1, Jan. 1983, p. 1.

34. Unger, S. "Engineering societies and the responsible engineer," in *The Social Responsibilities of Engineers Annals of the New York Academy of Sciences*, vol. 196, no. 10, Harold Fruchtbaum, ed., 1973, p. 435.

35. Nelkin, D., "Some social and political dimensions of nuclear power: examples from Three Mile Island," *American Political Science Review*, vol. 75, no. 1, March 1981, p. 132.

36. Payne, J., "Kemeny commission: a bright amber light," *Nuclear News*, vol. 22, no. 15, Dec. 1979, p. 25.

15 Ethical Responsibilities of Engineers in Large Organizations: The Pinto Case

Richard T. De George

The myth that ethics has no place in engineering has been attacked, and at least in some corners of the engineering profession has been put to rest.[1] Another myth, however, is emerging to take its place—the myth of the engineer as moral hero. A litany of engineering saints is slowly taking form. The saints of the field are whistle blowers, especially those who have sacrificed all for their moral convictions. The zeal of some preachers, however, has gone too far, piling moral responsibility upon moral responsibility on the shoulders of the engineer. This emphasis, I believe, is misplaced. Though engineers are members of a profession that holds public safety paramount,[2] we cannot reasonably expect engineers to be willing to sacrifice their jobs each day for principle and to have a whistle ever by their sides ready to blow if their firm strays from what they perceive to be the morally right course of action. If this is too much to ask, however, what then is the actual ethical responsibility of engineers in a large organization?

I shall approach this question through a discussion of what has become known as the Pinto case, i.e., the trial that took place in Winamac, Indiana, and that was decided by a jury on March 16, 1980.

In August 1978 near Goshen, Indiana, three girls died of burns in a 1973 Pinto that was rammed in traffic by a van. The rear-end collapsed "like an accordian,"[3] and the gas tank erupted in flames. It was not the first such accident with the Pinto. The Pinto was introduced in 1971 and its gas tank housing was not changed until the 1977 model. Between 1971 and 1978 about fifty suits were brought against Ford in connection with rear-end accidents in the Pinto.

What made the Winamac case different from the fifty others was the fact that the

From *Business and Professional Ethics Journal*, vol. 1, no. 1 (1981), pp. 1–14. Copyright © 1981 by Richard T. De George. Reprinted by permission of the author.

State prosecutor charged Ford with three (originally four, but one was dropped) counts of reckless homicide, a *criminal* offense, under a 1977 Indiana law that made it possible to bring such criminal charges against a corporation. The penalty, if found guilty, was a maximum fine of $10,000 for each count, for a total of $30,000. The case was closely watched, since it was the first time in recent history that a corporation was charged with this criminal offense. Ford spent almost a million dollars in its defense.

With the advantage of hindsight I believe the case raised the right issue at the wrong time.

The prosecution had to show that Ford was reckless in placing the gas tank where and how it did. In order to show this the prosecution had to prove that Ford consciously disregarded harm it might cause and the disregard, according to the statutory definition of "reckless," had to involve "substantial deviation from acceptable standards of conduct."[4]

The prosecution produced seven witnesses who testified that the Pinto was moving at speeds judged to be between 15 and 35 mph when it was hit. Harly Copp, once a high ranking Ford engineer, claimed that the Pinto did not have a balanced design and that for cost reasons the gas tank could withstand only a 20 mph impact without leaking and exploding. The prosecutor, Michael Cosentino, tried to introduce evidence that Ford knew the defects of the gas tank, that its executives knew that a $6.65 part would have made the car considerably safer, and that they decided against the change in order to increase their profits.

Federal safety standards for gas tanks were not introduced until 1977. Once introduced, the National Highway Traffic Safety Administration (NHTSA) claimed a safety defect existed in the gas tanks of Pintos produced from 1971 to 1976. It ordered that Ford recall 1.9 million Pintos. Ford contested the order. Then, without ever admitting that the fuel tank was unsafe, it "voluntarily" ordered a recall. It claimed the recall was not for safety but for "reputational" reasons.[5] Agreeing to a recall in June, its first proposed modifications failed the safety standards tests, and it added a second protective shield to meet safety standards. It did not send out recall notices until August 22. The accident in question took place on August 10. The prosecutor claimed that Ford knew its fuel tank was dangerous as early as 1971 and that it did not make any changes until the 1977 model. It also knew in June of 1978 that its fuel tank did not meet federal safety standards; yet it did nothing to warn owners of this fact. Hence, the prosecution contended, Ford was guilty of reckless homicide.

The defense was led by James F. Neal who had achieved national prominence in the Watergate hearings. He produced testimony from two witnesses who were crucial to the case. They were hospital attendants who had spoken with the driver of the Pinto at the hospital before she died. They claimed she had stated that she had just had her car filled with gas. She had been in a hurry and had left the gas station without replacing the cap on her gas tank. It fell off the top of her car as she drove down the highway. She noticed this and stopped to turn around to pick it up. While stopped, her car was hit by the van. The testimony indicated that the car was stopped. If the car was hit by a van going 50 mph, then the rupture of the gas tank was to be expected. If the cap was off the fuel tank, leakage would be more than otherwise. No small vehicle was made to withstand such impact. Hence, Ford claimed, there was no recklessness involved. Neal went on to produce films of tests that indicated that the amount of damage the Pinto suffered meant that the impact must have been caused by the van's going at least 50 mph. He further argued that the Pinto gas tank was at least as safe as the gas tanks on the 1973 American Motors Gremlin, the Chevrolet Vega, the Dodge Colt, and the Toyota Corolla, all of which suffered comparable damage when hit from the rear at 50 mph. Since no federal safety standards were in effect in 1973, Ford was not reckless if its safety standards were comparable to those of similar cars made by competitors; that standard represented the state of the art at that time, and it would be inappropriate to apply 1977 standards to a 1973 car.[6]

The jury deliberated for four days and finally came up with a verdict of not guilty. When the verdict was announced at a meeting of the Ford Board of Directors then taking place, the members broke out in a cheer.[7]

These are the facts of the case. I do not wish to second-guess the jury. Based on my reading of the case, I think they arrived at a proper decision, given the evidence. Nor do I wish to comment adversely on the judge's ruling that prevented the prosecution from introducing about 40% of his case because the evidence referred to 1971 and 1972 models of the Pinto and not the 1973 model.[8]

The issue of Ford's being guilty of acting recklessly can, I think, be made plausible, as I shall indicate shortly. But the successful strategy argued by the defense in this case hinged on the Pinto in question being hit by van at 50 mph. At that speed, the defense successfully argued, the gas tank of any subcompact would rupture. Hence that accident did not show that the Pinto was less safe than other subcompacts or that Ford acted recklessly. To show that would require an accident that took place at no more than 20 mph.

The contents of the Ford documents that Prosecutor Cosentino was not allowed to present in court were published in the *Chicago Tribune* on October 13, 1979. If they are accurate, they tend to show grounds for the charge of recklessness.

Ford had produced a safe gas tank mounted over the rear axle in its 1969 Capri in Europe. It tested that tank in the Capri. In its over-the-axle position, it withstood impacts of up to 30 mph. Mounted behind the axle, it was punctured by projecting bolts when hit from the rear at 20 mph. A $6.65 part would help make the tank safer. In its 1971 Pinto, Ford chose to place the gas tank behind the rear axle without the extra part. A Ford memo indicates that in this position the Pinto has more trunk space, and that production costs would be less than in the over-the-axle position. These considerations won out.[9]

The Pinto was first tested it seems in 1971, after the 1971 model was produced, for rear-end crash tolerance. It was found that the tank ruptured when hit from the rear at 20 mph. This should have been no surprise, since the Capri tank in that position had ruptured at 20 mph. A memo recommends that rather than making any changes Ford should wait until 1976 when the government was expected to introduce fuel tank standards. By delaying making any change, Ford could save $20.9 million, since the change would average about $10 per car.[10]

In the Winamac case Ford claimed correctly that there were no federal safety standards in 1973. But it defended itself against recklessness by claiming its car was comparable to other subcompacts at that time. All the defense showed, however, was that all the subcompacts were unsafe when hit at 50 mph. Since the other subcompacts were not forced to recall their cars in 1978, there is *prima facie* evidence that Ford's Pinto gas tank mounting was substandard. The Ford documents tend to show Ford knew the danger it was inflicting on Ford owners; yet it did nothing, for profit reasons. How short-sighted those reasons were is demonstrated by the fact that the Pinto thus far in litigation and recalls alone has cost Ford $50 million. Some forty suits are still to be settled. And these figures do not take into account the loss of sales due to bad publicity.

Given these facts, what are we to say about the Ford engineers? Where were they when all this was going on, and what is their responsibility for the Pinto? The answer, I suggest, is that they were where they were supposed to be, doing what they were supposed to be doing. They were performing tests, designing the Pinto, making reports. But do they have no moral responsibility for the products they design? What after all is the moral responsibility of engineers in a large corporation? By way of reply, let me emphasize that no engineer can morally do what is immoral. If commanded to do what he should not morally do, he must resist and refuse. But in the Ford Pinto situation no engineer was told to produce a gas tank that would explode and kill people. The engineers were not instructed to make an unsafe car. They were morally responsible for knowing the state of the art, including that connected with placing and mounting gas tanks. We can assume that the Ford engineers were cognizant of the state of the art in producing the model they did. When tests were made in 1970 and 1971, and a memo was written stating that a $6.65 modification could make the gas tank safer,[11] that was an engineering assessment. Whichever engineer proposed the modification and initiated the memo acted ethically in doing so. The next step, the administrative decision not to make the modification, was, with hindsight, a poor one in almost every way. It ended up costing Ford a great deal more not to put in the part than it would have cost to put it in. Ford still claims today that its gas tank was as safe as the accepted standards of the industry at that time.[12] It must say so, otherwise the suits pending against it will skyrocket. That it was not as safe seems borne out by the fact that only the Pinto of all the subcompacts failed to pass the 30 mph rear impact NHTSA test.

But the question of wrongdoing or of malicious intent or of recklessness is not so easily solved. Suppose the ordinary person were told when buying a Pinto that if he paid an extra $6.65 he could increase the safety of the vehicle so that it would withstand a 30 mph rear-end impact rather than a 20 mph impact, and that the odds of suffering a rear-end impact of between 20 and 30 mph was 1 in 250,000. Would we call him or her reckless if he or she declined to pay the extra $6.65? I am not sure how to answer that question. Was it reckless of Ford to wish to save the $6.65 per car and increase the risk for the consumer? Here I am inclined to be clearer in my own mind. If I choose to take a risk to save $6.65, it is my risk and my $6.65. But if Ford saves the $6.65 and I take the risk, then I clearly lose. Does Ford have the right to do that without informing me, if the going standard of safety of subcompacts is safety in a rear-end collision up to 30 mph? I think not. I admit, however, that the case is not clear-cut, even if we add that during 1976 and 1977 Pintos suffered 13 fiery fatal rear-end collisions, more than double that of other U.S. comparable cars. The VW Rabbit and Toyota Corolla suffered none.[13]

Yet, if we are to morally fault anyone for the decision not to add the part, we would censure not the Ford engineers but the Ford executives, because it was not an engineering but an executive decision.

My reason for taking this view is that an engineer cannot be expected and cannot have the responsibility to second-guess managerial decisions. He is responsible for bringing the facts to the attention of those who need them to make decisions. But the imput of engineers is only one of many factors that go to make up managerial decisions. During the trial, the defense called as a witness Francis Olsen, the assistant chief engineer in charge of design at Ford, who testified that he bought a 1973 Pinto for his eighteen-year-old daughter, kept it a year, and then traded it in for a 1974 Pinto which he kept two years.[14] His testimony and his actions were presented as an indication that the Ford engineers had confidence in the Pinto's safety. At least this one had enough confidence in it to give it to his daughter. Some engineers at Ford may have felt that the car could have been safer. but this is true of almost every automobile. Engineers in large firms have an ethical responsibility to do their jobs as best they can, to report their observations about safety and improvement of safety to management. But they do not have the obligation to insist that their perceptions or their standards be accepted. They are not paid to do that, they are not expected to do that, and they have no moral or ethical obligation to do that.

In addition to doing their jobs, engineers can plausibly be said to have an obligation of loyalty to their employers, and firms have a right to a certain amount of confidentiality concerning their internal operations. At the same time engineers are required by their professional ethical codes to hold the safety of the public paramount. Where these obligations conflict, the need for and justification of whistle blowing arises.[15] If we admit the obligations on both sides, I would suggest as a rule of thumb that engineers and other workers in a large corporation are morally *permitted* to go public with information about the safety of a product if the following conditions are met:

1. if the harm that will be done by the product to the public is serious and considerable;
2. if they make their concerns known to their superiors; and
3. if, getting no satisfaction from their immediate superiors, they exhaust the channels available within the corporation, including going to the board of directors.

If they still get no action, I believe they are morally *permitted* to make public their views; but they are not morally *obliged* to do so. Harly Copp, a former Ford executive and engineer, in fact did criticize the Pinto from the start and testified for the prosecution against Ford at the Winamac trial.[16] He left the company and voiced his criticism. The criticism was taken up by Ralph Nader and others. In the long run it led to the Winamac trial and probably helped in a number of other suits filed against Ford.

Though I admire Mr. Copp for his actions, assuming they were done from moral motives, I do not think such action was morally required, nor do I think the other engineers at Ford were morally deficient in not doing likewise.

For an engineer to have a moral *obligation* to bring his case for safety to the public, I think two other conditions have to be fulfilled, in addition to the three mentioned above.[17]

4. He must have documented evidence that would convince a reasonable, impartial observer that his view of the situation is correct and the company policy wrong.

Such evidence is obviously very difficult to obtain and produce. Such evidence, however, takes an engineer's concern out of the realm of the subjective and precludes that concern from being simply one person' opinion based on a limited point of view. Unless such evidence is available, there is little likelihood that the concerned engineer's view will win the day simply by public exposure. If the testimony of Francis Olsen is accurate, then even among the engineers at Ford there was disagreement about the safety of the Pinto.

5. There must be strong evidence that making the information public will in fact prevent the threatened serious harm.

This means both that before going public the engineer should know what source (government, newspaper, columnist, TV reporter) will make use of his evidence and how it will be handled. He should also have good reason to believe that it will result in the kind of change or result that he believes is morally appropriate. None of this was the case in the Pinto situation. After much public discussion, five model years, and failure to pass national safety standards tests, Ford plausibly defends its original claim that the gas tank was acceptably safe. If there is little likelihood of his success, there is no moral obligation for the engineer to go public. For the harm he or she personally incurs is not offset by the good such action achieves.[18]

My first substantive conclusion is that Ford engineers had no moral *obligation* to do more than they did in this case.

My second claim is that though engineers in large organizations should have a say in setting safety standards and producing cost-benefit analyses, they need not have the last word. My reasons are two. First, while the degree of risk, e.g., in a car, is an engineering problem, the acceptability of risk is not. Second, an engineering cost-benefit analysis does not include all the factors appropriate in making a policy decision, either on the corporate or the social level. Safety is one factor in an engineering design. Yet clearly it is only one factor. A Mercedes-Benz 280 is presumably safer than a Ford Pinto. But the difference in price is considerable. To make a Pinto as safe as a Mercedes it would probably have to cost a comparable amount. In making cars as in making many other objects some balance has to be reached between safety and cost. The final decision on where to draw the balance is not only an engineering decision. It is also a managerial decision, and probably even more appropriately a social decision.

The difficulty of setting standards raises two pertinent issues. The first concerns federal safety standards. The second concerns cost-benefit analyses. The state of the art of engineering technology determines a floor below which no manufacturer should ethically go. Whether the Pinto fell below that floor, we have already seen, is a controverted question. If the cost of achieving greater safety is considerable—and I do not think $6.65 is considerable—there is a built-in temptation for a producer to skimp more than he should and more than he might like. The best way to remove that temptation is for there to be a national set of standards. Engineers can determine what the state of the art is, what is possible, and what the cost of producing safety is. A panel of informed people, not necessarily engineers, should decide what is acceptable risk and hence what acceptable minimum standards are. Both the minimum standards and the standards attained by a given car should be a matter of record that goes with each car. A safer car may well cost more. But unless a customer knows how much safety he is buying for his money, he may not know which car he wants to buy. This information, I believe, is information a car buyer is entitled to have.

In 1978, after the publicity that Ford received with the Pinto and the controversy surrounding it, the sales of Pintos fell dramatically. This was an indication that consumers preferred a safer car for comparable money, and they went to the competition. The state of Oregon took all its Pintos out of its fleet and sold them off. To the surprise of one dealer involved in selling turned-in Pintos, they went for between $1000 and $1800.[19] The conclusion we correctly draw is that there was a market for a car with a dubious safety record even though the price was much lower than for safer cars and lower than Ford's manufacturing price.

The second issue is the way cost-benefit analyses are produced and used. I have already mentioned one cost-benefit analysis used by Ford, namely, the projection that by not adding a part and by placing the gas tank in the rear the company could save $20.9 million. The projection, I noted, was grossly mistaken for it did not consider litigation, recalls, and bad publicity which have already cost Ford over $50 million. A second type of cost-benefit analysis sometimes estimates the number and costs of suits that will have to be paid, adds to it fines, and deducts that total amount from the total saved by a particular practice. If the figure is positive, it is more profitable not to make a safety change than to make it.

A third type of cost-benefit analysis, which Ford and other auto companies produce, estimates the cost and benefits of specific changes in their automobiles. One study, for instance, deals with the cost-benefit analysis relating to fuel leakage associated with static rollover. The unit cost of the part is $11. If that is included in 12.5 million cars, the total cost is $137 million. That part will prevent 180 burn deaths, 180 serious burn injuries and 2100 burned vehicles. Assigning a cost of $200,000 per death, $67,000 per major injury, and $700 per vehicle, the benefit is $49.5 million. The cost-benefit ratio is slightly over 3-1.[20]

If this analysis is compared with a similar cost-benefit analysis for a rear-end collision, it is possible to see how much safety is achieved per dollar spent. This use is legitimate and helpful. But the procedure is open to very serious criticism if used not in a comparative but in an absolute manner.

The analysis ignored many factors, such as the human suffering of the victim and of his or her family. It equates human life to $200,000, which is based on average lost future wages. Any figure here is questionable, except for comparative purposes, in which case as long as the same figure is used it does not change the information as to relative benefit per dollar. The ratio, however, has no *absolute* meaning, and no decision can properly be based on the fact that the resulting ratio of cost to benefit in the above example is 3 to 1. Even more important, how can this figure or ratio be compared with the cost of styling? Should the $11 per unit to reduce death and injury from roll-over be weighed against a comparable $11 in rear-end collision or $11 in changed styling? Who decides how much more to put into safety and how much more to put into styling? What is the rationale for the decision?

In the past consumers have not been given an opportunity to vote on the matter. The automobile industry has decided what will sell and what will not, and has decided how much to put on safety. American car dealers have not typically put much emphasis on safety features in selling their cars. The assumption that American drivers are more interested in styling than safety is a decision that has been made for them, not by them. Engineers can and do play an important role in making cost-benefit analyses. They are better equipped than anyone else to figure risks and cost. But they are not better equipped to figure the acceptability of risk, or the amount that people should be willing to pay to eliminate such risk. Neither, however, are the managers of automobile corporations. The amount of acceptable risk is a public decision that can and should be made by representatives of the public or by the public itself.

Since cost-benefit analyses of the types I have mentioned are typical of those used in the auto industry, and since they are inadequate ways of judging the safety a car should have, given the state of the art, it is clear that the automobile companies should not have the last word or the exclusive word in how much safety to provide. There must be national standards set and enforced. The National Highway Traffic Administration was established in 1966 to set standards. Thus far only two major standards have been established and implemented: the 1972 side impact standard and the 1977 gasoline tank safety standard. Rather than dictate standards, however, in which process it is subject to lobbying, it can mandate minimum standards and also require auto manufacturers to inform the public about the safety quotient of each car, just as it now requires each car to specify the miles per gallon it is capable of achieving. Such an approach would put the onus for basic safety on the manufacturers, but it would also make additional safety a feature of consumer interest and competition.

Engineers in large corporations have an important role to play. That role, however, is not usually to set policy or to decide on the acceptability of risk. Their knowledge and expertise are important both to the companies for which they work and to the public. But they are not morally responsible for policies and decisions beyond their competence and control. Does this view, however, let engineers off the moral hook too easily?

To return briefly to the Pinto story once more, Ford wanted a subcompact to fend off the competition of Japanese imports. The order came down to produce a car of 2,000 pounds or less that would cost $2000 or less in time for the 1971 model. This allowed only 25 months instead of the usual 43 months for design and production of a new car.[21] The engineers were squeezed from the start. Perhaps this is why they did not test the gas tank for rear-end collision impact until the car was produced.

Should the engineers have refused the order to produce the car in 25 months? Should they have resigned, or leaked the story to the newspapers? Should they have refused to speed up their usual routine? Should they have complained to their professional society that they were being asked to do the impossible—if it were to be done right? I am not in a position to say what they should have done. But with the advantage of hindsight, I suggest we should ask not only what they should have done. We should especially ask what changes can be made to prevent engineers from being squeezed in this way in the future.

Engineering ethics should not take as its goal the producing of moral heroes. Rather it should consider what forces operate to encourage engineers to act as they feel they should not; what structural or other features of a large corporation squeeze them until their consciences hurt? Those features should then be examined, evaluated, and changes proposed and made. Lobbying by engineering organizations would be appropriate, and legislation should be passed if necessary. In general I tend to favor voluntary means where possible. But where that is utopian, then legislation is a necessary alternative.

The need for whistle-blowing in a firm indicates that a change is necessary. How can we preclude the necessity for blowing the whistle?

The Winamac Pinto case suggests some external and internal modifications. It was the first case to be tried under a 1977 Indiana law making it possible to try corporations as well as individuals for the criminal offenses of reckless homicide. In bringing the charges against Ford, Prosecutor Michael Cosentino acted courageously, even if it turned out to have been a poor case for such a precedent-setting trial. But the law concerning reckless homicide, for instance, which was the charge in question, had not been rewritten with the corporation in mind. The penalty, since corporations cannot go to jail, was the maximum fine of $10,000 per count—hardly a significant amount when contrasted with the 1977 income of Ford International which was $11.1 billion in revenues and $750 million in profits. What Mr. Cosentino did *not* do was file charges against individuals in the Ford Company who were responsible for the decisions he claimed were reckless. Had highly placed officials been charged, the message would have gotten through to management across the country that individuals cannot hide behind corporate shields in their decisions if they are indeed reckless, put too low a price on life and human suffering, and sacrifice it too cheaply for profits.

A bill was recently proposed in Congress requiring managers to disclose the existence of life-threatening defects to the appropriate Federal agency.[22] Failure to do so and attempts to conceal defects could result in fines of $50,000 or imprisonment for a minimum of two years, or both. The fine in corporate terms is negligible. But imprisonment for members of management is not.

Some argue that increased litigation for product liability is the way to get results in safety. Heavy damages yield quicker changes than criminal proceedings. Ford agreed to the Pinto recall shortly after a California jury awarded damages of $127.8 million after a youth was burned over 95% of his body. Later the sum was reduced, on appeal, to $6.3 million.[23] But criminal proceedings make the litigation easier, which is why Ford spent $1,000,000 in its defense to avoid paying $30,000 in fines.[24] The possibility of going to jail for one's actions, however, should have a salutary effect. If someone, the president of a company in default of anyone else, were to be charged in criminal suit, presidents would soon know whom they can and should hold responsible below them. One of the difficulties in a large corporation is knowing who is responsible for particular decisions. If the president were held responsible, outside pressure would build to reorganize the corporation so that responsibility was assigned and assumed.

If a corporation wishes to be moral or if society or engineers wish to apply pressure for organizational changes such that the corporation acts morally and responds to the moral conscience of engineers and others within the organization, then changes must be made. Unless those at the top set a moral tone, unless they insist on moral conduct, unless they punish immoral conduct and reward moral conduct, the corporation will function without considering the morality of questions and of corporate actions. It may by accident rather than by intent avoid immoral actions, though in the long run this is unlikely.

Ford's management was interested only in meeting federal standards and having these as low as possible. Individual federal standards should be both developed and enforced. Federal fines for violations should not be token but comparable to damages paid in civil suits and should be paid to all those suffering damage from violations.[25]

Independent engineers or engineering societies—if the latter are not co-opted by auto manufacturers—can play a significant role in supplying information on the state of the art and the level of technical feasibility available. They can also develop the safety index I suggested earlier, which would represent the relative and comparative safety of an automobile. Competition has worked successfully in many areas. Why not in the area of safety? Engineers who work for auto manufacturers will then have to make and report the results of standard tests such as the ability to withstand rear-end impact. If such information is required data for a safety index to be affixed to the windshield of each new car, engineers will not be squeezed by management in the area of safety.

The means by which engineers with ethical concerns can get a fair hearing without endangering their jobs or blowing the whistle must be made part of a corporation's organizational structure. An outside board member with primary responsibility for investigating and responding to such ethical concerns might be legally required. When this is joined with the legislation pending in Congress which I mentioned, the dynamics for ethics in the organization will be significantly improved. Another way of achieving a similar end is by providing an inspector general for all corporations with an annual net income of over $1 billion. An independent committee of an engineering association might be formed to investigate charges made by engineers concerning the safety of a product on which they are working;[26] a company that did not allow an appropriate investigation of employee charges would become subject to cover-up proceedings. Those in the engineering industry can suggest and work to implement other ideas. I have elsewhere outlined a set of ten such changes for the ethical corporation.[27]

In addition to asking how an engineer should respond to moral quandaries and dilemmas, and rather than asking how to educate or train engineers to be moral heroes, those in engineering ethics should ask how large organizations can be changed so that they do not squeeze engineers in moral dilemmas, place them in the position of facing moral quandaries, and make them feel that they must blow the whistle.

The time has come to go beyond sensitizing students to moral issues and solving and resolving the old, standard cases. The next and very important questions to be asked as we discuss each case is how organizational structures can be changed so that no engineer will ever again have to face *that* case.

Many of the issues of engineering ethics within a corporate setting concern the ethics of organizational structure, questions of public policy, and so questions that frequently are amenable to solution only on a scale larger than the individual—on the scale of organization and law. The ethical responsibilities of the engineer in a large organization have as much to do with the organization as with the engineer. They can be most fruitfully approached by considering from a moral point of view not only the individual engineer but the framework within which he or she works. We not only need moral people. Even more importantly we need moral structures and organizations. Only by paying more attention to these can we adequately resolve the questions of the ethical responsibility of engineers in large organizations.

NOTES

1. The body of literature on engineering ethics is now substantive and impressive. See *A Selected Annotated Bibliography of Professional Ethics and Social Responsibility in Engineering*, compiled by Robert F. Ladenson, James Choromokos, Ernest d'Anjou, Martin Pimsler, and Howard Rosen (Chicago: Center for the Study of Ethics in the Professions, Illinois Institute of Technology, 1980). A useful two-volume collection of readings and cases is also available: Robert J. Baum and Albert Flores, *Ethical Problems in Engineering*, 2nd edition (Troy, N.Y.: Rensselaer Polytechnic Institute, Center for the Study of the Human Dimensions of Science and Technology, 1980. See also Robert J. Baum's *Ethics and Engineering Curricula* (Hastings-on-Hudson, N.Y.: Hastings Center, 1980).

2. See, for example, the first canon of the 1974 Engineers Council for Professional Development Code, the first canon of the National Council of Engineering Examiners Code, and the draft (by A. Oldenquist and E. Slowter) of a "Code of Ethics for the Engineering Profession" (all reprinted in Baum and Flores, *Ethical Problems in Engineering*.

3. Details of the incident presented in this paper are based on testimony at the trial. Accounts of the trial as well as background reports were carried by both the *New York Times* and the *Chicago Tribune*.

4. *New York Times*, February 17, 1980, IV, p. 9.

5. *New York Times*, February 21, 1980, p. A6. *Fortune*, September 11, 1978, p. 42.

6. *New York Times*, March 14, 1980, p. 1.

7. *Time*, March 24, 1980, p. 24.

8. *New York Times*, January 16, 1980, p. 16; February 7, 1980, p. 16.

9. *Chicago Tribune*, October 13, 1979, p. 1, and Section 2, p. 12.

10. *Chicago Tribune*, October 13, 1979, p. 1; *New York Times*, October 14, 1979, p. 26.

11. *New York Times*, February 4, 1980, p. 12.

12. *New York Times*, June 10, 1978, p. 1; *Chicago Tribune*, October 13, 1979, p. 1, and Section 2, p. 12. The continuous claim has been that the Pinto poses "no serious hazards."

13. *New York Times*, October 26, 1978, p. 103.

14. *New York Times*, February 20, 1980, p. A16.

15. For a discussion of the conflict, see Sissela Bok, "Whistleblowing and Professional Responsibility," *New York University Educational Quarterly*, pp. 2–10. For detailed case studies see, Ralph Nader, Peter J. Petkas, and Kate Blackwell, *Whistle Blowing* (New York: Grossman Publishers, 1972); Charles Peters and Taylor Branch, *Blowing the Whistle: Dissent in the Public Interest* (New York: Praeger Publishers, 1972); and Robert M. Anderson, Robert Perrucci, Dan E. Schendel and Leon E. Trachtman, *Divided Loyalties: Whistle-Blowing at BART* (West Lafayette, Indiana: Purdue University, 1980).

16. *New York Times*, February 4, 1980, p. 12.

17. The position I present here is developed more fully in my book *Business Ethics* (New York: Macmillan, [1982]). It differs somewhat from the dominant view expressed in the existing literature in that I consider whistle-blowing an extreme measure that is morally obligatory only if the stringent conditions set forth are satisfied. Cf. Kenneth D. Walters, "Your Employees' Right to Blow the Whistle," *Harvard Business Review*, July-August, 1975.

18. On the dangers incurred by whistle-blowers, see Gene James, "Whistle-Blowing: Its Nature and Justification," *Philosophy in Context*, 10 (1980), pp. 99–117, which examines the legal context of whistle-blowing; Peter Raven-Hansen, "Dos and Don'ts for Whistleblowers: Planning for Trouble," *Technology Review*, May 1980, pp. 34–44, which suggests how to blow the whistle; Helen Dudar, "The Price of Blowing the Whistle," *The New York Times Magazine*, 30 October, 1977, which examines the results for whistle-blowers; David W. Ewing, "Canning Directions," *Harpers*, August, 1979, pp. 17–22, which indicates "how the government rids itself of troublemakers" and how legislation protecting whistle-blowers can be circumvented; and Report by the U.S. General Accounting Office, "The Office of the Special Counsel Can Improve Its Management of Whistleblower Cases," December 30, 1980 (FPCD-81-10).

19. *New York Times*, April 21, 1978, IV, p. 1, 18.

20. See Mark Dowie, "Pinto Madness," *Mother Jones*, September/October, 1977, pp. 24–28.

21. *Chicago Tribune*, October 13, 1979, Section 2, p. 12.

22. *New York Times*, March 16, 1980, IV, p. 20.

23. *New York Times*, February 8, 1978, p. 8.

24. *New York Times*, February 17, 1980, IV, p. 9; January 6, 1980, p. 24; *Time*, March 24, 1980, p. 24.

25. *The Wall Street Journal*, August 7, 1980, p. 7, reported that the Ford Motor Company "agreed to pay a total of $22,500 to the families of three Indiana teen-age girls killed in the crash of a Ford Pinto nearly two years ago. . . . A Ford spokesman said the settlement was made without any admission of liability. He speculated that the relatively small settlement may have been influenced by certain Indiana laws which severely restrict the amount of damages victims or their families can recover in civil cases alleging wrongful death."

26. A number of engineers have been arguing for a more active role by engineering societies in backing up individual engineers in their attempts to act responsibly. See Edwin Layton, *Revolt of the Engineers* (Cleveland: Case Western Reserve, 1971); Stephen H. Unger, "Engineering Societies and the Responsible Engineer," *Annals of the New York Academy of Sciences*, 196 (1973), pp. 433–37 (reprinted in Baum and Flores, *Ethical Problems in Engineering*, pp. 56–59); and Robert Perrucci and Joel Gerstl, *Profession Without Community: Engineers in American Society* (New York: Random House, 1969).

27. Richard T. De George, "Responding to the Mandate for Social Responsibility," *Guidelines for Business When Societal Demands Conflict* (Washington, D.C.: Council for Better Business Bureaus, 1978), pp. 60–80.

16 Moral Responsibility for Engineers

Kenneth D. Alpern

I

Technological knowledge gives us new and greater powers both to benefit and, as we have become increasingly aware, to harm ourselves. How are we to obtain the benefits and avoid the harm? One popular answer focuses on the individuals who design the products, conduct quality and safety tests, and directly oversee production. These individuals—practicing engineers, technicians, low-level managers[1]—it is claimed, have to be guardians of society. They are thought to stand under a special—if not exclusive—moral obligation to protect society from the harms that could result from technological development. They must be ready and willing to risk their jobs and make other personal sacrifices in order to protect and promote public welfare.

This conception of engineers' moral responsibility is common not only in the public mind but among engineers themselves—at least in their public pronouncements. (Virtually every one of the many codes of ethics proposed by engineers gives paramount place to serving the public good.)[2] But does this conception of the moral responsibility of practicing engineers survive criticism? Given the nature of engineering activity and the nature of the organizations in which it is normally carried out, aren't these demands excessive, misplaced, and unrealistic? Why should engineers have to bear a *special* burden for the benefit of society? Indeed, can't it be argued that the nature of the corporate organization,[3] with its specialization of labor and delegation of authority, insulates practicing engineers from moral responsibility? And, even if there is an ideal according to which engineers are guardians of society, isn't the suggested moral demand in fact unreasonable and impractical given the realities of corporate competition and job insecurity?

From *Business and Professional Ethics Journal*, vol. 2, no. 2 (1983), pp. 39–48. Copyright © 1983 by Kenneth D. Alpern. Reprinted by permission of the author.

In this paper I shall defend a strong conception of the moral responsibility of practicing engineers and the others I have mentioned who are active in the creation and production of technology. I will argue that though engineers are bound by no special moral obligations,[4] ordinary moral principles as they apply in the engineer's circumstances stipulate that they nonetheless be ready to make greater personal sacrifices than can normally be demanded of other individuals. Having made that argument I will defend it against common objections that seek to show that this demand is misplaced or unreasonable.

The "ordinary moral principles" stated in section II below are, I claim, quite general in scope, applying to anyone whose actions may contribute to harming others. However, to argue adequately for that claim would require a much longer paper. Instead, a few examples are provided as suggestive. The objections to the application of the principles, which I turn to in section III, are those most often heard in defense of or as excuses for questionable actions by engineers in corporations. These objections and the responses to them can, I think, easily be extended to cover the others mentioned above who are directly involved in developing and producing technological artifacts. I suspect, though, that further, often involved, arguments would be necessary to defend the principles in application to others in corporations (e.g., lawyers, accountants, janitors, secretaries), whose work is less directly related to technological production, and to professionals who are not in the corporation but hired by it for special purposes.[5]

Before turning to the arguments, I want to make perfectly clear just what sort of thesis I am arguing for. My thesis is that engineers have a strong moral obligation, where strength of obligation is to be understood in terms of the degree of personal sacrifice that can be demanded. I will say nothing, however, about how the public welfare is to be determined and little about the sorts of circumstances in which moral responsibility is to be exercised. These are quite different tasks from the one I have set and they require their own careful treatment.[6] My main aim is just to *establish* that engineers must meet a high standard of moral performance. Detailed argument on the proper exercise of their moral responsibility awaits another occasion.

II

I begin from the assumption that, other things being equal, it is morally wrong to harm others. This principle is a feature of popular morality (e.g., it is a sentiment behind the Golden Rule) and of virtually all types of ethical theory—utilitarian, intuitionistic, contractarian, axiological, etc.—and I take it that no argument for it is necessary here.[7] Somewhat more carefully stated, the principle—which I will call the Principle of Care—is this:

> Other things being equal, one should exercise due care to avoid contributing to significantly harming others.

This principle has, of course, only *prima facie* force and is acceptable only with certain qualifications that would allow for legitimate competition, the voluntary assumption of risks, etc.

The "due care" clause of the principle designates such things as apprising oneself of the harm that may result from one's actions, taking precautions to avoid such harm, and being ready and willing to make sacrifices in order to reduce the likelihood of harm. One may think in terms of the responsibilities assumed in driving a car: one must recognize the dangers, attend to the driving, be skillful in controlling the car, and be willing to risk one's property and, to some extent, person in order to avoid injury to others.

The Principle of Care is stated in terms of *contributing* to harm rather than in terms of *causing* harm because, as I see it, we have a basic obligation to avoid playing *any part* in the production of harm: both to avoid playing a direct causal role and to avoid creating conditions from which harm can reasonably be expected to arise.[8] Either sort of failure can result in culpability.[9] Of particular importance in the present context is that moral obligation does not hold only of those who "make the decisions." More on this point later.

As the Principle of Care stands, it is vague. What counts as due care? When is harm significant? What are the relevant types of contribution to harm? A bit of the vagueness of the principle can be removed by noting that the degree of care due is a function of the magnitude of the harm threatened and of the centrality of one's role in the production of that harm. For example, the driver of a gasoline truck must be more attentive and have greater skill than an ordinary motorist. This is true for the simple reason that the truck driver is in a position to create greater harm than is the ordinary motorist. Similarly, journalists must exercise special care in their behavior because of the critical role they may play in the formation of the beliefs and attitudes of the public. The general rule here, a corollary to the Principle of Care, may be called the Corollary of Proportionate Care:

> When one is in a position to contribute to greater harm or when one is in a position to play a more critical part in producing harm than is another person, one must exercise greater care to avoid so doing.

The consequences of the principle of Care and the Corollary of Proportionate Care are, I think, easy to draw. Practicing engineers exercise considerable control over technological developments. Though they may not be the ones who decide which projects shall be worked on, they do design, test for quality and safety of, employ, and maintain technology. Their actions (or refusal to act) can greatly affect public welfare. And, given the nature of much technology, their work affects the public welfare, for better or worse, to a greater extent than do the activities of most other citizens. Managers and higher-level executives, of course, likewise affect the public welfare (through directing rather than creating and testing), and so they are similarly subject to this higher standard. Thus, by the Corollary of Proportionate Care, practicing engineers can be held to a higher standard of care; that is, it can be demanded that they be willing to make greater sacrifices than others for the sake of public welfare.

This higher standard against which engineers are to be judged does not require supererogation of them; it is merely the consequence of the *ordinary* moral requirements of care and proportionate care as they apply to the circumstances of engineers. However, since significant disincentives and obstacles will often stand in the way of meeting these ordinary moral requirements, engineers can expect to have to exhibit a certain degree of moral courage in the course of their everyday work. This does not mean that any and all demands on engineers to sacrifice their personal good for the public good are justified. But it does *raise* the standard for them.

These principles do not single out engineers. The same principles and conclusion hold for anyone in a position of power—power to harm—from truck driver to president. If one is not willing and able to make the sacrifices, then one should not seek or accept the position of power. To do so would be to act immorally.

III

Many objections can be raised against the application I have made of the Principle of Care and the Corollary of Proportionate Care to the circumstances of practicing engineers. For the rest of this paper I will consider several attempts to deflate engineers' responsibility or to shield them from it.

"I'd lose my job if I didn't." Criticized for acting immorally at his job—say, for falsifying a report on safety tests—an engineer might offer the excuse, "But I'd lose my job if I didn't. It's unfair to expect me to jeopardize my job." This response is just a version of the immemorial complaint that morality often conflicts with self-interest. The traditional reply is to point out that moral considerations are just the sort of things that override self-interest and that is that: it is time to exhibit moral courage.

Though I am arguing in this paper that engineers must be prepared to exhibit moral courage, I think the situation is a bit more complex than the traditional response allows. Two sorts of case must be distinguished. First is the case in which the engineer himself conceives the idea of falsifying the report in order to gain advantage for himself. It is to this sort of case that the traditional response most directly applies, and that, indeed, is all that needs to be said. The pursuit of personal gain (greed) is no excuse for wrongdoing.

But now consider the sort of case in which the initial impetus for falsifying the report comes from another person who has authority over the engineer. Taking the crudest case (from which the main point emerges most clearly), we can imagine the engineer's supervisor to have threatened to fire him if he doesn't sign the report. It is still wrong, and a breach of moral integrity, for the engineer to sign the false report, but, in the circumstances, he deserves sympathy, for he is in one sense a *victim* faced with having to make a sacrifice because of *another* person's immorality.

Now the question is, Should the engineer receive more than sympathy? Should he receive positive support of some kind from society? Why, the engineer may ask, must he alone and unsupported have to bear the burden of vigilance and sacrifice for society's sake? One answer is that he has entered and continues his employment voluntarily, full well knowing that his chosen job has certain benefits and certain liabilities. One of the liabilities is that his moral integrity will likely be put to the test. Recognizing this, he is free to choose not to take that particular job or not to embark on that sort of career. But if he does choose that employment, then the responsibility to bear the burden is solely his.

This answer is, I think, basically sound, but qualifications are necessary. For one thing, society *needs* the moral vigilance of individual practicing engineers. Government regulation, for example, does not replace it: regulations cannot be sufficiently detailed, flexible, or up to date; regulators who enforce the rules cannot be present to evaluate each significant decision. (And besides, what would insure that the regulators would apply the regulations conscientiously?) So, society needs moral engineers. How are moral engineers to be secured? Higher salaries may attract some, but, by and large, if it's moral engineers that we want, then we will have to make it possible to practice engineering morally, and this means providing support for engineers when moral action is difficult.

There is a further argument not only that society should provide support out of considerations of prudence, but that, at least at the present time, society *owes* support to engineers. This conclusion follows from the fact that society is not neutral in the choice to become an engineer. Young people are encouraged, formally and informally, to pursue professional careers such as engineering. Having entered a university engineering program—usually without the knowledge or ability for much mature reflection—students are channeled into a rigorous engineering curriculum that usually offers them little idea of what to expect on the job while extolling the virtues of the profession. Society takes advantage of immature decisions, fosters only limited development of reflective abilities, and provides only selective knowledge of what work will be like. In such circumstances it is difficult for aspiring engineers to gain an adequate appreciation of the moral pressures that they will encounter, and so they do not have a proper opportunity to judge whether they are willing to take on the responsibility that goes with the job. Understanding one's moral predicament comes, if ever, further down the line when more substantial career and life commitments have been made and there is much more to lose in changing employers or careers. This is not a fair position for a person to be placed in and is, in fact, likely to be most trying for the morally conscientious engineer. In this situation, then, society not only ought to provide support out of considerations of prudence, but also is morally bound to provide at least some degree of assistance.

I do not, however, want to overestimate the degree to which engineering students are misled about the moral demands of the jobs they are training for. They have some responsibility to ascertain the facts for themselves. Enough stories of spectacular corruption and the tragedies of unforeseen consequences have been publicized to provide a general awareness of the potential for moral problems. However, I still find startling the credulity of many of my engineering students and attribute it, to a significant extent, to the limited and exploitive education they often receive.

There are a number of mechanisms of support for engineers which society may provide. These include effective government regulation, legal remedies, and the activities of professional organizations willing to take strong measures, such as censure, boycott, and strike. It is not my purpose, however, to discuss these mechanisms at this time.[10]

I have claimed that engineers should be held to higher standards of care than others and argued that they should receive some measure of support from society in trying to meet those standards. To this I add the observation that not much effective support is presently available and there is not soon likely to be much more. This justifies sympathy for engineers in their predicament. It may even on occasion provide an excuse for certain sorts of complicity in wrongdoing. But it does not license total acquiescence to immorality. Nor do these allowances nullify the general requirement of a higher standard of care for engineers.

"If I don't do it, someone else will." Next, a very brief comment on the defense, "If I don't do it, someone else will."[11] Obviously, the fact that someone else will perform an immoral action if one declines does not make the action right. The defense could be couched in other terms: "Why should *I* have to be the one to sacrifice when the bad consequences are inevitable anyhow?" One answer is, of course, that moral integrity requires it. Another reply is to challenge the inevitability of the worst consequences. Generally, one may comply grudgingly while doing the best one can to temper the bad consequences and to combat further activities of the same sort (rather than to promote immoral practices through cheerful complicity). When some improvement can be effected, grudging compliance may be the morally best path, but at other times disengagement may be the only morally acceptable course of action.

It is possible that one may be the victim of bad moral luck and may keep finding oneself in situations that demand sacrifice, but there are things that one can do to reduce the chances. Some of these will be mentioned in the course of my reply to the next defense.

"It's not my job." This defense attempts to undercut the applicability of the principles I have stated. The claim here is that the engineer just does not have the power that I assert he has. According to this defense, the structure of corporations (as well as governments and other large hierarchical organizations) is such that people other than the practicing engineer make the critical decisions. Upper-level managers and executives are the ones who determine what projects shall be worked on, how work shall proceed, and what shall be done with the result. The engineer does not have and should not have discretionary power.[12] For example, engineers design an automobile within general guidelines that have been specified *for* them. The design they produce will have virtues and defects. They are responsible for pointing out the defects to the best of their abilities, but it is the managers and executives who decide whether or not to use the design and market the product. These individuals have control of technology, not the engineers.

The proper response to all this is to point out that discretionary power is not the only form of control. The harm that results from a dangerous product comes about not only through the decision to employ the design, but through the formulation and submission of the design in the first place. Harm could not come about if the engineers had refused to submit the design when they had good reason to believe that it was dangerous.

But now one might reply to this by acknowledging that the engineer does have the *power* to forestall harm, but then claiming that it is not the engineer's *responsibility* to exercise this power. Indeed, it would be wrong for him to do so. A corporation is structured so that people perform various limited and specialized functions, thus taking advantage of special talents and defining (supposedly) clear lines of authority and responsibility. Engineers are trained, hired, and paid to do engineering work. Their responsibilities and prerogatives extend no further.

In response, I will allow that corporations can (morally) be structured in this way. But allowing this still does not relieve engineers either from moral responsibility for harm that may result from their work or from the moral necessity of their taking appropriate action on the basis of that responsibility. When one gets into a position in which one abdicates or delegates control over choice of work, how that work shall be done, what shall be done with it, and so on, it is morally incumbent on one to have good reason to believe that control will be exercised morally. When there is reason to believe that those who exercise the powers one has relinquished are not to be trusted to act morally, then one has a responsibility to press for recognition of moral values, to withhold one's contribution, or to sever one's relationship altogether, depending on the gravity of the case. Indeed, even where one's work does not directly contribute to harmful results, one may be subject to moral criticism for indirectly supporting an immoral organization.

There is an important implication of this argument for the criteria by which one should evaluate prospective employment. In considering employment one must weigh not only economic and career opportunities, but also the morality of the organization and the prospects for moral action within it. One must consider the morality of the structure and goals of the organization and of the particular individuals involved—colleagues, supervisors, managers, and executives. One must also reckon on changes that are likely to occur. Selecting a job merely on the basis of personal preferences for salary, location, potential for advancement, or challenge and interest of the work leaves one completely open to moral criticism. And this process of moral evaluation does not end at the point of employment. Reevaluation of the potential for moral action in one's work is a continuing responsibility.

"There's no alternative." Pointing out the responsibility of engineers to judge the morality of the organizations they enter leads to the final attempt I will consider to defend an engineer's morally questionable activities. The defense is this. What if there is reason to believe that virtually any employment will place one in a morally compromising position? Such a circumstance does not necessarily mean that all potential employers are evil. The situation may rather be the result of structural deficiencies in the corporate form of organization or of the pressures of competition on vulnerable people who have insufficient support. In such a situation, what is even the most moral and well-intentioned engineer to do? Having prepared in good faith for a career in engineering, is he now required by morality to abandon that career?

The answer, I think, is yes. Of course, it is a matter of degree. But in the extreme case the conclusion is clear: if one's only alternative for an engineering career is to design fire bombs for the destruction of London, then it's time to try to emigrate or to change career. The point is that the degree of one's commitment and the good faith with which one has dedicated one's talents do not change the morality of the case. One may, perhaps, blame others for misleading one about the moral situation, but this does not alter what is the moral course of action.

There is one other option. This is to accept employment, but to maintain a crusading attitude. This alternative can be morally acceptable if one can hope to have good effects while not contributing to greater evils.

The general conclusion I hope to have established, however, is that moral considerations must always be borne in mind. Engineers, managers, and the others within the corporate structure who develop and manage technology are never mere "animate machines" in the service of corporate ends.[13] Moral responsibility cannot be abdicated; corporate structure cannot shield one from responsibility as an autonomous moral agent.

NOTES

This is a revised version of a paper presented at the Second National Conference on Ethics in Engineering in Chicago, in March 1982. The Conference was made possible by an EVIST grant from the National Science Foundation and was directed by Vivian Weil, Center for the Study of Ethics in the Professions, Illinois Institute of Technology.

1. For simplicity, I will usually refer hereafter only to (practicing) engineers and will consider specific objections with them primarily in mind.

2. A sample of codes of ethics in engineering can be found in Albert Flores, ed., *Ethical Problems in Engineering*, vol. I, 2nd ed. (Troy, NY: Rensselaer Polytechnic Institute, Center for the Study of the Human Dimensions of Science and Technology, 1980), pp. 63–75.

3. Most engineers practicing in the United States work for private corporations. Similar arguments to the ones I give can be applied to the public sector. For a treatment of moral responsibility in government, see Dennis Thompson, "Moral Responsibility of Public Officials: The Problem of Many Hands," *American Political Science Review*, vol. 74 (1980), pp. 905–16.

4. In a sense that would constitute "strong role differentiation" as defined by Alan H. Goldman in *The Moral Foundations of Professional Ethics* (Totowa, NJ: Rowman and Littlefield, 1980), pp. 2–3.

5. Still further afield would be application of the principles to professionals (e.g., physicians, journalists) whose work is not in the development of technology.

6. Some of the main problems are raised crisply in Samuel Florman's *Existential Pleasures of Engineering* (New York: St. Martin's Press, 1976), chap. 3, especially pp. 21–22. I would not, however, endorse the solutions proposed there.

7. Readers unfamiliar with the philosophical literature may usefully consult *The Encyclopedia of Philosophy* (New York: Macmillan, 1967). See articles and bibliographies under such headings as "Golden Rule," "Problems of Ethics," "History of Ethics."

8. That other people's negligence or misconduct may be the critical factor through which harm results enormously complicates matters. I can offer only a brief comment. Take a case such as the illegal sale of hospital drugs by hospital personnel. Does this affect what a chemical engineer should do? To a certain extent the answer depends on the balance of good over evil that results from the engineer's work. True, other people are responsible for controlling illegal drug traffic, but, as I discuss below, morality requires that one consider and modify one's actions in light of the (fallible) workings of the *whole* system of which one is a part. In extreme cases, when great harm is likely to result, even though it be through other people's ignorance, negligence, or evil, one may have a moral responsibility not to continue. For example, I can see little moral justification for having *any* role in the rocketry work in Libya carried out by the German firm Otrag.

9. On culpability, see Kurt Baier, "Responsibility and Action," in *The Nature of Human Action*, ed. Myles Brand (Glenview, IL: Scott, Foresman, and Company, 1970), pp. 121–23.

10. A number of these mechanisms are discussed in Stephen H. Unger, *Controlling Technology: Ethics and the Responsible Engineer* (New York: Holt, Rinehart, and Winston, 1982), chap. 4, 5, and 6.

11. A number of perspectives on this defense in general are analyzed in the contributions of Jonathan Glover and M. Scott-Taggart to the symposium "It Makes No Difference Whether Or Not I Do It," *Proceedings of the Aristotelian Society*, suppl. vol. 49 (1975), pp. 171–209. See also section I of Michael Scriven, "Business Responsibilities in Product Design and Manufacture," in *Responsibilities in Product Design and Manufacture: Proceedings of the Second Panel Discussion of the Council of Better Business Bureaus* (Washington, DC: Council of Better Business Bureaus, 1978), pp. 92–103.

12. For a view of this sort, see Florman, especially chap. 3.

13. The "mechanical view" of corporate rationality is set out clearly in John Ladd, "Morality and the Ideal of Rationality in Formal Organizations," *Monist*, vol. 54 (1970), pp. 488–516. Ladd's article contains several useful references to the management literature on this topic.

17 Engineering as Social Experimentation

Mike W. Martin

Roland Schinzinger

As it departed on its maiden voyage in April 1912 the *Titanic* was proclaimed the greatest engineering achievement ever. Not merely was it the largest ship the world had seen, having a length of two and a half football fields, it was also the most glamorous of ocean liners, complete with a tropical vinegarden restaurant and the first seagoing masseuse. It was supposed to be the first fully safe ship. Since the worst collision envisaged was at the juncture of two of its sixteen watertight compartments, and since it could float with any four compartments flooded, the *Titanic* was confidently believed to be virtually unsinkable.

Buoyed by such confidence, the captain allowed the ship to sail full speed at night in an area of reported icebergs, one of which tore a large gap in its side, directly or indirectly[1] flooding five compartments. Time remained to evacuate the ship, but there were not enough lifeboats to accommodate all the passengers and crew. British regulations then in effect did not foresee vessels of this size. Accordingly only 825 places were required in lifeboats, sufficient for a mere one-quarter of the *Titanic*'s capacity of 3547 passengers and crew. No extra precautions had seemed necessary for a practically unsinkable ship. The result: 1522 dead (drowned or frozen) out of the 2227 on board for the *Titanic*'s first trip (Lord, 1976; Wade, 1980; Davie, 1986).

In his poem written shortly after the event, "The Convergence of the Twain," Thomas Hardy portrayed the meeting of the ship and iceberg as determined by unpredictable fate: "No mortal eye could see/The intimate welding of their later history." Yet greater imagination and prudence could have prevented the disaster.

Interestingly enough, novelists did not lack the imaginative foresight to describe scenarios that paralleled the later real events in shocking detail. In Morgan Robertson's

---

1898 novel *Futility*, a ship almost identical in size to the *Titanic* was wrecked by an iceberg on a cold April night. The ship in the book was named the *Titan*; it too had a less than sufficient number of lifeboats. Mayn Clew Garnett's story "The White Ghost of Disaster" was being readied for publication in *Popular Magazine* while the *Titanic* was on her maiden voyage. It is said that Garnett had dreamed the story while traveling on the *Titanic*'s sister ship, the *Olympic*. Again, circumstances, similar to those surrounding the sinking of the *Titanic*, as well as an insufficient number of life-boats to save all the passengers, were key elements in the narrative (Wade, 1980, 70–71).

The *Titanic* remains a haunting image of technological complacency. Perhaps all we can take for granted today is Murphy's law that if anything can go wrong, it will—sooner or later. All products of technology present some potential dangers, and thus engineering is an inherently risky activity. In order to underscore this fact and help in exploring its ethical implications, we suggest that engineering should be viewed as an experimental process. It is not, of course, an experiment conducted solely in a laboratory under controlled conditions. Rather, it is an experiment on a social scale involving human subjects.

ENGINEERING AS EXPERIMENTATION

Experimentation is commonly recognized to play an essential role in the design process. Preliminary tests or simulations are conducted from the time it is decided to convert a new engineering concept into its first rough design. Materials and processes are tried out, usually employing formal experimental techniques. Such tests serve as the basis for more detailed designs, which in turn are tested. At the production stage further tests are run, until a finished product evolves. The normal design process is thus iterative, carried out on trial designs with modifications being made on the basis of feedback information acquired from tests. Beyond those specific tests and experiments, however, each engineering project taken as a totality may itself be viewed as an experiment.

Similarities to Standard Experiments

Several features of virtually every kind of engineering practice combine to make it appropriate to view engineering projects as experiments. First, any project is carried out in partial ignorance. There are uncertainties in the abstract model used for the design calculations; there are uncertainties in the precise characteristics of the materials purchased; there are uncertainties about the nature of the stresses the finished product will encounter. Engineers do not have the luxury of waiting until all the relevant facts are in before commencing work. At some point theoretical exploration and laboratory testing must be bypassed for the sake of moving ahead on a project. Indeed, one talent crucial to an engineer's success lies precisely in the ability to accomplish tasks with only a partial knowledge of scientific laws about nature and society.

Second, the final outcomes of engineering projects, like those of experiments, are generally uncertain. Often in engineering it is not even known what the possible outcomes may be, and great risks may attend even seemingly benign projects. A reservoir may do damage to a region's social fabric or to its ecosystem. It may not even serve its intended purpose if the dam leaks or breaks. An aqueduct may bring about a population explosion in a region where it is the only source of water, creating dependency and vulnerability without adequate safeguards. An aircraft may become a status symbol that ultimately bankrupts its owners. A special-purpose fingerprint reader may find its main application in the identification and surveillance of dissidents by totalitarian regimes. A nuclear reactor, the scaled-up version of a successful smaller model, may exhibit unexpected problems that endanger the surrounding population, leading to its untimely shutdown at great cost to owner and consumers alike. A hair dryer may expose the unknowing or unwary user to lung damage from the asbestos insulation in its barrel.

Third, effective engineering relies upon knowledge gained about products both before and after they leave the factory—knowledge needed for improving current products and creating better ones. That is, ongoing success in engineering depends upon gaining new knowledge, just as does ongoing success in experimentation. Monitoring is thus as essential to engineering as it is to experimentation in general. *To monitor* is to make periodic observations and tests in order to check for both successful performance and unintended side effects. But since the ultimate test of a product's efficiency, safety, cost-effectiveness, environmental impact, and aesthetic value lies in how well that product functions within society, monitoring cannot be restricted to the development or testing phases of an engineering venture. It also extends to the stage of client use. Just as in experimentation, both the intermediate and final results of an engineering project deserve analysis if the correct lessons are to be learned from it.

Learning from the Past

It might be expected that engineers would learn not only from their own earlier design and operating results, but also from those of other engineers. Unfortunately that is frequently not the case. Lack of established channels of communication, misplaced pride in not asking for information, embarrassment at failure, and plain neglect often impede the flow of such information and lead to many repetitions of past mistakes. Here are a few examples:

1. The *Titanic* lacked a sufficient number of lifeboats decades after most of the passengers and crew on the steamship *Arctic* had perished because of the same problem (Wade, 1980, 417).
2. "Complete lack of protection against impact by shipping caused Sweden's worst ever bridge collapse on Friday as a result of which eight people were killed." Thus reported the *New Civil Engineer* on January 24, 1980. On May 15 of the same year it also reported the following: "Last Friday's disaster at Tampa Bay, Florida, was the largest and most tragic of a growing number of incidents of errant ships colliding

with bridges over navigable waterways." While collisions of ships with bridges do occur—other well-known cases being those of the Maracaibo Bridge (Venezuela, 1964) and the Tasman Bridge (Australia, 1975)—Tampa's Sunshine Skyline Bridge was not designed with horizontal impact forces in mind because the code did not require it. Floating concrete bumpers which can deflect ships have been proposed by Laura and Nava (1981).

3. In June 1966 a section of the Milford Haven bridge in Wales collapsed during construction. A bridge of similar design was being erected by the same bridge builder (Freeman Fox and Partners) in Melbourne, Australia, when it too partially collapsed, killing thirty-three people and injuring nineteen. This happened in October of the same year, shortly after chief construction engineer Jack Hindshaw (also a casualty) had assured worried workers that the bridge was safe (Yarrow Bridge, 415).

4. Valves are notorious for being among the least reliable components of hydraulic systems. It was a pressure relief valve, and lack of positive information regarding its open or shut state, which helped lead to the nuclear reactor accident at Three Mile Island on March 28, 1979. Similar malfunctions had occurred with identical values on nuclear reactors at other locations. The required reports had been filed with Babcock and Wilcox, the reactor's manufacturer, but no attention had been given to them (Sugarman, 1979, 72).

5. The Bureau of Reclamation, which built the ill-fated Teton Dam, allowed it to be filled rapidly, thus failing to provide sufficient time to monitor for the presence of leaks in a project constructed out of less than ideal soil. The Bureau did not heed the lesson of its Fontenelle Dam, where 10 years earlier massive leaks had also developed and caused a partial collapse (Shaw, 1977; Boffey, 1977).

These examples, and others to be given in later chapters, illustrate why it is not sufficient for engineers to rely on handbooks alone. Engineering, just like experimentation, demands practitioners who remain alert and well informed at every stage of a project's history.

Contrasts with Standard Experiments

To be sure, engineering differs in some respects from standard experimentation. Some of those very differences help to highlight the engineer's special responsibilities. And exploring the differences can also aid our thinking about the moral responsibilities of all those engaged in engineering.

Experimental Control. One great difference has to do with experimental control. In a standard experiment this involves the selection, at random, of members for two different groups. The members of one group receive the special, experimental treatment. Members of the other group, called the *control group*, do not receive that special treatment although they are subjected to the same environment as the first group in every other respect.

In engineering this is not the usual practice, unless the project is confined to laboratory experimentation, because the experimental subjects are humans out of the range of the experimenter's control. Indeed, clients and consumers exercise most of the control because it is they who choose the product or item they wish to use. This makes it impossible to obtain a random selection of participants from various groups. Nor can parallel control groups be established based on random sampling. Thus no careful study of the effects of changing variables on two or more comparison groups is possible, and one must simply work with the available historical and retrospective data about various groups that use the product.

This suggests that the view of engineering as a social experiment involves a somewhat extended usage of the concept of experimentation. Nevertheless, "engineering as social experimentation" should not be dismissed as a merely metaphorical notion. There are other fields where it is not uncommon to speak of experiments whose original purpose was not experimental in nature and that involve no control groups.

For example, social scientists monitor and collect data on differences and similarities between existing educational systems that were not initially set up as systematic experiments. In doing so they regard the current diversity of systems as constituting what has been called a "natural experiment" (as opposed to a deliberately initiated one) (Rivlin, 1970, 70). Similarly, we think that engineering can be appropriately viewed as just such a "natural experiment" using human subjects, despite the fact that most engineers do not currently consider it in that light.

Informed Consent.   Viewing engineering as an experiment on a societal scale places the focus where it should be: on the human beings affected by technology. For the experiment is performed on persons, not on inanimate objects. In this respect, albeit on a much larger scale, engineering closely parallels medical testing of new drugs and techniques on human subjects.

Society has recently come to recognize the primacy of the subject's safety and freedom of choice as to whether to participate in medical experiments. Even since the revelations of prison and concentration camp horrors in the name of medicine, an increasing number of moral and legal safeguards have arisen to ensure that subjects in experiments participate on the basis of informed consent.

But while current medical practice has increasingly tended to accept as fundamental the subject's moral and legal rights to give informed consent before participating in an experiment, contemporary engineering practice is only beginning to recognize those rights. We believe that the problem of informed consent, which is so vital to the concept of a properly conducted experiment involving human subjects, should be the keystone in the interaction between engineers and the public. We are talking about the *lay public.* When a manufacturer sells a new device to a knowledgeable firm which has its own engineering staff, there is usually an agreement regarding the shared risks and benefits of trying out the technological innovation.

Informed consent is understood as including two main elements: knowledge and voluntariness. First, subjects should be given not only the information they request, but all the information which is needed for making a reasonable decision. Second, subjects must enter into the experiment without being subjected to force, fraud, or deception. Respect for the fundamental rights of dissenting minorities and compensation for harmful effects are taken for granted here.

The mere purchase of a product does not constitute informed consent, any more than does the act of showing up on the occasion of a medical examination. The public and clients must be given information about the practical risks and benefits of the product in terms they can understand. Supplying complete information about the product is neither necessary nor in most cases possible. In both medicine and engineering there may be an enormous gap between the experimenter's and the subject's understanding of the complexities of an experiment. But while this gap most likely cannot be closed, it should be possible to convey all pertinent information needed for making a reasonable decision on whether to participate or not.

We do not propose a proliferation of lengthy environmental impact reports. We favor the kind of sound advice a responsible physician gives a patient when prescribing a course of drug treatment that has possible side effects. The physician must search beyond the typical sales brochures from drug manufacturers for adequate information; hospital management must allow the physician the freedom to undertake different treatments for different patients, as each case may constitute a different "experiment" involving different circumstances; finally, the patient must be readied to receive the information.

Likewise, an engineer cannot succeed in providing essential information about a project or product unless there is cooperation by management and a receptivity on the part of those who should have the information. Management is often understandably reluctant to provide more information than current laws require, fearing disclosure to potential competitors and exposure to potential lawsuits. Moreover, it is possible that, paralleling the experience in medicine, clients or the public may not be interested in all of the relevant information about an engineering project, at least not until a crisis looms. It is important nevertheless that all avenues for disseminating such information be kept open and ready.

We note that the matter of informed consent is surfacing indirectly in the continuing debate over acceptable forms of energy. Representatives of the nuclear industry can be heard expressing their impatience with critics who worry about reactor malfunction while engaging in statistically more hazardous activities such as driving automobiles and smoking cigarettes. But what is being overlooked by those representatives is the common enough human readiness to accept risks voluntarily undertaken (as in daring sports), even while objecting to involuntary risks resulting from activities in which the individual is neither a direct participant nor a decision maker. In other words, we all prefer to be the subjects of our own experiments rather than those of somebody else. When it comes to approving a nearby oil-drilling platform or a nuclear plant, affected parties expect their consent to be sought no less than it is when a doctor contemplates surgery.

Prior consultation of the kind suggested can be effective. When Northern States Power Company (Minnesota) was planning a new power plant, it got in touch with local citizens and environmental groups before it committed large sums of money to preliminary design studies. The company was able to present convincing evidence regarding the need for a new plant and then suggested several sites. Citizen groups responded with a site proposal of their own. The latter was found acceptable by the company. Thus informed consent was sought from and voluntarily given by those the project affected, and the acrimonious and protracted battle so common in other cases where a company has already invested heavily in decisions based on engineering studies alone was avoided (Borrelli, 36–39). Note that the utility company interacted with groups that could serve as proxy for various segments of the ratepaying public. Obviously it would have been difficult to involve the ratepayers individually.

We endorse a broad notion of informed consent, or what some would call *valid consent* (Culver and Gert), defined by the following conditions:

1.   The consent was given voluntarily.
2.   The consent was based on the information that a rational person would want, together with any other information requested, presented to them in understandable form.
3.   The consenter was competent (not too young or mentally ill, for instance) to process the information and make rational decisions.

We suggest two requirements for situations in which the subject cannot be readily identified as an individual:

4.   Information that a rational person would need, stated in understandable form, has been widely disseminated.
5.   The subject's consent was offered in proxy by a group that collectively represents many subjects of like interests, concerns, and exposure to risk.

Knowledge Gained

Scientific experiments are conducted to gain new knowledge, while "engineering projects are experiments that are not necessarily designed to produce very much knowledge," according to a valuable interpretation of our paradigm by Broome (1987). When we carry out an engineering activity as if it were an experiment, we are primarily preparing ourselves for unexpected outcomes. The best outcome in this sense is one which tells us nothing new but merely affirms that we are right about something. Unexpected outcomes send us on a search for new knowledge—possibly involving an experiment of the first (scientific) type. For the purposes of our model the distinction is not vital because we are concerned about the manner in which the experiment is conducted, such as that valid consent of human subjects is sought, safety measures are taken, and means exist for terminating the experiment at any time and providing all participants a safe exit. . . .

ENGINEERS AS RESPONSIBLE EXPERIMENTERS

What are the responsibilities of engineers to society? Viewing engineering as social experimentation does not by itself answer this question. For while engineers are the main technical enablers or facilitators, they are far from being the sole experimenters. Their responsibility is shared with management, the public, and others. Yet their expertise places them in a unique position to monitor projects, to identify risks, and to provide clients and the public with the information needed to make reasonable decisions. . . .

We want to know what is involved in displaying the virtue of being a responsible person while acting as an engineer. From the perspective of engineering as social experimentation, what are the general features of morally responsible engineers?

At least four elements are pertinent: a conscientious commitment to live by moral values, a comprehensive perspective, autonomy, and accountability (Haydon, 1978, 50–53). Or, stated in greater detail as applied to engineering projects conceived as social experiments:

1. A primary obligation to protect the safety of and respect the right of consent of human subjects
2. A constant awareness of the experimental nature of any project, imaginative forecasting of its possible side effects, and a reasonable effort to monitor them.
3. Autonomous, personal involvement in all steps of a project
4. Accepting accountability for the results of a project

It is implied in the foregoing that engineers should also display technical competence and other attributes of professionalism. Inclusion of these four requirements as part of engineering practice would then earmark a definite "style" of engineering. In elaborating upon this style, we will note some of the contemporary threats to it.

Conscientiousness

People act responsibly to the extent that they conscientiously commit themselves to live according to moral values. But moving beyond this truism leads immediately to controversy over the precise nature of those values. In Chap. 1 we adopted the minimal thesis that moral values transcend a consuming preoccupation with a narrowly conceived self-interest. Accordingly, individuals who think solely of their own good to the exclusion of the good of others are not moral agents. By *conscientious* moral commitment is meant a sensitivity to the full range of moral values and responsibilities that are relevant to a given situation, and the willingness to develop the skill and expend the effort needed to reach the best balance possible among those considerations.

The contemporary working conditions of engineers tend to narrow moral vision solely to the obligations that accompany employee status. As stated earlier, some 90 percent of engineers are salaried employees, most of whom work within large bureaucracies under great pressure to function smoothly within the organization. There are obvious benefits in terms of prudential self-interest and concern for one's family that make it easy to emphasize as primary the obligations to one's employer. Gradually the minimal negative duties, such as not falsifying data, not violating patent rights, and not breaching confidentiality, may come to be viewed as the full extent of moral aspiration.

Conceiving engineering as social experimentation restores the vision of engineers as guardians of the public interest, whose professional duty it is to guard the welfare and safety of those affected by engineering projects. And this helps to ensure that such safety and welfare will not be disregarded in the quest for new knowledge, the rush for profits, a narrow adherence to rules, or a concern over benefits for the many that ignores harm to the few.

The role of social guardian should not suggest that engineers force, paternalistically, their own views of the social good upon society. For, as with medical experimentation on humans, the social experimentation involved in engineering should be restricted by the participant's consent—voluntary and informed consent.

Relevant Information

Conscientiousness is blind without relevant factual information. Hence showing moral concern involves a commitment to obtain and properly assess all available information pertinent to meeting one's moral obligations. This means, as a first step, fully grasping the *context* of one's work which makes it *count* as an activity having a moral import.

For example, there is nothing wrong in itself with being concerned to design a good heat exchanger. But if I ignore the fact that the heat exchanger will be used as part of a still involved in the manufacture of a potent, illegal hallucinogen, I am showing a lack of moral concern. It is this requirement that one be aware of the wider implications of one's work which makes participation in, say, a design project for a superweapon morally problematic—and which makes it sometimes convenient for engineers self-deceivingly to ignore the wider context of their activities, a context that may rest uneasily with an active conscience.

Another way of blurring the context of one's work results from the ever increasing specialization and division of labor which makes it easy to think of someone else in the organization as responsible for what otherwise might be a bothersome personal problem. For example, a company may produce items with obsolescence built into them, or the items might promote unnecessary energy usage. It is easy to place the burden on the sales department: "Let *them* inform the customers—if the customers ask." It may be natural to thus rationalize one's neglect of safety or cost considerations, but it shows no moral concern.

These ways of losing perspective on the nature of one's work also hinder acquiring a full perspective along a second dimension of factual information: the *consequences* of what one does. And so while regarding engineering as social experimentation points out the importance of context, it also urges the engineer to view his or her specialized activities in a project as part of a larger whole having a social impact—an impact that may involve a variety of unintended effects. Accordingly, it emphasizes the need for wide training in disciplines related to engineering and its results, as well as the need for a constant effort to imaginatively foresee dangers.

It might be said that the goal is to practice what Chauncey Starr once called "defensive engineering." Or perhaps more fundamental is the concept of "preventive technology" as described by Ruth Davis, who could have addressed the following lines equally well to engineers as she did to scientists and physicians:

> The solution to the problem is not in successive cures to successive science-caused problems; it is in their prevention. Unfortunately, cures for scientific ills are generally more interesting to scientists than is the prevention of those ills. We have the unhappy history of the medical community to show us the difficulties associated with trying to establish preventive medicine as a specialty.
>
> Scientists probably had more fun developing scientific defenses against nuclear weapons (that is, cures) than they would have had practicing preventive nuclear science during the development of the atomic bomb. Computer scientists find it more attractive to develop technological safeguards, after the fact, to prevent invasions of privacy associated with computer data banks than to develop good information practices along with the computer systems.
>
> However, it now seems quite clear that public patience with the cure always following after the ill has worn thin. The public wants to see some preventive measures taken. Indeed, individuals have taken what can be called preventive technology into their own hands. We have seen the public in action in this way in its handling of the supersonic transport issue and its reaction toward siting of nuclear power plants. This is the reactive mode of practicing preventive technology, and it hinges on public recognition that technology is fallible (Davis, 1975, 213).

No amount of disciplined and imaginative foresight, however, can serve to anticipate all dangers. Because engineering projects are inherently experimental in nature, it is crucial for them to be monitored on an ongoing basis from the time they are put into effect. While individual practitioners cannot privately conduct full-blown environmental and social impact studies, they can choose to make the extra effort needed to keep in touch with the course of a project after it has officially left their hands. This is a mark of *personal* identification with one's work, a notion that leads to the next aspect of moral responsibility.

Moral Autonomy

People are morally autonomous when their moral conduct and principles of action are their *own*, in a special sense deriving from Kant. That, is, moral beliefs and attitudes must be held on the basis of critical reflection rather than merely through passive adoption of the particular conventions of one's society, church, or profession. This is often what is meant by "authenticity" in one's commitment to moral values.

Those beliefs and attitudes, moreover, must be integrated into the core of an individual's personality in a manner that leads to committed action. They cannot be agreed to abstractly and formally and adhered to merely verbally. Thus, just as one's principles are not passively imbibed from others when one is morally autonomous, so too one's actions are not treated as something alien and apart from oneself.

It is a comfortable illusion to think that in working for an employer, and thereby performing acts directly serving a company's interests, one is no longer morally and personally identified with one's actions. Selling one's labor and skills may make it seem that one has thereby disowned and forfeited power over one's actions (Lachs, 1978, 201–213).

Viewing engineering as social experimentation can help one overcome this tendency and can help restore a sense of autonomous participation in one's work. As an experimenter, an engineer is exercising the sophisticated training that forms the core of his or her identity as a professional. Moreover, viewing an engineering project as an experiment that can result in unknown consequences should help inspire a critical and questioning attitude about the adequacy of current economic and safety standards. This also can lead to a greater sense of personal involvement with one's work.

The attitude of management plays a decisive role in how much moral autonomy engineers feel they have. It would be in the long-term interest of a high-technology firm to grant its engineers a great deal of latitude in exercising their professional judgment on moral issues relevant to their jobs (and, indeed, on, technical issues as well). But the yardsticks by which a manager's performance is judged on a quarterly or yearly basis most often militate against this. This is particularly true in our age of conglomerates, when near-term profitability is more important than consistent quality and long-term retention of satisfied customers.

In government-sponsored projects it is frequently a deadline which becomes the ruling factor, along with fears of interagency or foreign competition. Tight schedules contributed to the loss of the U.S. space shuttle *Challenger*. . . .

Accordingly engineers are compelled to look to their professional societies and other outside organizations for moral support. Yet it is no exaggeration to claim that the blue-collar worker with union backing has greater leverage at present in exercising moral autonomy than do many employed professionals. A steel plant worker, for instance, who refused to dump oil into a river in an unauthorized manner was threatened with dismissal, but his union saw to it that the threat was never carried out (Nader, 1972, 189). Or take the case of the automobile plant inspector who repeatedly warned his supervisors about poorly welded panels which allowed carbon monoxide from the exhaust to leak into the cab. Receiving no satisfactory response from the company, he blew the whistle. The company wanted to fire him, but pressure from the union allowed him to keep his job. (The union, however, did not concern itself with the safety issue. It was probably as surprised as the company by the number of eventual fatalities traceable to the defect, the recall order those deaths necessitated, and the tremendous financial loss ultimately incurred by the company.) (Nader, 1972, 75–89)

Professional societies, originally organized as learned societies dedicated to the exchange of technical information, lack comparable power to protect their members, although most engineers have no other group to rely on for such protection. Only now is the need for moral and legal support of members in the exercise of their professional obligations being recognized by those societies. Unger (1987) describes how engineering societies can proceed, even in the face of difficulties such as litigation.

Accountability

Finally, responsible people accept moral responsibility for their actions. Too often "accountable" is understood in the overly narrow sense of being culpable and blameworthy for misdeeds. But the term more properly refers to the general disposition of being willing to submit one's actions to moral scrutiny and be open and responsive to the assessments of others. It involves a willingness to present morally cogent reasons for one's conduct when called upon to do so in appropriate circumstances.

Submission to an employer's authority, or any authority for that matter, creates in many people a narrowed sense of accountability for the consequences of their actions. This was documented by some famous experiments conducted by Stanley Milgram during the 1960s (Milgram, 1974). Subjects would come to a laboratory believing they were to participate in a memory and learning test. In one variation two other people were involved, the "experimenter" and the "learner." The experimenter was regarded by the subject as an authority figure, representing the scientific community. He or she would give the subject orders to administer electric shocks to the "learner" whenever the latter failed in the memory test. The subject was told the shocks were to be increased in magnitude with each memory failure. All this, however, was a deception—a "setup." There were no real shocks and the apparent "learner" and the "experimenter" were merely acting parts in a ruse designed to see how far the unknowing experimental subject was willing to go in following orders from an authority figure.

The results were astounding. When the subjects were placed in an adjoining room separated from the "learner" by a shaded glass window, over half were willing to follow orders to the full extent: giving the maximum electric jolt of 450 volts. This was in spite of seeing the "learner," who was strapped in a chair, writhing in (apparent) agony. The same results occurred when the subjects were allowed to hear the (apparently) pained screams and protests of the "learner," screams and protests which became intense from 130 volts on. There was a striking difference, however, when subjects were placed in the same room within touching distance of the "learner." Then the number of subjects willing to continue to the maximum shock dropped by one-half.

Milgram explained these results by citing a strong psychological tendency in people to be willing to abandon personal accountability when placed under authority. He saw his subjects ascribing all initiative, and thereby all accountability, to what they viewed as legitimate authority. And he noted that the closer the physical proximity, the more difficult it becomes to divest oneself of personal accountability.

The divorce between causal influence and moral accountability is common in business and the professions, and engineering is no exception. Such a psychological schism is encouraged by several prominent features of contemporary engineering practice.

First, large-scale engineering projects involve fragmentation of work. Each person makes only a small contribution to something much vaster. Moreover, the final product is often physically removed from one's immediate workplace, creating the kind of "distancing" that Milgram identified as encouraging a lessened sense of personal accountability.

Second, corresponding to the fragmentation of work is a vast diffusion of accountability within large institutions. The often massive bureaucracies within which most engineers work are designed to diffuse and delimit areas of personal accountability within hierarchies of authority.

Third, there is frequently pressure to move on to a new project before the current one has been operating long enough to be observed carefully. This promotes a sense of being accountable only for meeting schedules.

Fourth, the contagion of malpractice suits currently afflicting the medical profession is carrying over into engineering. With this comes a crippling preoccupation with legalities, a preoccupation which makes one wary of becoming morally involved in matters beyond one's strictly defined institutional role.

We do not mean to underestimate the very real difficulties these conditions pose for engineers who seek to act as morally accountable people on their jobs. Much less do we wish to say engineers are blameworthy for all the bad side effects of the projects they work on, even though they partially cause those effects simply by working on the projects. That would be to confuse accountability with blameworthiness, and also to confuse causal responsibility with moral responsibility. But we do claim that engineers who endorse the perspective of engineering as a social experiment will find it more difficult to divorce themselves psychologically from personal responsibility for their work. Such an attitude will deepen their awareness of how engineers daily cooperate in a risky enterprise in which they exercise their personal expertise toward goals they are especially qualified to attain, and for which they are also accountable.

NOTES

1. Some investigators believe the *Titanic* left England with a coal fire on board, that this made the captain rush the ship to New York, and that water entering the coal bunkers through the gash caused an explosion and thereby greater damage to the compartments.

REFERENCES

BOFFEY, PHILIP M. 1977. "Teton Dam Verdict: Foul-up by the Engineers," *Science*, vol. 195 (21 January):270–72.

BORRELLI, PETER, MAHLON EASTERLING, BURTON H. KLEIN, LESTER LEES, GUY PAUKER, and ROBERT POPPE. 1971. *People, Power, and Pollution: Environmental and Public Interest Aspects of Electronic Power Plant Siting.* Pasadena: Environmental Quality Lab, California Institute of Technology.

BROOME, TAFT H. 1987. "Engineering Responsibility for Hazardous Technologies," *Journal of Professional Issues in Engineering*, vol. 113, No. 2 (April):139–49.

CULVER, CHARLES M., and BERNARD GERT. 1982. "Valid Consent," in Charles M. Culver and Bernard Gert (eds.), *Conceptual and Ethical Problems in Medicine and Psychiatry.* New York: Oxford University Press.

DAVIE, MICHAEL. 1986. *The Titanic.* London: The Bodley Head.

DAVIS, RUTH M. 1975. "Preventative Technology: A Cure for Specific Ills," *Science*, vol. 188 (18 April). Quotation in text used with permission of author.

HAYDON, GRAHAM. 1978. "On Being Responsible," *The Philosophical Quarterly*, vol. 28:46–57.

LACHS, JOHN 1978. " 'I Only Work Here': Mediation and Irresponsibility," in Richard T. De George and Joseph. A. Pichler (eds.), *Ethics, Free Enterprise, and Public Policy*, pp. 201–13. New York: Oxford.

LORD, WALTER. 1976. *A Night to Remember*, illustrated edition. New York: Holt.

MILGRAM, STANELY. 1974. *Obedience to Authority.* New York: Harper and Row.

NADER, RALPH, PETER J. PETKAS, and KATE BLACKWELL. 1972. *Whistle Blowing*. New York: Grossman.

RIVLIN, ALICE M. 1971. *Systematic Thinking for Social Action*. Washington, D.C.: The Brookings Institution.

SHAW, GAYLORD. 1977. "Bureau of Reclamation Harshly Criticized in New Report on Teton Dam Collapse," *Los Angeles Times*, 4 June, Part I, p. 3.

SUGARMAN, ROBERT. 1979. "Nuclear Power and the Public Risk," *IEEE Spectrum*, vol. 16, no. 11 (November):59–79.

UNGER, STEPHEN H. 1987. "Would Helping Ethical Professionals Get Professional Societies Into Trouble?" *IEEE Technology and Society Magazine* (September):17–20.

WADE, WYNN C. 1980. *The Titanic: End of a Dream*. New York: Penguin.

"Yarrow Bridge." 1970. Editorial, *The Engineer* 210 (23 October):415.

18 The Social and Professional Responsibility of Engineers

Deborah G. Johnson

INTRODUCTION

One of the most difficult of the "ethical issues associated with scientific research for the military" has to do with a researcher's decision whether or not to become involved in such research at all, and, if so, whether to draw a line between research she is willing to do for the military and research she is not willing to do. My aim in this paper is not to decide these questions, but rather to argue for a framework for thinking about them, a framework which facilitates analysis and brings the important issues to the fore. The framework I propose places these matters in the context of broader questions about the social responsibilities of researchers.

The focus here will be on engineers, though most, if not all, of what is said applies to other researchers. The special emphasis on engineers is useful for a number of reasons. First, social responsibilities are often understood to arise from membership in a profession, because of the special expertise or unique role of the profession in society. Thus, focusing on a particular profession allows us to see how the very conception of a profession implies criteria for choosing projects. Second, a large portion of American engineers are employed by the military or by companies with contracts from the military, and a large portion of the research being done for the military is done by engineers. (There are important differences in the circumstances of academic engineers, corporate engineers and government engineers, but these will not be emphasized here.)

From the ethics codes of engineering professional organizations and from the engineering ethics literature, it is clear that·engineers generally see themselves as having responsibilities to society, to employers, to clients, and to co-professionals or

Reprinted from *Annals of the New York Academy of Sciences*, 577 (1989), pp. 106–14, with permission.

the profession as a whole. Many of the codes specify that the responsibility to protect the safety and welfare of society is paramount. It is this responsibility that we refer to when we talk about "the social responsibilities of engineers." And, it is this responsibility that comes into play in decisions about participation in military research.

This responsibility can be understood to fall on the shoulders of individual engineers, and/or on the shoulders of the profession, i.e., members of the profession collectively. In the latter case it falls to engineering professional organizations to take appropriate action (of a kind different from that taken by individuals) to protect the safety and welfare of society. While the primary concern here is with individual responsibility, the role and importance of collective action should not be missed.

The question of this paper is, then, what do the social responsibilities of engineers call for when it comes to military research? The idea here is to infer from the social responsibilities of engineers a rule or principle which engineers could use in making choices about whether or not to, or under what conditions to, undertake research for the military. At first glance, it may seem that such a framework will not address the importance of individual conscience in the decision process, but it will become clear that this is not the case.

The paper aims to make some progress towards development of a principle which would apply to all engineers, and to do this by evaluating several principles which have been put forth in the engineering ethics literature. The three principles considered are roughly stated as follows:

1. Engineers should not impose their moral views on society; they should let society decide what projects are undertaken.
2. Engineers should refuse to work on projects which they deem, on balance, to conflict with their moral values.
3. Engineers should refuse to work on projects which increase risk unless the public is informed about the risk and given the opportunity to consent to the project.

THE "GUNS FOR HIRE" VIEW

The view suggested by the first principle can be called the "guns for hire" view of the social responsibilities of engineers, since it suggests that engineers should make their skills available to whomever is willing to pay for them, presumably as long as the projects are within the law. Samuel Florman (1978) comes very close to adopting this view in "Moral Blueprints: On Regulating the Ethics of Engineers." Florman is concerned about engineers imposing their own personal values on the rest of society. He writes,

> The problem-solver cannot factor his personal fancy into each equation. He must operate within constraints and expectations set by those who commission his work.

He also writes,,

> Should we risk oil spills and increase our reserves by offshore drilling? Accept the hazards of pesticides in order to feed hungry people? Stop building a dam and thus protect an endangered fish? These are political questions: it is pathetic and a little frightening to see citizens abdicate their responsibilities by assigning them to the realm of engineering ethics.

and,

> If each person is entitled to medical care and legal representation, is it not equally important that each legitimate business entity, government agency, and citizens' group should have access to expert engineering advice? If so, then it follows that engineers (within the limits of conscience) will sometimes labor on behalf of causes in which they do not believe.

Florman's position sounds very much like Milton Friedman's view (1970) in "The Social Responsibility of Business is to Increase Profits." Friedman argues that the only social responsibility that a business has is to increase profits while staying within the limits of the law, and that corporate executives impose their personal views on stockholders and others when they use corporate profits to give to charity or to contribute to other social programs. Friedman claims that when corporate executives use corporate profits in this way, they, in effect, tax stockholders "without representation," and, of course, no one has the right to do this. Similarly, we might say of engineers that their only social responsibility is to refuse to work on illegal projects and to do otherwise is to impose their personal values on the rest of the world.

On this view it is never wrong for an engineer to work on a project which has been endorsed by the public through the marketplace or filtered through government regulation. And, of course, this would seem to suggest that it is never wrong to work on a military project, since military projects are presumably projects endorsed by society through representative government.

Perhaps Florman is right to worry about individual engineers imposing their personal values on society, but it is often impossible to separate personal from professional values and judgments. Professions are not value neutral, nor would we want them to be. The very idea of a profession implies commitment to a social good or value, e.g., health, justice, truth, human well-being, etc. (Questions can be and have been raised about whether or not engineering is a "profession," but I do not want to get side-tracked by that issue, especially since all sides of the controversy generally agree that the more engineering becomes a profession, the better.)

The problem with the "guns for hire" model is that it presupposes that individuals can and should become amoral in their professional roles. This contradicts the very idea of "professions" which are socially recognized and granted special privileges by the state, precisely because they are directed at a social good. We would not want a value-neutral profession of engineering any more than we would want value-neutral professions of medicine or law. We want doctors who are committed to a healthy society, lawyers committed to justice (as defined in our system) and engineers committed to safety and human well-being.

The "guns for hire" view of engineering is also objectionable because it assumes, as does Friedman, that the marketplace and government regulation will do a good job of filtering out projects which should not be undertaken. It assumes that anything which makes it through the filter is good for society. If this were so, of course, there would be no reason for engineers to have a responsibility for the safety and welfare of society. "The system" would, so to speak, bear the full responsibility. However, we know that the system sometimes errs and that the marketplace and government regulation are not all-knowing and often lag well behind current knowledge relating to the safety and health of society. We also know that engineers (scientists, researchers, experts) are in a much better position to evaluate the safety and appropriateness of technological undertakings than are consumers and the public. They have the relevant knowledge and experience to evaluate the safety, credibility, and reliability of engineering projects. Of course, they are not "all-knowing." Their knowledge has limits. Nevertheless, it seems clear that we are better off if engineers act on our behalf and not as "guns for hire."

Thus, the "guns for hire" view of engineering is unacceptable. Engineers (and other researchers) should have a say about projects that are to be undertaken and they should certainly not absolve themselves of responsibility for the effects of projects on which they work. It is in the interests of all that they conceive of themselves as having, and act as if they have, responsibility for the safety and welfare of society.

PERSONAL AND PROFESSIONAL VALUES

In *Controlling Technology* Stephen Unger (1982) presents a model code of engineering ethics. Article 1 begins with the statement that "Engineers shall regard their responsibility to society as paramount and shall: . . ." This is followed by a series of sub-articles. Sub-article 1.2 reads as follows:

> Endeavor to direct their professional skills toward conscientiously chosen ends they deem, on balance, to be of positive value to humanity; declining to use those skills for purposes they consider, on balance, to conflict with their moral values.

Unger seems here to take a view in direct opposition to Florman's. The principle he asserts makes it clear that engineers should not be neutral. It asserts not only that engineers should refuse to work on certain projects, but that they should use their skills (perhaps "only") for projects of positive value to humanity.

This principle is a significant improvement over Florman's account insofar as it commits all engineers to a shared value, the good of humanity. Of course, there will be disagreements about what is good for humanity; nevertheless, the importance of a commitment to even such a general value, as the good of humanity, should not be underestimated. It defines the framework within which members of the profession must make their decisions. It provides the common ground upon which individual engineers or groups of engineers may disagree.

Still, while Unger asserts this value in the first part of sub-article 1.2, he seems to take it away in the second half, when he asserts that engineers should decline using their skills for purposes they consider "on balance, to conflict with their moral values." Here Unger seems to retreat from the idea of the profession having a value at its core, to individuals being the only entities with moral values. In the discussion about the model code, he explains his concern that professional codes of ethics should leave room for individual variation and conscience, so that the profession does not constrain individual freedom. Still, the point is that there may be professional as well as personal reasons for declining to use your skills.

While Unger's concern for individual freedom and individual variation within professions is appropriate, he draws an untenable line between personal and professional values and judgments. The principle says that one should not participate in projects which conflict with one's moral values, implying that one's moral values are personal and not professional. He separates concern for the good of humanity from one's personal moral values. However, generally when researchers refuse to work on projects or publicly oppose them on grounds of conscience (their own personal values), it is because they believe the project to be *not* good for humanity (or some subset of humanity). These are matters of professional judgment (at least, partially) and not just matters of conscience. For example, those who have opposed the construction of nuclear power plants are surely expressing their technical judgement about the degree of safety obtainable in such plants. The Strategic Defense Initiatives (SDI) is an even better example for here the opponents have not been researchers opposed to all military research. Rather, they have been opposed on grounds that the system could not be built to an appropriate level of reliability (Parnas 1987). Matters of conscience and matters of safety and welfare of society are inextricably connected.

Because Unger does not recognize the difficulty of drawing a line between personal and professional values, he does not seem to recognize the significance of the profession itself being committed to a value. But, our concern here should not be with interpretations of Unger. What is at stake are two different conceptions of the place of professions in the world, and two different conceptions of engineering. One vision is of professions as value neutral, with the values directing them coming from outside. On this model it follows that engineers can and should be "guns for hire." (Of course, on this view, there is little difference between professionals and non-professionals.)

The other conception is of professions as enterprises committed to a social good and being structured (constrained in various ways, privileged in others) so as to achieve that social good. On this view, there will be some projects which are antithetical to the profession itself, and it would be "unprofessional" to participate in them. In this conception of a profession and only in this conception, can we understand engineering as a morally worthy enterprise, worthy, that is, of individual commitment and social recognition.

Florman is clearly an adherent of the first conception. Unger is hard to place. He leans towards the latter, but does not seem to recognize the distinction.

Another problem with Unger's principle, related to the previous problem, has to do with its usefulness to engineers. Unger's principle is, to some extent, empty of content. That is, it does not tell engineers what their moral values should be. After all, the hard part about being moral is not just acting on one's conscience, but figuring out what one's conscience ought to be. It is precisely for assistance with this that a professional might turn to a professional code.

Unger does not seem to realize that he has begun to supply this content just by placing the matter in the context of the good of humanity. Of course, as mentioned before, there can be genuine disagreements about what is good for humanity, but this should not paralyze those who have expertise relevant to the good of humanity. In particular, it should not paralyze them from making the good of humanity their end.

Thus, while Unger's principle is an improvement over Florman's insofar as it allows and expects individuals to remain moral beings in their professional roles, it is problematic for other reasons. It is empty of content in helping engineers figure out what their moral values ought to be, and it does not recognize that professional values should play an important role here. It does not adequately recognize a value at the heart of the profession. In this respect it pushes responsibility too much to the personal realm and not enough to the professional.

RISK AND PUBLIC CONSENT

In "Engineers Who Kill: Professional Ethics and the Paramountly of Public Safety," a third principle is offered by Kipnis (1981), whose concerns are somewhat different from those of Florman and Unger. Kipnis argues that:

> Engineers shall not participate in projects that degrade ambient levels of public safety unless information concerning those degradations is made generally available.

Kipnis recognizes that risk pervades our lives, and that this must be taken into account when we consider the risks of various engineering endeavors. He argues, in effect, that the real issue for engineers has to do with projects which increase the extant level of risk. And, he thinks the informed consent of those who will be put at increased risk by such engineering projects ought to be sought before such projects are undertaken. However, he does not think that engineers, as engineers, have the responsibility for determining whether or not adequate consent has been given. Hence, he does not insist that engineers work only on projects in which consent has been obtained. Rather, he argues that "information about risks should not be withheld from the public" and that engineers should not participate in "covert degradation of public safety."

Kipnis's account is close to, and seemingly consistent with, Martin and Schinzinger's (1988) idea of engineering as social experimentation. Martin and Schinzinger argue that engineering endeavors always involve risk. Engineers learn by trying something and seeing if it works, then learning from what goes wrong. We never know with certainty all the effects which will result from a project.

According to Martin and Schinzinger, once we recognize the experimental nature of engineering, we can model it on medical experimentation and draw on recent analyses of the ethical issues there. Analyses of medical experimentation make clear that researchers should not be allowed to experiment on subjects without their consent, that is, their informed and uncoerced consent. This imposes important responsibilities on medical researchers, and by analogy on engineers. Martin and Schinzinger conceive of these responsibilities broadly. However, they seem to believe that management and the public, as well as engineers, bear the responsibility to ensure that those affected by a project are informed and given an opportunity to consent. Thus, while their account seems consistent with Kipnis's account, they shy away from asserting a principle of the kind Kipnis proposes.

The attraction of Kipnis's principle lies in its responsiveness both to Florman's concerns about individual engineers imposing their personal views on the rest of the world and my concerns about the lack of content in Unger's principle. This third principle would not have engineers impose their views on the rest of the world. It would have those who will be affected by a project determine (or, at least, have a say in) what projects are undertaken. On the other hand, it does not make engineers into "guns for hire" because it imposes on engineers a distinct and substantive professional responsibility to ensure that the public is informed about projects which will affect its well-being. Hence, it gives engineers professional grounds for refusing to work on certain projects. Engineers are in a good position to ensure that the public is adequately informed because they understand better than non-engineers what the risks of a project will be.

The principle does not explicitly put forth the good of humanity as a value at the heart of engineering, but one could argue that it is implicit. It is implicit in the idea that those who are affected by a project should be informed and have a say. In effect, the principle specifies that whether or not a project is, on balance, good for humanity ought to be decided by humanity rather than engineers alone. This rightly suggests that the good at issue is not wholly a technical or engineering matter. It suggests that the decision about whether or not to take a risk and how to balance risks against benefits involves more than technical expertise.

The major problem with the Kipnis-Martin-Schinzinger approach is that the responsibility they assign to engineers is much weaker than their analyses would seem to indicate. This is, no doubt, due to the fact that the ideas are so difficult to implement. Both analyses suggest that those who are being put at risk by a project ought to be informed about the risks and given the opportunity to consent or say "no" to the project. But, this is wholly impractical, as Kipnis, Martin and Schinzinger are well aware. How can we obtain the informed and uncoerced consent of the public? What do we do when there is less than unanimous consent (for example, when some people in a community think the benefits of a nuclear power plant or pesticides factory being located in their community outweigh the risks, and other people do not)? And, what do we do when there is some question about the voluntariness of the consent (for example, when there is high unemployment in the community in which many want the risky factory)? And, will government approval count as representative consent? Will the political process be adequate for cases where there is a mixture of public approval and disapproval?

These are primarily practical, not theoretical issues, albeit very real. They lead both Kipnis and Martin and Schinzinger to propose something quite short of the full involvement of all individuals who will be affected by a project. It is important to note that this somewhat weakens the line between these authors and Florman for if the political process, and perhaps the marketplace, will count as indirect forms of consent, then Kipnis, Martin and Schinzinger would not be far from Florman. The public, through government and the marketplace, would be deciding what projects are undertaken. Still, neither Kipnis nor Martin and Schinzinger seem to have quite this in mind, for they argue for broader responsibilities for engineers.

Thus, Kipnis's principle is still better than the first and second, and closer to the mark in identifying and giving some substance to the social responsibilities of engineers. It would be even better if it were coupled *explicitly* to a commitment to the good of humanity. Thus, a fourth principle might combine the first part of Unger's principle (strengthened with the addition of the word "only") with Kipnis's principle roughly as follows:

> Engineers should only direct their professional skills to projects they deem, on balance, to be of positive value to humanity and should refuse to work on projects that put people at risk, unless information about such projects is made generally available.

IMPLICATIONS

Now, what does all of this mean for an engineer's (or any researcher's) responsibility with regard to research for the military? The final principle indicates that a researcher contemplating participation in a military project should ask herself (1) whether the endeavor is good for humanity, and (2) whether those affected by the project are informed about it. Each of these questions brings an important issue of military research to the fore. The first raises the question whether all military research is bad (or good) for humanity. That is, can we say that military research just because it is for the military is bad (or good) for humanity, or must we take each project on its own and consider its potential impact? The second question brings to the fore the special problem of secrecy in research, for secret research would seem to violate the condition that information be publicly available.

Satisfactory analyses of these issues will require a good deal more analysis than can be undertaken here, though some important parameters seem clear. On the first issue, it seems very important to distinguish claims to the effect that research for the military, simply because it is for the military, is bad for humanity, from the claim that a particular project is good or bad for humanity. Recognition of this distinction is critical for intelligent discussion and coherent points of view.

The matter of secrecy is no less complicated. Some may argue that any principle ruling out secret research is unacceptable because there are times and cases when secrecy in research is necessary and, even perhaps, good for humanity. This might be so; nevertheless, a distinction might be drawn between the generic features of a project and the details. With this distinction, we can insist that researchers should not work on projects the generic features of which have not been made public, though the details may well remain secret.

CONCLUSION

Both of these questions call for much more analysis and debate, but the aim here was to provide a framework for thinking about the issues associated with military research and not to settle them. The framework proposed is that of the social responsibilities of researchers. While it is no simple matter to figure out what these are, it seems clear that researchers should not abdicate responsibility and act as if they are "guns for hire." It also seems clear that we should not think that the ethical issues in military research are simply matters of personal conscience. They can be matters of professional judgement and professional commitment. The principle that I propose calls for researchers to consider whether their work is good for humanity and whether the public is adequately informed about the projects on which they work. These are considerations that ought to be at the core of the debate on military research. They ought to define the common ground and thereby focus disagreement.

REFERENCES

FLORMAN, S. C. 1978. "Moral Blueprints: On Regulating the Ethics of Engineers." *Harper's* (October):30–33.

FRIEDMAN, M. 1970. "The Social Responsibility of Business is to Increase Profits." *New York Times Magazine* (September 13).

UNGER, S. H. 1982. *Controlling Technology: Ethics and the Responsible Engineer.* New York: Holt, Rinehart and Winston.

PARNAS, D. L. 1987. "SDI: A Violation of Professional Responsibility." *Abacus*, vol. 4, no. 2:46–52.

KIPNIS, K. 1981. "Engineers Who Kill: Professional Ethics and the Paramountcy of Public Safety." *Business & Professional Ethics Journal*, vol. 1, no. 1:77–91.

MARTIN, M. and R. SCHINZINGER. 1988. *Ethics in Engineering*, 2nd Ed. New York: McGraw-Hill Book Company.

5

The Engineer's Obligations of Loyalty to Employer

─────────────────────────── **Spying on the Boss** ───────────────────────────

"I don't know," Fred Watson said to Ted Moore, the well-dressed man sitting across the table from him. "Old man Barnett's been pretty good to me."

Watson was right. When jobs were hard to get, especially for ex-cons, Milt Barnett, president of Barnett's Drug Exchange had employed Watson as a shipping clerk. "Others are more qualified than you are," Barnett had told Watson while examining his job application, "but you seem to need the job more than they do." Watson was understandably impressed with Barnett's concern for him, an impression that Barnett did nothing to tarnish in the two years that Watson had been in his employment. In fact, Barnett had recently intimated to Watson that he was next in line for the job of purchasing manager that promised to open in the next year. Now he was being asked to violate Barnett's trust and to endanger his own livelihood.

"Let's get this straight," Watson said to Moore, "you want me to spy on my boss."

"What we at Schilling Laboratories would like you to do, Mr. Watson, is to help us determine whether or not our suspicions of irregularities in Barnett's distribution of drugs is founded."

As he explained it, Schilling's franchised distributors were entitled to specific discounts for selling directly to retailers. But Schilling had reason to believe that these distributors were getting their discounts while actually selling to Barnett. "What we'd like you to do," he told Watson, "is to report to us the contents of the cartons shipped to and from the Barnett company."

"Well, the whole thing strikes me as pretty underhanded, if you want to know the truth," Watson told him.

219

"Let me assure you, Mr. Watson, that we find such surveillance equally as repugnant as you do. But at the same time we've an obligation to enforce wholesale distribution agreements under law, and since we've exhausted every other means of doing this short of espionage, we're left with no alternative." Then he added, "I should point out that what you're doing will be kept in the strictest confidence and should you in any way suffer as a result of your activities, Schilling will adequately compensate you for the inconveniences."

Watson shook his head slowly before muttering, "I don't know."

Reprinted from Vincent Barry, Moral Issues in Business, 2nd ed. (Belmont, Calif.: Wadsworth Publishing Co., Inc., 1983), p. 256, with permission. Copyright © 1983, 1979 by Wadsworth, Inc.

Covering Design Flaws

Engineer Jody, fresh out of school, is assigned by her new firm to design reinforcing bars for a cantilever beam that is to be part of a hospital entrance. Her superior, engineer Robert, looks over her calculations and, without checking them closely, passes the drawings on to the drafting department. The plans are drawn and sealed by Robert, and the beam poured. By chance, another member of the firm, engineer Pat, discovers a serious error in the plans and points it out to Robert. The beam apparently has half as many reinforcing bars as good design would dictate. Robert notes that the beam seems to be holding and instructs the drafting department to add the missing reinforcing bars to the "as-built" set of drawings.

Reprinted from Elizabeth M. Endy and P. Aarne Vesilind, "Ethics in the Field," Civil Engineering, December 1985, p. 64, with permission.

Who Owns Your Knowledge?

John Doe, an engineer employed by the ABC Manufacturing Company, in the course of his work as a design engineer conceived an idea which in his opinion would produce a commercial product manufactured by his employer at much lower cost. Doe was also of the opinion that the idea was patentable. However, he did not disclose the idea to his superiors in the company and shortly thereafter left the employ of the ABC Manufacturing Company to develop his idea and to initiate action to obtain a patent on it. When first employed by the ABC Manufacturing Company, Doe had signed the usual agreement that he would disclose to his employer any inventions developed or conceived by him in the course of his employment and would assign to his employer all rights, title, and interest to such inventions. In consideration of Doe's agreement, the ABC Manufacturing Company agreed to pay Doe the sum of $50 upon disclosure of the invention and an additional $100 when and if a patent was granted.

Reprinted from the National Society of Professional Engineers, Opinions of the Board of Ethical Review, Case No. 68-1 (Washington, D.C.: National Society of Professional Engineers, 1971), III, 25, with permission.

_____ **The Costs of Keeping a Secret** _____

Philip Cortez reread the engineering director's memo with considerable anxiety. It read: "Call me at your earliest convenience about design specs for new radial."

"New radial"—that could mean only one thing: that his employer, National Rubber and Tire, wanted to beat its biggest competitor, Lifeworth, in getting an 80,000-mile, puncture-proof tire on the market.

Ordinarily such a memo would signal a challenge for an employee as conscientious and industrious as Phil Cortez. But until six months ago Cortez had been employed by Lifeworth. While there, he had been instrumental in drawing up designs for a similar tire that Lifeworth was not only interested in producing but was also counting on to revitalize its sagging profit posture. In fact, so important did Lifeworth consider Cortez's work that when he announced his departure, Lifeworth's president reminded him of an agreement which Cortez had entered into when undertaking his work with Lifeworth. He had promised to refrain from disclosing any classified information directly or indirectly to competitors for a period of two years after his termination with Lifeworth. In no uncertain terms the president indicated that he considered Cortez's work on the new radial highly classified. Cortez assured the president that he anticipated no conflict of interests since National had given him every reason to believe that it wanted him primarily in a managerial capacity.

And now the memo was staring him in the face. Cortez responded to it that very afternoon and had his worst fears realized. As he'd suspected, the engineering director solicited Cortez's input on the matter of a new radial.

Cortez unhesitatingly explained his dilemma. While sympathetic to Cortez's predicament, the director broadly hinted that refusal to provide constructive input would result in a substantial disservice to National and was bound to affect Cortez's standing with the firm. "After all," the director said, "it's very difficult to justify paying a man a handsome salary and expediting his movement up the organizational ladder when his allegiances obviously lie elsewhere."

INTRODUCTION

Many of the readings in earlier chapters suggest that the commonest dilemma of engineers is a conflict between the engineer's responsibility to society and his or her obligation of loyalty to an employer. Chapter 4 was devoted to an in-depth exploration of the responsibility for the safety and welfare of society. Chapter 5 is devoted to loyalty to employer.

The readings have been selected and arranged so as to begin with the broadest questions about "loyalty." What is it? Why is it valuable? What are its dangers? What might create an obligation of loyalty? Subsequent readings consider problems surrounding loyalty to employer, in particular those dealing with dissent and whistle-blowing, and trade secrecy. The idea here is that loyalty to employer is one of the factors that must figure into an engineer's decisions, and the more an engineer understands about loyalty, the better he or she will be able to balance its importance against other responsibilities.

The piece by Marcia Baron, entitled "The Moral Status of Loyalty," introduces the topic and lays out good and bad aspects of acting out of loyalty. Baron sees loyalty as an obligation, but clearly not one that is absolute. She seems to think that loyalty might be a prima facie obligation in the sense that one should hold to it unless other considerations take priority.

Ronald Duska focuses specifically on loyalty to employer, but he gives a different account of the role of loyalty in human relationships. He argues that loyalty only arises in special relationships based on mutual enrichment. Loyalty is not appropriate in relationships in which the parties are pursuing their self-interest. He then argues that employee-employer relationships are based on self-interest. They are not for the purpose of mutual enrichment, at least not from the viewpoint of corporate employers. Hence, we should feel no obligation of loyalty to our corporate employers. Corporations would like employees to believe that they have an obligation of loyalty to their employers, for such a belief serves the interest of the corporation, but Duska is quick to try to dissuade us of such beliefs.

Duska's account of loyalty is most provocative, but it needs to be scrutinized carefully. We should, for example, consider whether we can classify all employers together as he does, or whether it isn't more accurate to say that some employers are better than others in the way they treat employees. For example, in the scenario entitled "Spying on the Boss," one may be reluctant to say that Fred Watson should feel no loyalty to his boss, when his boss had helped him out in hard times. It would seem that his boss, in hiring ex-convict Watson, took a risk that could have seriously interfered with his self-interest. Some employers are better than others in recognizing the needs and interests of their employees—for example, in recognizing the importance of opportunities for advancement or in keeping people on the payroll during long illnesses. Hence, it might be that loyalty to employer is sometimes appropriate, not just because the person or company is your employer, but rather because the person or company has treated you well, doing more than is required or expected of an employer.

The real issue for employed engineers may be not so much in deciding whether or not they have an obligation of loyalty to their employer, but rather in deciding how much weight to give to this obligation, and what to do when it comes into conflict with other interests or responsibilities. In the second set of readings in this chapter, the focus is on dissent in organizations. Here we explore what happens when employees disagree with their employers and express their differences. Alfred G. Feliu discusses recent changes in the law that give more protection to employees when they express ideas that their employers do not want them to express. Feliu's account gives a sense of the various issues on which employers and employees may disagree.

It sometimes seems that individual rights cease to exist in the workplace, and Feliu's account indicates that, indeed, historically the law has favored the employer's right to control the workplace. Although his description of the recent changes in the law—precedent-setting cases and new regulation—give cause for optimism about the situation changing so that employees such as engineers may have more freedom to express their concerns, real limitations exist on how much the law can do to protect dissenting employees.

The next selection focuses on a topic that has recurred in many of the preceding readings, whistle-blowing. Here it might be a good idea to go back and look at Richard T. De George's piece and others to compare their accounts of whistle-blowing with that of Gene G. James.

After defining whistle-blowing and explaining the limitations of laws that might protect whistle-blowers, Gene G. James focuses on the moral justification of acts of whistle-blowing. In his analysis, James takes issue with De George's account of when whistle-blowing is permissible and when obligatory. He also disagrees with De George's analysis of the Pinto case. James argues that we have a prima facie obligation to disclose organizational wrongdoing we are unable to prevent. According to James, the degree of the obligation depends on the extent to which we are capable of foreseeing the consequences of organizational actions and our own acts or failures to act are causes of those consequences.

In the final set of readings in this chapter, we turn to trade secrecy and the challenge it poses to the employer-employee relationship. Readers may find this one of the most interesting issues in this anthology, as it raises a deep and fascinating question about who owns knowledge—especially when the knowledge is in the brain of a human being. This issue also calls for a delicate balancing of the interests of employers and those of employees. Employers have a legitimate need to protect the ideas that they are developing for the marketplace. If their ideas are stolen, the time, effort, and money they have invested in developing a new product will be lost. How far can employers go, however, to protect their new ideas? Can they go so far as to claim, in effect, that they own a piece of your mind because they have paid your salary while you have been acquiring knowledge? Can they stop you from working for other companies? Here we begin to test the real limits of loyalty, for we may recognize the legitimate claims of employers to trade secrets and recognize an employee's obligation to keep those secrets; yet, we may be reluctant to say that an employer can have a say about where an employee may go to work when the employee quits or what inventions an ex-employee can create. It would seem only reasonable to say that going to work for a company should not entail a life-long commitment, and yet employers sometimes believe that they need such a commitment to protect their legitimate trade secrets.

Michael S. Baram gives us a survey of the problem and explains many of the techniques employers use to protect themselves. He suggests that employers will have a difficult time winning cases in court except when they can show that employees have physically taken documents from the workplace.

In "Trade Secrets, Patents, and Morality" Robert E. Frederick and Milton Snoeyenbos delve into the complexity of the problems surrounding ownership of knowledge. Although they do not explicitly say so, it becomes clear from reading their piece that claims to ownership of ideas cannot be understood to be dictated by nature. Instead, what can and should be owned is a matter of law or social convention. Frederick and Snoeyenbos make clear that the law concerning patents and trade secrecy is aimed at social utility. We give people the right to own ideas because we think doing this will encourage the development of new ideas and inventions. Conversely, we must limit this concept because we do not want to interfere with individual rights to liberty. In addition to discussing the underlying basis of patent and trade secrecy law, Frederick and Snoeyenbos also discuss the employment contracts that individuals sign, promising to keep secret what they learn at work.

19 The Moral Status of Loyalty

Marcia Baron

BACKGROUND

In a 1973 CBS report on Phillips Petroleum, Inc., one of its chief executives was asked to describe what sort of qualities his company looks for in prospective employees. He responded without hesitation that above all else, what Phillips wants and needs is loyalty on the part of its employees. A loyal employee, he elaborated, would buy only Phillips' products. (I take it that he did not mean this literally, but meant, rather, that the employee would not buy any products from a company other than Phillips if Phillips produced products of the same type.) Moreover, a loyal employee would vote in local, state, and national elections in whatever way was most conducive to the growth and flourishing of Phillips. And, of course, a loyal employee would never leave Phillips unless it was absolutely unavoidable. To reduce the likelihood of that happening, prospective employees were screened to make sure their respective wives did not have careers which might conflict with life-long loyalty to Phillips.[1]

Phillips does not appear to be anomalous in its expectations of loyalty, although times have changed somewhat since the early 1970s, thanks to the efforts of Ralph Nader and others. Nader and Mark Green (1979) report that the Gilman Paper Company of Saint Mary's, Georgia, demanded that their personnel manager find out who planned to vote against the candidate backed by the Gilman Company. The personnel manager refused to comply and finally quit, but another mill worker took on the task that the former had refused, and several people were subsequently fired for voting for the "wrong" candidate.[2]

Serious though the demand of loyalty is for all of those in business, the problem is particularly acute for engineers. Engineers are in a position of public trust. Compliance with the company's expectation of loyalty may, in some circumstances, have far-reaching consequences for those who trust the engineer to see to it that the product inspected by his or her department is safe.

Consider the following case reported by Kermit Vandivier (1972) in Robert Heilbroner's *In the Name of Profit*.[3] Rather than risk losing a sale by delaying delivery of the four-disk brake to the LTV Aerospace Corporation and explaining that, in the interest of safety, a new brake design would have to be drawn up, the B.F. Goodrich plant at Troy, Ohio opted to "fudge" the data from the qualifying tests. Vandivier, who was among the engineers told to co-operate "or else," entitles his essay in Heilbroner's book "Why Should My Conscience Bother Me?"[4] His task was to issue the formal qualification report on the brake. The brake had failed the tests abysmally, even after it was "helped along": fans were used to cool it during the test and a conveniently miscalibrated instrument was employed to measure the brake pressure. Vandivier buckled under the severe pressure of his superiors and reluctantly handed in the fraudulent report. Later, however, he submitted a letter of resignation, citing the "atmosphere of deceit and distrust in which it is impossible to work" (p. 28). The resignation was to take effect a few weeks later, but the chief engineer informed Vandivier that in view of Vandivier's " 'disloyalty,' " he had decided to accept the resignation " 'right now' " (p. 29).

Vandivier and his cohorts were lucky. No one was (physically) injured when, predictably enough, the brakes failed. Such good fortune does not come to all those who succumb to the pressure and do what is said to be in the best interest of the company and to be required by loyalty. Many engineers who were loyal to Lee Iacocca and to Ford have more on their consciences than does Vandivier: between 1970 and 1977 Pinto crashes caused somewhere between 500 and 900 burn deaths. Yet the Pinto design was known to be faulty before any of the Pintos were sold (Dowie 1980; De George 1981).

The Issues for Engineers

While loyalty is a significant moral issue for everyone—why this is so will become evident shortly—it is of paramount importance that engineers come to grips with it since the impact of an engineer's decision to put loyalty to his or her company before (other) moral demands can have far-reaching and even life-and-death consequences.

There are two clusters of abstract questions that a responsible engineer should ponder:

1. What, if anything, is good about loyalty? If it is good to be loyal, is it always good to be loyal? If there are circumstances in which it is wrong to act loyally, how can we identify or be on the alert for such circumstances?
2. What should one do if conflicting loyalties make demands on one? How, if at all, can one weigh the relative importance of one claim of loyalty against another?[5]

Let us first consider how the cluster of questions that 2 raises bears on engineering ethics. A look at the code of the National Society of Professional Engineers (NSPE), or virtually any other code of ethics for engineers, will make this plain. The NSPE Code begins: "The Engineer, to uphold and advance the honor and dignity of the engineering profession and in keeping with the high standards of ethical conduct . . . will be honest and impartial, and will serve with devotion his employer, his clients, and the public. . . ." Can an engineer, no matter how heroic, always serve *each* of these parties with devotion? Can he or she, in other words, always be loyal to all three? The answer is clearly "No." Loyalty to their clients required that the engineers at B.F. Goodrich live up to the trust that LTV placed in them: it required, among other things, that they adhere to the methods of qualification testing that the military specifies, rather than concoct their own "tests." Loyalty to the public required the Ford engineers to "blow the whistle," that is, to inform the public of the hidden danger in the Pinto, or perhaps collectively refuse to cooperate in completing the Pinto, given Iacocca's refusal to remodel the gas tank.

In order to answer the questions raised in 2 we must first address the more abstract ones which 1 raises. We cannot expect to make any headway in adjudicating between conflicting loyalties unless we first figure out how to evaluate the extent to which various claims of loyalty really do make a legitimate claim on us. To do this, we will analyze the concept of loyalty, isolate its positive features from its negative features and determine, within broad parameters, when it is right to act loyally and when, because of other moral considerations, it is wrong to do so. But first we must ask what loyalty is.

The Nature of Loyalty

In asking what loyalty is we have two aims: (1) to pin down what we shall mean, for the purposes of this discussion, when we use the words "loyal," "loyalty," and "loyally"; and (2) to try to capture the idea that most of us have when we speak of loyalty and the idea of loyalty that is relevant to the issues in engineering ethics, as indicated above. In other words, we want to avoid using the words in question loosely and vaguely: it is crucial that we be clear on what it is that we are talking about. In addition, though we do not need to take on the task of giving a full analysis of what loyalty is, we do not want to "change the subject" and end up discussing the moral status of something other than what is generally meant by "loyalty" when the term is used in connection with issues in engineering ethics.[6]

Loyalty and Its Objects

To accomplish our aims we must first decide what objects loyalty can take; that is, what sorts of things one can be loyal *to*. Immediately we encounter disagreement among those who have written on loyalty. Josiah Royce, a turn-of-the-century American philosopher and one of the few philosophers to write an entire book on loyalty, stipulates that the object of loyalty must be some *cause* or other. "Loyalty shall mean . . . *The willing and practical and thoroughgoing devotion of a person to a cause* (16–17, Italics in text)," the cause being something "beyond your private self, greater than you are . . . personal and . . . superpersonal" (Royce 1908, pp. 55–56).

> Instances of loyalty are: The devotion of a patriot to his country, when this devotion leads him actually to live and perhaps to die for his country; the devotion of a martyr to his religion; the devotion of a ship's captain to the requirements of his office when, after a disaster, he works steadily for his ship, for the saving of his ship's company until the last possible service is accomplished, so that he is the last man to leave the ship, and is ready if need be to go down with his ship (Royce 1908, p. 17).

John Ladd, a contemporary philosopher, disagrees. So does another contemporary thinker, Andrew Oldenquist. In his *Encyclopedia of Philosophy* article on loyalty, Ladd differs from Royce as to the object of loyalty. Far from having as its objects impersonal and superpersonal causes, loyalty, Ladd thinks, is interpersonal. Both historically and in our ordinary moral language, "loyalty" is "taken to refer to a relationship between persons—for instance, between a lord and his vassal, between a parent and his children, or between friends. Thus the object of loyalty is ordinarily taken to be a person or group of persons" (Ladd 1967, p. 97). Loyalty, Ladd adds, is "also specific; a man is loyal to *his* lord, *his* father, or *his* comrades. It is conceptually impossible to be loyal to people in general (to humanity) or to a general principle, such as justice or democracy" (p. 97).[7]

Oldenquist joins Ladd in rejecting the view that ideals can be the object of loyalty. His explanation makes it clear that the issue is a deep one, involving much more than the simple question of how we should use the term "loyalty." In his explanation, Oldenquist contrasts being loyal to something (or as he puts it, "having a loyalty") with having an ideal. The test by which one can distinguish loyalties from ideals is as follows:

> If I say that I ought to defend my country, I have a putative loyalty. But if I am willing to replace "my country" with, e.g., "a democratic country" or "a Christian country," I have not a loyalty but an ideal; in this case what I am committed to is a kind of thing, not some particular thing. If I am unwilling to replace "my country" with a characterizing expression, I have a genuine loyalty and not an ideal; my normative judgment is self-dependent (Oldenquist 1982, p. 175).

To put Oldenquist's point more generally, loyalties involve an ineliminable first-person (possessive) pronoun: "my" (or "our"). This means that I can only be loyal to *my* X, but more importantly that to be loyal to my X, I must think of it under the description "my X" rather than merely as an X which has the qualities a, b, and c. The reason is that otherwise I am committed to a kind of X, not to this X. If I am committed to a kind of X but not to some particular X, then I do not yet have any reason for preferring my X to other X's of the same kind. And yet if I am loyal to my X (e.g., my country) I *do*, Oldenquist thinks, prefer it or value it more than other X's of the same kind (e.g., other democratic countries). So this must mean that if I have a loyalty to X, I value it as my X, not just as an X which is valuable independently of being mine. This is what Oldenquist means when he argues that the objects of loyalty contain "unelimi-nable [*sic*] egocentric particulars" (p. 175).

Ladd and Oldenquist thus seem roughly to agree on what sorts of objects loyalty can take. Loyalties, on their view, are to people, not to ideals. Oldenquist might deny that one can only be loyal to people or groups of people, for he might deny that loyalty to one's country is really just loyalty to a group of people. But we can ignore such differences for now. We must focus instead on this question: What bearing does the disagreement between Royce, on the one hand, and Ladd and Oldenquist, on the other, have on the issues concerning loyalty in engineering ethics? Once we answer that question we can decide which characterizations of loyalty and its objects to accept for the purposes of this essay.

On Oldenquist's analysis, the demand that an engineer be loyal—if it really is a demand for loyalty—amounts to something like this: an engineer is to be loyal to his company because it is his company, and not solely because it is an important, socially useful company, or because he has been treated well by "the company" (i.e., the people who constitute it). His reasons for being loyal to it must include the fact that it is *his* company. Ladd would agree: the engineer must, to be loyal, be loyal to some particular group of people. In contrast, Royce's view is that this is elliptical and inaccurate. What the engineer is supposed to be loyal to, he thinks, is a cause—not a person, not a group of people, not an organization of people. Which characterization better captures (a) our ordinary conception of loyalty, and (b) the notion of loyalty which is relevant to engineering ethics? I believe that Ladd's and Oldenquist's characterization does. It outstrips Royce's characterizations with respect to both (a) and (b).

Consider (b) first. When Vandivier's superior at Goodrich told him that he was being disloyal, he surely did not mean that Vandivier was failing (either by having a cause to which he was disloyal or by having no cause) to fight for some cause—indeed, that is part of what Vandivier was doing in deciding to quit the company! What the superior meant is that he was being disloyal to his superiors and co-workers at Goodrich. The relevant notion of loyalty in that instance is loyalty to certain people or to a group of people, not loyalty to an ideal or a cause.

The Ladd-Oldenquist characterization also accounts well for our ordinary use of "loyalty" and "loyal." A friend is loyal to another person, not to the cause of friendship, or to any other cause. The loyal dog is loyal to his master. When we speak of causes (or ideals) we are more apt to say that people are committed to them or devoted to them than that they are loyal to them.

The Case Against Loyalty

There are good philosophical reasons for worrying about the moral status of loyalty. Moral reasoning and moral conduct demand that one be impartial, that one not play favorites. Professors are not to give high grades to students just because they are family friends or members of the same political organization or Bible study group. Nor are jobs to be filled on the basis of whether the candidate is "my kind." Indeed, depending on the "kind" in question, it can be illegal to hire on that basis—and for good reason. If the members of group A have most of the power in a certain society and if out of loyalty to their co-members they try always to give the jobs to members of group A and to rent or sell residential property only to members of group A (or to reserve the only decent housing for members of group A), those who are not in group A will be, at the very best, second-class citizens.[8] Unfortunately, such scenarios are far from merely hypothetical.

What all this points to is the link between loyalty to X's and discrimination against non-X's. It is worth taking note of a special feature of the link between loyalty to X's and discrimination against non-X's: the link does not rely on any beliefs to the effect that non-X's are in some relevant (or irrelevant) respect inferior to X's. Whereas discrimination against non-X's commonly is nurtured by a belief that the people in question are less bright or lazier or somehow morally inferior, loyalty to X's provides its own potentially independent basis for discrimination. The "old buddy system" of hiring makes this clear: if, out of loyalty, I hire my nephews and sons-in-law whenever I can (and perhaps my nieces and daughters-in-law as well), I need not have anything against the better-qualified people whom I turn down. I need not believe that they are "a greater risk" or in some other respect less qualified. I simply am being loyal to my family. One problem with loyalty, then, is that it invites unfairness and threatens to contribute to social injustice.

There is a second and closely related reason for questioning the value of loyalty. Loyalty seems to eschew another central feature of morality: reliance on good reasons. If I am to justify some action that I took, I must be able to show that I had good reasons for taking it and that the reasons for taking it outweighed the reasons against taking it. Consider what happens if the action in question was performed out of loyalty. We have already seen that if I act from loyalty, I act partially; that is, I act on behalf of some particular person(s) or constellation of persons—my sister, my boss, my friend, my university, my company, my country. But putting partiality to one side, we note another feature of acting loyally: I act on behalf of one of these parties not because the party deserves it, because I promised it, because it will help the people in question while hurting no one else, but for a very different sort of reason (if indeed for a *reason* at all!): because the party is question is *my X*.

Recall Oldenquist's distinction between loyalties and ideals. If my reason for defending my country is that my country is democratic, then, he says, "I have not a loyalty but an ideal," for "what I am committed to is a kind of thing, not some particular thing." I have a genuine loyalty only if I am dedicated to X under the description "my X"; otherwise, I would have to say, any other X of the same kind (e.g., any democratic country) would have an equal claim on me. But what kind of reason is "Because it is mine"? If to act loyally is to act with a special regard for something because it is mine—only because it is mine—loyalty seems at best silly. Suppose someone asked me why I favor the type of government that I do favor or why I think so highly of my thesis student. If to either question I responded, "Because it (s/he) is my _____," the appropriate response would be an amused smile. And the only sensible way to comprehend my answer would be to regard it as a refusal to give a reason—perhaps an evasion. Hence it is hard to see how loyalty generates reasons. An appeal to loyalty seems to reject or evade the request for a reason. No wonder David Hume thought loyalty a virtue that holds "less of reason, than of bigotry, and superstition" (Hume 1888, p. 562). At its core this is just the sort of narrowness of vision that we are supposed to escape *through* moral reasoning!

This last point can be expanded on if we take a look at Hume's account of how moral reasoning enables us to be more impartial. Hume saw that while we are, as humans, very social creatures, our affections are partial. They pick and choose: we do not love everybody equally. It is natural to prefer certain people to others. He also noticed that we are more impressed by admirable men and women who live in our part of the world and our era, and more disturbed by horrible deeds done "close to home" than by those that happened hundreds of years ago. And yet, he noticed (speaking as a Briton), "we give the same approbation to the same moral qualities in China as in England" (p. 581). The fact that one wicked person lives in our town and another lives thousands of miles away does not prompt us to think of the first as more wicked, even though we *feel* more shaken up and more outraged by the spectacle of wicked deeds close to home. We don't say that cruelty of the same type and degree is worse if far away from us than if it is right in our neighborhood; yet our feelings towards the one instance of cruelty are quite different from our feelings towards the other instance. Hume noticed that what happens in such instances is that we take ourselves *beyond* those feelings by abstracting from them. We try to ignore the aspects of our feelings that are occasioned by the nearness or remoteness of the crime or character (or whatever) that is in question.

> Our servant, if diligent and faithful, may excite stronger sentiments of love and kindness than Marcus Brutus, as represented in history; but we say not upon that account, that the former character is more laudable than the latter. We know, that were we to approach equally near to that remown'd patriot, he wou'd command a much higher degree of affection and admiration. Such corrections are common with regard to all the senses; and indeed 'twere impossible we cou'd ever make use of language, or communicate our sentiments to one another, did we not correct the momentary appearances of things, and overlook our present situation (Hume 1888, p. 582).

In moral reasoning we try to leave behind the irrelevant considerations. We try not to let such factors as the person's "looks" affect our judgment of guilt or innocence for a certain crime; in allocating academic honors or 4–H awards we try not to be affected in our decisions by considerations of how much we like the candidates, from which part of the country they hail, etc. Of course, I may *feel* like awarding the honor to the student who babysits my children, but I realize that the fact that she is our babysitter is not a good reason for favoring her over someone else who is a candidate for this honor. Hume would say that moral reasoning extends my natural sympathy—or if the "passions do not always follow our correction . . . these corrections serve sufficiently to regulate our abstract notions, and are alone regarded, when we pronounce in general concerning the degrees of vice and virtue" (p. 585).

The trouble with loyalty is that it seems to force our sympathies back into their initial partiality. It seems to undo or oppose all the good that fair-minded moral reasoning strives to accomplish.

Yet a third and related problem with loyalty is that it seems to invite irresponsibility: acting out of loyalty to X without a concern for whether in doing so we act fairly, and without heeding the likely consequences of our action. In his ebullient praise of and call for loyalty, Josiah Royce (1908, p. 106) urges:

> Let this so possess you that . . . you can say . . . "I am the servant of this cause, its reasonable, its willing, its devoted instrument, and being such, I have neither eyes to see nor tongue to speak save as this cause shall command." Let this be your bearing, and this your deed. Then, indeed, you . . . have won the attitude which constitutes genuine personal dignity.

How can I act responsibly if I make myself a willing instrument of something else? If I say "No, I will not consider what dangers there are in nuclear power; I will promote the cause of my company without any regard to what happened at Browns Ferry," can I be acting responsibly? The answer is clearly "No." I cannot act responsibly if I avert my eyes from all warning signs. It is crucial that I remain open to new information and that I be willing to revise my plans—revise a design for a bridge or urge that the company alter its plans to keep the cost of the Pinto from exceeding two thousand dollars and the weight from exceeding two thousand pounds[9]—if I find that things are not quite as they seemed. To charge ahead despite indications that all will not go well is irresponsible. If loyalty demands such ostrich-like behavior, that only goes to show that loyalty needs to be tempered by other considerations.

It is worth noting that such instances of loyalty to one's company frequently end up hurting the company in the long run, as well as hurting consumers. This was the case, for instance, with the refusal to take seriously the very worrisome test results on the Corvair. The proposal to install a stabilizing bar in the rear of each car to correct the Corvair's tendency to flip over was long regarded as too costly—at fifteen dollars a car. When it finally was accepted and executed, it was too late for the Corvair to regain credibility. Losses in sales and legal expenses and out-of-court settlements for those maimed and killed were enormous (Wright 1980).

It is a sad fact about loyalty that it invites—according to Royce, *demands*—single-mindedness. Single-minded pursuit of a goal is sometimes delightfully romantic, even a real inspiration. But it is hardly something to advocate to engineers, whose impact on the safety of the public is so very significant. Irresponsibility, whether caused by selfishness or by magnificently unselfish loyalty, can have most unfortunate consequences.

The Case For Loyalty

The preceding pages expose loyalty's darker side. But there is also much to be said *for* loyalty, as the following examples will demonstrate.

Imagine a parent who, perhaps as a result of reading the previous section of this essay, felt that the mere fact that her son was *her son* was no reason for her to pay thousands of dollars a year for four years to send him to college, despite the fact that he is bright and eager to go to college. Imagine that she considers the idea of spending the money on him rather than using it to help bright orphans to get an education to be "irrational prejudice" in favor of her son. Clearly there would be something wrong here. It is terrific of her to devote large sums of money to the education of orphans; but what about her son? Surely she shouldn't regard him just as one of the promising young people in the world, as someone who has no greater claim to her pocketbook (and to her love and her attention) than anyone else.[10] To take a different example, imagine a parent who felt that there was no more reason to throw a birthday party for his six-year-old than for any other child. Here again, the fact that it is *his* child *should* make a difference to him.

From these considerations it emerges that "The Case Against Loyalty" stands in need of qualification. "Because it is my X" can, in some situations, for some instances of X, be a good reason for doing something for that person that one would not do for anyone else. "Because it is my child" is a good reason for me to spend much more time with him or her than with any other child (assuming that I have no other children) and, more generally, to make considerable sacrifices which I would not make for anyone else.

Consider, too, something that psychologists frequently point out: children need unconditional love, i.e., love that isn't conditional on the child's behavior. Yet someone who, disdaining the element of "blind affection" in loyalty, felt that the mere fact that it is his son was not sufficient reason to love him, would be incapable of unconditional love—unless his affections got the better of his judgment.

Parental responsibilities are not the only reason why loyalty is of great value. Relationships between equals—spouses, siblings, friends, lovers—could not flourish (or even count as *relationships* in the usual sense of the word) without the "favoritism" or "bias" which is central to loyalty. What kind of friend would I be if I were no more willing to help a friend in need than to help a stranger in the same way? And there are many other situations and instances of X for which "Because it is my X" is a good reason for the sort of favoritism which is at the heart of loyalty. "Because she is my friend" is a good reason for me to put in a good (but honest) word for her when she applies for a job in the company where I work, or to give her a lift to the airport—something that I would be less likely to do for a mere acquaintance (depending on the degree of need and the distance to the airport).

So far we have focussed on interpersonal, one-to-one relationships in presenting the case for loyalty. But loyalty is valuable in other arenas, as well. Memberships and fellowship in a community—be it a club, a church, an athletic team, a women's (or men's) support group, a town, (a division of) a company or university—is a significant part of human life. It would not be possible to feel that one is really a part of such a group if one did not have a special concern for that group because (at least *partly* because) it is one's group.

This is true even if one draws the important distinction between loyalty to the group and commitment to the ideal (if any) that it stands for. If I am in a local political action group and feel a real membership in and fellowship with that group, I would not be likely to quit that group for another which works for the same ideal. If I feel identification and affiliation with that group, if I am interested in its success or well-being as a group, I would feel a certain loyalty to it. This is a phenomenon that many of us experience in connection with the organizations for which we work—unless, of course, we are very unhappy with our work situations. And the organizations for which we work count on this feeling. They count on the fact that most of us will feel a certain amount of loyalty to the organization, and that this will help to deter us from quitting if some "nice opportunity" comes along. Despite its apparent lack of a rational basis, a bit of a "Rah! Rah!" attitude or a "I don't know why I'm attached to it; I just am" seems appropriate and desirable.

All of the above examples of loyalty emphasize the value of certain *attitudes and affections* which are central to loyalty. It can also be pointed out that many facets of human interaction would be impossible if we could not rely on each other to *act* loyally. Thus it is not just the *feeling* in loyalty that is important for human relationships, but also the *actions* which loyalty prompts. Friends would not confide in each other if they did not expect loyalty in the form of the keeping of these confidences.

The same is true on a large scale: a company needs to be able to count on its employees not to divulge trade secrets. Suppose that Engineer A and Engineer B are friends who are engaged in similar design projects at their respective businesses. Suppose, moreover, that the businesses are rivals. Under certain conditions it could be quite harmful to the company that employs Engineer A if she were to share with Engineer B the innovative plans that she and others at her company are working on. Her company depends on her special consideration for her company just because it is her company. In other words, it counts on her to be loyal. Imagine what would happen if Engineers A and B thought of the research that they were engaged in simply as research, and not as something that was being done *for* a certain company. It would be impossible for a company to compete successfully if too much vital information were leaked. Of course in a much less capitalistic society, where businesses did not compete as ours do, trade secrets would not have the same importance. Only if there is competition, and only if that competition is important, does information have to be thought of as "owned." But that hardly justifies American Engineer A in sharing such information with American Engineer B, or vice versa.

Note that on a yet larger scale, where the "company" is a country, the vital information concerns defense matters, and the information is leaked to someone regarded by the government as an enemy, the person suspected of leaking the information is regarded as a traitor. It is important to recognize that the concept of a traitor only makes sense given a background expectation of loyalty. It is considered so very serious to be "disloyal" to one's country in this manner (leaking security information) that in the United States, at least, the punishment imposed is sometimes death.[11] If all countries were at perpetual peace with one another, if there were no animosity, then here again, the situation would not arise.

Expectations of loyalty from an employee last even after the employee quits one company to join another. The former company has to count on the former employee for a certain amount of loyalty. This becomes evident when one ponders the following hypothetical case, posed by Richard T. De George in his *Business Ethics* (1982, p. 204):

> John Knosit was head of a research team of CDE Electric. His team was working on developing a cheaper and more effective filament for light bulbs. Six months ago, a rumor circulated in the industry that the team had made a breakthrough and all that was required was final testing. This would put CDE Electric far ahead of its competitors. Five months ago, X Electric hired John away from CDE, offering him $25,000 a year more than he had been getting. No mention was made of his work on the new filament. After being in his new position for three months, his superior approached him and said that X Electric had hired him because of his work on the filament and that he would have to develop the filament

quickly for X Electric or be fired. John knows how to develop the filament. Is he morally justified in developing it for X Electric?

Companies cannot control the departures of their employees: they can usually fire them at will, but they cannot force an employee to stay.[12] Nor can they keep someone from taking a job elsewhere (except, perhaps, by blackmailing, blackballing, or some other nefarious technique). Nor can they erase certain bits of information from the employee's memory. (Once again there are elaborate methods (hypnosis, electric shock "therapy"), but at least for the purposes of this paper, these are not worth regarding as options.) Companies simply must count on a certain modicum of loyalty on the part of those employees who, as employees, have important "trade secrets."

The dependence of companies on the loyalty of their employees is actually just an instance of a more general phenomenon. Our world is shaped by competition: there are goods which I—and my group—cannot have unless certain others do not get some of the same goods. Not everyone who applies for a fellowship gets it; not every team can win the championship. Those on the team count on each other to stick with the group, to aid it and not the opposing groups. A group member who refused to recognize the boundaries—i.e., who refused to think in terms of "us" and "them"—would, in some instances, be good cause for worry; a group leader who insisted on impartiality vis-à-vis other groups, on playing no favorites, would quickly be deposed. Imagine a department head in a university who refused additional travel money offered to the department by the Dean, on the grounds that a different department was more in need! Imagine a team captain who offered to have one of his best players take the place of someone on the opposing team who had been injured! Need we say more? These examples—as well as many others presented in this section—show that impartiality and a refusal to play (or have?) favorites can easily be overrated.

THE SYNTHESIS

At this stage we seem to be stuck in a dialectic, or a sort of tug-of-war. Loyalty seems so bad and yet so good. We must now tackle the really challenging question: Under what conditions is it wrong, on balance, to act as loyalty would demand—and under what conditions is it right to do so? What's a well-meaning, thoughtful engineer to do when faced with demands or expectations to be loyal, or when plagued by worries that a certain move (e.g., to quit a job she's recently begun for a more lucrative one) would be disloyal?

One answer will be based on a distinction commonly drawn in ethical theory: a distinction between *duties of justice* and *duties of benevolence.*

Among our duties of justice are duties to be fair, to be honest and to avoid inflicting or contributing to the needless suffering of others. These are strict duties; that is, they are duties which we owe to everyone. The violation of such a duty constitutes a violation of someone's right(s). If I deceive or rob someone, I violate his or her rights.[13]

Compare the duties just named with the duty to be kind and generous and to help those in need. I cannot help *everyone*; time, financial considerations, professional demands and the like preclude that. I can discharge the duty to help those in need without helping all who are in need. So it does not follow from the fact that I have a duty to be generous that I owe it to be generous to any particular person; more broadly, from the fact that I have duties of benevolence, it does not follow that I have a duty or duties of benevolence to any particular person. This being the case, no one to whom I have been unkind or ungenerous can correctly claim that (in itself) my lack of generosity or unkindness to him or her constituted a violation of his or her *rights*. It may be true that I've behaved badly, that I've been unkind and that this is an expression of a moral defect in my character; but if the duty that I failed to fulfill was a duty of benevolence and not a duty of justice, I have not violated anyone's rights. It may be true, of course, that I wasn't really behaving badly—I may simply have been unable to sacrifice my time or money to help this person in *these* circumstances, especially since I was helping a number of others. I am culpable only if I refuse the cases where people are most desperate and where the cost to me is quite low, *or* if I refuse far too often to help others and am just plain selfish. An example of the first type is the case of the thirty-eight witnesses who didn't bother even to call the police when Kitty Genovese slowly died in an alley from the wounds received in a stabbing. An example of the latter type would be someone who would perhaps phone the police in the sort of situation just described, but would never contribute to a charity or a political cause (unless, perhaps, the political cause was one which directly affected that person's interests), would never offer to give directions to someone who appeared to be lost, or help a blind person who, waiting to cross a busy street, is unaware that the light has turned green. The important thing for the reader to bear in mind, however, is simply that duties of justice are duties that one owes to everyone, and a failure to fulfill such duties to S constitutes an infringement of S's rights; whereas duties of benevolence are owed to no one in particular, and a failure to be benevolent to someone, no matter how culpable, does not in itself constitute a violation of that person's (or anyone else's) rights.

Applying the Distinction

Armed with the distinction between duties of justice and duties of benevolence, we can proceed to examine the duties of engineers vis-à-vis loyalty by asking: (1) Should an engineer act as loyalty directs if in doing so (s)he must violate a duty of justice, i.e., violate someone's rights? (2) Should one do what loyalty asks if in doing so one must violate a duty of benevolence?

It is vital to bear in mind that duties of justice and benevolence are matters of degree: some duties of justice (e.g., duties not to kill) are more important than others (e.g., a duty to keep one's promise to return a book to the library the next day), and likewise with duties of benevolence. Moreover, it is sometimes hard to say whether a certain duty is a duty of justice, or instead, a duty of benevolence.[14] And sometimes it isn't clear whether an alleged duty is a duty at all. This should not worry us as long as we do not expect (or even hope) to find a mechanical solution to the problem of precisely when one should act as loyalty dictates. If we expect *parameters* for decision-making, the classifications of duties of justice and duties of benevolence should prove useful.

I will argue that duties of justice override considerations of loyalty[15] and that duties of benevolence (other than loyalty) sometimes do and sometimes do not. In part for the reasons why it is difficult to come up with any useful, general principles which rank duties of benevolence, it is not easy to say in advance when the claims of loyalty trump duties of benevolence. Some guidelines can be provided, however, for adjudicating among such conflicting claims. The guidelines will also be of assistance in situations where loyalties themselves conflict, or where demands of loyalty clash with the engineer's own wishes.

Loyalty and Duties of Justice

That duties of justice override considerations of loyalty becomes quickly apparent when we recall what we are counting as considerations of loyalty. A consideration of loyalty is a consideration that because X is mine—my company, team, club, neighborhood, etc.—I should promote it and should concern myself more with its needs than with the needs of other parties (except insofar as they are also, in some meaningful way, mine). How do such considerations compete with duties of justice? It is clear, I think, that my obligation to respect the rights of others has to come before considerations of what is best for my company, family, neighborhood, etc. What I owe to everyone must supersede what I may do to promote the welfare of my "group," or my spouse or friend or sibling.[16] None of this should be taken as denying that we should promote the welfare of our group, and more will be said shortly which will underscore the importance of such loyal actions. All that I have said so far is that duties of justice must come first.

If this is right, we now have an explanation (and justification) for our intuitions on such dilemmas in engineering ethics as the one in which Kermit Vandivier found himself, or that in which those who worked on the Pinto found themselves. If loyalty to the company—"My company, right or wrong"—mandated that the engineers at Ford who knew of the Pinto's built-in dangers keep quiet about them, it is nonetheless the case that the rights of the consumers to *know* about any unusual dangers in the car that they were driving (or thinking about buying) must come first.[17] The engineers at B.F. Goodrich had a duty of justice *not* to deceive those who had commissioned the qualification test (the test as specified by the military, not as "re-created" by employees of Goodrich). This duty of justice trumps considerations of loyalty to one's superiors or to the company.[18] Similarly, the thesis that duties of justice override considerations of loyalty explains our intuition that illegal dumping of hazardous wastes is wrong, especially if it threatens to contaminate the water supply, and that it is wrong not simply because it is illegal. It violates the right of those who drink the water to have drinking water which is safe—at least as safe as the government is willing to insist that it must be. But the thesis helps us out only in instances where the claims of loyalty clash with duties of justice. So, much more needs to be said. . . .

NOTES

[Baron pursues questions about other claims of loyalty in sections not included here. See Marcia Baron, *The Moral Status of Loyalty* (Dubuque, Iowa. Kendall/Hunt Publishing Co., 1984)—ED.]

1. "The Corporation," CBS Reports, December 6, 1973.

2. Nader and Green do not indicate in what year this occurred. They said "recently" and their paper was first printed in 1973. For a plethora of stories of this sort, see Ewing (1977). One of the cases that Ewing reports is that of Louis V. McIntire, a chemical engineer who was fired by the Du Pont company when his supervisors came across the novel that he and his wife co-authored and published, *Scientists and Engineers: The Professionals Who Are Not.* The novel indirectly criticizes Du Pont by portraying in vivid detail a fictitious company, Logan Chemical, which resembles Du Pont.

3. See also Vandivier (1980).

4. Vandivier (1972, p. 233). Vandivier was at the time actually a data analyst and instrumentation writer. He started at Goodrich as an instrumentation engineer.

5. Rather than address this question directly, I will leave it to the reader to ponder the matter after reading my essay.

6. Of course, it could be that the notion of loyalty that is relevant to engineering ethics is *not* what is usually meant by "loyalty." But I do not think that this will turn out to be the case.

7. Alasdair MacIntyre takes a similar view in his Lindlay Lecture "Is Patriotism a Virtue?" (Lawrence, Kans.: The University of Kansas, 1984). For discussions of MacIntyre's and Oldenquist's views, see Marcia Baron, "Patriotism and 'Liberal' Morality," in David Weissbord, ed., *Mind, Value and Culture: Essays in Honor of E.M. Adams* (Atascadero, Calif.: Ridgeview Publishing Co., 1989) and Stephen Nathanson, "In Defense of 'Moderate' Patriotism," *Ethics*, vol. 99, no. 3 (April 1989), pp. 535–52.

8. It should be noted that like most motives, the motive of loyalty rarely operates by itself, and so when I speak, here and elsewhere, of people acting from or out of loyalty, I should not be taken to mean that they are then motivated *only* by loyalty. Loyalty may mix with self-interest.

9. According to Dowie (1980, p. 170), all proposals to improve the Pinto's safety—one of which would have cost only one dollar per car and added only one pound to each car's weight—were rejected out of hand because Iacocca was determined not to exceed the "limits of 2,000" that he had set. See also the chronology of events in the development and production of the Pinto in the *Chicago Tribune* (1979).

10. I do not mean to imply that this evaluative judgment is valid independently of the social structure in which the woman and the son live. Within a different social framework where there was nothing resembling the nuclear family, adults (or perhaps only those who are parents) might regard themselves as having a duty of benevolence (explained below) to children in general, without any special duties to their children in particular.

11. Julius and Ethel Rosenberg were executed on June 19, 1953, amidst widespread protest and proclamation of their innocence. They were accused of having given the Soviet Union the secret of the atom bomb.

12. In some instances employers can ask new employees to sign "noncompetitive agreements" requiring that in the event that the engineer leaves the company he or she may not work for any other company in the area for a certain length of time, both to be specified in the agreement. Feld (1980) sketches the conditions under which such a noncompetition agreement is valid.

13. My use of "right" and "rights" here follows common philosophical usage. A right is, roughly, a title or a "trump." If you have a right to X, the fact that millions of people will be

happier if your right isn't honored is irrelevant (assuming, of course, that you *really do* have a right to *X*). Your right trumps all considerations except competing rights. As Sharon Bishop Hill puts it (Hill 1975, p. 177), "The considerations [that a right] picks out as relevant mark off an area in which we do not allow considerations about either the general good or an individual's good to be decisive."

14. There are further problems with the distinction between duties of justice and duties of benevolence. First, the distinction is only as clear as the notion of rights, since duties of justice are duties to honor rights. And that notion is, at least in the opinion of many philosophers, itself riddled with problems. Secondly, it may not even be *that* clear, since if there are positive rights as well as negative rights—duties to do *X* for others as well as duties to refrain from doing *Y* to others—duties of justice may turn out to be duties to honor only a certain type of rights, viz., negative rights.

15. My position parallels and was to some extent inspired by Alan Goldman's position on the adversary system, as put forth in his discussion of legal ethics (1980).

16. Two clarifications are in order. First, things are different if the *rights* of (members of) my company, family, group are at stake. A subsistence right—a right to have the requisite food and shelter to stay alive—is at the *very least* in strong competition with a property right. Second, if two parties' rights compete and neither right appears to trump the other, it is presumably quite okay to favor one's loved ones. Hence, in a catastrophe in which, say, I can only save only one of two people, the other of whom will die without my aid, I do not act wrongly if I choose to save the person to whom I bear some special relation (friend, traveling companion, spouse, etc.). There is a growing literature in philosophy on these and related topics. See Anscombe (1967) and Bernard Williams (1976). In Baron (1984) I caution against some conclusions that Williams and others draw.

17. That at least some Ford engineers knew of the Pinto's dangers long before any accidents happened is documented by Mark Dowie (1980). See also De George (1981) and the *Chicago Tribune* (1979).

18. I have chosen my words carefully so as *not* to say that one must never act as loyalty directs if doing so violates someone's rights. I am inclined to this latter position, but I would not espouse it without thoroughly considering the complexities which arise because of the deplorable risk to whistleblowers—loss of job and, in some instances, profession. I will not discuss the question of whether an engineer should blow the whistle at great cost to herself or himself, since that is discussed in a different module in this series.

REFERENCES

ANSCOMBE, G.E.M. 1967. "Who Is Wronged?" *Oxford Review* 5:16–17.
BARON, MARCIA. 1984. "The Alleged Moral Repugnance of Acting from Duty." *The Journal of Philosophy* 81 (4):197–220.
BAUM, ROBERT, and ALBERT FLORES, eds. 1980. *Ethical Problems in Engineering*, 2nd ed. Troy, N.Y.: The Center for the Study of the Human Dimensions of Science and Technology.
Chicago Tribune. 1979. "Ignored Pinto danger, secret memos." October 14, p. 1.
DE GEORGE, RICHARD T. 1981. "Ethical Responsibilities to Engineers in Large Organizations: The Pinto Case." *Business and Professional Ethics Journal* 1(1):1–14.
———. 1982. *Business Ethics.* New York: MacMillan Publishing Company.
DOWIE, MARK. 1980. "Pinto Madness." In *Ethical Problems in Engineering*, ed. Baum and Flores, vol. II, pp. 167–74.
EWING, DAVID. 1977. *Freedom Inside the Organization.* New York: E. P. Dutton.
FELD, LIPMAN G. 1980. "Responsibilities to Former Employers." In *Ethical Problems in Engineering*, ed. Baum and Flores, vol. I, pp. 166–67.

GOLDMAN, ALAN. 1980. *The Moral Foundations of Professional Ethics*. Totowa, N.J.: Rowman and Littlefield.

HEILBRONER, ROBERT, ed. 1972. *In the Name of Profit*. Garden City, N.Y.: Doubleday and Company, Inc.

HILL, SHARON BISHOP. 1975. "Self-Determination and Autonomy." In *Today's Moral Problems*, ed. Richard Wasserstrom, pp. 171–86. New York: MacMillan Publishing Company.

HUME, DAVID. 1888. *Treatise of Human Nature*. (Many editions; citations here are to the Selby-Bigge edition.)

LADD, JOHN. 1967. "Loyalty." In *Encyclopedia of Philosophy*, ed. Paul Edwards, vol. V, pp. 97–98. New York: The MacMillan Company and The Free Press.

NADER, RALPH, and MARK GREEN. 1979. "Owing Your Soul to the Company Store." In *Ethical Issues in Business: A Philosophical Approach*, ed. Thomas Donaldson and Patricia H. Werhane, pp. 197–206. Englewood Cliffs, N.J.: Prentice Hall.

OLDENQUIST, ANDREW. 1982. "Loyalties." *The Journal of Philosophy* 79(4):179–93.

ROYCE, JOSIAH. 1908. *The Philosophy of Loyalty*. New York: The MacMillan Company.

VANDIVIER, KERMIT. 1972. "Why Should My Conscience Bother Me?" In *In the Name of Profit*, ed. Heilbroner, pp. 3–31.

———. 1980. "Engineers, Ethics and Economics." In *Ethical Problems in Engineering*, ed. Baum and Flores, vol. II, pp. 136–38.

WILLIAMS, BERNARD. 1976. "Persons, Character and Morality." In *The Identities of Persons*, ed. Amelie O. Rorty, pp. 197–215. Berkeley: University of California Press.

WRIGHT, J. PATRICK. 1980. "On a Clear Day You Can See General Motors." In *Ethical Problems in Engineering*, ed. Baum and Flores, vol. II, pp. 155–58.

20 Whistle-Blowing and Employee Loyalty

Ronald Duska

Three Mile Island. In early 1983, almost four years after the near meltdown at Unit 2, two officials in the Site Operations Office of General Public Utilities reported a reckless company effort to clean up the contaminated reactor. Under threat of physical retaliation from superiors, the GPU insiders released evidence alleging that the company had rushed the TMI cleanup without testing key maintenance systems. Since then, the Three Mile Island mop-up has been stalled pending a review of GPU's management.[1]

The releasing of evidence of the rushed cleanup at Three Mile Island is an example of whistle-blowing. Norman Bowie defines whistle-blowing as "the act by an employee of informing the public on the immoral or illegal behavior of an employer or supervisor."[2] Ever since Daniel Ellsberg's release of the Pentagon Papers, the question of whether an employee should blow the whistle on his company or organization has become a hotly contested issue. Was Ellsberg right? Is it right to report the shady or suspect practices of the organization one works for? Is one a stool pigeon or a dedicated citizen? Does a person have an obligation to the public which overrides his obligation to his employer or does he simply betray a loyalty and become a traitor if he reports his company?

There are proponents on both sides of the issue—those who praise whistle-blowers as civic heroes and those who condemn them as "finks." Glen and Shearer who wrote about the whistle-blowers at Three Mile Island say, "Without the *courageous* breed of assorted company insiders known as whistle-blowers—workers who often risk their livelihoods to disclose information about construction and design flaws—the Nuclear Regulatory Commission itself would be nearly as idle as Three Mile Island.

. . . That whistle-blowers deserve both gratitude and protection is beyond disagreement."[3]

Still, while Glen and Shearer praise whistle-blowers, others vociferously condemn them. For example, in a now-infamous quote, James Roche, the former president of General Motors said:

> Some critics are now busy eroding another support of free enterprise—the loyalty of a management team, with its unifying values and cooperative work. Some of the enemies of business now encourage an employee to be *disloyal* to the enterprise. They want to create suspicion and disharmony, and pry into the proprietary interests of the business. However this is labelled—industrial espionage, whistle blowing, or professional responsibility—it is another tactic for spreading disunity and creating conflict.[4]

From Roche's point of view, whistle-blowing is not only not "courageous" and deserving of "gratitude and protection" as Glen and Shearer would have it, it is corrosive and not even permissible.

Discussions of whistle-blowing generally revolve around four topics: (1) attempts to define whistle-blowing more precisely; (2) debates about whether and when whistle-blowing is permissible; (3) debates about whether and when one has an obligation to blow the whistle; and (4) appropriate mechanisms for institutionalizing whistle-blowing.

In this paper I want to focus on the second problem, because I find it somewhat disconcerting that there is a problem at all. When I first looked into the ethics of whistle-blowing it seemed to me that whistle-blowing was a good thing, and yet I found in the literature claim after claim that it was in need of defense, that there was something wrong with it, namely that it was an act of disloyalty.

If whistle-blowing was a disloyal act, it deserved disapproval, and ultimately any action of whistle-blowing needed justification. This disturbed me. It was as if the act of a good Samaritan was being condemned as an act of interference, as if the prevention of a suicide needed to be justified. My moral position in favor of whistle-blowing was being challenged. The tables were turned and the burden of proof had shifted. My position was the one in question. Suddenly instead of the company being the bad guy and the whistle-blower the good guy, which is what I thought, the whistle-blower was the bad guy. Why? Because he was disloyal. What I discovered was that in most of the literature it was taken as axiomatic that whistle-blowing was an act of disloyalty. My moral intuitions told me that axiom was mistaken. Nevertheless, since it is accepted by a large segment of the ethical community it deserves investigation.

In his book *Business Ethics*, Norman Bowie, who presents what I think is one of the finest presentations of the ethics of whistle-blowers, claims that "whistleblowing . . . violate[s] a *prima facie* duty of loyalty to one's employer." According to Bowie, there is a duty of loyalty which prohibits one from reporting his employer or company. Bowie, of course, recognizes that this is only a *prima facie* duty, i.e., one that can be overridden by a higher duty to the public good. Nevertheless, the axiom that whistle-blowing is disloyal is Bowie's starting point.

Bowie is not alone. Sisela Bok, another fine ethicist, sees whistle-blowing as an instance of disloyalty.

The whistleblower hopes to stop the game; but since he is neither referee nor coach, and since he blows the whistle on his own team, his act is seen as a *violation of loyalty* [italics mine]. In holding his position, he has assumed certain obligations to his colleagues and clients. He may even have subscribed to a loyalty oath or a promise of confidentiality. . . . Loyalty to colleagues and to clients comes to be pitted against loyalty to the public interest, to those who may be injured unless the revelation is made.[5]

Bowie and Bok end up defending whistle-blowing in certain contexts, so I don't necessarily disagree with their conclusions. However, I fail to see how one has an obligation of loyalty to one's company, so I disagree with their perception of the problem, and their starting point. The difference in perception is important because those who think employees have an obligation of loyalty to a company fail to take into account a relevant moral difference between persons and corporations and between corporations and other kinds of groups where loyalty is appropriate. I want to argue that one does not have an obligation of loyalty to a company, even a *prima facie* one, because companies are not the kind of things which are proper objects of loyalty. I then want to show that to make them objects of loyalty gives them a moral status they do not deserve and in raising their status, one lowers the status of the individuals who work for the companies.

But why aren't corporations the kind of things which can be objects of loyalty? . . .

Loyalty is ordinarily construed as a state of being constant and faithful in a relation implying trust or confidence, as a wife to husband, friend to friend, parent to child, lord to vassal, etc. According to John Ladd "it is not founded on just *any* casual relationship, but on a specific kind of relationship or tie. The ties that bind the persons together provide the basis of loyalty."[6] But all sorts of ties bind people together to make groups. I am a member of a group of fans if I go to a ball game. I am a member of a group if I merely walk down the street. I am in a sense tied to them, but don't owe them loyalty. I don't owe loyalty to just anyone I encounter. Rather I owe loyalty to persons with whom I have special relationships. I owe it to my children, my spouse, my parents, my friends and certain groups, those groups which are formed for the mutual enrichment of the members. It is important to recognize that in any relationship which demands loyalty the relationship works both ways and involves mutual enrichment. Loyalty is incompatible with self-interest, because it is something that necessarily requires we go beyond self-interest. My loyalty to my friend, for example, requires I put aside my interests some of the time. It is because of this reciprocal requirement which demands surrendering self-interest that a corporation is not a proper object of loyalty.

A business or corporation does two things in the free enterprise system. It produces a good or service and makes a profit. The making of a profit, however, is the primary function of a business as a business. For if the production of the good or service was not profitable the business would be out of business. Since non-profitable goods or services are discontinued, the providing of a service or the making of a product is not done for its own sake, but from a business perspective is a means to an end, the making of profit. People bound together in a business are not bound together for mutual fulfillment and support, but to divide labor so the business makes a profit.

Since profit is paramount if you do not produce in a company or if there are cheaper laborers around, a company feels justified in firing you for the sake of better production. Throughout history companies in a pinch feel no obligation of loyalty. Compare that to a family. While we can jokingly refer to a family as "somewhere they have to take you in no matter what," you cannot refer to a company in that way. "You can't buy loyalty" is true. Loyalty depends on ties that demand self-sacrifice with no expectation of reward, e.g., the ties of loyalty that bind a family together. Business functions on the basis of enlightened self-interest. I am devoted to a company not because it is like a parent to me. It is not, and attempts of some companies to create "one big happy family" ought to be looked on with suspicion. I am not "devoted" to it at all, or should not be. I *work* for it because it pays me. I am not in a family to get paid, but I am in a company to get paid.

Since loyalty is a kind of devotion, one can confuse devotion to one's job (or the ends of one's work) with devotion to a company.

I may have a job I find fulfilling, but that is accidental to my relation to the company. For example, I might go to work for a company as a carpenter and love the job and get satisfaction out of doing good work. But if the company can increase profit by cutting back to an adequate but inferior type of material or procedure, it can make it impossible for me to take pride in my work as a carpenter while making it possible for me to make more money. The company does not exist to subsidize my quality work as a carpenter. As a carpenter my goal may be good houses, but as an employee my goal is to contribute to making a profit. "That's just business!"

This fact that profit determines the quality of work allowed leads to a phenomenon called the commercialization of work. The primary end of an act of building is to make something, and to build well is to make it well. A carpenter is defined by the end of his work, but if the quality interferes with profit, the business side of the venture supercedes the artisan side. Thus profit forces a craftsman to suspend his devotion to his work and commercializes his venture. The more professions subject themselves to the forces of the marketplace, the more they get commercialized, e.g., research for the sake of a more profitable product rather than for the sake of knowledge jeopardizes the integrity of academic research facilities.

The cold hard truth is that the goal of profit is what gives birth to a company and forms that particular group. Money is what ties the group together. But in such a commercialized venture, with such a goal there is no loyalty, or at least none need be expected. An employer will release an employee and an employee will walk away from an employer when it is profitable to do so. That's business. It is perfectly permissible. Contrast that with the ties between a lord and his vassal. A lord could not in good conscience wash his hands of his vassal, nor could a vassal in good conscience abandon his lord. What bound them was mutual enrichment, not profit.

Loyalty to a corporation, then, is not required. But even more it is probably misguided. There is nothing as pathetic as the story of the loyal employee who, having given above and beyond the call of duty, is let go in the restructuring of the company. He feels betrayed because he mistakenly viewed the company as an object of his loyalty. To get rid of such foolish romanticism and to come to grips with this hard but accurate assessment should ultimately benefit everyone.

One need hardly be an enemy of business to be suspicious of a demand of loyalty to something whose primary reason for existence is the making of profit. It is simply the case that I have no duty of loyalty to the business or organization. Rather I have a duty to return responsible work for fair wages. The commercialization of work dissolves the type of relationship that requires loyalty. It sets up merely contractual relationships. One sells one's labor but not one's self to a company or an institution.

To think we owe a company or corporation loyalty requires us to think of that company as a person or as a group with a goal of human enrichment. If we think of it in this way we can be loyal. But this is just the wrong way to think. A company is not a person. A company is an instrument, and an instrument with a specific purpose, the making of profit. To treat an instrument as an end in itself, like a person, may not be as bad as treating an end as an instrument, but it does give the instrument a moral status it does not deserve, and by elevating the instrument we lower the end. All things, instruments and ends, become alike.

To treat a company as a person is analogous to treating a machine as a person or treating a system as a person. The system, company, or instrument get as much respect and care as the persons for whom they were invented. If we remember that the primary purpose of business is to make profit, it can be seen clearly as merely an instrument. If so, it needs to be used and regulated accordingly, and I owe it no more loyalty than I owe a word processor.

Of course if everyone would view business as a commercial instrument, things might become more difficult for the smooth functioning of the organization, since businesses could not count on the "loyalty" of their employees. Business itself is well served, at least in the short run, if it can keep the notion of a duty to loyalty alive. It does this by comparing itself to a paradigm case of an organization one shows loyalty to, the team.

Remember that Roche refers to the "management team" and Bok sees the name "whistleblowing" coming from the instance of a referee blowing a whistle in the presence of a foul. What is perceived as bad about whistle-blowing in business from this perspective is that one blows the whistle on one's own team, thereby violating team loyalty. If the company can get its employees to view it as a team they belong to, it is easier to demand loyalty. The rules governing teamwork and team loyalty will apply. One reason the appeal to a team and team loyalty works so well in business is that businesses are in competition with one another. If an executive could get his employees to be loyal, a loyalty without thought to himself or his fellow man, but to the will of the company, the manager would have the ideal kind of corporation from an organizational standpoint. As Paul R. Lawrence, the organizational theorist says, "Ideally, we would want one sentiment to be dominant in all employees from top to bottom, namely a complete loyalty to the organizational purpose."[7] Effective motivation turns business practices into a game and instills teamwork.

But businesses differ from teams in very important respects, which makes the analogy between business and a team dangerous. Loyalty to a team is loyalty within the context of sport, a competition. Teamwork and team loyalty require that in the circumscribed activity of the game I cooperate with my fellow players, so that pulling all together, we can win. The object of (most) sports is victory. But the winning in sports is a social convention, divorced from the usual goings on of society. Such a winning is most times a harmless, morally neutral diversion.

But the fact that this victory in sports, within the rules enforced by a referee (whistle-blower), is a socially developed convention taking place within a larger social context makes it quite different from competition in business, which, rather than being defined by a context, permeates the whole of society in its influence. Competition leads not only to winners but to losers. One can lose at sport with precious few serious consequences. The consequences of losing at business are much more serious. Further, the losers in sport are there voluntarily, while the losers in business can be those who are not in the game voluntarily (we are all forced to participate) but are still affected by business decisions. People cannot choose to participate in business, since it permeates everyone's life.

The team model fits very well with the model of the free-market system because there competition is said to be the name of the game. Rival companies compete and their object is to win. To call a foul on one's own teammate is to jeopardize one's chances of winning and is viewed as disloyalty.

But isn't it time to stop viewing the corporate machinations as games? These games are not controlled and are not over after a specific time. The activities of business affect the lives of everyone, not just the game players. The analogy of the corporation to a team and the consequent appeal to team loyalty, although understandable, is seriously misleading at least in the moral sphere, where competition is not the prevailing virtue.

If my analysis is correct, the issue of the permissibility of whistle-blowing is not a real issue, since there is no obligation of loyalty to a company. Whistle-blowing is not only permissible but expected when a company is harming society. The issue is not one of disloyalty to the company, but the question of whether the whistle-blower has an obligation to society if blowing the whistle will bring him retaliation. I will not argue that issue, but merely suggest the lines I would pursue.

I tend to be a minimalist in ethics, and depend heavily on a distinction between obligations and acts of supererogation. We have, it seems to me, an obligation to avoid harming anyone, but not an obligation to do good. Doing good is above the call of duty. In-between we may under certain conditions have an obligation to prevent harm. If whistle-blowing can prevent harm, then it is required under certain conditions.

Simon, Power and Gunneman set forth four conditions:[8] need, proximity, capability, and last resort. Applying these, we get the following.

1. There must be a clear harm to society that can be avoided by whistle-blowing. We don't blow the whistle over everything.

2. It is the "proximity" to the whistle-blower that puts him in the position to report his company in the first place.

3. "Capability" means that he needs to have some chance of success. No one has an obligation to jeopardize himself to perform futile gestures. The whistle-blower needs to have access to the press, be believable, etc.

4. "Last resort" means just that. If there are others more capable of reporting and more proximate, and if they will report, then one does not have the responsibility.

Before concluding, there is one aspect of the loyalty issue that ought to be disposed of. My position could be challenged in the case of organizations who are employers in non-profit areas, such as the government, educational institutions, etc. In this case my commercialization argument is irrelevant. However, I would maintain that any activity which merits the blowing of the whistle in the case of non-profit and service organizations is probably counter to the purpose of the institution in the first place. Thus, if there were loyalty required, in that case, whoever justifiably blew the whistle would be blowing it on a colleague who perverted the end or purpose of the organization. The loyalty to the group would remain intact. Ellsberg's whistle-blowing on the government is a way of keeping the government faithful to its obligations. But that is another issue.

NOTES

1. Maxwell Glen and Cody Shearer, "Going After the Whistle-blowers," *The Philadelphia Inquirer*. Tuesday, Aug. 2, 1983, Op-ed Page, p. 11a.

2. Norman Bowie, *Business Ethics* (Englewood Cliffs, N.J.: Prentice-Hall, 1982), p. 140. For Bowie, this is just a preliminary definition. His fuller definition reads, "A whistle blower is an employee or officer of any institution, profit or non-profit, private or public, who believes either that he/she has been ordered to perform some act or he/she has obtained knowledge that the institution is engaged in activities which a) are believed to cause unnecessary harm to third parties, b) are in violation of human rights or c) run counter to the defined purpose of the institution and who inform the public of this fact." Bowie then lists six conditions under which the act is justified. pp. 142–143.

3. Glen and Shearer, *op. cit.*

4. James M. Roche, "The Competitive System, to Work, to Preserve, and to Protect," *Vital Speeches of the Day* (May 1971), 445. This is quoted in Bowie, p. 141 and also in Kenneth D. Walters, "Your Employee's Right to Blow the Whistle," *Harvard Business Review*, 53, no. 4.

5. Sisela Bok, "Whistleblowing and Professional Responsibilities," *New York University Education Quarterly*, Vol. II, 4 (1980), p. 3.

6. John Ladd, "Loyalty," *The Encyclopedia of Philosophy*, Vol. 5, p. 97.

7. Paul R. Lawrence, *The Changing of Organizational Behavior Patterns: A Case Study of Decentralization* (Boston: Division of Research, Harvard Business School, 1958), p. 208, as quoted in Kenneth D. Walters, op. cit.

8. John G. Simon, Charles W. Powers, and Jon P. Gunnemann, *The Ethical Investor: Universities and Corporate Responsibility* (New Haven: Yale University Press, 1972).

21 The Role of the Law in Protecting Scientific and Technical Dissent

Alfred G. Feliu

Dissent in private employment, it is assumed by those who want to keep their corporate noses clean, is to be avoided at all costs. For a nation of free thinkers with a taste for the underdog, we are notably intolerant of outspokenness in the workplace. The First Amendment of the Constitution, the cornerstone of American civil liberties, limits *government* interference with free expression, but does not reach the activities of large, "government-like" private corporations. Management discretion, rather than government restrictions, define the bounds of dissent in corporate America.

Scientists and engineers are particularly burdened by this state of affairs. Trained to rely on their professional skills and senses, and required by statutes and ethical codes to act in the public interest, scientists and engineers make problematic employees. Management's need for flexibility is clear; the public's interest in independent-minded professionals is compelling. The resulting tension seems inevitable and hopelessly incurable.

The law has traditionally sided with management when dissent spilled over into (perceived) insubordination. In recent years, however, the law has increasingly intervened in defense of the responsible employee dissenter in situations in which the employee is acting to further an acknowledged public interest. I will review these legal developments, focusing particularly on one area of legal protection of special significance to scientists and engineers—namely, whistle-blower protection in federal health, safety, and environmental protection legislation enacted since 1970. A review of the leading cases in the area, keeping in mind the scope of the protection offered and the strengths and weaknesses of this type of anti-reprisal legislation, leads to the conclusion that, despite recent developments, the law, by its nature and by the nature of the problem, is an inadequate tool for protecting scientific and technical dissent in the corporation and for fostering a workplace in which the expression of unorthodox or minority points of view are not only tolerated, but encouraged.

BASIC ASSUMPTIONS

Three basic assumptions underlie this analysis.

First, that dissent in the workplace is not, like fair treatment or due process, an innately positive value to be applauded in all instances. One employee's dissent may very well be a co-worker's or manager's contentiousness. To be worthy of legal protection, a dissenting view should be: sincerely held and offered in good faith, based on credible data or information, and related to the safe and adequate performance of the job. Chronic naysayers tend to make speeches rather than exchange views or discuss problems. Neither the law nor management need strain to protect the merely contentious worker.

Second, in order to properly perform their jobs and by the very nature of their professions, scientists and engineers are on occasion required to express a differing professional view. Expressing their professional opinion on a subject within their expertise is often the essence of what they are paid to do, and the structural engineer, industrial chemist, or marine biologist who fails to bring to management's attention a differing view affecting the success of the project may properly be subject not only to dismissal, but to professional disciplining as well.

Finally, the expression of a differing professional opinion is not whistle-blowing, although an ignored or rejected dissenter may at some point resort to blowing the whistle. Dissent is the expression of a differing view; whistle-blowing is the disclosure to one in authority of a violation of law or threat to public health and safety in the hope of correcting the ill. Whistle-blowing, by definition, is an extraordinary act, usually involving going out of established channels with a concern related to the public interests. An employee who takes a differing view to a company official empowered to address such concerns is less the whistle-blower and more the customer at the company dispute-resolution store.

With these assumptions in mind, a review of the legal setting in which scientific and technical dissent occur is appropriate.

LEGAL BACKGROUND

Since the late 19th century, employers have been able to dismiss workers at will without incurring liability [1]; no reason need be offered the employee. Even a "bad" reason would not confer a right of redress on the employee. Underlying the employment-at-will doctrine is the freedom of contract notion that both parties benefited by being able to freely sever the relationship. Employees can move to a better position if one becomes available; employers, in turn, gain the flexibility to respond to shifting business needs. The perceived equality of this bargain faded with the pre-industrial workplace. Workers' ties to a job today, such as seniority rights and pension and medical benefits, further render illusory the assumed free mobility between jobs. Nonetheless, the employment-at-will doctrine remains the centerpiece of American employment law.

Employer discretion has, however, been somewhat restricted in ensuing decades. Congress, in the 1930s, 1940s, and 1950s, limited employers' ability to retaliate against workers who collectively seek to protect their rights through unionization [2]. Further job protection was provided to workers who asserted their rights under minimum wages/maximum hours laws [3]. In the 1960s, both the federal and state levels emphasized the protection of group rights, and employers were precluded from discriminating on the basis of race, color, sex, nationality, religion, age, and, to a lesser extent, handicap [4].

In the 1970s, the focus shifted to the individual rights of employees. For example, privacy legislation was enacted in some states guaranteeing workers access to their personnel files and restricting the use of polygraphs by employers [5]. Two developments particularly inform this discussion, namely, the development of a public policy exception to the employment-at-will doctrine, and, second, the enactment of statutory whistle-blower protection.

1. Public Policy Exception

Courts embraced the dismissal-at-will doctrine over a century ago. In the 1970s, courts began to create limited exceptions to the doctrine where a particular discharge violated a significant and identifiable public policy. For example, damages were awarded to employees who were dismissed for performing jury duty [6], for filing workers' compensation claims [7], and for rejecting the sexual advances of a supervisor [8]. Whistle-blowers were also protected in a number of notable cases. The following whistle-blowers who were discharged were allowed to sue their ex-employers: a quality control inspector who urged his employer to comply with Connecticut's food and drug act [9]; a West Virginia bank employee who furnished information to bank auditors regarding overcharged accounts [10]; an Illinois employee who reported co-worker thefts to the police, and then assisted in the subsequent investigation [11]; and a sales representative who refused to participate in an illegal scheme to fix retail gas prices in California [12]. The following trilogy of cases from New Jersey involving professional or health care employees is instructive.

In 1978, Frances O'Sullivan, an X-ray technician at Washington Memorial Hospital, was discharged for refusing to perform catheterizations on patients, a procedure that she was neither trained nor permitted—under New Jersey's Medical Practices Act—to perform. The New Jersey Board of Nursing issued a cease and desist order preventing further such actions by the hospital, but lacked the authority to reinstate O'Sullivan. A New Jersey appellate court ruled that an employee who is asked to perform an illegal act may not be terminated for refusing to do so [13]. The court found this to be particularly true where patient care was implicated, an area already extensively regulated by the government.

The most significant New Jersey case in this area arose out of the constructive discharge of the Director of Medical Research at Ortho Pharmaceutical Corporation, Dr. A. Grace Pierce. The New Jersey Supreme Court ruled that an employee whose dismissal violates a significant public policy may sue for wrongful discharge [14]. Unfortunately for Dr. Pierce, the facts of her case were found not to fit within the newly created exception to the dismissal-at-will rule.

Dr. Pierce was the only physician on a research team developing a new liquid treatment for chronic diarrhea in children and the aged. She objected to the use of large amounts of the suspected carcinogen saccharin in the drug. When she refused to give in to management's demand that she continue work on the drug, she was demoted and told she had no future with the company. She resigned and sued.

In court, Dr. Pierce argued that the standards of her profession demanded that she not continue work on the drug. In particular, she pointed to the Hippocratic Oath. The court, while recognizing an employee's right to sue for wrongful discharge, concluded that the Hippocratic Oath was an insufficient basis upon which to rely. Instead, the court required that the employee's action be based on specific legislation, regulations, court decisions, or, in certain instances, professional codes of ethics. Professional codes that were self-serving or administrative in character would not be sufficient. Actions based on personal morals rather than a professional code were also outside of the new protection. The court commented in this regard that employees responding to "a call of conscience should recognize that other employees and their employer might heed a different call." [15] In Dr. Pierce's case, the court determined that she was acting out of the mandates of her conscience and not in response to the ethical mandates of her profession. The court noted that there was no immediate threat to the public in that the drug had not yet been marketed, nor even approved by the FDA. In ruling against Dr. Pierce, the court expressed its fear that "[c]haos would result if a single doctor engaged in research were allowed to determine, according to his or her individual conscience, whether a project should continue."[16]

The third case is an interesting application of the *Pierce* decision. A New Jersey appellate court allowed a pharmacist who claimed he was discharged for forcing his employer to comply with the state Board of Pharmacy regulations to sue for wrongful discharge [17].

Sidney Kalman was the pharmacist-in-charge in a Grand Union store in Paramus, NJ. The store wanted to keep the pharmacy closed on July 4th while the remainder of the store was open. Kalman checked with the state Board and determined that the pharmacy was required to be open when the store was open. The pharmacy remained open on July 4th, and Kalman was fired when he appeared for work the next day.

Kalman was able to persuade the court that the relevant regulation implicated a significant public policy. He argued that an unsecured, unsupervised drug counter in a large store created the risk that potentially hazardous drugs would be sold by unqualified persons. The court noted that both the state regulations and the Code of Ethics of the American Pharmaceutical Association required Kalman to report the store's attempt to allow the pharmacy to remain unattended. The court concluded that this was "an instance where a code of ethics coincides with public policy." [18]

New Jersey is just one of a growing number of states, now approximately 20, that have recognized a public policy exception to the "dismissal-at-will" rule. New York is perhaps the most notable example of a state that has expressly refused to create such a limitation on employer's discharge rights. Just last year, the highest court in New York State rejected a suit by an assistant treasurer alleging a fraud of over $50 million resulting from illegal account manipulation by high management [19]. The court determined that such a radical departure from a century's worth of case law should await action by the state legislature. [Note that the employment-at-will doctrine was created and has been dutifully applied by the courts for over a century, and that half the other states modified the doctrine judicially.]

In sum, the public policy exception is just that—an exception to the general rule, and a limited one at that. Scientists or engineers whose expressions of differing views get them into personnel trouble will be unlikely to make use of this legal remedy, unless they meet the following three conditions: (1) they get themselves fired; being transferred, harassed, demeaned, or ignored is generally not enough; (2) they raise an issue clearly implicating a recognized and substantial public policy; and (3) they are willing to pursue litigation that will most likely take one to three years to complete. The public policy exception is more appropriately suited for martyrs than dissenters.

2. Whistle-Blower Protection Laws

The legislatures of three states—Michigan, Connecticut, and Maine—have enacted whistle-blower protection legislation that covers workers in the private sector [20]. This type of legislation protects employees against discrimination on the job for having reported a violation of law or regulation to a government body, or for having assisted in a government investigation. These laws parallel the protection offered by the court-created remedy just discussed, with one exception—the employee need not be fired, but merely discriminated against, to support a claim. These laws are so new that little can be said about the type of cases that have been filed. More such legislation can be expected in the coming years.

EMPLOYEE FREE SPEECH

As mentioned earlier, the First Amendment's free speech guarantee is not enforceable in the workplace. That is not to say that you lose your First Amendment rights upon entering the workplace; just that, in exercising your rights, you may lose your job.

What would a workplace with an enforceable First Amendment look like? Somewhat like a government workplace (putting aside for the moment other variables). Free speech rights are guaranteed to public sector employees. A differing opinion on an issue of public interest may be protected against retaliatory acts by superiors. For example, a federal appeals court in New York recently ruled that the director of nursing at Harlem Hospital, a municipal facility, could not be discriminated against because she disclosed illegal or wasteful practices at the hospital [21].

Two very recent developments indicate that the ether of free speech may be entering the corporate atmosphere. First, a federal appeals court in Pennsylvania ruled in October 1983 that an employee may not be fired for refusing to join his employer's lobbying effort [22]. In that case, an insurance agent was urged by his employer to lobby the state legislature for enactment of certain no-fault insurance law revisions. The employee was discharged, and was allowed to sue under the public policy exception described above. Those scientists and engineers active, for example, in the anti-nuclear movement or other political/social causes may find solace in such developments in the law.

Second, Connecticut has become the first state to enact statutory free speech protection for private sector employees [23]. Discipline or discharge for the exercise by employees of their constitutional free speech rights is prohibited insofar as the speech does not substantially or materially interfere with job performance or the working relationship between management and the employee.

The Connecticut statute tries to balance management's broad discretion in personnel matters with workers' right of expression. This is a difficult task. Employees who report violations of law are protected; the persistent complainer with a personal gripe that interferes with job performance presumably would not be.

The day-to-day experience of professional employees seems in special need of such protection. The toxicity of certain chemical substances may or may not be anticipated; the design problems presented by wind sheer for jumbo jets may not be easily resolved. Unless there is only one acceptable answer to the question posed, differing views within the professional staff must not only be expected, but encouraged.

To complete this overview of recent legal developments, attention to the legal protection for scientific and technical dissent in private sector employment—namely whistleblower protection, found in all major federal environmental protection and health and safety legislation enacted since 1970—is appropriate. The substantial experience gained under these legislative provisions supports the broader thesis on what we can and should expect of the law in relation to scientific and technical dissent.

WHISTLE-BLOWER PROTECTION IN FEDERAL LEGISLATION

The Occupational Safety and Health Act was enacted in 1970 with the laudable goal of ensuring a safe and healthful workplace for all Americans. Section 11(c) of the Act prohibits an employer from discharging or discriminating against an employee who exercises "any right afforded by" the Act [24]. Workers who complain to OSHA about what they believe to be hazardous conditions on the worksite, or who refuse to perform an assigned task because of a reasonable apprehension of serious injury, are protected under this provision. Similar protection exists in the Federal Mine Safety and Health Act Amendment of 1977 [25]. Workers making claims under both these whistle-blower provisions tend to be blue collar and on the construction site, working in factories or, in the case of the Mine Act, in the coal mines.

The whistle-blower protection that is most appropriate for use by scientists and engineers is found in the environmental protection and nuclear safety legislation enacted through the 1970s, such as the Clean Air Act [26], the Federal Water Pollution

Control Act [27], the Safe Drinking Water Act [28], the Toxic Substances Control Act [29], and the Energy Reorganization Act [30]. The cases under these provisions are instructive.

What type of employee has made effective use of these laws so far? Those in highly regulated work settings working in safety sensitive positions—for example, a quality control inspector or welder at a nuclear plant [31]; a chemist at the water pollution treatment plant [32]; a coordinator of environmental safety reports for a major coal company [33]; and a radiation safety officer at a hospital [34].

In order to be protected, the employee must raise an issue or perform an act in furtherance of the purposes of the federal environmental protection or nuclear safety legislation listed above [35]. The employees need not directly contact a government official or agency, but must do something more affirmative than merely discussing the topic over lunch with a buddy [36]. For example, a protected act may be the filing of a nonconformance report in a nuclear plant [37], discussion of safety issues with an on-site inspector [38], or establishing a policy for staff of apprising state regulatory officials of improper waste discharges at a treatment plant [39]. In expressing the view or taking the action, the employee must be acting to further the purposes of the legislation, although he or she need not specifically rely on the statute. Just as one can buy an item on sale without knowing it is on sale and still be entitled to the discount, protection against whistleblowing in certain settings can benefit the unknowing.

The employee need not be right on the merits, nor need the claim be meritorious. The claim need only be objectively reasonable [40]. Dissent would be unduly inhibited if the dissenting view were required to be correct, particularly when issues do not lend themselves to precise calculation, as is typically the case with scientific dissent.

The scope of employer action triggering the protection of the legislation is broad. Basically, any discriminatory personnel action will suffice, such as an unjustified bad performance review [41], a baseless denial of a leave application [42], the retaliatory transfer of the employee [43], the withdrawal of a previously approved raise [44], or, most dramatically, the firing of the dissenting employees [45].

Are there ways in which protection to which an employee may be entitled may nonetheless be lost? Yes, several ways.

As with all rights, the protection offered by this legislation is most often lost out of ignorance of its existence. Unknown rights cannot be asserted. With no outreach effort by the Department of Labor, which enforces these laws, widespread ignorance of this form of protection may be assumed. Tardiness may also result in loss of this protection, as employees are allowed only 30 days to file a claim [46].

Some employees have lost their rights by coupling their protected acts with abuses of their own. For example, a quality control inspector whose reports of serious non-compliances with specifications were ignored finally reported the problem to the Nuclear Regulatory Commission [47]. When his employer learned of the report, the inspector was reassigned. Two days later, the employee was found trying to remove the personnel records of 15 dismissed quality control inspectors. He was immediately suspended for this act of self-help, then terminated. The judge reviewing the case concluded that the inspector's act of removing the files constituted sufficient reason for his dismissal apart from his protected activity of reporting hazards to the NRC.

Finally, workers hired to monitor their employers' compliance with government regulations are prone to losing the protection to which they would otherwise be entitled by performing their job too well—by crusading rather than cooperating. A company-hired safety inspector is still the employer's employee. An insubordinate employee can be fired whether he or she is a clerk/typist or the director of environmental health. A safety inspector who nitpicks [48], an electrician who complains of a hazard not within his bailiwick [49], or a supervisor who antagonizes staff or seems to derive undue pleasure in discovering flaws in underlings' work product [50] can expect unsympathetic hearings from a judge following allegedly discriminatory treatment. As an example, a drinking-water inspector, although competent, was reassigned following numerous complaints about his attitude [51]. He was characterized as overbearing, volatile, as one who came on too strong, and who tended to require unnecessary procedures and remedies in his work. As described by the judge, the engineer tended to "extrapolate" beyond the point that his employer could support him [52]. The judge concluded that the transfer was designed to further enforcement of water system regulations which had been hindered by the engineer's attitude. Thus, a troublesome employee who injects personality into his scientific and technical dissent runs the risk of confusing the issue upon legal review, allowing form to prevail over substance, personality over performance. The legal issue must not be confused with the substantive technical issue upon which the dissenting view is based.

CASE STUDIES: RICHTER AND THOMAS

Two of the more notable cases arising under this legislation brought by professionals involve a medical physicist for a state cancer hospital and a DuPont chemist. A review of these cases and the factors prompting different legal results may be instructive.

1. Dr. Clifford Richter [53]

Ellis Fischel State Cancer Hospital in Columbia, MO, was licensed by the NRC to use radioactive materials for medical therapy purposes. Highly radioactive irridium seeds were implanted in a cancer patient in December 1977 to be removed prior to her discharge from the hospital. Over three months later, Dr. Clifford Richter, the Chief Medical Physicist and the Radiation Safety Officer at the hospital, discovered that four seeds had been mistakenly left in her body. As Radiation Safety Officer, Dr. Richter was required to report this incident to the NRC, which he did. It was later discovered that a suture needle had also been left in the patient. The presence of irridium seeds in the patient's body was hazardous not only to her, but to those with whom she came in contact after her discharge. After a review of the incident, the NRC concluded that the failure to remove the irridium from the patient's body violated a condition of the hospital's license to use radioactive materials, and sanctioned the hospital.

Dr. Richter, in his four years with the hospital, had consistently received outstanding ratings in reviews conducted by his peers. The hospital administration had requested a $10,000 raise for him just prior to his report to the NRC. (Dr. Richter never received that raise.) Six days after his report to the NRC, the hospital executive committee met to discuss the incident. Dr. Richter, though a member, was not invited. The committee directed Dr. Richter to clear further reports to the NRC through the hospital administration. At the same time, the Department of Medical Physics which he headed was abolished as an independent entity and made a division of the Radiation Therapy Department. Dr. Richter's next three job performance evaluations became progressively less favorable. Seven months later, the position of Chief Medical Physicist was eliminated; Dr. Richter was terminated two months after that.

Dr. Richter filed a claim with the Department of Labor alleging a violation of the employee protection provision of the Energy Reorganization Act. An administration law judge and later a federal appeals court found that the hospital had discriminated against Dr. Richter because of his actions in furtherance of the aims of that law—in this case, the safe medical use of radioactive materials. Dr. Richter was reinstated to his position as Chief Medical Physicist, awarded back pay and attorneys' fees, and had all adverse references in his personnel file removed. This case serves as a paradigm of how the law may serve to protect scientific and technical dissent.

2. Lovick Thomas [54]

Lovick Thomas, a chemist and DuPont employee for 35 years, prepared material safety data sheets at a DuPont chemicals, dye, and pigments laboratory. In September 1978, Thomas first expressed the view that DuPont's zircon mineral sands products presented a radioactive hazard. He later asked whether the alleged hazards should be included on the material safety data sheet on the substance. After its own review, DuPont determined that mention of the hazard was not necessary, and because Thomas disagreed, preparation of the material safety data sheet would be reassigned. Thomas received a satisfactory rating on his next performance review. His reviewer wrote, "Tends to be overly defensive vs. criticism and argues opposing views excessively—should concentrate on major priorities of job. Should take a more active role in moving his program." [55] The reviewer also noted that Thomas should consider an assignment with another division, the pigments group.

Thomas persisted. He wrote letters and memoranda to supervisors regarding new OSHA regulations in the area, and his continued belief in the hazards of zircon sands. Finally, Thomas indicated that he felt compelled to go to OSHA with his concern. Thomas was soon after reassigned to the pigments division, in part because he was dissatisfied with his recent performance ratings. Eight other members of the professional staff were reassigned at the same time. Thomas filed a claim alleging discrimination under the Toxic Substances Control Act.

As stated by the reviewing judge, the issue was not "whether Mr. Thomas is right or wrong, but rather whether he was discriminated against because he threatened to, or did, report a hazardous material made by DuPont." [56] The judge found no basis for the discrimination claim. Discrimination, the judge noted, means treating similarly-situated individuals differently. Thomas' performance ratings, while not what he thought he deserved, were not shown to be discriminatory. Further, his reassignment, contemporaneous with that of others, was not shown to be the result of his threat to go to OSHA with his complaint. The judge also noted that his salary had not been decreased. Finally, Thomas had earlier acknowledged that he would accept reassignment to the pigments division. The judge offered no opinion on the strength of Thomas' views regarding zircon sands, a question over which he had no jurisdiction.

LAW AS AN INADEQUATE TOOL

This review compels the conclusion that the law is an inadequate tool to foster and support scientific and technical dissent in the private sector. The law does have a role to play in protecting those employees who are retaliated against for expressing a differing view. The more significant factor, however, in assuring that differing views will be encouraged and listened to in the American workplace is a new management ethic that recognizes employees' views and experiences for what they are—a valuable resource upon which to draw. This does not require that a view contrary to office orthodoxy be adopted—only that it be listened to and rejected on the merits, if appropriate. The law can encourage this development primarily by focusing public attention on the issue— for example, through large damage awards to deserving employees—but cannot mandate it.

Why is the law inadequate? I suggest three reasons. First, the law is a cumbersome tool. Litigation is expensive and time-consuming, and drains the resources of the parties and the courts. Barring settlement, a case can be expected on the average to take two years to complete. Answers to personnel decisions cannot realistically wait that long. Also, legal action creates adversaries where once colleagues stood. Further, an effective employment relationship can rarely be reestablished after litigation, so that the seemingly inviting remedy of reinstatement is illusory. Finally, with the law as unsympathetic to employees' rights claims as it is at the current time, despite recent developments, it will be difficult to find a lawyer to take a case with so little law in its favor and so limited a prospective financial reward.

Secondly, legal remedies tend to be (for lack of a better term) issue-specific—that is, concerned only with the immediate question of whether the claim presented sets forth a violation of law as defined by statute or court decision. The policy question of whether dissent in the corporation should be encouraged or protected is not before a court on review. Only the subject of the speech, and not the speech itself, is protected. In contrast, the First Amendment protects generic "speech" and not particular speeches. A speech by an American Nazi party official and one by a Girl Scout troop leader are both entitled to the same protection. Only the time, place, and manner of the speech may be regulated. With employee free speech, it is the substance of the speech that determines its entitlement to protection. One of the ironies of the current state of the law is that to be protected, an employee is usually required to do the extraordinary, such as blow the whistle in a very public way, which in turn hastens the breakdown of the employment relationship. Under the current law, this public display may be required to entitle an employee to protection. If the worker stays within channels, works diligently within the system, and fails to leave a paper trail, he or she may be without a remedy.

Conversely, employers who respond dramatically, for example, by promptly and vehemently retaliating against an employee who performs a protected act, are more likely to be sued and lose than the subtle retaliator who waits a period of time and then makes life so miserable for the employee that he or she resigns in frustration. Of all the recent legal developments, only the Connecticut free speech law holds out the potential of focusing the issue on protecting dissent, and not merely selected dissenting views. Whether it and similar legislation will succeed will not be apparent for years.

Finally, the law is an inadequate tool because the legal issue does not parallel the substantive professional dispute prompting the dissenting view. An amazing metamorphosis takes place: a simple technical dispute involving, for example, the discharge of an effluent into a stream, becomes, for a judge applying existing law, a fact question involving such matters as motives, work histories, and the intent of Congress. Just as a rape trial seems to victimize the victim by requiring her to account for her sexual history and proclivities, so a whistle-blower or wrongful discharge suit turns on matters unrelated to the substance of the original dispute. As the judge in the *Thomas* case said, the issue is not whether the employee was right or wrong, but rather whether there was discrimination under the law [57]. Thomas lost, despite very sympathetic facts—an experienced chemist speaking out forcefully about a perceived hazard. There is a lesson in that for scientists and engineers who expect to win a lawsuit simply because they feel that they are right on the merits of the case, believing the scientific/ technical issue encompasses the legal issue. Dr. Richter, in contrast, won his case because 1) his actions furthered the purposes of a particular federal law, 2) the hospital's actions were egregiously discriminatory, and 3) the hospital's actions were in direct retaliation for his protected activity. The fact that Dr. Richter's claims proved meritorious was of little consequence in the lawsuit. Legal rights and scientific truth need not cross paths. This fact became particularly clear to me in speaking to the Chief Administrative Law Judge for the Department of Labor [58]. When asked if the complex technical issues often present in these cases turned the matter into a battle of experts, he assured that it did not. The sole issue for the judge is the question of discrimination, and side trips into the intricacies of a scientific or technical disagreement only get in the judge's way. In legal terms, evidence offered on the substance of the technical dispute, depending on the circumstances, may not be allowed into evidence as simply not being relevant to the discrimination question, which is the focus of the lawsuit. The law and science make, at times, awkward bedfellows.

PROPER ROLE OF THE LAW

The proper role for the law, then, is that of teacher, standard-setter, and, when necessary and solely for its therapeutic value, punisher of flagrant violators.

The law unquestionably can prohibit discrimination on the basis of race, sex, or age, factors for which no legitimate grounds exist. The law can prohibit the use of lie detectors in the workplace, since management has no overpowering need to use them to run its business effectively. The law can even protect against hazards in the workplace so that management cannot improperly threaten worker safety. To mandate the recognition of the value of dissenting views in the workplace, however, is a more delicate task requiring a less blunt tool than the law. The law has long recognized that management must be given broad prerogatives in running its business as it sees fit. A company's acceptance and recognition of differing views in the workplace has traditionally been viewed solely as a question of management style. The law cannot effectively mandate an open workplace marked by the free and willing exchange of views. To require management to hear is not to assure that it will listen.

[. . .] Robert Jackall has persuasively demonstrated how the bureaucratic ethic, which extolls fealty to one's immediate superiors and the perception of being a team player, works to dilute personal and moral responsibility for corporate decisions [59]. The idealogue, the stickler for detail, the noble dissenter—the resister in one form or another—is discredited, shunned, and inevitably (in personnel manager's jargon) "separated" in this setting.

The law, in contrast, has a tradition of the noble dissenter—Oliver Wendell Holmes, Louis Brandeis, William O. Douglas—whose views in dissent have come to be adopted by future generations. Litigation, adversarial in nature, lends itself naturally to prevailing and dissenting views. The American workplace typically does not. Production schedules, to those who live by them, determine continued employment, not retroactive acceptance of their views. Making widgets and making law are not comparable, at least in this respect. The physicist, the marine biologist, and the chemical engineer, working in the corporate setting, are more often in the role of widget-makers rather than lawmakers. Dissenting views like Dr. Pierce's and Mr. Thomas' are likely to be resented rather than respected.

FREE SPEECH AS GOOD POLICY

The laws reviewed above are, to a limited extent, able to protect the dissenting employee. One form of protection, the statutory whistleblower protection found in major federal environmental and health and safety legislation, is particularly suited to the needs of the dissenting scientist and engineer working in certain highly regulated industries. This protection has the further advantage of being relatively efficient and inexpensive. Nonetheless, less than half of the claims filed that have not already been withdrawn or dismissed result in a finding of discrimination. In the three years since enactment of the Michigan whistleblowing protection law, only a handful of lawsuits have been filed, and none as yet have resulted in a reported court decision. This is not to say that such legislation is not desirable or worthy of support. Rather, it is to emphasize the limited nature of the protection it promises.

These laws do, however, establish public policy, setting standards against which behavior should be measured. Laws in the employment environment, as elsewhere, have a way, after an initial period of assimilation, of becoming policy. What major respected chemical concern today would not make a serious effort to assure that it produced a safe product while providing a safe workplace for its workers? Fourteen years after enactment of OSHA, occupational safety and health have become part of the cost of doing business and an integral part of corporate planning, and not merely a liability concern of counsel. So, too, with Title VII of the Civil Rights Act of 1964 and employment discrimination. Equal employment opportunity has become part of the personnel management function of any good, profitable firm, not simply because it is the law, but because it is good policy.

Free expression in the workplace must follow the same course. We as a society can enact, and should enact, further legislation to protect legitimate employee dissent. Such legislation has a way of publicizing the need for protection and of punishing in a very public way egregious (or unlucky) offenders of the law. Publicity is good. Public awareness is good. Legislation in this area, as in the occupational safety and health and employment discrimination areas, will eventually lead, I believe, to good management policies and practices. Fair treatment of employees is also being encouraged by competition from abroad. Progressive companies are instituting a variety of employee participation models, such as quality control circles. Some have gone further and established internal dispute-resolution systems in which scientific and technical disagreements may get a full airing. Further, publicity surrounding the enactment of whistle-blower protection or free speech legislation may encourage both the general public and management policy makers to value more highly free expression in the workplace.

But what of the individual scientist or engineer in the interim? Differing views are too infrequently welcome in the workplace. With or without legal protection, the question of whether to speak out is an intensely personal one depending on the nature and importance of the issue and the strength of the convictions and character of the prospective dissenter. Noble causes do not require noble characters, only individuals with strong senses of personal responsibility. We may, with Professor Stephen Unger, hope for "an enhanced sense of responsibility on the part of the individual." [60] We should also work towards making the expression of a dissenting view easy rather than extraordinary or bold. Dissenters should not have to be martyrs, sacrificed for the cause of full disclosure.

Until that time, the expression of dissenting views will be left to the courageous and the foolhardy. And until that time, the law should be broadened, as it has been in the state of Connecticut, to come to the aid of the brave and foolhardy who do what it would seem should be expected of every employee—namely, to express his or her opinion on a work-related issue without fear of reprisal.

NOTES

1. See, e.g., *Payne v. Western & A.R.R.*, 81 Tenn. 507, 519–20 (1884), overruled on other grounds, *Hutton v. Watters*, 132 Tenn. 527, 179 S.W. 134 (1915).
2. National Labor Relations Act, 29 U.S.C. §151, *et seq.*
3. Fair Labor Standards Act, 29 U.S.C. §215.
4. Civil Rights Act of 1964, 42 U.S.C. §2000e; Rehabilitation Act of 1973, 29 U.S.C. §794.
5. Personnel file statutes: Cal. Lab. Code §1198.5; Conn. Gen. Stat. Ann. §31-1238 (b); Pa. Stat. Ann. tit. 43 §1321. Polygraph statutes: Mass. Gen. Laws Ann. ch. 149, §19B; N.J.S.A. §2A:170–90.1.

6. See, e.g., *Reuther v. Fowler & Williams, Inc.*, 255 Pa. Super. Ct. 28, 386 A. 2d 119 (1978).

7. *Frampton v. Central Indiana Gas Co.*, 260 Ind. 249, 297 N.E.2d 425 (1973).

8. *Monge v. Beebe Rubber*, 114 N.H. 130, 316 A.2d 549 (1974).

9. *Sheets v. Teddy's Frosted Foods, Inc.*, 179 Conn. 471, 427 A.2d 385 (1980).

10. *Harless v. First National Bank in Fairmont*, 246 S.E.2d 270 (W. Va. 1978).

11. *Palmateer v. International Harvester Co.*, 85 Ill.2d 124, 421 N.E.2d 876 (1981).

12. *Tameny v. Atlantic Richfield Co.*, 27 Cal.3d 167, 164 Cal. Rptr. 839, 610 P.2d 1330 (1980).

13. *O'Sullivan v. Mallon*, 160 N.J. Super. 416, 390 A.2d 149 (1978).

14. *Pierce v. Ortho Pharmaceutical Corp.*, 84 N.J. 58, 417 A.2d 505 (1980). *See* Feliu, "Discharge of Professional Employees: Protecting Against Dismissal for Acts Within a Professional Code of Ethics," 11 *Colum. Hum. Rts. L. Rev.* 149 (1979/1980).

15. *Id.* at 75, 417 A.2d at 514.

16. *Id.*

17. *Kalman v. Grand Union Company*, 183 N.J. Super. 153, 443 A.2d 728 (1982).

18. 443 A.2d at 730.

19. *Murphy v. American Home Products*, 58 N.Y.2d 293, 461 N.Y.S.2d 232 (1983).

20. Mich. Stat. Ann, §§17.428.1-9; 1982 Conn. Pub. Acts §2-289; Me. Stat. ch. 452 §821 *et seq.*

21. *Rookard v. Health and Hospitals Corporation*, 710 F.2d 41 (2d Cir. 1983).

22. *Novosel v. Nationwide Insurance Co.*, 721 F.2d 894 (3d Cir. 1983).

23. Conn. Pub. Act 83-578 (Oct. 1, 1983).

24. 29 U.S.C. §660.

25. 30 U.S.C. §§815, 820(b).

26. 42 U.S.C. §§7401, 7622.

27. 33 U.S.C. §1367.

28. 42 U.S.C. §300j-9.

29. 15 U.S.C. §26622.

30. 42 U.S.C. §5851.

31. See, e.g., *Atchison v. Brown & Root, Inc.*, 82 ERA 9; *Crider v. Pullman Power Products Corp.*, 82 ERA 7.

32. *Ray v. Harrington*, 79 SDWA 2; *Ray v. Metropolitan Government*, 80 SDWA 1.

33. *Murphy v. Consolidated Coal*, 83 ERA 4.

34. *Richter v. Ellis Fischel State Cancer Hospital*, 79 ERA 1, *aff'd*, 629 F.2d 563 (8th Cir. 1980), *cert. denied*, 450 U.S. 1040 (1981) (hereinafter "*Richter*").

35. See 29 C.F.R. 24.2.

36. See *Murphy v. Consolidated Coal*, 83 ERA 4.

37. See *Atchison v. Brown & Root, Inc.*, 82 ERA 9.

38. *DeFord v. Tennessee Valley Authority*, 81 ERA 1; *Hedden v. Conam Inspection*, 82 ERA 3.

39. *Fischer v. Town of Steilacoom*, 83 WPCA 2.

40. *Id.*

41. *Richter, supra*, note 34.

42. *Hanna v. School District*, 79 TSCA 1, *rev'd*, 657 F.2d 16 (3d Cir. 1981).

43. *DeFord v. Tennessee Valley Authority*, 81 ERA 1.

44. *Richter, supra*, note 34.

45. *Cotter v. Con Edison*, 81 ERA 6.

46. *Greenwald v. City of North Miami Beach*, 587 F.2d 779 (5th Cir.), *cert. denied*, 444 U.S. 826 (1979).

47. *Dartey* v. *Zack Company*, 82 ERA 2.

48. *Murphy* v. *Consolidated Coal*, 83 ERA 4.

49. *In the Matter of William Wood*, 79 ERA 3.

50. *Mackowiak* v. *University Nuclear Systems*, 82 ERA 8; *Murphy* v. *Consolidated Coal*, 83 ERA 4.

51. *Bauch* v. *Landers*, 79 SDWA 1.

52. *Id.* at p. 5.

53. *Richter, supra,* note 34. *See Science,* March 1980.

54. *Thomas* v. *DuPont*, 81 TSCA 1.

55. *Id.* at p. 3.

56. *Id.* at p. 5.

57. *Id.*

58. Meeting with Chief Administrative Law Judge Nahum Litt, April 19, 1982.

59. Jackall, Robert, "Moral Mazes: bureaucracy and managerial work," *Harvard Business Review*, Sept./Oct. 1983, p. 118.

60. Unger, Stephen H., *Controlling Technology: Ethics and the Responsible Engineer*, p. 137 (Holt, Rinehart & Winston, New York), 1982.

22 Whistle-Blowing: Its Moral Justification

Gene G. James

Whistle-blowing may be defined as the attempt of an employee or former employee of an organization to disclose what he or she believes to be wrongdoing in or by the organization. Like blowing a whistle to call attention to a thief, whistle-blowing is an effort to make others aware of practices one considers illegal or immoral. If the wrongdoing is reported to someone higher in the organization, the whistle-blowing may be said to be *internal*. If the wrongdoing is reported to outside individuals or groups, such as reporters, public interest groups, or regulatory agencies, the whistle-blowing is *external*. If the harm being reported is primarily harm to the whistle-blower alone, such as sexual harassment, the whistle-blowing may be said to be *personal*. If it is primarily harm to other people that is being reported, the whistle-blowing is *impersonal*. Most whistle-blowing is done by people currently employed by the organization on which they are blowing the whistle. However, people who have left an organization may also blow the whistle. The former may be referred to as *current* whistle-blowing, the latter as *alumni* whistle-blowing. If the whistle-blower discloses his or her identity, the whistle-blowing may be said to be *open*; if the whistle-blower's identity is not disclosed, the whistle-blowing is *anonymous*.

Whistle-blowers almost always experience retaliation. If they work for private firms and are not protected by unions or professional organizations, they are likely to be fired. They are also likely to receive damaging letters of recommendation and may even be blacklisted so that they cannot find work in their profession. If they are not fired, they are still likely to be transferred, given less interesting work, denied salary increases and promotions, or demoted. Their professional competence is usually attacked. They are said to be unqualified to judge, misinformed, etc. Since their actions may threaten both the organization and their fellow employees, attacks on their personal lives are also frequent. They are called traitors, rat finks, disgruntled, known trouble makers, people who make an issue out of nothing, self-serving, and publicity seekers. Their life-styles, sex lives, and mental stability may be questioned. Physical assaults, abuse of their families, and even murder are not unknown as retaliation for whistle-blowing.

WHISTLE-BLOWING AND THE LAW[1]

The law does not at present offer whistle-blowers very much protection. Agency law, the area of common law which governs relations between employees and employers, imposes a duty on employees to keep confidential any information learned through their employment that might be detrimental to their employers. However, this duty does not hold if the employee has knowledge that the employer either has committed or is about to commit a felony. In this case the employee has a positive obligation to report the offense. Failure to do so is known as misprision and makes one subject to criminal penalties.

One problem with agency law is that it is based on the assumption that unless there are statutes or agreements to the contrary, contracts between employees and employers can be terminated at will by either party. It therefore grants employers the right to discharge employees at any time for any reason or even for no reason at all. The result is that most employees who blow the whistle, even those who report felonies, are fired or suffer other retaliation. One employee of thirty years was even fired the day before his pension became effective for testifying under oath against his employer, without the courts doing anything to aid him.

This situation has begun to change somewhat in recent years. In *Pickering v. Board of Education* in 1968 the Supreme Court ruled that government employees have the right to speak out on policy issues affecting their agencies provided doing so does not seriously disrupt the agency. A number of similar decisions have followed, and the right of government employees to speak out on policy issues now seems firmly established. But employees in private industry cannot criticize company policies without risking being fired. In one case involving both a union and a company doing a substantial portion of its business with the federal government, federal courts did award back pay to an employee fired for criticizing the union and the company but did not reinstate or award him punitive damages.

A few state courts have begun to modify the right of employers to dismiss employees at will. Courts in Oregon and Pennsylvania have awarded damages to employees fired for serving on juries. A New Hampshire court granted damages to a woman fired for refusing to date her foreman. A West Virginia court reinstated a bank employee who reported illegal interest rates. The Illinois Supreme Court upheld the right of an employee to sue when fired for reporting and testifying about criminal activities of a fellow employee. However, a majority of states still uphold the right of employers to fire employees at will unless there are statutes or agreements to the contrary. To my knowledge only one state, Michigan, has passed a law prohibiting employers from retaliating against employees who report violations of local, state, or federal laws.

A number of federal statutes contain provisions intended to protect whistle blowers. The National Labor Relations Act, Fair Labor Standards Act, Title VII of the 1964 Civil Rights Act, Age Discrimination Act, and the Occupational Safety and Health Act all have sections prohibiting employers from taking retaliatory actions against employees who report or testify about violations of the acts. Although these laws seem to encourage and protect whistle blowers, to be effective they must be enforced. A 1976 study[2] of the Occupational Safety and Health Act showed that only about 20 percent of the 2300 complaints filed in fiscal years 1975 and 1976 were judged valid by OSHA investigators. About half of these were settled out of court. Of the sixty cases taken to court at the time of the study in November 1976, one had been won, eight lost, and the others were still pending. A more recent study[3] showed that of the 3100 violations reported in 1979, only 270 were settled out of court and only sixteen litigated.

Since the National Labor Relations Act guarantees the right of workers to organize and bargain collectively, and most collective bargaining agreements contain a clause requiring employers to have just cause for discharging employees, these agreements would seem to offer some protection for whistle blowers. In fact, however, arbitrators have tended to agree with employers that whistle blowing is an act of disloyalty which disrupts business and injures the employer's reputation. Their attitude seems to be summed up in a 1972 case in which the arbitrator stated that one should not "bite the hand that feeds you and insist on staying for future banquets."[4] One reason for this attitude, pointed out by David Ewing, is that unions are frequently as corrupt as the organizations on which the whistle is being blown. Such unions he says, "are not likely to feed a hawk that comes to prey in their own barnyard."[5] The record of professional societies is not any better. They have generally failed to come to the aid or defense of members who have attempted to live up to their codes of professional ethics by blowing the whistle on corrupt practices.

THE MORAL JUSTIFICATION OF WHISTLE-BLOWING

Under what conditions, if any, is whistle blowing morally justified? Some people have argued that whistle blowing is never justified because employees have absolute obligations of confidentiality and loyalty to the organization for which they work. People who argue this way see no difference between employees who reveal trade secrets by selling information to competitors and whistle blowers who disclose activities harmful to others.[6] This position is similar to another held by some business people and economists that the sole obligation of corporate executives is to make a profit for stockholders. If this were true, corporate executives would have no obligations to the public. However, no matter what one's special obligations, one is never exempt from the general obligations we have to our fellow human beings. One of the most fundamental of these obligations is to not cause avoidable harm to others. Corporate executives are no more exempt from this obligation than other people.

Just as the special obligations of corporate executives to stockholders cannot override their more fundamental obligations to others, the special obligations of employees to employers cannot override their more fundamental obligations. In particular, obligations of confidentiality and loyalty cannot take precedence over the fundamental duty to act in ways that prevent unnecessary harm to others. Agreements to keep something secret have no moral standing unless that which is to be kept secret is itself morally justifiable. For example, no one can have an obligation to keep secret a conspiracy to murder someone, because murder is an immoral act. It is for this reason also that employees have a legal obligation to report an employer who has committed or is about to commit a felony. Nor can one justify participation in an illegal or immoral activity by arguing that one was merely following orders. Democratic governments repudiated this type of defense at Nuremberg.

It has also been argued that whistle blowing is always justified because it is an exercise of the right to free speech. However, the right to free speech is not absolute. An example often used to illustrate this is that one does not have the right to shout "Fire" in a crowded theater because that is likely to cause a panic in which people may be injured. Analogously, one may have a right to speak out on a particular subject, in the sense that there are no contractual agreements which prohibit one from doing so, but it nevertheless be the case that it would be morally wrong for one to do so because it would harm innocent people, such as one's fellow workers and stockholders who are not responsible for the wrongdoing being disclosed. The mere fact that one has the right to speak out does not mean that one ought to do so in every case. But this kind of consideration cannot create an absolute prohibition against whistle blowing, because one must weigh the harm to fellow workers and stockholders caused by the disclosure against the harm to others caused by allowing the organizational wrong to continue. Furthermore, the moral principle that one must consider all people's interests equally prohibits giving priority to one's own group. There is, in fact, justification for not giving as much weight to the interests of the stockholders as to those of the public, because stockholders investing in corporate firms do so with the knowledge that they undergo financial risk if management acts in imprudent, illegal, or immoral ways. Similarly, if the employees of a company know that it is engaged in illegal or immoral activities and do not take action, including whistle blowing, to terminate the activities, then they too must bear some of the guilt for the actions. To the extent that these conditions hold, they nullify the principle that one ought to refrain from whistle blowing because speaking out would cause harm to the organization. Unless it can be shown that the harm to fellow workers and stockholders would be *significantly greater* than the harm caused by the organizational wrongdoing, the obligation to avoid unnecessary harm to the public must take precedence. Moreover, as argued above, this is true even when there are specific agreements which prohibit one from speaking out, because such agreements are morally void if the organization is engaged in illegal or immoral activities. In that case one's obligation to the public overrides one's obligation to maintain secrecy.

CRITERIA FOR JUSTIFIABLE WHISTLE-BLOWING

The argument in the foregoing section is an attempt to show that unless special circumstances hold, one has a obligation to blow the whistle on illegal or immoral actions—an obligation that is grounded on the fundamental human duty to avoid preventable harm to others. In this section I shall attempt to spell out in greater detail the conditions under which blowing the whistle is morally obligatory. Since Richard De George has previously attempted to do this, I shall proceed by examining the criteria he has suggested.[7]

De George believes there are three conditions that must hold for whistle-blowing to be morally permissible and two additional conditions that must hold for it to be morally obligatory. The three conditions that must hold for it to be morally permissible are:

1. The firm, through its product or policy, will do serious and considerable harm to the public, whether in the person of the user of its product, an innocent bystander, or the general public.
2. Once an employee identifies a serious threat to the user of a product or to the general public, he or she should report it to his or her immediate superior and make his or her moral concern known. Unless he or she does so, the act of whistle blowing is not clearly justifiable.
3. If one's immediate superior does nothing effective about the concern or complaint, the employee should exhaust the internal procedures and possibilities within the firm. This usually will involve taking the matter up the managerial ladder, and, if necessary—and possible—to the board of directors.

The two additional conditions which De George thinks must hold for whistle-blowing to be morally obligatory are:

4. The whistle blower must have, or have accessible, documented evidence that would convince a reasonable, impartial observer that one's view of the situation is correct and that the company's product or practice poses a serious and likely danger to the public or to the user of the product.
5. The employee must have good reason to believe that by going public the necessary changes will be brought about. The chance of being successful must be worth the risk one takes and the danger to which one is exposed.[8]

De George intends for the proposed criteria to apply to situations in which a firm's policies or products cause physical harm to people. Indeed, the first criterion he proposes is intended to restrict the idea of harm even more narrowly to threats of serious bodily harm or death.

De George apparently believes that situations which involve threats of serious bodily harm or death are so different from those involving other types of harm, that the kind of considerations which justify whistle-blowing in the former situations could not possibly justify it in the latter. Thus, he says, referring to the former type of whistle-blowing: "As a paradigm, we shall take a set of fairly clear-cut cases, namely, those in which serious bodily harm—including possible death—threatens either the users of a product or innocent bystanders."[9]

One problem in restricting discussion to clear-cut cases of this type, regarding which one can get almost universal agreement that whistle blowing is justifiable, is that it leaves us with no guidance when we are confronted with more usual situations involving other types of harm. Although De George states that his "analysis provides a model for dealing with other kinds of whistle blowing as well,"[10] his criteria in fact provide no help in deciding whether one should blow the whistle in situations involving such wrongs as sexual harassment, violations of privacy, industrial espionage, insider trading, and a variety of other harmful actions.

No doubt, one of the reasons De George restricts his treatment the way he does is to avoid having to define harm. This is indeed a problem. For if we fail to put any limitations on the idea of harm, it seems to shade into the merely offensive or distasteful and thus offer little help in resolving moral problems. But, on the other hand, if we restrict harm to physical injury, as De George does, it then applies to such a limited range of cases that it is of minimal help in most of the moral situations which confront us. One way of dealing with this problem is by correlating harm with violations of fundamental human rights such as the rights to due process, privacy, and property, in addition to the right to freedom from physical harm. Thus, not only situations which involve threats of physical harm, but also those involving actions such as sexual harassment which violates the right to privacy and causes psychological harm, compiling unnecessary records on people, and financial harm due to fraudulent actions, are situations which may justify whistle-blowing.

A still greater problem with De George's analysis is that even in cases where there is a threat of serious physical harm or death, he believes that this only makes whistle-blowing morally permissible, rather than creating a strong *prima facie* obligation in favor of whistle-blowing. His primary reasons for believing this seem to be those stated in criterion 5. Unless one has reason to believe that the whistle-blowing will eliminate the harm, and the cost to oneself is not too great, he does not believe whistle-blowing is morally obligatory. He maintains that this is true even when the person involved is a professional whose code of ethics requires her or him to put the public good ahead of private good. He argued in an earlier article, for example, that:

> The myth that ethics has no place in engineering has . . . at least in some corners of the engineering profession . . . been put to rest. Another myth, however, is emerging to take its place—the myth of the engineer as moral hero. . . . The zeal . . . however, has gone too far, piling moral responsibility upon moral responsibility on the shoulders of the engineer. This emphasis . . . is misplaced. Though engineers are members of a profession that holds public safety paramount, we cannot reasonably expect engineers to be willing to sacrifice their jobs each day for principle and to have a whistle ever at their sides.[11]

He contends that engineers have only the obligation "to do their jobs the best they can."[12] This includes reporting their concerns about the safety of products to management, but does not include "the obligation to insist that their perceptions or . . .

standards be accepted. They are not paid to do that, they are not expected to do that, and they have no moral or ethical obligation to do that."[13]

To take a specific case, De George maintains that even though some Ford engineers had grave misgivings about the safety of Pinto gas tanks, and several people had been killed when tanks exploded after rear-end crashes, the engineers did not have an obligation to make their misgivings public. De George's remarks are puzzling because the Pinto case would seem to be exactly the kind of clear-cut situation which he says provides the paradigm for justified whistle blowing. Indeed, if the Ford engineers did not have an obligation to blow the whistle, it is difficult to see what cases could satisfy his criteria. They knew that if Pintos were struck from the rear by vehicles traveling thirty miles per hour or more, their gas tanks were likely to explode, seriously injuring or killing people. They also knew that if they did not speak out, Ford would continue to market the Pinto. Finally, they were members of a profession whose code of ethics requires them to put public safety above all other obligations.

De George's remarks suggest that the only obligation the Ford engineers had was to do what management expected of them by complying with their job descriptions and that so long as they did that no one should find fault with them or hold them accountable for what the company did. It is true that when people act within the framework of an organization, it is often difficult to assess individual responsibility. But the fact that one is acting as a member of an organization does not relieve one of moral obligations. The exact opposite is true. Because most of the actions we undertake in organizational settings have more far-reaching consequences than those we undertake in our personal lives, our moral obligation to make sure that we do not harm others is *increased* when we act as a member of an organization. The amount of moral responsibility one has for any particular organizational action depends on the extent to which: (1) the consequences of the action are foreseeable, and (2) one's own action or failure to act is a cause of those consequences. It is important to include failure to act here, because frequently it is easier to determine what will happen if we do not act than if we do, and because we are morally responsible for not preventing harm as well as for causing it.

De George thinks that the Ford engineers would have had an obligation to blow the whistle only if they believed doing so would have been likely to prevent the harm involved. But we have an obligation to warn others of danger even if we believe they will ignore our warnings. This is especially true if the danger will come about partly because we did not speak out. De George admits that the public has a right to know about dangerous products. If that is true, then those who have knowledge about such products have an obligation to inform the public. This is not usurping the public's right to decide acceptable risk; it is simply supplying people with the information necessary to exercise that right.

De George's comments also seem to imply that in general it is not justifiable to ask people to blow the whistle if it would threaten their jobs. It is true that we would not necessarily be justified in demanding this if it would place them or their families' lives in danger. But this is *not* true if only their jobs are at stake. It is especially not true if the people involved are executives and professionals, who are accorded respect and high salaries, not only because of their specialized knowledge and skills, but also because of the special responsibilities we entrust to them. Frequently, as in the case of engineers, they also subscribe to codes of ethics which require them to put the public good ahead of their own or the organization's good. Given all this, it is difficult to understand why De George does not think the Ford engineers had an obligation to blow the whistle in the Pinto case.

The belief that whistle-blowing is an act of disloyalty and disobedience seems to underlie De George's second and third criteria for justifiable whistle-blowing: The whistle-blower must have first reported the wrongdoing to his or her immediate superior and, if nothing was done, have taken the complaint as far up the managerial ladder as possible. Some of the problems with adopting these suggestions as general criteria for justified whistle-blowing are: (1) It may be one's immediate supervisor who is responsible for the wrongdoing. (2) Organizations differ considerably in both their procedures for reporting, and how they respond to, wrongdoing. (3) Not all wrongdoing is of the same type. If the wrongdoing is of a type that threatens people's health or safety, exhausting channels of protest within the organization may result in unjustified delay in correcting the problem. (4) Exhausting internal channels of protest may give people time to destroy evidence needed to substantiate one's allegations. (5) Finally, it may expose the employee to possible retaliation, against which she or he might have some protection if the wrongdoing were reported to an external agency.

His fourth criterion, that the whistle-blower have documented evidence which would convince an impartial observer, is intended to reduce incidence of whistle-blowing by curbing those who would blow the whistle on a mere suspicion of wrong-doing. It is true that one should not make claims against an organization based on mere guesses or hunches, because if they turn out to be false one will have illegitimately harmed the organization and innocent people affiliated with it. But, De George also wishes to curb whistle-blowing, because he thinks that if it were widespread, that would reduce its effectiveness. De George's fourth and fifth criteria are, therefore, deliberately formulated in such a way that if they are satisfied, "people will only rarely have the moral obligation to blow the whistle."[14]

De George's fear, that unless strict criteria of justification are applied to whistle-blowing it might become widespread, is unjustified. If it is true, as he himself claims, that there is a strong tradition in America against "ratting," that most workers consider themselves to have an obligation of loyalty to their organization, and that whistle-blowers are commonly looked upon as traitors, then it is unlikely that whistle-blowing will ever be a widespread practice. De George believes that if one is unable to document wrongdoing without recourse to illegal or immoral means, this relieves one of the obligation to blow the whistle. He argues:

> One does not have an obligation to blow the whistle simply because of one's hunch, guess, or personal assessment of possible danger, if supporting evidence and documentation are not available. One may, of course, have the obligation to attempt to get evidence if the harm is serious. But if it is unavailable—or unavailable without using illegal or immoral means—then one does not have the obligation to blow the whistle.[15]

I have already indicated above that I do not think one has an obligation to blow the whistle on possible wrongdoing on the basis of a mere guess or hunch because this might harm innocent people. But if one has good reason to believe that wrongdoing is occurring even though one cannot document it without oneself engaging in illegal or immoral actions, this does not relieve one of the obligation to blow the whistle. Indeed, if this were true one would almost never have an obligation to blow the whistle, because employees are rarely in a position to satisfy De George's fourth criterion that the whistle-blower "must have, or have accessible, documented evidence that would convince a reasonable, impartial observer that one's view of the situation is correct." Indeed, it is precisely because employees are rarely ever in a position to supply this type of documentation without themselves resorting to illegal or immoral actions, that they have an obligation to inform others who have the authority to investigate the possible wrongdoing. The attempt to secure such evidence on one's own may even thwart the gathering of evidence by the proper authorities. Thus, instead of De George's criterion being a necessary condition for justifiable whistle-blowing, the attempt to satisfy it would prevent its occurrence. One has an obligation to gather as much evidence as one can so that authorities will have probable cause for investigation. But, if one is convinced that wrongdoing is occurring, one has an obligation to report it even if one is unable to adequately document it. One will have then done one's duty even if the authorities ignore the report.

The claim that it is usually necessary for the whistle-blower to speak out openly for whistle-blowing to be morally justified implies that anonymous whistle-blowing is rarely, if ever, justified. Is this true? It has been argued that anonymous whistle-blowing is never justified because it violates the right of people to face their accusers. But, as Frederick Elliston has pointed out, although people should be protected from false accusations, it is not necessary for the identity of whistle-blowers to be known to accomplish this. "It is only necessary that accusations be properly investigated, proven true or false, and the results widely disseminated."[16]

Some people believe that because the whistle-blower's motive is not known in anonymous whistle-blowing, this suggests that the motive is not praiseworthy and in turn raises questions about the moral justification of anonymous whistle-blowing. De George apparently believes this, because in addition to stating that only public whistle-blowing by previously loyal employees who display their sincerity by their willingness to suffer is likely to be effective and morally justified, he mentions at several places that he is restricting his attention to whistle-blowing for moral reasons. He says, e.g., that "the only motivation for whistle blowing we shall consider . . . is moral motivation."[17] However, in my opinion, concern with the whistle-blower's motive is irrelevant to the moral justification of whistle-blowing. It is a red herring which takes attention away from the genuine moral issue involved: whether the whistle-blower's claim that the organization is doing something harmful to others is true. If the claim is true, then the whistle-blowing is justified regardless of the motive. If the whistle-blower's motives are not moral, that makes the act less praiseworthy, but this is a totally different issue. As De George states, whistle-blowing is a "practical matter." But precisely because this is true, the justification of whistle-blowing turns on the truth or falsity of the disclosure, not on the motives of the whistle-blower. Anonymous whistle-blowing is justified because it can both protect the whistle-blower from unjust attacks and prevent those who are accused of wrongdoing from shifting the issue away from their wrongdoing by engaging in an irrelevant *ad hominem* attack on the whistle-blower. Preoccupation with the whistle-blower's motives facilities this type of irrelevant diversion. It is only if the accusations prove false or inaccurate that the motives of the whistle-blower have any moral relevance. For it is only then, and not before, that the whistle-blower rather than the organization should be put on trial.

The view that whistle-blowing is *prima facie* wrong because it goes against the tradition that "ratting" is wrong is indefensible because it falsely assumes both that we have a general obligation to not inform others about wrongdoing and that this outweighs our fundamental obligation to prevent harm to others. The belief that whistle-blowers should suffer in order to show their moral sincerity, on the other hand, is not only false and irrelevant to the issue of the moral justification of whistle-blowing, but is perverse. There are *no* morally justifiable reasons a person who discloses wrongdoing should be put at risk or made to suffer. The contradictory view stated by De George that "one does not have an obligation to put oneself at serious risk without some compensating advantage to be gained,"[18] is also false. Sometimes doing one's duty requires one to undertake certain risks. However, both individuals and society in general should attempt to reduce these risks to the minimum. In the next section I consider some of the actions whistle-blowers can take to both make whistle-blowing effective and avoid unnecessary risk. In the last section I briefly consider some of the ways society can reduce the need for whistle-blowing.

FACTORS TO CONSIDER IN WHISTLE-BLOWING

Since whistle-blowing usually involves conflicting moral obligations and a wide range of variables and has far-reaching consequences for everyone concerned, the following is not intended as a recipe or how-to-do list. Like all complicated moral actions, whistle-blowing cannot be reduced to such a list. Nevertheless, some factors can be stated which whistle-blowers should consider in disclosing wrongdoing if they are to also act prudently and effectively.

Make Sure the Situation Is One That Warrants Whistle-Blowing

Make sure the situation is one that involves illegal or immoral actions which harm others, rather than one in which you would be disclosing personal matters, trade secrets, customer lists, or similar material. If the disclosure would involve the latter as well, make sure that the harm to be avoided is great enough to offset the harm from the latter.

Examine Your Motives

Although it is not necessary for the whistle-blower's motives to be praiseworthy for whistle-blowing to be morally justified, examining your motives can help in deciding whether the situation is one that warrants whistle-blowing.

Verify and Document Your Information

Try to obtain information that will stand up in regulatory hearings or court. If this is not possible, gather as much information as you can and indicate where and how additional information might be obtained. If the *only* way you could obtain either of these types of information would be through illegal procedures, make sure the situation is one in which the wrongdoing is so great that it warrants this risk. Although morality requires that in general we obey the law, it sometimes requires that we break it. Daniel Ellsberg's release of the Pentagon papers was a situation of this type in my opinion. If you do have to use illegal methods to obtain information, try to find alternative sources for any evidence you uncover so that it will not be challenged in legal hearings. Keep in mind also that if you use illegal methods to obtain information you are opening yourself to *ad hominem* attacks and possible prosecution. In general illegal methods should be avoided unless substantial harm to others is involved.

Determine the Type of Wrongdoing Involved and to Whom It Should Be Reported

Determining the exact nature of the wrongdoing can help you both decide what kind of evidence to obtain and to whom it should be reported. For example, if the wrongdoing consists of illegal actions such as the submission of false test reports to government agencies, bribery of public officials, racial or sexual discrimination, violation of safety, health, or pollution laws, then determining the nature of the law being violated will help indicate which agencies have authority to enforce the law. If, on the other hand, the wrongdoing is not illegal, but is nevertheless harmful to the public, determining this will help you decide whether you have an obligation to publicize the actions and if so how to go about it. The best place to report this type of wrongdoing is usually to a public interest group. Such an organization is more likely than the press to: (1) be concerned about and advise the whistle-blower how to avoid retaliation, (2) maintain confidentiality if that is desirable, (3) investigate the allegations to try to substantiate them, rather than sensationalizing them by turning the issue into a "personality dispute." If releasing information to the press is the best way to remedy the wrongdoing, the public interest group can help with or do this.

State Your Allegations in an Appropriate Way

Be as specific as possible without being unintelligible. If you are reporting a violation of law to a government agency, and it is possible to do so, include technical data necessary for experts to verify the wrongdoing. If you are disclosing wrongdoing that does not require technical data to substantiate it, still be as specific as possible in stating the type of illegal or harmful activity involved, who is being harmed and how.

Stick to the Facts

Avoid name calling, slander, and being drawn into a mud-slinging contest. As Peter Raven-Hansen wisely points out: "One of the most important points . . . is to focus on the disclosure. . . . This rule applies even when the whistle-blower believes that certain individuals are responsible. . . . The disclosure itself usually leaves a trial for others to follow the miscreants."[19] Sticking to the facts also helps the whistle-blower minimize retaliation.

Decide Whether the Whistle-Blowing Should Be Internal or External

Familiarize yourself with all available internal channels for reporting wrongdoing and obtain as much data as you can both on how people who have used these channels were treated by the organization and what was done about the problems they reported. If people who have reported wrongdoing in the past have been treated fairly and the problems corrected, use internal channels. If not, find out which external agencies would be the most appropriate to contact. Try to find out also how these agencies have treated whistle-blowers, how much aid and protection they have given them, etc.

Decide Whether the Whistle-Blowing Should Be Open or Anonymous

If you intend to blow the whistle anonymously, decide whether partial or total anonymity is required. Also document the wrongdoing as thoroughly as possible. Finally, since anonymity may be difficult to preserve, anticipate what you will do if your identify becomes known.

Decide Whether Current or Alumni Whistle-Blowing Is Required

Sometimes it is advisable to resign one's position and obtain another before blowing the whistle. This is because alumni whistle-blowing helps protect one from being fired, receiving damaging letters of recommendation, or even being blacklisted in one's profession. However, changing jobs should not be thought of as an alternative to whistle-blowing. If one is aware of harmful practices, one has a moral obligation to try to do something about them, which cannot be escaped by changing one's job or location. Many times people who think the wrongdoing involved is personal, harming only them, respond to a situation by simply trying to remove themselves from it. They believe that "personal whistle blowing is, in general, morally permitted but not morally required."[20] For example, a female student subjected to sexual harassment, and fearful that she will receive low grades and poor letters of recommendation if she complains, may simply change departments or schools. However, tendencies toward wrongdoing are rarely limited to specific victims. By not blowing the whistle the student allows a situation to exist in which other students are likely to be harassed also.

Make Sure You Follow Proper Guidelines in Reporting the Wrongdoing

If you are not careful to follow any guidelines that have been established by organizations or external agencies for a particular type of whistle-blowing, including using the proper forms, meeting deadlines, etc., wrongdoers may escape detection or punishment because of "technicalities."

Consult a Lawyer

Lawyers are advisable at almost every stage of whistle-blowing. They can help determine if the wrongdoing violates the law, aid in documenting it, inform you of any laws you might break in documenting it, assist in deciding to whom to report it, make sure reports are filed correctly and promptly, and help protect you from retaliation. If you cannot afford a lawyer, talk with an appropriate public interest group that may be able to help. However, lawyers frequently view problems within a narrow legal framework, and decisions to blow the whistle are moral decisions, so in the final analysis you will have to rely on your own judgment.

Anticipate and Document Retaliation

Although not as certain as Newton's law of motion that for every action there is an equal reaction, whistle-blowers whose identities are known can expect retaliation. Furthermore, it may be difficult to keep one's identity secret. Thus whether the whistle-blowing is open or anonymous, personal or impersonal, internal or external, current or alumni, one should anticipate retaliation. One should, therefore, protect oneself by documenting every step of the whistle-blowing with letters, tape recordings of meetings, etc. Without this documentation, the whistle-blower may find that regulatory agencies and the courts are of little help in preventing or redressing retaliation.

BEYOND WHISTLE-BLOWING

What can be done to eliminate the wrongdoing which gives rise to whistle-blowing? One solution would be to give whistle-blowers greater legal protection. Another would be to change the nature of organizations so as to diminish the need for whistle-blowing. These solutions are of course not mutually exclusive.

Many people are opposed to legislation to protect whistle-blowers because they think that it is unwarranted interference with the right to freedom of contract. However, if the right to freedom of contract is to be consistent with the public interest, it cannot serve as a shield for wrongdoing. It does this when threat of dismissal prevents people from blowing the whistle. The right of employers to dismiss at will has been previously restricted by labor laws which prevent employers from dismissing employees for union activities. It is ironic that we have restricted the right of employers to fire employees who are pursuing their economic self-interest but allowed them to fire employees acting in the public interest. The right of employers to dismiss employees in the interest of efficiency should be balanced against the right of the public to know about illegal, dangerous, and unjust practices of organizations. The most effective way to achieve this goal would be to pass a federal law protecting whistle-blowers.

Laws protecting whistle-blowers have also been opposed on the grounds that: (1) employees would use them to mask poor performance, (2) they would create an "informer ethos," and (3) they would take away the autonomy of business, strangling it in red tape.

The first objection is illegitimate because only those employees who could show that an act of whistle-blowing preceded their being penalized or dismissed, and that their employment records were adequate up to the time of the whistle-blowing, could seek relief under the law.

The second objection is more formidable but nevertheless invalid. A society that encourages snooping, suspicion, and mistrust does not conform to most people's idea of the good society. Laws which encourage whistle-blowing for self-interested reasons, such as the federal tax law which pays informers part of any money that is collected, could help bring about such a society.[21] However, laws protecting whistle-blowers from being penalized or dismissed are quite different. They do not reward the whistle-blower; they merely protect him or her from unjust retaliation. It is unlikely that state or federal laws of this type would promote an informer society.

The third objection is also unfounded. Laws protecting whistle-blowers would not require any positive duties on the part of organizations—only the negative duty of not retaliating against employees who speak out in the public interest.

However not every act of apparent whistle-blowing should be protected. If (1) the whistle-blower's accusations turn out to be false and, (2) it can be shown that she or he had no probable reasons for assuming wrongdoing, then the individual should not be shielded from being penalized or dismissed. Both of these conditions should be satisfied before this is allowed to occur. People who can show that they had probable reasons for believing that wrongdoing existed should be protected even if their accusations turn out to be false. If the accusation has not been disproved, the burden of proof should be on the organization to prove that it is false. If it has been investigated and proven false, then the burden of proof should be on the individual to show that she or he had probable reasons for believing wrongdoing existed. If it is shown that the individual did not have probable reasons for believing wrongdoing existed, and the damage to the organization from the false charge is great, it should be allowed to sue or seek other restitution. Since these provisions would impose some risks on potential whistle-blowers, they would reduce the possibility of frivolous action. If, on the other hand, it is found that the whistle-blower had probable cause for the whistle-blowing and the organization has penalized or fired him or her, then that person should be reinstated, awarded damages, or both. If there is further retaliation, additional sizable damages should be awarded.

What changes could be made in organizations to prevent the need for whistle-blowing? Some of the suggestions which have been made are that organizations develop effective internal channels for reporting wrongdoing, reward people with salary increases and promotions for using these channels, and appoint senior executives, board members, ombudspersons, etc., whose primary obligations would be to investigate and eliminate organizational wrongdoing. These changes could be undertaken by organizations on their own or mandated by law. Other changes which might be mandated are requiring that certain kinds of records be kept, assessing larger fines for illegal actions, and making executives and other professionals personally liable for filing false reports, knowingly marketing dangerous products, failing to monitor how policies are being implemented, and so forth. Although these reforms could do much to reduce the need for whistle-blowing, given human nature it is highly unlikely that this need can ever be totally eliminated. Therefore, it is important to have laws which protect whistle-blowers and for us to state as clearly as we can both the practical problems and moral issues pertaining to whistle-blowing.

NOTES

1. For discussion of the legal aspects of whistle-blowing see Lawrence E. Blades, "Employment at Will vs. Individual Freedom: On Limiting the Abusive Exercise of Employer Power," *Columbia Law Review*, vol. 67 (1967); Philip Blumberg, "Corporate Responsibility and the Employee's Duty of Loyalty and Obedience: A Preliminary Inquiry," *Oklahoma Law Review*, vol. 24 (1967); Clyde W. Summers, "Individual Protection Against Unjust Dismissal: Time for a Statute," *Virginia Law Review*, vol. 62 (1976); Arthur S. Miller, "Whistle Blowing and the Law," in Ralph Nader, Peter J. Petkas, and Kate Blackwell, *Whistle Blowing*, New York: Grossman Publishers, 1972; Alan F. Westin, *Whistle Blowing!*, New York: McGraw-Hill, 1981. See also vol. 16, no. 2, Winter 1983, *University of Michigan Journal of Law Reform*, special issue, "Individual Rights in the Workplace: The Employment-At-Will Issue."

2. For a discussion of this study which was conducted by Morton Corn see Frank von Hipple, "Professional Freedom and Responsibility: The Role of the Professional Society," *Newsletter on Science, Technology and Human Values*, vol. 22, January 1978.

3. See Westin, *Whistle Blowing!*

4. See Martin H. Marlin, "Protecting the Whistle-blower from Retaliatory Discharge," in the special issue of the *University of Michigan Journal of Law Reform*.

5. David W. Ewing, *Freedom inside the Organization*, New York: E. P. Dutton, 1977, pp. 165–166.

6. For a more detailed discussion of this argument see Gene G. James, "Whistle Blowing: Its Nature and Justification," *Philosophy in Context*, vol. 10 (1980).

7. See Richard T. De George, 2d ed., *Business Ethics*, New York: Macmillan, 1986. Earlier versions of De George's criteria can be found in the first edition (1982), and in "Ethical Responsibilities of Engineers in Large Organizations," *Business and Professional Ethics Journal*, vol. 1, no. 1, Fall 1981.

8. De George, *Business Ethics*, pp. 230–234.

9. *Ibid.*, p. 223.

10. *Ibid.*, p. 237.

11. De George, "Ethical Responsibilities of Engineers," p. 1.

12. *Ibid.*, p. 5.

13. *Ibid.*

14. De George, *Business Ethics*, p. 235.

15. *Ibid.*, p. 234.

16. Frederick A. Elliston, "Anonymous Whistleblowing," *Business and Professional Ethics Journal*, vol. 1, no. 2, Winter 1982.

17. De George, *Business Ethics*, p. 223.

18. *Ibid.*, p. 234.

19. Peter Raven-Hansen, "Dos and Don'ts for Whistleblowers: Planning for Trouble,"

Technology Review, May 1980, p. 30. My discussion in this section is heavily indebted to this article.

20. De George, *Business Ethics*, p. 222.

21. People who blow the whistle on tax evaders in fact rarely receive any money because the law leaves payment to the discretion of the Internal Revenue Service.

23 Trade Secrets: What Price Loyalty?

Michael S. Baram

In 1963, the Court of Appeals of Ohio heard an appeal of a lower court decision from The B.F. Goodrich Company. The lower court had denied Goodrich's request for an injunction, or court order, to restrain a former employee, Donald Wohlgemuth, from disclosing its trade secrets and from working in the space suit field for any other company.

This case, as it was presented in the Court of Appeals, is a fascinating display of management issues, legal concepts, and ethical dilemmas of concern to research and development organizations and their scientist and engineer employees. The case also represents an employer-employee crisis of increasing incidence in the young and vigorous R&D sector of U.S. industry. Tales of departing employees and threatened losses of trade secrets or proprietary information are now common.

Such crises are not surprising when one considers the causes of mobility. The highly educated employees of R&D organizations place primary emphasis on their own development, interests, and satisfaction. Graduates of major scientific and technological institutions readily admit that they accept their first jobs primarily for money and for the early and brief experience they feel is a prerequisite for seeking more satisfying futures with smaller companies which are often their own. Employee mobility and high personnel turnover rates are also due to the placement of new large federal contracts and the termination of others. One need only look to the Sunday newspaper employment advertisements for evidence as to the manner in which such programs are used to attract highly educated R&D personnel.

This phenomenon of the mobile employee seeking fulfillment reflects a sudden change in societal and personal values. It also threatens industrial reliance on trade secrets for the protection of certain forms of intellectual property. There are no union solutions, and the legal framework in which it occurs is an ancient structure representing values of an earlier America. The formulation of management responses—with cognizance of legal, practical, and ethical considerations—is admittedly a difficult task, but one which must be undertaken.

In this article I shall examine the basic question of industrial loyalty regarding trade secrets, using the Goodrich-Wohlgemuth case as the focal point of the challenge to the preservation of certain forms of intellectual property posed by the mobile employee, and then offer some suggestions for the development of sound management policies.

THE APPEALS CASE

Donald Wohlgemuth joined the B.F. Goodrich Company as a chemical engineer in 1954, following his graduation from the University of Michigan, and by 1962 he had become manager of the space suit division. As the repository of Goodrich know-how and secret data in space suit technology, he was indeed a key man in a rapidly developing technology of interest to several government agencies. Nevertheless, he was dissatisfied with his salary ($10,644) and the denial of his requests for certain additional facilities for his department.

A Goodrich rival, International Latex, had recently been awarded the major space suit subcontract for the Apollo program. Following up a contact from an employment agency hired by Latex, Wohlgemuth negotiated a position with Latex, at a substantial salary increase. In his new assignment he would be manager of engineering for industrial products, which included space suits. He then notified Goodrich of his resignation, and was met with a reaction he apparently did not expect. Goodrich management raised the moral and ethical aspects of his decision, since the company executives felt his resignation would result in the transfer of Goodrich trade secrets to Latex.

After several heated exchanges, Wohlgemuth stated that "loyalty and ethics have their price and International Latex has paid this price. . . ." Even though Goodrich threatened legal action Wohlgemuth left Goodrich for Latex. Goodrich thereupon requested a restraining order in the Ohio courts.

At the appeals court level, the Goodrich brief sought an injunction that would prevent Wohlgemuth from working in the space suit field for *any* other company, prevent his disclosure of *any* information on space suit technology to *anyone*, prevent his consulting or conferring with *anyone* on Goodrich trade secrets, and finally, prevent *any* future contact he might seek with Goodrich employees.

These four broad measures were rejected by the Ohio Court of Appeals. All were too wide in scope, and all would have protected much more than Goodrich's legitimate concern of safeguarding its trade secrets. In addition, the measures were speculative, since no clear danger seemed imminent. In sum, they represented a form of "overkill" that would have placed undue restraints on Wohlgemuth.

The court did provide an injunction restraining Wohlgemuth from disclosure of Goodrich trade secrets. In passing, the court noted that in the absence of any Goodrich employment contract restraining his employment with a competitor, Wohlgemuth could commence work with Latex. With ample legal precedent, the court therefore came down on both sides of the fence. Following the decision, Wohlgemuth commenced his career with Latex and is now manager of the company's Research and Engineering Department.

COMMON-LAW CONCEPTS

The two basic issues in crises such as the Goodrich-Wohlgemuth case appear irreconcilable: (1) the right of the corporation to its intellectual property—its proprietary data or trade secrets; and (2) the right of the individual to seek gainful employment and utilize his abilities—to be free from a master-servant relationship.

There are no federal and but a few state statutes dealing with employment restraints and trade secrets. The U.S. courts, when faced with such issues, have sought to apply the various common-law doctrines of trade secrets and unfair competition at hand to attain an equitable solution. Many of these common-law doctrines were born in pre-industrial England and later adopted by English and U.S. courts to meet employment crises of this nature through ensuing centuries of changing industrial and social patterns. In fact, some of the early cases of black smiths and barbers seeking to restrain departing apprentices are still cited today.

To the courts, the common legal solution, as in *Goodrich* v. *Wohlgemuth*, is pleasing because it theoretically preserves the rights of both parties. However, it is sadly lacking in practicality, since neither secrets nor individual liberty are truly preserved.

The trade secrets which companies seek to protect have usually become an integral portion of the departing employee's total capabilities. He cannot divest himself of his intellectual capacity, which is a compound of information acquired from his employer, his co-workers, and his own self-generated experiential information. Nevertheless, all such information, if kept secret by the company from its competition, may legitimately be claimed as corporate property. This is because the employer-employee relationship embodied in the normal employment contract or other terms of employment provides for corporate ownership of all employee-generated data, including inventions. As a result, a departing employee's intellectual capacity may be, in large measure, corporate property.

Once the new position with a competitor has been taken, the trade secrets embodied in the departing employee may manifest themselves quite clearly and consciously. This is what court injunctions seek to prohibit. But, far more likely, the trade secrets will manifest themselves subconsciously and in various forms—for example, as in the daily decisions by the employee at his new post, or in the many small contributions he makes to a large team effort—often in the form of an intuitive sense of what or what not to do, as he seeks to utilize his overall intellectual capacity. Theoretically, a legal injunction also serves to prohibit such "leakage." However, the former employer faces the practical problem of securing evidence of such leakage, for little will be apparent from the public activities and goods of the new employer. And if the new employer's public activities or goods appear suspicious, there is also the further problem of distinguishing one's trade secrets from what may be legitimately asserted as the self-generated technological skills or state of the art of the new employer and competitor which were utilized.

This is a major stumbling block in the attempt to protect one's trade secrets, since the possessor has no recourse against others who independently generate the same information. It is therefore unlikely that an injunction against disclosure of trade secrets to future employers prevents any "unintentional" transfer (or even intentional transfer) of information, except for the passage of documents and other physical embodiments of the secrets. In fact, only a lobotomy, as yet not requested nor likely to be sanctioned by the courts, would afford security against the transfer of most trade secrets.

Conversely, the departing employee bears the terrible burden of sensitivity. At his new post, subconscious disclosure and mental and physical utilization of what he feels to be no more than his own intellectual capacity may result in heated exchanges between companies, adverse publicity, and litigation. He is marked, insecure, and unlikely to contribute effectively in his new position. In fact, new co-workers may consider him to be a man with a price, and thus without integrity. Frequently, caution on the part of his new employer will result in transfer to a nonsensitive post where he is unlikely to contribute his full skills, unless he has overall capability and adaptability.

The fact that neither secrets nor individual liberty will be truly preserved rarely influences the course of litigation. Similarly, these practical considerations are usually negligible factors in the out-of-court settlements which frequently terminate such litigation, because the settlements primarily reflect the relative bargaining strengths of disputing parties.

Finally, there is the full cost of litigation to be considered. In addition to the obvious court costs and attorney's fees, there is the potentially great cost to the company's image. Although the drama enacted in court reflects legitimate corporate concerns, the public may easily fail to see more than an unequal struggle between the powerful corporate machine and a lonely individual harassed beyond his employment tenure. Prospective employees, particularly new and recent graduates whose early positions are stepping stones, may be reluctant to accept employment with what appears to be a vindictive and authoritarian organization.

Practical and Legal Aspects

Trade secrets are, of course, a common form of intellectual property. Secrecy is the most natural and the earliest known method of protecting the fruits of one's intellectual labors. Rulers of antiquity frequently had architects and engineers murdered, after completion of their works, to maintain secrecy and security. The medieval guilds and later the craftsmen of pre-industrial Europe and America imposed severe restraints on apprentices and their future activities.

Recognition and acceptance of the practice of protecting intellectual property by secrecy is found throughout Anglo-American common or judge-made law, but statutory protection has not been legislated. Perhaps the failure to do so is because of the recognition by the elected officials of industrial societies that secrecy is not in the public interest and that the widest dissemination of new works and advances in technology and culture is necessary for optimal public welfare.

Coincidentally with the industrial revolution, British and U.S. copyright and patent legislation was enacted and represents to this day enlightened efforts to diminish the practice of secrecy. Such legislation was designed to stimulate creativity and disclosure by providing limited commercial monopolies of copyright and patent to authors and inventors, in exchange for immediate public disclosure of their works following acceptance by copyright and patent agencies. However, the copyright and patent systems have failed to meet changing technologies, societal concepts, and industrial practices. A current example is the inadequate response of both agencies to computer software.

Dual standards for patent and copyright protection have arisen, since courts have applied strict standards of validity to the patents and copyrights that are challenged and litigated. The result is a high incidence of findings of subsequently invalid patents and copyrights issued by the federal systems. Further, the 17-year period of patent protection is often insufficient because inventions normally require a longer period of time, following reduction to practice and patentability, before commercial acceptance occurs. Thus early disclosure of the invention through the award of a patent only serves to inform the competition of one's state of the art. Industry has therefore continued to rely on secrecy and the persistent and ill-defined concepts of the common law of trade secrets and unfair competition to protect its intellectual property.

To summarize this common law briefly, virtually all information—ranging from full descriptions of inventions to plant layouts, shop know how, methods of quality control, customer and source lists, and marketing data—is eligible for protection as trade secrets. No standards of invention or originality are required. If such information is not known to the public or to the trade (or it is known but its utility is not recognized), and if such information is of value to its possessor, it is eligible for protection by the courts.

Further, and of greatest importance in terms of favorably impressing the courts, there must be evidence that the possessor recognized the value of his information and treated it accordingly. In the context of confidential relationships, "treatment" normally means that the possessor provided for limited or no disclosure of trade secrets. This means many things: for example, total prohibition of disclosure except to key company people on a need-to-know basis; provision of the information to licensees, joint ventures, or employees having contractual restraints against their unauthorized disclosure or use, division of employee responsibilities so that no employee is aware of more than a small segment of a particular process, and use in labs of unmarked chemicals and materials.

There must also be evidence that particular efforts were expended for the purpose of preserving secrecy for the specific data claimed as trade secrets. General company policies indiscriminately applied to data and employees or licensees will not suffice in the legal sense to convince the courts of the presence of trade secrets.

When the possessor and his information do fulfill such criteria, court recognition and the award of compensation to damaged parties, or injunctive restraints to protect parties in danger of imminent or further damage, will follow. If there is evidence of (a) breach of confidential relationships (contracts or licenses) which were established to preserve the secrecy of company information, (b) unauthorized copying and sale of secrets, or (c) conspiracy to damage the possessor, the courts will act with greater certitude. But in many cases, such as in the Goodrich-Wohlgemuth litigation, no such evidence is present.

Finally, the courts will not move to protect trade secrets when an action is brought by one party against another who independently generated similar information, or who "reverse-engineered" the publicly sold products of the party petitioning the court, unless there is some contractual, fiduciary, or other relationship based on trust connecting the parties in court.

Other Considerations

In addition to the foregoing practical and legal aspects, basic questions of industrial ethics and the equitable allocation of rights and risks should be examined to provide management with intelligent and humane responses to employer-employee crises that involved intellectual property. The patent and copyright systems for the stimulation and protection of such property are premised on dissemination of information and subsequent public welfare. These systems reflect public concern with the proper use of intellectual property, which the common law of trade secrets lacks.

Will the courts continue to utilize common-law concepts for the protection of trade secrets, when such concepts are based solely on the rights of the possessors of secret information, and when the application of such concepts has a detrimental effect on both the rights of employees and the public welfare? Since current court practice places the burden of industrial loyalty solely on the employee, the skilled individual has to pay the price. In other words, the law restricts the fullest utilization of his abilities. And the detrimental effect on public welfare can be inferred from recent federal studies of technology transfer, which indicate that employee mobility and the promotion of entrepreneurial activities are primary factors in the transfer of technology and the growth of new industries.

The continuation of trade secret concepts for the preservation of property rights in secret information at the expense of certain basic individual freedoms is unlikely. The law eventually reflects changing societal values, and the mobile R&D employee who seeks career fulfillment through a succession of jobs, frequently in sensitive trade secret areas, is now a reality—one not likely to disappear. Thus it is probable that the courts will eventually adopt the position that those who rely on trade secrets assume the realities or risks in the present context of public concern with technological progress and its relationship to the public good, and with the rights of the individual. Resulting unintentional leakage of secret information through the memory of a departing employee is now generally accepted as a reasonable price to pay for the preservation of these societal values. However, the courts will never condone the theft or other physical appropriation of secret information, nor are the courts likely to condone fraud, conspiracy, and other inequitable practices resulting in some form of unfair competition.

The failings of the statutory systems serve, not as justification for the inequitable application of medieval trade secret concepts, but as the basis for legislative reform. Injunctive restraints against the unintentional leakage of secrets and the harassment of departing employees through litigation should not be part of our legal system. This is especially true when there is a growing body of evidence that management can respond, and has intelligently done so, to such crises without detriment to the individual employee, the public good, or the company itself.

MANAGEMENT RESPONSE

How then shall managers of research and development organizations respond to the reality of the mobile employee and his potential for damage to corporate trade secrets?

Contractual Restraints

Initial response is invariably consideration of the use of relevant contractual prohibitions on employees with such potential. For a minority of companies, this means the institution of employment contracts or other agreements concerning terms of employment. For most, a review of existing company contracts, which at a minimum provide for employee disclosure of inventions and company ownership of subsequent patents, will be called for to determine the need for relevant restraints.

Contractual prohibitions vary somewhat, but they are clearly of two general types: (1) restraints against unauthorized disclosure and use of company trade secrets or proprietary information by employees during their employment tenure or at any time thereafter, (2) restraints against certain future activities of employees following their employment tenure.

A restraint against unauthorized disclosure or use is normally upheld in the courts, provided it is limited to a legitimate company concern—trade secrets. But it is usually ineffective, due to the unintentional leakage and subconscious utilization of trade secrets, and the difficulties of "policing" and proving violation, as discussed earlier. In fact, several authorities feel that this type of restraint is ineffective unless coupled with a valid restraint against future employment with competitors.

Restraints limiting future activities are more difficult to generalize since little consistency—and hence, predictability—as to validity is provided by the common law. Nevertheless, when held valid, a limitation on employment with competitors can be totally effective. In the past, such restraints limited certain activities of the departing employee for a period of time and within a geographical sector. Thus, such a restraint as "no competing activities for five years, and thereafter not within a 50-mile radius of Cambridge" may have served a colonial craftsman. But now that corporate interests are nationwide, a geographical limitation is meaningless to the employer. It is therefore the reasonableness of the scope of restricted activities and of the time limitation that is at issue in all such cases today.

Is enforced abstinence from competing activities of, say, five years, or three, or one, a reasonable price to exact from the departing employee to protect his former employer's trade secrets? Let me point out that the trend over the last several decades has been toward a position that no time limitation is a reasonable one.

The *Encyclopedia of Patent Practice and Invention Management*, in discussing "restrictions on future employment," states:

> It is understood that no contract is valid that withdraws from a man the right to earn a living. This may be expressed in the words that a man's tools cannot be taken for debt or that the operations of his brain may not be mortgaged. . . . Such limitation as that an engineer may not accept other work in the engineering industry or a chemist in chemistry is obviously improper and void. Restrictions on future employment, if they are to have any chance for enforceability, must define the forbidden field clearly and with severe limitations.
>
> One company is reported to have attempted to modify its research chemists's contracts, so as to require approval by the company of any employment accepted by the chemist for two years after leaving the company. Employment within two of the less industrialized states was excepted . . . the attempt was unsuccessful.[1]

In *Donahue* v. *Permacil Tape* Corporation, the court said in regard to an ex-employee's knowledge and overall capability:

> They belong to him as an individual for the transaction of any business in which he may engage, just the same as any part of the skill, knowledge, information or education which was received by him before entering the employment. . . . On terminating his employment, he has a right to take them with him.[2]

Courts have been naturally reluctant to extend protection to trade secrets when the freedom of an individual to use his overall capability is at stake. In addition, the former employer faces the practical difficulty of convincing almost any court that a prohibition of future employment is necessary, since the court will look for clear and convincing evidence that the ex-employee has, or inevitably will, exercise more than the ordinary skill a man of his competence possesses. A few states—such as California by statute and others by consistent court action—now prohibit future employment restraints.

It therefore appears that a contractual prohibition of future employment in a broad area which prevents an ex-employee from using his overall capability, is invalid in most states. And a request for an injunction to prohibit such employment, without a prior contractual provision, stands an even poorer chance of success, as Goodrich learned when it sought to prevent Wohlgemuth from working in the space suit field for any other company.

Nevertheless, there are occasional cases in which provisions in employment contracts restraining a narrow scope of activity—i.e., work on a particular process or machine—for up to two years have been upheld. These cases are often distorted by the presence of highly charged factors such as the employee's departure with copies of company trade secrets in his possession, or evidence of his enticement by a competitor to garner the trade secrets he bears, to the direct detriment of his former employer. In the absence of such distortions, and in the presence of evidence that even such narrowly defined prohibited activities would prevent the individual from a reasonable pursuit of his career, it is doubtful if even the most skillfully drawn contractual prohibition would prevail.

Few scientists and engineers possess sufficient strength at the time of negotiating a new position to demand excision of contractual restraints on their post-employment futures. Yet the restraint is a deterrent, and its impact, though unmeasured, on the sensitivities of the creative, highly motivated employees in demand by R&D organizations can be anticipated.

Management must therefore consider the opprobrium connected to contractual restraints on employees. It is worth noting that in the most intensive trade secret area—the chemical industry—a recent survey revealed that only 1 of 24 companies utilized contractual restraints on future employment.

Government classification of company contract work serves no purpose toward the protection of company trade secrets. The intellectual property arising from government-funded work is, in Department of Defense terminology, "unlimited rights data." Since it is the property of the government, it is available to other cleared government contractors who are competitors and potential employers.

In sum, there is low predictability and low security in management reliance on the employment contract as protection against the loss of trade secrets through the departure of key employees.

Internal Policies

Another response of R&D management to the mobile employee and his potential for damage to corporate trade secrets is the formulation of internal company policies for the handling of intellectual property of trade secret potential. Such policies may call for the prior review of publications and addresses of key employees, prohibition of consulting and other "moonlighting," dissemination of trade secrets on a strict "need to know" basis to designated employees, and prohibitions on the copying of trade secret data. More "physical" policies may restrict research and other operational areas to access for designated or "badge" employees only and divide up operations to prevent the accumulation of extensive knowledge by any individual—including safety and other general plant personnel. Several companies I know of distribute unmarked materials—particularly chemicals—to employees.

Although internal policies do not necessarily prevent future employment with competitors, they can serve to prevent undue disclosures and lessen the criticality of the departure of key personnel. All must be exercised with a sophisticated regard for employee motivation, however, because the cumulative effect may result in a police state atmosphere that inhibits creativity and repels prospective employees.

Several farsighted R&D organizations are currently experimenting with plans which essentially delegate the responsibility for nondisclosure and nonuse of their trade secrets to the key employees themselves. These plans include pension and consulting programs operative for a specified post-employment period. In one company, for example, the pension plan provides that the corporate monies which are contributed to the employee pension fund in direct ratio to the employee's own contributions will remain in his pension package following his term of employment, provided he does not work for a competing firm for a specified number of years. In another company, the consulting plan provides that certain departing employees are eligible to receive an annual consulting fee for a given number of years following employment if they do not work for a competitor. The consulting fee is a preestablished percentage of the employee's annual salary at the time of his departure.

Obviously, such corporate plans are subject to employee abuse, but if limited to truly key employees, they may succeed without abuse in most cases. They not only have the merit of providing the employee with a choice, an equitable feature likely to incur employee loyalty, but they also have no apparent legal defects.

Another valid internal practice is the debriefing of departing employees. The debriefing session, carried out in a low-key atmosphere, affords management an excellent opportunity to retrieve company materials and information in physical form, to impart to the employee a sense of responsibility regarding trade secrets and sensitive areas, and to discuss mutual anxieties in full.

External Procedures

Several management responses relating to external company policies are worth noting, as they also serve to protect trade secrets in cases involving employee departures. Among several industries, such as in the chemical field, it is common to find gentlemen's agreements which provide mutuality in the nonhiring of competitor's key employees, following notice. Employees who have encountered this practice have not found the experience a pleasant one. This same practice is also found in other areas, such as the industrial machinery industry, that are in need of innovation, and it appears that the presence of such agreements helps to depict these industries in an unappealing fashion to the types of employees they need.

Another external response for management consideration is company reliance on trademarks. Given a good mark and subsequent public identification of the product with the mark, a company may be able to maintain markets despite the fact that its intellectual property is no longer a trade secret. Competitors may be hesitant about utilizing the former trade secrets of any company whose products are strongly identified with trademarks and with the company itself.

Some trade secrets are patentable, and management faced with the potential loss of such secrets should consider filing for patent protection. The application is treated confidentially by the U.S. Patent Office and some foreign patent offices up to the time of award. Moreover, if the application is rejected, the secrecy of the information is not legally diminished. In any case, the subject matter of the application remains secret throughout the two-to-three year period of time normally involved in U.S. Patent Office review.

CONCLUSION

A major concern of our society is progress through the promotion and utilization of new technology. To sustain and enhance this form of progress, it is necessary to optimize the flow of information and innovation all the way from conception to public use. This effort is now a tripartite affair involving federal agencies, industry, and universities. A unique feature of this tripartite relationship is the mobility of R&D managers, scientists, and engineers who follow contract funding and projects in accordance with their special competence. Neither the federal agencies nor the universities rely on trade secret concepts for the protection of their intellectual property. However, industry still does, despite the fact that trade secret concepts bear the potential ancillary effect of interfering with employee mobility.

It is becoming increasingly clear that new societal values associated with the tripartite approach to new technology are now evolving, and that the common law dispensed by the courts has begun to reflect these values. A victim of sorts is trade secret law, which has not only never been clearly defined, but which has indeed been sustained by court concepts of unfair competition, equity, and confidence derived from other fields of law. The day when courts restrict employee mobility to preserve industrial trade secrets appears to have passed, except—as we noted earlier—in cases involving highly charged factors such as conspiracy, fraud, or theft.

In short, it is now unwise for management to rely on trade secret law and derivative employee contractual restraints to preserve trade secrets. Companies must now carefully weigh the nature and value of their intellectual property, present and potential employees, competition, and applicable laws in order to formulate sound management policies.

Programmed Approach

Regarding the challenge to the preservation of trade secrets posed by the mobile employee, sophisticated management will place its primary reliance on the inculcation of company loyalty in key employees, and on the continual satisfaction of such key employees. For example, management might consider adopting the following five-step basis for developing an overall approach to the challenge:

1. Devise a program for recognition of employee achievement in the trade secret area. At present, this form of recognition is even more neglected than is adequate recognition of employee inventions.
2. Make an appraisal of trade secret activities. This should result in a limitation of (a) personnel with access to trade secrets, (b) the extent of trade secrets available to such personnel, and (c) information which truly deserves the label of trade secret.
3. Review in-house procedures and the use of physical safeguards, such as restrictions on access to certain specified areas and on employee writings for outside publication. Restriction may tend to stifle creativity by inhibiting communication and interaction conducive to innovation. Striking the balance between too few and

too many safeguards is a delicate process and depends on employee awareness of what is being sought and how it will benefit them.

4. Appraise the legal systems available for the protection of intellectual property. Utility and design patents may be advisable in some cases. The copyright system now offers some protection to certain types of industrial designs and computer software. Trademarks may be adroitly used to maintain markets.

5. Recognize that all efforts may fail to persuade a key employee from leaving. To cope with this contingency, the "gentle persuasion" of a pension or consulting plan in the post-employment period has proved effective and legally sound. A thorough debriefing is a further safeguard. Other cases wherein employee mobility is accompanied by fraud, unfair competition, or theft will be adequately dealt with by the courts.

The problem of the departing employee and the threatened loss of trade secrets is not solved by exhortations that scientists and engineers need courses in professional ethics. Management itself should display the standards of conduct expected of its employees and of other companies.

Finally, let me stress again that success probably lies in the inculcation of company loyalty in key employees, not in the enforcement of company desires or in misplaced reliance on the law to subsidize cursory management. Better employee relations—in fact, a total sensitivity to the needs and aspirations of highly educated employees— requires constant management concern. In the long run, total sensitivity will prove less costly and more effective than litigation and the use of questionable contractual restraints.

NOTES

1. R. P. Calvert, editor (New York, Reinhold Publishing Company, 1964), p. 230.
2. 127 N.E. (2), p. 235.

24 Trade Secrets, Patents, and Morality

Robert E. Frederick

Milton Snoeyenbos

Suppose that company M develops a super-computer that gives it a competitive advantage, but decides that, rather than marketing it, it will use the computer to provide services to users. In doing so, it keeps its technical information secret. If another company, N, were to steal the computer, N would be subject to moral blame as well as legal penalty. But suppose that, without M's consent, N obtained M's technical information, which thereby enabled N to copy M's computer. Should N then be subject to moral blame and legal penalty?

At first glance it seems that N should be held morally and legally accountable; but N has a line of defense which supports its position. Information, or knowledge, unlike a physical asset, can be possessed by more than one individual or firm at any one time. Thus, in obtaining M's information N did not diminish M's information; since M possesses exactly the same information it had before, N cannot be said to have stolen it. Furthermore, everyone regards the dissemination of knowledge as a good thing; it has obvious social utility. M's competitive advantage, moreover, was not a good thing, since it could have enabled M to drive other firms out of the computer service business; M might have established a monopoly. Thus, M has no right to keep the information to itself, and, in the interests of social utility, N had a right to obtain M's information. Hence, N should be praised rather than blamed for its act.

This defense of N raises the general question of whether a firm's use of trade secrets or patents to protect information is justifiable. If it is not, then N may at least be morally justified in using clandestine means to obtain M's information. If there is a justification for allowing trade secrets and patents, then, not only is N's act unjustifi-

From *Business Ethics: Corporate Values and Society*, edited by Milton Snoeyenbos, Robert Almeder, and James Humber (Buffalo, N.Y.: Prometheus Books, 1983). Copyright © 1983 by Milton Snoeyenbos, Robert Almeder, and James Humber. Reprinted by permission of the publisher.

able, but we also have a basis for saying that the release of certain information in certain contexts to N by an employee of M is unjustifiable. In this paper we argue that there are both consequentialist and nonconsequentialist reasons for allowing firms to protect *their* proprietary information via patents and trade secrets. On the other hand, an individual has a right to liberty and a right to use *his* knowledge and skills to better himself. These rights place certain constraints on what can qualify as a trade secret or patentable item of information. We begin with a discussion of present patent and trade secret law.

Patents differ significantly from trade secrets. A patent provides a legal safeguard of certain information itself, but the information must be novel. Some internal information generated by a firm may not meet the U.S. Patent Office's standards of inventiveness. Then, too, even if an item is patentable, there may be disadvantages to the firm in seeking and securing a patent on it and/or advantages to the firm in just trying to keep the information secret. There are legal costs in securing a patent, and patents have to be secured in every country in which one wishes to protect the information. In the U.S. a patent expires in 17 years, and, since it is not renewable, the information then becomes public domain. Furthermore, since a patent is a public document, it both reveals research directions and encourages competitors to invent related products that are just dissimilar enough to avoid a patent infringement suit. So there are ample reasons for a firm to keep information secret and not attempt to secure a patent. If a firm can keep the information secret, it may have a long-term advantage over competitors. The disadvantage is that, unlike a patented device or information, the law provides no protection for a trade secret itself. A competitor can analyze an unpatented product in any way, and, if it discovers the trade secret, it is free to use that information or product. For example, if a firm analyzes Coca-Cola and uncovers the secret formula, it can market a product chemically identical to it, although, of course, it cannot use the name "Coca-Cola," since that is protected by trademark law.

It is, however, unlawful to employ "improper means" to secure another's trade secret. Legal protection of trade secrets is based on the agent's duty of confidentiality. Section 395 of the *Restatement of Agency* imposes a duty on the agent "not to use or communicate information confidentially given to him by the principal or acquired by him during the course of or on account of his agency . . . to the injury of the principal, on his own account or on behalf of another . . . unless the information is a matter of general knowledge." This duty extends beyond the length of the work contract; if the employee moves to a new job with another firm, his obligation to not disclose his previous principal's trade secrets is still in effect.

Since patents are granted by the U.S. Patent Office in accordance with the U.S. Patent Code, patent law cases are federal cases, whereas trade secrets cases are handled by state courts in accordance with state laws. Although there is no definition of "trade secret" adopted by every state, most follow the definition in Section 757 of the *Restatement of Torts*, according to which a trade secret consists of a pattern, device, formula or compilation of information used in business and designed to give the employer an opportunity to obtain an advantage over his competitors who neither know nor use the information. On this definition virtually anything an employer prefers to keep confidential could count as a trade secret.

In practice, however, the *Restatement* specifies several factors it suggests that courts should consider in deciding whether information is legally protectable: (1) the extent to which the information is known outside the business, (2) the extent to which it is known to employees in the firm, (3) the extent to which the firm used measures to guard secrecy of the information, (4) the value of the information to the firm and to its competitors, (5) the amount of money the firm spent to develop the information, and (6) how easily the information may be developed or properly duplicated.

According to (1), (2), (4), (5), and (6), not all internally generated information will count legally as a trade secret. And, via (3), the firm must take measures to guard its secrets: ". . . a person entitled to a trade secret . . . must not fail to take all proper and reasonable steps to keep it secret. He cannot lie back and do nothing to preserve its essential secret quality, particularly when the subject matter of the process becomes known to a number of individuals involved in its use or is observed in the course of manufacturing in the plain view of others" (*Gallowhur Chemical Corp. v. Schwerdle*, 37 N. J. Super. 385, 397, 117 A2d 416, 423; *J. T. Healy & Son, Inc., v. James Murphy & Son, Inc.*, 1970 Mass. Adv. Sheets 1051, 260 NE2d 723 (Ill. App. 1959)). In addition to attempting to keep its information secret, the firm must inform its employees as to what data are regarded as secret: there "must be a strong showing that the knowledge was gained in confidence," (*Wheelabrator Corp. v. Fogle*, 317 F. Supp. 633 (D. C. La. 1970)), and employees must be warned that certain information is regarded as a trade secret (*Gallo v. Norris Dispensers, Inc.*, 315 F. Supp. 38 (D. C. Mo. 1970)). Most firms have their employees sign a document that (a) specifies what its trade secrets or types of trade secrets are, and (b) informs them that improper use of the trade secrets violates confidentiality and subjects them to litigation.

If a firm has information that really is a legitimate trade secret, if it informs its employees that this information is regarded as secret, and informs them that improper use violates confidentiality, then it may be able to establish its case in court, in which case it is entitled to injunctive relief and damages. But the courts also typically examine how the defendant in a trade secret case obtained the information. For example, if an employee transfers from company M to company N, taking M's documents with him to N, then there is clear evidence of a breach of confidentiality (or "bad faith") if the evidence can be produced by M. But trade secret law is equity law, a basic principle of which is that bad faith cannot be presumed. In equity law the maxim "Every dog has one free bite" obtains, i.e., a dog cannot be presumed to be vicious until he bites someone. Thus, if the employee took no producible hard evidence in the form of objects or documents, but instead took what was "in his head" or what he could memorize, then M may have to wait for its former employee to overtly act. By then it may be very difficult to produce convincing evidence that would establish a breach of confidentiality.

In considering possible justifications of patents and trade secrets, we have to take into consideration the public good or social utility, the firm's rights and interests, and the individual's rights and interests. Our aim should be to maximize utility while safeguarding legitimate rights.

As Michael Baram has noted, "A major concern of our society is progress through the promotion and utilization of new technology. To sustain and enhance this form of progress, it is necessary to optimize the flow of information and innovation all the way from conception to public use."[1] Given the assumption that technological progress is conducive to social utility, and that the dissemination of technological information is a major means to progress, the key issue is how to maximize information generation and dissemination.

One answer is to require public disclosure of all important generated information, and allow unrestricted use of that information. In some cases this is appropriate, e.g., government sponsored research conducted by a private firm is disclosed and can be used by other firms. Within a capitalistic context, however, it is doubtful that a general disclosure requirement would maximize social utility. The innovative firm would develop information leading to a new product only to see that product manufactured and marketed by another firm at a lower price because the latter firm did not incur research costs. The proposal probably would also result in less competition; only firms with strong financial and marketing structures would survive. Small, innovative firms would not have the protection of their technological advantages necessary to establish a competitive position against industry giants. If both research effort and competition were diminished by this proposal, then the "progress" Baram mentions would not be maximized—at least not in the area of marketable products.

In a market economy, then, there are reasons grounded in social utility for allowing firms to have some proprietary information. The laws based on such a justification should, in part, be structured with an eye to overall utility, and in fact they are so structured. Patents, for example, expire in 17 years. While the patent is in force it allows the firm to recoup research expenses and generate a profit by charging monopolistic prices. Patent protection also encourages the generation of new knowledge. The firm holding the patent, and realizing profits because of it, is encouraged to channel some of those profits to research, since its patent is of limited duration. Given that its patent will expire, the firm needs to generate new, patentable information to maximize profits. Competitors are encouraged to develop competing products that are based on new, patentable information.

Patent protection should not, however, extend indefinitely; it would not only extend indefinitely the higher costs that consumers admittedly bear while a patent is in force, but in certain cases, it could also stifle innovation. A firm holding a basic patent might either "sit on" it or strengthen its monopoly position. A company like Xerox, for example, with the basic xerography patent, might use its profits to fund research until it had built up an impenetrable patent network, but then cut reproductive graphics research drastically and rest relatively secure in the knowledge that its competitors were frozen out of the market. Patents allow monopoly profits for a limited period of time, but patent law should not be structured to forever legitimatize a monopoly.

Richard De George has recently offered another argument to the conclusion that the right to proprietary information is a limited right:

> Knowledge is not an object which one can keep locked up as long as one likes. . . . Whatever knowledge a company produces is always an increment to the knowledge developed by society or by previous people in society and passed from one generation to another. Any new invention is made by people who learned a great deal from the general store of knowledge before they could bring what they knew to bear on a particular problem.

Though we can attribute them to particular efforts of individuals or teams, therefore, inventions and discoveries also are the result of those people who developed them and passed on their knowledge to others. In this way every advance in knowledge is social and belongs ultimately to society, even though for practical purposes we can assign it temporarily to a given individual or firm.[2]

Allowing the firm to use proprietary information has utility, but the right to such information is limited. In point of fact, although we have stressed the utility of allowing use of proprietary information, U.S. patent and copyright laws were enacted during the industrial revolution to reduce secrecy. Patent laws allow limited monopolies in return for public disclosure of the information on which the patent is based. Thus, patent laws provide information to competitors and encourage them to develop their own patentable information that not only generates new products, but also adds to the store of available knowledge.

If allowing limited use of proprietary information has utility, it is still an open question as to the proper limits of such use. Does the present 17 years patent limit maximize utility? This is an empirical question that we will not attempt to answer. Although most experts and industry representatives believe the present limit is about right, U.S. drug firms have recently argued that research and development time and Federal Drug Administration (FDA) testing and licensing requirements are so extensive that social disutility results, as well as disutility for innovative firms.

Although patents expire and the information protected can then be used by anyone, trade secrets can extend indefinitely according to present law. In 1623, the Zildjian family in Turkey developed a metallurgical process for making excellent cymbals. Now centered in Massachusetts, the family has maintained their secret to the present day, and they still produce excellent cymbals. Preservation of such secrets may well have utility for firms holding the secrets, but does it have social utility? Not necessarily, as the following case illustrates. Suppose that Jones, a shadetree mechanic, develops a number of small unpatentable improvements in the internal combustion engine's basic design. The result is an engine that is cheap, reliable, and gets 120 miles per gallon. With no resources to mass produce and market his engine, Jones decides to sell to the highest bidder. XYZ oil company, with immense oil reserves, buys the information. To protect its oil interests, it keeps the information secret. Now suppose it is in fact against XYZ's interests to divulge the information Then, to calculate overall utility we have to weigh the social disutility of keeping the information secret against the social utility of keeping the existing oil industry intact. Although utility calculations are difficult, it seems clear that disutility would arise from allowing the information to be kept secret.

If the preservation of *some* secrets has social disutility, it also seems clear that requiring immediate disclosure of *all* trade secrets in a capitalistic context would have disutility as well. The arguments here parallel those we developed in discussing patents. Again, specification of the appropriate duration of a trade secret is a utility calculation. The calculation will, however, have to take into consideration the fact that the law provides no protection for the secret itself. The firm with a significant investment in a trade secret always runs the risk that a competitor may legitimately uncover and use the secret.

Allowing patents and trade secrets has obvious utility for the firm that possesses them, but the firm also has a *right* to at least the limited protection of its information. It has a *legal* right to expect that its employees will live up to their work contracts, and employees have a correlative duty to abide by their contracts. The work contract is entered into voluntarily by employer and employee; if a prospective employee does not like the terms of a (legitimate) trade secret provision of a contract, he does not have to take the job. The normal employment contract specifies that the firm owns all employee-generated information. Even if the employee transfers from firm M to firm N, M still owns the information produced when he was employed there, and the employee is obligated not to reveal that information.

The moral basis of contract enforceability, including contractual provisions for the protection of proprietary information, is twofold. First, as argued, allowing trade secrets has social utility in addition to utility for the firm. The institution of contract compliance is necessary for the systematic and orderly functioning of business, and a sound business environment is essential to general social utility. However, if only a few people broke their contracts, business would continue to survive. This leads to the second moral basis for adhering to the provisions of one's contract.

If an individual breaks his contract, then he must either regard himself as an exception to the rule banning contract-breaking, or he must believe, in Kant's terms, that a maxim concerning contract-breaking is universalizable. But if we agree that in moral matters everyone ought to adopt the moral point of view, and that point of view requires that one not make himself an exception to the rule, it follows that the person in question is not justified in breaking the rule. On the other hand, if he claims that breaking the contract is in accordance with a maxim, then we can properly demand to have the maxim specified. Clearly the maxim cannot be something like: "I will keep my promises, except on those occasions where it is not to my advantage to keep the promises." For if everyone followed this maxim, there would be no institution of promising or promise-keeping. Since the maxim is not universalizable, it cannot legitimately be appealed to as a sanction for action. Of course, other maxims are available, and the contract-breaker may claim that his act is in accordance with one of these maxims. But note that this reply at least tacitly commits the person to the moral point of view; he is agreeing that everyone ought to act only on universalizable maxims. The only dispute, then, is whether his maxim is in fact universalizable. If we can show him that it is not, he is bound to admit that he is not morally justified in breaking the contract. As a standard, then, contracts should be kept, and where an individual breaks, or contemplates breaking, a contract, the burden is on him to produce a universalizable maxim for his action.

Our analysis does not, however, imply that a person is morally obligated to abide by all contracts; some contracts, or provisions of certain contracts, may be morally and/or legally unacceptable. A person does have a right to liberty and a right to use his knowledge and skills to earn a living. Thus, firm M cannot legitimately specify that *all* knowledge an employee gains while at M is proprietary. This would prohibit the person from obtaining employment at another firm; in effect the work contract would amount to a master-slave relationship. As the *Restatement of Torts* appropriately specifies, only certain information qualifies as a legitimate trade secret. Furthermore, the employee brings to his job certain knowledge and skills that typically are matters of public domain, and, on the job, the good employee develops his capacities. As the court noted in *Donahue v. Permacil Tape Corporation:* an ex-employee's general knowledge and capabilities "belong to him as an individual for the transaction of any business in which he may engage, just the same as any part of the skill, knowledge, information or education which was received by him before entering the employment. . . . On terminating his employment, he has a right to take them with him."[3]

Given that an individual's rights to liberty and to use his knowledge and skills to better himself are primary rights, and hence cannot be overridden by utility considerations, the burden clearly is on the firm to: (1) specify to employees what it regards as its trade secrets, and (2) make sure the secrets are legitimate trade secrets. In addition, a company can employ certain pragmatic tactics to protect its trade secrets. It can fragment research activities so that only a few employees know all the secrets. It can restrict access to research data and operational areas. It can develop pension and consulting policies for ex-employees that motivate them not to join competitors for a period of time. More importantly, it can develop a corporate atmosphere that motivates the individual to remain with the firm.

We began by sketching an argument that company N was justified in obtaining information about company M's computer without M's consent. Our conclusion is that N's argument is specious. Utility considerations justify allowing M to keep its information secret for a period of time, and any employee of M who divulges M's secret information to N is morally blameworthy because he violates his contractual obligations to M.

NOTES

1. Michael Baram, "Trade Secrets: What Price Loyalty," *Harvard Business Review*, vol. 46, No. 6 (Nov.–Dec., 1968), pp. 66–74.

2. Richard T. De George, *Business Ethics* (New York: Macmillan, 1982), p. 207.

3. Cited in Baram, p. 71.

6

Obligations to Clients
and Fair Play in Engineering

SCENARIOS

Public Employment

John Doe, a professional engineer, is a county engineer and a member of the county planning board. He also engages in part-time consulting practice. Doe prepared the plans for a subdivision development in his capacity as a consulting engineer, then as county engineer recommended approval of his plans to the county planning board. As a member of the county planning board he later voted to approve these plans.

Reprinted from the National Society of Professional Engineers, Opinions of the Board of Ethical Review, *Case No. 67-1 (Washington, D.C.: National Society of Professional Engineers, 1971), III, 1, with permission.*

Ownership of Another Firm

Firm A, an incorporated consulting engineering firm with five owners, offers the usual type of consulting engineering services to the public. The owners of Firm A, acting as individuals, organize a new and separate corporation (Company B) for the purpose of marketing several products which are used in the construction of engineering projects. The products are manufactured by a national company which contracts with Company B for the dealership rights to market its products in a specified geographical area. Company B is operated separately from Firm A by individuals other than the owners of Firm A, but under their general direction.

Firm A specifies by name the products of Company B in its specifications for a project which it designed, but with a provision that products of equal acceptability may be used. The relationship between the ownership of Firm A and Company B is made known to the owner of the project.

In a different but related situation, the principals of Firm A suggest to one of their clients that Company B has some products that the client may wish to use in a development, also disclosing to the client the relationship between Firm A and Company B.

Reprinted from the National Society of Professional Engineers, Opinions of the Board of Ethical Review, *Case No. 69-8 (Washington, D.C.: National Society of Professional Engineers, 1971), III, 61, with permission.*

_____ **Charging Your Time to Another Project** _____

A New Jersey consulting engineering firm had a contract to provide engineering services that included field and office engineering. Since the project was complex and the amount of engineering manpower was indeterminate at the signing of the contract, the award was made on the basis of a fixed fee per man-hour of engineering. This required each engineer in the firm to record on a time sheet the hours he worked on the project. The time record was to be audited periodically by the governmental agency.

One of the partners in the firm instructed a departmental head who in turn instructed a subordinate to have some engineers who were working on a separate fixed-fee contract charge their time to the government contract. The department head and his assistant wondered about the illegality of this action and even questioned the partner. His reply was that it was just a bookkeeping procedure and in the end it would all even out. These two engineers were born and educated in a foreign country and were unsure of the business procedures in the United States. They trusted the head of the firm and had the individual engineers charge their time to the wrong project number. Government officials eventually suspected the wrongdoing and in the following legal investigation both of these directed employees confessed to the wrong action and became witnesses against the firm and especially the partner. The resulting trial led to a conviction of fraud for the partner and a jail sentence. The two subordinate engineers were not indicted but legal fees in presenting their cases in the grand jury investigation were costly. The firm was dissolved as a result of this illegal action. All three engineers' ethical conduct was set for trial by ASCE Board of Direction. The partner resigned from ASCE before the hearing and his resignation was received with prejudice (no future membership without a hearing before the Board). The department head had a professional conduct hearing and received a one-year suspension from ASCE. The other engineer received a letter of reprimand from the Board of ASCE.

Both members were found guilty by the Board of ASCE of violation of the ASCE Code of Ethics in that they acted in a manner derogatory to the honor, integrity, and dignity of the engineering profession.

Reprinted from D. Allan Firmage, Modern Engineering Practice: Ethical, Professional, and Legal Aspects (New York: Garland STPM Press, 1980), with permission.

Working in Saudi Arabia

A computer security consultant and citizen of the USA signed a contract, including a confidentiality and non-disclosure agreement, with a client company in Saudi Arabia to assist the company in protecting its information. As a consequence, U.S. government efforts to obtain information about the company were thwarted. The U.S. government complained to the consultant about his work and asked him to reveal what he did. He refused, claiming a duty to his client. The government claimed he had a higher duty to his country.

Reprinted from Donn Parker, Susan Swope, and Bruce Baker, "Ethical Conflicts in Information and Computer Science, Technology, and Business," Final Report for the National Science Foundation, SRI International, August 1988, with permission.

Wife's Investment in Project

John Doe, P.E., is the city engineer of a municipality. His duties include review of plans and specifications prepared for developers of housing projects, and recommendations to the city council on approval of such projects.

Doe's wife has an investment in one of the development companies operating in the jurisdiction of the city, and plans for one of its projects were reviewed by him and approved by the city council. His wife's investment in the project was not known to the city officials or the public until after his review, recommendation for approval of the project, and the approval of the city council. When the fact of his wife's investment was disclosed at a later date, Doe was requested to resign his position on the grounds of unethical conduct.

Reprinted from the National Society of Professional Engineers, Opinions of the Board of Ethical Review, Case No. 66-5 (Washington, D.C.: National Society of Professional Engineers, 1967), II, 55, with permission.

Catching Up with a Lucky Star

"You understand, of course," the island's representative was saying, "that a modest gratuity would—how shall we put it?—speed things up?"

Ellen Reuster smiled charmingly, but she was thinking: "This is extortion." Not that his proposition shocked her. On the contrary, officials at Lucky Star Bottling had warned her and other negotiators who'd be involved in securing outlets for Star's soft drinks abroad to be prepared for such demands. "Officially," the firm's president had remarked, "we must disapprove of and resist such overtures," Then he added wryly, "Officially." The unanswered laughter which met this comment underscored the clear intent of the president's message: while publicly condemning such practices, Lucky Star nonetheless expected its negotiators to "deal constructively" with the "peculiar nature" of host country customs and practices in order to ensure that Star would make substantial inroads into the international soft-drink market.

"How modest?" Reuster asked the jolly, robust representative.

"Oh," he said, folding his hands contentedly over his ample paunch, "a few hundred American dollars."

"Not even the cost of my air-fare here," Reuster thought as she produced her checkbook.

It was thus that Lucky Star captured the exclusive right to market its soft drinks on the island—a truly insignificant investment when one realizes that other island neighbors quickly followed suit. Within three years Lucky Star had not only established itself in the island chain but was doing a far more profitable business than it had ever dreamed.

In the interim, Lucky Star was engaging in a round of corporate musical chairs at home. The result was a new president, Winston Arnett. Not long after assuming his new position, Arnett learned of how opportunistic the firm had been in securing its enviable trade in the islands. What's more, he discovered that what were once "modest gratuities" had developed into a full-scale greasing and bribing operation, consisting of a wide variety of favors and services bestowed on local officials instrumental in perpetuating Star's lucrative position.

Arnett immediately sent for Ellen Reuster, who by this time had risen to chief operations officer in the islands. While informing Reuster that without doubt her initiative had vastly enriched the firm's international interests, Arnett indicated that Lucky Star was paying a small price for the huge dividends it was reaping. "Furthermore," she told Arnett, "we're doing no more down there than what's expected of anyone who wishes to fit in with local custom and practice." Nevertheless, Arnett was intent on suspending all activities that smacked of bribery.

"You realize, of course," Reuster pointed out," it would mean the end of Lucky Star's interest in the islands," a point that wasn't lost on the new president who wished to avoid anything that would seriously undo the firm's profits.

Arnett still was not convinced. He wanted to take a strong stand against bribery.

"If you won't think of the firm," Reuster finally cautioned, "consider the catastrophic impact that our withdrawal will have on those island economies." She reminded Arnett not only of the number of natives that the firm employed but also of the sizable taxes it was paying, which almost single-handedly underwrote many social welfare programs the islands desperately needed.

Reprinted from Vincent Barry, Moral Issues in Business, *2nd ed. (Belmont, Calif.: Wadsworth Publishing Company Inc., 1983), p. 254–55, with permission.*

INTRODUCTION

When engineers are not employed in corporations or government bureaucracies, they are often self-employed, as consultants, or they work as employees of engineering firms that supply engineering services to clients. Engineers may have contact with clients in all these contexts, but most of what has been written about obligations to clients, even the statements in the professional codes of conduct, seem to have been written for engineers who are self-employed or employed by other engineers (in consulting firms). This is unfortunate because obligations to clients get more complicated when the client is not exactly yours but a client of the company for whom you work. Which should be your primary priority, the good of the client or the good of the corporation? In most cases these interests will not conflict, but now and then they do. For example, suppose you work for a company that sells computer products. You are assigned to a client company and your job is to help the client company make decisions about how to automate their various units. After working with people in one of the units, you realize that the best way to automate the unit's operations (allowing them to do what they want with ease and less expense) would be to use a product that is sold not by your company but by your company's competitor. If you make this recommendation you will be serving your client well, but you will not be furthering the interests of your employer.

We begin this chapter with a selection by Michael Bayles from his book *Professional Ethics*. In *Professional Ethics*, Bayles does not focus exclusively on one profession. He provides an analysis that cuts across many professions. In the chapter excerpted here, Bayles explores the proper relationship between a professional and a client. He considers several models of this relationship and argues for the fiduciary model. According to this model, the professional's superior knowledge is recognized, but the client retains significant authority and responsibility in decision making. The professional has a responsibility to provide information to the client but must not take decision making out of the client's hands. With this understanding of the professional-client relationship, it becomes clear, according to Bayles, that professionals have the special obligation to be worthy of the client's trust; this leads to obligations of honesty, candor, competence, diligence, loyalty, and discretion. It is important to note that these are the very obligations repeatedly mentioned in the codes of conduct of engineering professional organizations. Thus, Bayles's analysis supplies the foundation for our understanding of many of the statements in professional codes.

Professional-client relationships are complex, but the one issue that seems to come up most frequently in engineering, both in relationships between consulting engineers and clients and between employed engineers and clients, is conflict of interest. In the professional-client relationship, the professional is expected to act in the interests of the client. At first glance, this may appear to imply that professionals are not to have interests of their own, or perhaps that the interests of the client and the professional are in harmony. One might argue that they are in harmony in the following way. A professional has an interest in serving a client well so that the professional will get the client's future business and will develop a good reputation (which assists him or her in getting other clients). The client has an interest in getting something done and so is willing to hire the professional, paying what is necessary so as to get the expertise or the labor of the professional. In theory this is all true, but in reality things are a bit more complicated. People have many short-term as well as long-term, interests, not to mention that their interests are multifaceted. The professional's legitimate interest, for example, in making money (as much as possible) is in tension with the client's interest in having to pay as little as possible. Hence, working out professional-client relationships that serve the interests of all is not a simple matter. The phrase "conflict of interest" usually applies to a situation in which the interests of professionals and clients (or employers) are especially problematic. A more rigorous definition is provided in a subsequent reading.

The important questions for this chapter are: What is a conflict of interest? What is wrong with a conflict of interest? When do the interests of the professional and the client conflict such that the professional has an obligation to inform the client or remove herself from the situation altogether?

To get a handle on these questions, we read Michael Davis's "Conflict of Interest." In this piece Davis tries to characterize conflicts of interest in a way that helps us to understand what is wrong with them. He begins with an analysis of the role of lawyers, then generalizes to all fields of business and professional ethics. The rough version of his account is that a person has a conflict of interest if: "a) he is in a relationship with another requiring him to exercise judgment in that other's service and b) he has an interest tending to interfere with the proper exercise of judgment in that relationship." Clearly, this account makes sense for engineers, as well as other professionals.

Another issue concerning engineering as a system of practices is bribery. Some may think it unnecessary in a book on the ethical issues in engineering to discuss bribery because it is illegal and not unique to engineering. Nevertheless, engineers do often find themselves in situations in which they are offered bribes or are expected to give bribes. For this reason it is important to understand *why* bribery is illegal, and to consider whether or not it would be immoral even if it were not illegal.

It may be useful to note that this section on bribery might have been included in the section on conflicts of interest, for accepting a bride often involves entering into a conflict of interest (perhaps the worst kind). When a bribe is offered to you, the offer creates an interest in you—an interest in acting or choosing as the briber wishes—for if you do as the briber wishes you will receive money, a car, or a favor. The bribe gives you a personal interest in choosing one way rather than another, when your choice should be based on the best interests of your client or employer.

This makes it fairly easy to see why bribery might be prohibited. It interferes with the exercise of professional judgment, and it interferes with the proper conduct of business. Still, some difficult cases challenge this account. For example, what about the case in which I am bribed to do what I would have done anyway, because it is in my employer's best interest to do what I will be bribed to do? Consideration of a case like this may help us to move our focus from the individual to the whole system of engineering.

The readings in this section begin with a piece by Robert Almeder entitled "Morality and Gift-Giving." In a few paragraphs, Almeder gives us the basic arguments against bribery. He then goes on to try to distinguish bribery from gift-giving, but in the end concludes that the wisest policy is to prohibit gift-giving. Perhaps the most important argument in Almeder's account is the argument to the effect that bribery "strikes at the heart of capitalism." Although we often take for granted that engineers practice engineering in the context of business (which means a capitalist system for American engineers), we too often forget that capitalism, itself, needs to be justified. The classic justification of capitalism is that it produces positive results. The system is based on the idea that in open competition, the best products (highest quality for least money) will survive, and this will benefit all concerned.

Bribery undermines open competition. It encourages those who make choices—about what products are purchased, what companies are allowed to sell their products in a country, what company receives a contract, and so forth—to choose not on the basis of the best product or service but rather on the basis of a personal benefit (a bribe) to the chooser. This is extraneous to the product or service. When such activities go on, we cannot be assured that the best products will survive.

The one form of bribery that has received the most public attention in recent years is that involving international business. Jack G. Kaikati's article "The Phenomenon of International Bribery" explains the problem and gives an overview of attempts that have been made to stop international bribery.

One of those attempts was passage of the Foreign Corrupt Practices Act (FCPA) in 1977. This act makes it a crime for American corporations to offer and provide payments to officials of foreign governments for the purpose of obtaining or retaining business. Mark Pastin and Michael Hooker take issue with this law. They examine international bribery from an ethical perspective, using what they call end-point ethics and rule assessment ethics, and they conclude that neither provides a clear basis for the FCPA.

After reading these selections, you will have a much better understanding of what bribery is and why it is considered wrong, but you may also be much more uncertain that all forms of bribery are morally equivalent because the readings point to the importance of the details in particular cases.

All the issues addressed in this chapter raise broad questions not so much about the behavior of individual engineers, but rather about the rules that are or should be operative in the system in which engineers practice. The rules should be such that engineering serves society. If they are, then engineers will have a reason for following them even if they go against the individual engineer's immediate self-interest. All engineers indirectly benefit from a system of engineering that serves humanity and commands the respect of the public.

25 Obligations Between Professionals and Clients

Michael D. Bayles

THE PROFESSIONAL–CLIENT RELATIONSHIP

The central issue in the professional–client relationship is the allocation of responsibility and authority in decision making—who makes what decisions. The ethical models are in effect models of different distributions of authority and responsibility in decision making. One can view the professional–client relationship as one in which the client has the most authority and responsibility in decision making, the professional being an employee; as one in which the professional and client are equals, either dealing at arm's length or at a more personal level; or as one in which the professional, in different degrees, has the primary role. Each of these conceptions has been suggested by some authors as the appropriate ethical model of the relationship. Each has some commonsense support.

Although the argument in this section supports one model over the others, it is not the only one that is ever appropriate. The others might be so for certain specialized types of situations. Indeed, a relationship between a professional and a client might move back and forth between two or more models as the situation changes. It does not follow, as one author has objected, that one can generate any number of models or that they are merely matters of style.[1] They are based on the logically possible divisions of responsibility and authority between professional and client. The models set a framework for determining what obligations pertain and so are not mere matters of style.

Agency

According to this view, the client has most of the authority and responsibility for decisions; the professional is an expert acting at the direction of the client.[2] The client hires a professional to protect or act for some interest; the professional provides services to achieve the client's goal—purchase of a house, marriage counseling, design of a building. According to this conception, not only does the professional act for or in behalf of the client, but also acts under the direction of the client, as in bureaucratic employer–employee relationships. This conception is especially plausible for lawyers. In filing a complaint or arguing for a client, a lawyer acts for and in behalf of the client. According to some people, a lawyer is merely a "mouthpiece" or "hired gun." This is not a plausible view of accountants performing public audits, for they are supposed to provide an independent review and statement of the clients' financial conditions.

In some contexts, professionals are prone to adopt the agency view of the professional–client relationship. Professionals are sometimes "identified" with their clients and charged with the clients' alleged moral failings. Lawyers offer the defense that, in representing clients, they do not thereby ascribe to or support clients' goals or aims.[3] They are merely employees hired to perform a specific task. If the projects are bad or immoral, the fault lies with the clients, or perhaps with the legal system for permitting the projects.

The agency model most clearly exemplifies what has been called the "ideology of advocacy." This ideology has two principles of conduct: (1) that the lawyer is neutral or detached from the client's purposes and (2) that the lawyer is an aggressive partisan of the client working to advance the client's ends.[4] This ideology is readily applicable to physicians, architects, social workers, and engineers. A physician, for example, should not evaluate the moral worth of patients but only work to advance their health. The second element of the ideology does not apply to accountants performing audits, for they are to present independent statements of clients' financial conditions. It applies in other accounting activities though. For example, an accountant preparing a client's income tax statement should try to take every plausible deduction on behalf of the client.

Some aspects of this ideology appear inescapable in professional ethics. If professionals accepted only clients whose purposes they approved of and did not consider clients' interests any more than those of others, many persons with unusual purposes (such as wanting an architectural style of a building that is completely inconsistent with those nearby) might be unable to obtain professional services. And even if they did, the services might not be worth much because no special consideration would be paid to their interests.[5] The chief problem with the ideology of advocacy, where it does become an ideology, is that devotion to a client's interests is sometimes thought to justify any lawful action advancing the client's ends, no matter how detrimental the effect on others.

The agency view of the professional–client relationship is unduly narrow. Four considerations indicate limits to a professional's proper devotion to a client's interests, and consequently to a client's authority in decision making.

1. Professionals have obligations to third persons that limit the extent to which they may act in behalf of client interest.

2. The agency view arises most often in the context of defending professionals, especially lawyers, from attribution of client sins. This focus is too narrow to sustain a general account of the professional–client relationship. It best pertains to an adversarial context in which two opposing parties confront one another. In counseling, a lawyer's advice "need not be confined to purely legal considerations. . . . It is often desirable for a lawyer to point out those factors which may lead to a decision that is morally just as well as legally permissible."[6]

3. Professionals emphasize their independence of judgment. Unlike soldiers, who are not expected to think for themselves but to do things the army's way, professionals should exercise their training and skills to make objective judgments. The agency view ignores this feature.

4. Except in cases of dire need—medical emergencies, persons charged with crimes —professionals may accept or reject specific clients. With a few restrictions, they may also cease the relationship. Consequently, the agency view is too strong. Professionals must also be ethically free and responsible persons. For their own freedom and the protection of others, they should not abdicate authority and responsibility in decision making.

Contract

If a client ought not to be viewed as having the most authority and responsibility, then perhaps the authority and responsibility should be shared equally. In law, a professional–client relationship is based on a contract, and the ethical concept of a just contract is of an agreement freely arrived at by bargaining between equals. If the relationship is a contractual one, then there are mutual obligations and rights, "a true sharing of ethical authority and responsibility."[7] Because it recognizes the freedom of two equals to determine the conditions of their relationship, the contract model accords well with the values of freedom and equality of opportunity.

However, no gain results from treating as equals people who are not relevantly equal in fact or from assuming a nonexistent freedom. The history of contracts of adhesion (the standard forms offered by monopolies or near monopolies such as airlines) indicates the injustice that can result from falsely assuming contracting parties have equal bargaining power. Many commentators have noted relevant inequalities between professionals and clients, especially in the medical context.[8] First, a professional's knowledge far exceeds that of a client. A professional has the special knowledge produced by long training, knowledge a client could not have without comparable training. Second, a client is concerned about some basic value—personal health, legal status, or financial status—whereas a professional is not as concerned about the subject matter of their relationship. The client usually has more at stake. Third, a professional often has a freedom to enter the relationship that a client lacks. A professional is often able to obtain other clients more easily than a client can obtain another professional. Especially if a potential client has an acute illness, has been referred to a social agency, or has just been charged with a crime, he or she is not free to shop around for another professional. From this point of view, the bargaining situation is more like that between an individual and a public utility.

These considerations are not as important for the usual situation in architecture, accounting, and engineering. The clients of these professionals are often better informed about the subject matter of the transaction than are clients of lawyers and physicians. For example, businesses and corporations have accountants working for them who can give advice about auditors. Firms hiring consulting engineers have often had previous experience working with engineers in that field. Governments, even local ones, frequently have one or two engineers working for them who can advise and help. Moreover, they are freer than the professional to conclude an arrangement with another firm. Thus, in these situations, the factual basis for the contract model is most nearly present. However, the consulting engineer or architect has some special knowledge and ability the client lacks, or else a professional would probably not be hired, so the contract model's empirical assumptions do not quite hold even in these cases. . . .

Paternalism

Once one abandons models that assume the professional and client are equal and accepts that the professional is to some extent in a superior position to the client, one faces the problem of the proper extent of professional authority and responsibility in decision making. Parents have knowledge and experience that children lack, and it is often ethically appropriate for them to exercise their judgment on behalf of their children. Similarly, because a professional has knowledge and experience a client lacks and is hired to further the client's interests, perhaps the relationship should be viewed as one of paternalism.

Paternalism is a difficult concept to analyze. A person's conduct is paternalistic to the extent his or her reasons are to do something to or in behalf of another person for that person's well-being. What is done can be any of a number of things, from removing an appendix to preventing the person from taking drugs. One can also have a paternalistic reason for acting in behalf of a person—for example, filing a claim for food stamps or asserting a legal defense. The key element of paternalism derives from the agent, X, acting regardless of the person's, Y's, completely voluntary and informed consent. X's reason is that he or she judges the action to be for Y's well-being regardless of Y's consent to it. Y might be incapable of consent (a young child or psychiatric patient), Y might never have been asked, or Y might have refused to consent to the act.[9] . . .

A voluminous literature exists concerning the justification of paternalism.[10] The brief discussion here will outline only the major arguments. Paternalism requires justification because it involves doing something to or in behalf of another person regardless of that person's consent. It thus denies people the freedom to make choices affecting their lives. They lack self-determination. . . . The loss of control over their own lives, especially to professionals, is one reason for people's concern about professional ethics. Thus, paternalism is of central importance in professional ethics.

Three arguments are often offered to justify paternalism.

1. The agent has superior knowledge as to what is in a person's best interest. Because the agent knows better than the person what is best, the agent is justified in acting to avoid significant harm to, or to procure a significant benefit for, the person. This argument is perhaps the central one in favor of paternalism by professionals. As noted before, a professional possesses a relevant knowledge the client lacks, so he or she is better able to perceive the advantages and disadvantages of alternative actions. Consequently, the professional rather than the client should have primary authority and responsibility for decisions.

2. The client is incapable of giving a sufficiently voluntary and informed consent. By "voluntary" is meant without duress, psychological compulsion, or other significant emotional or psychological disturbance. By "informed" is meant with appreciation of the consequences of a course of conduct and its alternatives. If people cannot give such consent, then their decisions will not adequately reflect their reasonable desires and will not be expressions of their "true selves.". . .

3. A person will later come to agree that the decision was correct. Although the person does not now consent, he or she will later. For example, an unconscious accident victim with a broken limb will agree that a physician was correct to set the bone. Parents often require their children to do things, such as take music lessons, on the ground that later the children will be glad they did—"You'll thank me later!" An engineer might see a way to improve an agreed on rough design to better serve a client's needs, although it involves a significant alteration from the rough design. She might make the change in the belief that the client will agree when he sees the completed design.

To decide whether these justifications support viewing the professional–client relationship as paternalistic, it is useful to consider when reasonable people would allow others to make decisions for them. First, a person might not wish to bother making decisions because the differences involved are trivial. For example, an executive authorizes a secretary to order any needed office supplies because the differences between brands of paper clips and so forth are not important. Second, the decisions might require knowledge or expertise a person does not possess. For example, an automobile mechanic knows whether a car's oil filter needs changing. One goes to a mechanic for knowledge and service. Third, a person might allow others to make judgments if he or she is or will be mentally incompetent. Some people voluntarily enter mental hospitals. One would, however, want some assurance in this and the previous case that the persons making judgments for one have values similar to one's own. For example, a woman might not want a physician to make decisions in childbirth if the physician believed in saving the fetus' life over the woman's. Often, even usually, one can assume that the values are those of reasonable or average persons in society.

The first of these reasons does not directly relate to the arguments for paternalism, but the second and third do relate to the first two arguments for paternalism. Reasonable persons would allow others to make decisions for them when they lack the capacity to make reasonable judgments. However, most clients do not have sufficiently impaired judgment reasonably to allow others to make important decisions for them. This incapacity argument has little or no plausibility for the common clients of architects, engineers, and accountants. Business and corporate clients are unlikely to have significantly impaired judgment, even if they are biased. Moreover, even with individuals, the view is not plausible for the common cases. A person who wants to purchase a house or make a will, or who has the flu or an infection, is rarely so distraught as to be unable to make reasonable decisions. Consequently, the argument from incapacity does not support adopting a paternalistic conception of the professional–client relationship for most cases, although it supports using that conception in special cases.

The first argument for paternalism, that from superior knowledge, fits with reasonable persons allowing others to make decisions when they lack knowledge. Moreover, clients go to professionals for their superior knowledge and skills; such knowledge and skill is a defining feature of a profession. However, many decisions require balancing legal or health concerns against other client interests. As many authors have noted, crucial professional decisions involve value choices.[11] They are not simple choices of technical means to ends, and even choices of means have a value component. Professionals have not had training in value choices. Even if they had, they might not know a client's value scheme sufficiently to determine what is best for him or her when everything is considered. An attorney might advise a client that he or she need not agree to such large alimony or child support payments, but the client might decide that for personal relations with the former spouse or the welfare of the children, the larger payments are best. Similarly, a physician can advise bed rest, but because of business interests, a client can decide his or her overall interests are best promoted by continuing to work on certain matters. The client might especially need the income or be on the verge of completing a business deal that will earn a promotion. Social workers are often distraught to learn that "bag ladies" and other "derelicts" prefer their life to one with the benefits that a social worker can provide. Physicians sometimes fail to realize that a patient's other concerns, even a vacation trip with the family, can precede health. They write and speak of the problem of patient noncompliance just as parents speak of noncompliance by children. Yet one does not have everything when one has health. Similarly, a client might want an engineering or architectural design to use one type of construction rather than another because its subsidiary supplies such materials.

Although a professional and client are not equals, sufficient client competence exists to undermine the paternalistic model as appropriate for their usual relationship. Clients can exercise judgment over many aspects of professional services. If they lack information to make decisions, professionals can provide it. Sometimes professionals argue that clients can never have the information they have. This is true, but not directly to the point. Much of the information professionals have is irrelevant to decisions that significantly affect client values. The precise name of a disease and its manner of action are not relevant to deciding between two alternative drug therapies, but the fact that one drug reduces alertness is. Similarly, clients of engineers do not need to know the full weight a structure will bear, only that it is more than sufficient for all anticipated stress. To deny clients authority and responsibility by adopting the paternalistic model is to deny them the freedom to direct their own lives. Clients are not capable of determining the precise nature of their problem, or of knowing the alternative courses of action and predicting their consequences or carrying them out on their own. They need and want the technical expertise of a professional to do so. However, they are capable of making reasonable choices among options on the basis of their total values. They need professionals' information to make wise choices to accomplish their purposes.

Finally, when the professional–client relationship is conducted on the paternalistic model, client outcomes are not as good as when the client has a more active role. Douglas E. Rosenthal studied settlement awards in personal injury cases.[12] The actual awards received were compared to an expert panel's judgments of the worth of the claims. The less the client participated in the case by not expressing wants, seeking information from the lawyers, and so on, the more the awards fell short of the panel's estimates of the worth of claims. Other studies have found that in medical care, disclosure of information (and consequent more informed participation of clients) also beneficially affects outcomes.[13] Not only does the paternalistic model sacrifice client freedom and autonomy, but as a result, client values and interests are also often sacrificed.

Fiduciary

As a general characterization of what the professional–client relationship should be, one needs a concept in which the professional's superior knowledge is recognized, but the client retains a significant authority and responsibility in decision making. The law uses such a conception to characterize most professional–client relationships, namely, that of a fiduciary. In a fiduciary relationship, both parties are responsible and their judgments given consideration. Because one party is in a more advantageous position, he or she has special obligations to the other. The weaker party depends on the stronger in ways in which the other does not and so must *trust* the stronger party.

In the fiduciary model, a client has more authority and responsibility in decision making than in the paternalistic model. A client's consent and judgment are required, and he or she participates in the decision-making process. But clients depend on the professional for much of the information upon which they give or withhold their consent. The term *consents* (the client consents) rather than *decides* (the client decides) indicates that it is the professional's role to propose courses of action. It is not the conception of two people contributing equally to the formulation of plans, whether or not dealing at arm's length. Rather, the professional supplies the ideas and information, and the client agrees or not. For the process to work, the client must trust the professional to analyze accurately the problem, canvass the feasible alternatives, know as well as one can their likely consequences, fully convey this information to the client, perhaps make a recommendation, and work honestly and loyally for the client to effectuate the chosen alternative. In short, the client must rely on the professional to use his or her knowledge and ability in the client's interests. Because the client cannot check most of the work of the professional or the information supplied, the professional has special obligations to the client to ensure that the trust and reliance are justified.

This is not to suggest that the professional simply presents an overall recommendation for a client's acceptance or rejection. Rather, a client's interests can be affected by various aspects of a professional's work, so the client should be consulted at various times. The extent of appropriate client participation and decision making can be determined by advertence to the reasons for allowing others to make decisions for one. Professionals do not have expertise in a client's values or in making value choices significantly affecting a client's life plans or style. However, they do have knowledge of technical matters. A patient will certainly let a physician determine the dosage of medicines. A client can reasonably allow an engineer to determine the general specifications of materials for a job. A lawyer may decide whether to stipulate facts or object to testimony.[14] Clients allow professionals to make these judgments because the effects on their values are small, and they do not wish to be bothered. In short, client consent and involvement are not necessary when (1) the value effect is not significant or (2) the matter is a technical one, and the professional's values do not differ significantly from the client's.

The literature on medical ethics is replete with discussions of informed consent, and it has been taken up as important for other professions such as engineering and law.[15] The legal doctrine of informed consent developed from medical malpractice and experimentation. Informed consent is legally necessary before one can perform procedures on a patient. However, informed consent has a strong ethical basis in protecting a client's self-determination. The elements of informed consent are (1) a capacity to understand and choose; (2) an explanation of a proposed course of action, its alternatives, and the risks and potential benefits of each option; and (3) free and voluntary consent.

Informed consent is not itself a model of the professional–client relationship. Instead, it is a method or technique to guard against paternalism and promote shared decision making. Doubt exists about the extent to which it has actually promoted these goals in medicine. The process can become a ritual of securing a patient's signature on a form. One might think that informed consent implies a contractual model of the professional–client relationship. However, as previously suggested, it better fits the fiduciary model. The client consents, agrees to, or accepts the professional's recommendation and explanation of it. The client does not participate in formulating a plan of action or developing alternatives and determining the risks and benefits of each. Nonetheless, the client's self-determination is retained because the client's consent is necessary.

The appropriate ethical conception of the professional–client relationship is one that allows clients as much freedom to determine how their life is affected as is reasonably warranted on the basis of their ability to make decisions. In most dealings of business and corporate clients with accountants, architects, engineers, and lawyers, the relationship is close to a contract between equals or even agency. As clients have less knowledge about the subject matter for which the professional is engaged, the special obligations of the professional in the fiduciary model become more significant. The professional must assume more responsibiilty for formulating plans, presenting their advantages and disadvantages, and making recommendations. Because of the increased reliance on the professional, he or she must take special care to be worthy of client trust. Thus, although the fiduciary model is appropriate throughout the range of competent clients and services, the less a client's knowledge and capacity to understand, the greater the professional's responsibilities to the client. . . .

OBLIGATIONS OF TRUSTWORTHINESS

The fiduciary ethical model of the professional–client relationship emphasizes a professional's special obligations to be worthy of client trust. Only if a professional deserves a client's initial and continuing trust has the ideal of the fiduciary conception been achieved. As should be clear from the rejection of paternalism, the sense of trust involved is not that of trusting a professional to make decisions for one.[16] One may always pertinently ask, "Trust to do what?" The answer is trust to fulfill the functions that the average client wants and for which a professional is hired. A client wants a professional to use expertise to analyze the problem, formulate alternative plans or courses of action, determine their probable consequences, make recommendations, or carry out certain activities (audit, surgery) in his or her behalf. A professional's obligations to a client are those necessary to deserve the client's trust that these activities will be performed in a manner to promote the client's interests—including the freedom to make decisions regarding his or her life. . . .

The fiduciary model's implication that professionals must be worthy of client trust provides a criterion for determining professionals' obligations to clients. Seven virtues and responsibilities of professionals to clients are honesty, candor, competence, diligence, loyalty, fairness, and discretion. By definition, a professional must be honest to be worthy of trust. Professionals can be dishonest toward clients by suggesting and providing services that are not useful, as well as by outright theft. Candor is probably a subclass of honesty and includes full disclosure to clients as well as truthfulness. Although lying to clients can probably never be justified, because it effectively destroys a trust relationship, information may be justifiably withheld from clients if necessary to prevent direct harm to them and if they are told as soon as possible.

Competence is not itself an ethical virtue, but the responsibility to keep current with one's field and not to undertake tasks for which one lacks competence is an ethical one. Moreover, to inform clients of alternative approaches, professionals have an obligation to be aware of developments in other professions pertaining to problems they handle. Diligence is the requirement that a professional work carefully and promptly. Self-employed professionals cannot properly argue that they lack time to consider each client's case adequately unless a shortage of professionals means some people would be denied services to which they have a right. Employed professionals such as teachers, nurses, and social workers often have no direct control over the number of clients they have. If they have more than they can ideally handle, they must provide services based on the priority of the value to the different clients.

Because professionals are hired by clients to protect and promote their interests, they must be loyal to their clients. A professional's loyalty can be affected by conflicts of interest between the client and the professional, other clients in that transaction or in other cases, or third party payers. Client consent to a professional acting in his or her behalf after disclosure of an actual or possible conflict of interest is a necessary but not sufficient condition to justify a professional accepting a case. The professional must also be able to exercise independent judgment in behalf of the client. Accountants performing audits, lawyers making independent evaluations, and journalists owe independence of judgment to the public.

Fairness, primarily an obligation to provide impartial service to clients, rests on the value of equality of opportunity. Bias can affect the quality of services professionals provide clients. Professionals should not favor one client over another. This obligation is especially important for teachers in grading.

Discretion rests on the clients' value of privacy in not having information about them conveyed to others without their consent. Even discussion of a client's public activities can be indiscreet. Confidential information about a client may be disclosed for the client's sake if (1) the client has been informed that the professional will do so when he or she judges it to be in the client's best interest and the client has not explicitly refused permission or (2) disclosure is necessary to prevent significant harm to the client. It may also be disclosed by a professional in order to collect a fee or in self-defense against a charge of wrongdoing. Confidential information may be disclosed to protect others from injury when required by law. For journalists, confidentiality pertains to sources of information, not to the audience that is plausibly the clients. Consequently, it does not rest on the privacy of clients, but on the privacy of sources and the interests of clients in information.

Finally, clients have three obligations to professionals. The first is to keep commitments they make to them, including to pay them. Clients also have an obligation to be truthful to professionals, but arguably not to full disclosure. Lastly, they may not request professionals to perform unethical acts. These obligations are all specifications of universal norms, not role-related ones, because in a fiduciary relationship, the special obligations are those of the advantaged party—the professional.

NOTES

1. See K. Danner Clouser, "Veatch, May, and Models: A Critical Review and a New View," in *The Clinical Encounter*, ed. Shelp, pp. 94–96.

2. See Veatch, "Models for Ethical Medicine," p. 5. Veatch calls this the engineering model of the physician, but this assumes it is appropriate for engineers.

3. ABA, *Model Rules*, Rule 1.2(b).

4. Simon, "The Ideology of Advocacy," p. 36.

5. Simon's proposed alternative to the ideology of advocacy suffers these defects to some extent. He does not allow for professional roles. Thus, all professional obligations are at best specifications of universal norms. "The foundation principle of non-professional advocacy is that problems of advocacy be treated as a matter of *personal* ethics. . . . Personal ethics apply to people merely by virtue of the fact that they are human individuals. The obligations involved may depend on particular circumstances or personalities, but they do not follow from social role or station." Ibid., p. 131.

6. ABA, *Code of Professional Responsibility*, EC 7-8; see also ABA, *Model Rules*, Rule 2.1 and comment.

7. Veatch, "Models for Ethical Medicine," p. 7; see also Veatch, *Theory of Medical Ethics*, esp. pp. 134–137.

8. See, for example, Masters, "Is Contract an Adequate Basis," p. 25; May, "Code, Covenant, Contract, or Philanthropy," p. 35; Engelhardt, "Rights and Responsibilities," pp. 16–17; Richard Wasserstrom, "Lawyers as Professionals: Some Moral Issues," in *1977 National Conference on Teaching Professional Responsibility*, ed. Goldberg, pp. 120–122.

9. Some authors contend that paternalism does not apply to persons incapable of consent because they define paternalism as limiting a person's autonomy, which incompetent persons lack; see, for example, Beauchamp and McCullough, *Medical Ethics*, p. 84. Such a definition makes it difficult for parents to be paternalistic and undercuts the grounds for some laws, such as compulsory commitment because persons are a danger to themselves.

10. See especially Feinberg, *Harm to Self*; Kleinig, *Paternalism*; and Van DeVeer, *Paternalistic Intervention*.

11. See, for example, Glenn C. Graber, "On Paternalism and Health Care," in *Contemporary Issues in Biomedical Ethics*, ed. Davis, Hoffmaster, and Shorten, p. 239; Buchanan, "Medical Paternalism," p. 381; and Goldman, *Moral Foundations*, pp. 179–186.

12. Rosenthal, *Lawyer and Client*, chap. 2.

13. President's Commission, *Making Health Care Decisions*, pp. 100–101.

14. See ABA, *Code of Professional Responsibility*, EC 7-7; but see ABA, *Model Rules*, Rules 1.2(a) and 1.4.

15. See Martin and Schinzinger, *Ethics in Engineering*, pp. 59–64. Strauss, "Toward a Revised Model of Attorney–Client Relationship"; and Spiegel, "Lawyers and Professional Autonomy."

16. Cooper, "Trust," distinguishes (1) entrusting someone with something, (2) deeming someone to be trustworthy as honest and so on, and (3) having confidence in abilities and so on. The sense involved in the test is being worthy of trust in senses (2) and (3).

REFERENCES

AMERICAN BAR ASSOCIATION. 1983. *Code of Professional Responsibility and Code of Judicial Conduct*. Chicago: American Bar Association.

——. 1983. *Model Rules of Professional Conduct*. Chicago: American Bar Association.

BEAUCHAMP, TOM L., AND LAURENCE B. McCULLOUGH. 1984. *Medical Ethics*. Englewood Cliffs, N.J.: Prentice Hall.

BUCHANAN, ALLEN. "Medical Paternalism." *Philosophy and Public Affairs* 7: 370–90.

COOPER, DAVID E. 1985. "Trust." *Journal of Medical Ethics* 11: 92–93.

DAVIS, JOHN W., BARRY HOFFMASTER, AND SARAH SHORTEN, eds. 1978. *Contemporary Issues in Biomedical Ethics*. Clifton, N.J.: Humana Press.

FEINBERG, JOEL. 1986. *Harm to Self*. Vol. 3 of *The Moral Limits of the Criminal Law*. New York: Oxford University Press.

GOLDBERG, STUART C., ed. 1977. *1977 National Conference on Teaching Professional Responsibility: Pre-Conference Materials*. Detroit: University of Detroit School of Law.

GOLDMAN, ALAN, H. 1980. *The Moral Foundations of Professional Ethics*. Totowa, N.J.: Rowman and Littlefield.

KLEINIG, JOHN. 1984. *Paternalism*. Totowa, N.J.: Rowman and Allanheld.

MARTIN, MIKE W., AND ROLAND SCHINZINGER. 1983. *Ethics in Engineering*. New York: McGraw-Hill.

PRESIDENT'S COMMISSION FOR THE STUDY OF ETHICAL PROBLEMS IN MEDICINE AND BIO-

MEDICAL AND BEHAVIORAL RESEARCH. 1982. *Making Health Care Decisions*, vol. 1, *Report*. Washington, D.C.: U.S. Government Printing Office.

ROSENTHAL, DOUGLAS E. 1974. *Lawyer and Client: Who's in Charge?* New York: Russell Sage Foundation.

SHELP, EARL E., ed. 1983. *The Clinical Encounter: The Moral Fabric of the Patient–Physician Relationship*. Boston: D. Reidel.

SIMON, WILLIAM H. 1978. "The Ideology of Advocacy: Procedural Justice and Professional Ethics." *Wisconsin Law Review*: 29–144.

SPIEGEL, MARK. 1987. "Lawyers and Professional Autonomy: Reflections on Corporate Lawyering and the Doctrine of Informed Consent." *Western New England Law Review* 9: 139–52.

STRAUSS, MARCY. 1987. "Toward a Revised Model of Attorney–Client Relationship: The Argument for Autonomy." *North Carolina Law Review* 65: 315–50.

VANDEVEER, DONALD. 1986. *Paternalistic Intervention: The Moral Bounds on Benevolence*. Princeton, N.J.: Princeton University Press.

VEATCH, ROBERT M. 1972. "Models for Ethical Medicine in a Revolutionary Age." *Hastings Center Report* 2 (June): 5–7.

26 Conflict of Interest

Michael Davis

Five years ago, Joseph Margolis began an important paper on conflict of interest with the observation:

> The notion of a conflict of interest is singularly ignored in most attempts to examine the nature of moral and legal constraints. In attempting to supply an analysis, therefore, we will be breaking relatively fresh ground.[1]

Had Margolis made that observation only yesterday, it would have been just as true. There is, of course, now much more being written about whether this or that is a conflict of interest. The practical literature of business and professional ethics is much richer than it was even five years ago. But Margolis was talking about "the *notion* of a conflict of interest," not about this or that particular conflict. He set out to supply an "analysis" missing from the literature. If Margolis was breaking relatively fresh ground five years ago, the ground remains relatively fresh. Margolis analyzed conflict of interest as an avoidable exploiting of conflicting roles. No one has (as far as I can tell) publicly disagreed with him.

But was Margolis breaking fresh ground? If one examines the literature of what is generally known as "business and professional ethics," it certainly seems he was. If, however, one examines instead the special literature of legal ethics, Margolis's fresh ground looks about as fresh as an Illinois corn field after harvest. Legal ethics long ago worked out an analysis of conflict of interest as a situation tending to undermine independent professional judgment. The analysis can, I think, easily be generalized to cover situations other than those lawyers face. So generalized, the analysis is both

---

importantly different from Margolis's and significantly better. The analysis is importantly different because it connects conflict of interest with undermined judgment within a role rather than with conflict between roles; and significantly better because it does not (as Margolis admits his does) require ascribing conflicts of interest to situations commonly thought not to be conflict-of-interest situations or imposing a number of more or less *ad hoc* restrictions on the basic analysis to avoid such ascriptions. That, at least, is what I shall try to show here.

I shall first state (what I shall call) "the lawyer's analysis"; then generalize it to fit business and professional ethics generally, giving some examples of its application; and last, draw from the exercise an interesting lesson for those working in business and professional ethics.

I. THE LAWYER'S ANALYSIS

The lawyer's analysis of conflict of interest is to be found in the American Bar Association's *Code of Professional Responsibility* as well as in numerous articles, books, court opinions, and opinions of various bar ethics committees.[2] The *Code*'s statement of the analysis, while not particularly subtle, is all we need here.

The *Code* understands a conflict of interest to require only a) one relatively formal role (with occupants), the role of being someone's lawyer, and b) at least one interest tending to interfere with acting properly in that role. The *Code* understands a lawyer's role to be exercising "professional judgment . . . , within the bounds of the law, solely for the benefit of his client and free of compromising influences and loyalties."[3] The emphasis is on the lawyer's judgment within *that* role. The lawyer's professional judgment must be "independent." The lawyer must be able to commit his legal training, knowledge, and sagacity fully to his client (within the bounds of the law and what the client wants done). Let us consider this analysis in detail.

The client is, of course, someone other than the lawyer himself. A lawyer acting for himself may well not be free of influences tending to undermine his professional judgment. His personal involvement may make him too emotional to think things through. Tender feelings may lead him to resolve doubts about the law against his own interests. And so on. That is the point of the lawyer's joke that "a lawyer who represents himself has a fool for a client." But a lawyer "representing himself" cannot have a conflict of interest however unreliable his judgment becomes. He cannot because (strictly speaking) he is not acting in his role as lawyer. He is simply acting for himself knowing what a lawyer knows. Being someone's lawyer is having someone to represent, someone in whose place one acts. To act for oneself is not to represent anyone. So, though conflict of interest is a fact about a lawyer's judgment and so, in that way, *intra*-personal, it is also a fact about the lawyer's judgment-in-his-role-as-lawyer-for-someone-else and so, in that way, *inter*-personal.

"Interest" is just short-hand for any influence, loyalty, or other concern capable of compromising a lawyer's ability to act for the benefit of his client (within the bounds of his role as a lawyer). Such concerns might include the temptation to turn the lawyer-client relation to the lawyer's advantage, the possibility of using confidence gained in one lawyer-client relation for the benefit of another client, or the necessity of sacrificing one of two clients whose interests have come in conflict. "Interest" does not, however, include *any* factor that might make judgment unreliable. For lawyers, all talk of conflict of interest presupposes a competent professional. Judgment made unreliable by ignorance of the law, poor training, drunkenness, or the like is incompetent, a failing of "*professional* judgment" rather than of "*independent* judgment." Conflict of interest is a problem of professional judgment, a problem of arranging things so that competent judgment can function as it ordinarily does. The "conflict" of conflict of interest is a collision between competent judgment and something that might make that judgment unable to function as the lawyer's role requires.

The ABA *Code of Professional Responsibility* implicitly distinguishes at least three kinds of conflict of interest. Some interests are such that they are certain to affect adversely the advice given or services rendered the prospective client. These create (what we may call) "actual" conflicts of interest. Other interests create only a "reasonable probability" of such adverse effects. Such interests create (what we may call) "latent" conflicts ("latent" because the conflict is already there, requiring only a change of circumstance to become actual). Other interests are such that a lawyer can "reasonably foresee" that an actual conflict may arise (even though there is not even a latent conflict yet). Such interests create (what we may call) "potential" conflicts ("potential" because circumstances must change for such conflicts even to become latent). The boundaries of these three sorts of conflict are, of course, rather indefinite. The distinction is nevertheless useful.

Let me illustrate the distinction (and its usefulness) by an example derived from Margolis. Suppose that a lawyer is considering becoming a candidate for Congress, that among his clients is an Indian tribe with a claim against the federal government, that the lawyer can foresee the Indians some day becoming dissatisfied with the slow pace of adjudication, and that under such circumstances it might be reasonable for them to try to get Congress to act on their claim directly. Such a lawyer already has a potential conflict of interest. He can reasonably foresee that he may some day have to choose between his client and his constituency. He may already have begun to feel the tug of constituent interests. There is already some reason for his client to be wary of depending upon his advice should the question of taking the claim to Congress arise. If the lawyer were then to run for Congress and win, the potential conflict would become latent. There would now be a reasonable probability that the lawyer-Congressman would have to advise on a question in which his interests as Congressman made his judgment as lawyer unreliable. But, so long as the Indians have no reason to become dissatisfied with the pace of adjudication, he does not have an actual conflict. He is not yet in a situation in which he will have to advise on the question of taking the claim to Congress. To be in a situation requiring advice on that question is to have a conflict of interest par excellence, an actual conflict.

The *Code* does not treat these three sorts of conflict of interest the same. The differences are instructive (especially because the *Code*'s treatment diverges from Margolis's in at least one important way). The *Code* looks with distrust upon *all* conflicts of interest, even those that are merely potential. For example, not only should a lawyer not accept proffered employment if his personal interests or desires will affect adversely the advice given or services rendered the prospective client, he should also not accept such employment if there is even a reasonable probability that they will have that effect.[4] A lawyer should not draw up a will in which he is named a beneficiary, or take a case where there is much chance that he will be called as a witness concerning any controversial point, or agree in advance to accept as payment for services any publication rights relating to the subject of employment.

The *Code* flatly condemns not only actual conflicts of interest but also latent conflicts. The *Code* sets a lower standard only for potential conflicts. A lawyer may properly accept a client even if he can reasonably foresee that an actual conflict may arise. He may accept, but only if he explains the situation to the client and the client consents to continuing the relationship with the lawyer nonetheless.[5] Thus, if a lawyer has a financial interest in a company competing with a client's, the lawyer may agree to draft contracts for that company only after making full disclosure of the potential conflict and receiving the client's permission to go ahead nevertheless.

The *Code* does not then agree with Margolis that "[pursuing] a course of conduct that leads to [an actual] conflict of interest is not itself a mark of any wrongdoing on the agent's part."[6] A lawyer who accepts a client without making full and timely disclosure of any conflict of interest that is more than merely potential, is subject to discipline under the *Code*.[7] The *Code* can be tougher on latent (and potential) conflict of interest than Margolis is because the lawyer's analysis makes latent (and potential) conflict less likely than the Margolis analysis does. Conflict of roles, especially if "role" is given its full elasticity, is much more common than an interest tending to undermine independent professional judgment. Only a special subclass of "role-conflict" makes a lawyer's judgment less reliable.

The *Code* also distinguishes between (what we may call) *having* a conflict of interest (potential, latent, or actual) and *acting* in a conflict-of-interest situation. Here too the treatment is interestingly different from Margolis's. The *Code* expressly allows a lawyer to act in situations of potential conflict as noted above (just as Margolis would). Such action is quite proper if there is full disclosure and the client consents nonetheless. The *Code*'s approach to acting in other conflict-of-interest situations is more complex. While it condemns most acting in situations of actual (or latent) conflict, it exempts much of it from discipline if the lawyer makes full disclosure and his client retains him nonetheless.[8] The *Code* does not (as Margolis does) treat divesting as the only permissible response to an actual (or latent) conflict. The *Code* sometimes permits a client to be as foolish as the lawyer who chooses to represent himself. The *Code* thus shows itself more sensitive than Margolis to the practicalities of divestiture.

The way the *Code* does that tells much about what the *Code* takes to be wrong with having a conflict of interest. What the *Code* says in effect is that while a lawyer *should* provide independent professional judgment, he *must* at least not betray the trust a client properly puts in him. If a lawyer has a conflict of interest (actual or latent), he must either refuse the proffered employment (as Margolis recommends) or let the client know that he cannot trust the lawyer to exercise his professional judgment as independently as lawyers ordinarily do (an alternative Margolis does not consider). To have a conflict of interest is bad, but to have one without putting the client on notice is worse. To be a lawyer is (the *Code* seems to say) to occupy a role traditionally understood to guarantee independent (professional) judgment. That guarantee is worth preserving. A conflict of interest makes the lawyer's judgment less reliable, endangering the client's interests whether the client is willing to tolerate the danger or not. So, a lawyer *should* (all else equal) divest. But, if a lawyer does not at least warn his client of the conflict, he does more than weaken a guarantee worth preserving. He presents himself as having a judgment more reliable than in fact it is. He invites a trust the invitation itself betrays. No matter how well things happen to turn out, the lawyer would not have behaved as his client had a right to expect him to behave. The lawyer would have taken risks his client did not know of, risks a client has a right to decide whether or not to take. If the lawyer does not realize he has a conflict (and that certainly is possible), he has failed to perform competently. Lawyers are supposed to recognize conflicts. If, however, the lawyer knows he has a conflict and chooses not to tell the client, having the conflict becomes an intentional wrong. The best analogue is not breach of etiquette (as Margolis suggests) but lying or promise-breaking. Disclosure and consent cannot end the conflict (because they cannot make judgment more reliable). But they can prevent automatic betrayal (because they allow the client to adjust his reliance to fit the circumstances).

II. GENERALIZING THE LAWYER'S ANALYSIS

That is enough of the lawyer's analysis for our purposes. Its main components should now be familiar: a) the role of being someone's lawyer and b) an interest tending to interfere with proper exercise of judgment required in that role. To generalize the analysis so that it covers all of business and professional ethics, we need to replace being-someone's-lawyer with the appropriate category of which being-someone's-lawyer is a special case. If we take being-someone's-lawyer to be (as seems reasonable) a special case of relationships-between-persons-requiring-one-to-exercise-judgment-in--the-other's-service, we get the following generalization of the lawyer's analysis:

I.   A person has a conflict of interest if a) he is in a relationship with another requiring him to exercise judgment in that other's service and b) he has an interest tending to interfere with the proper exercise of judgment in that relationship.

This formulation is too rough to be final. But it is good enough to start with. Let us consider it term by term to see what it entails. Having done that, we should be able to provide a fuller and (for purposes of this paper) final formulation.

The generalized analysis does not, as formulated, refer to "role" at all, only to "relationship" of a certain kind. That is no accident. Though "lawyer" is a traditionally defined role, there is no reason to limit conflict of interest to traditionally defined roles (as Margolis eventually does). Quite informal roles, mere relationships among persons, can, it seems, involve relatively clear conflicts of interest. For example: Suppose that I have been raising black angus bulls with the intention of competing with you in the next cattle show. Suppose too that you do not know of my intention, that you ask me to look after your bulls while you are away, and that I agree. Taking care of cattle requires exercise of judgment now and then. If your bull looks a bit weak, I may have to decide whether it would be better to bring the bulls in from the field now or wait a little longer to be sure there will be a storm. And so on. Given my interest in beating you at the next cattle show, I may not be as good a judge of such things as I would otherwise be. My own interests would tend to make my judgment on such questions less reliable than it would otherwise be. I have, then, a conflict of interest as soon as I agree to put myself in your service. If it is not too likely that I will have to exercise judgment while looking after your bulls, the conflict will be potential. But, even so, it will be there, informal role or not.

Though the generalized analysis does not refer to "role," the analysis does imply role if "role" is allowed its full elasticity. "Role" can be allowed its full elasticity here (as it could not in the Margolis analysis) because our concern is not roles as such but a certain sort of role, that is, relationships requiring the exercise of judgment in the service of another. "Judgment," not "role," is the crucial term.

What is judgment? Judgment must, of course, be something that lawyers exercise, but something too that not only lawyers exercise. For our purposes, judgment may be thought of as the capacity to make correctly decisions not as likely to be made correctly by a simple clerk with a book of rules and access to all the facts (and only the facts) the actual decision maker has. Judgment implies discretion. A policeman does not need judgment (in this sense) to decide whether to issue me a speeding ticket once I have been clocked well over the limit, pulled over, and found to have no valid excuse. A bank president does not need judgment to decide whether she (as president) should embezzle the bank's money. And so on. For questions such as these, such persons cannot have a conflict of interest, however hard the question may be for them. In contrast, a critic needs judgment to decide how good a play or actor is. A member of Congress needs judgment to decide how to vote on a certain bill. And so on. Such persons can be subject to a conflict of interest in any situation where they are charged with deciding such questions.

Judgment is, of course, always judgment relative to certain questions, not judgment in the abstract. A conflict of interest is always a situation where someone is charged with deciding something or other. Acting in a situation of conflict is always deciding *that* something or other. For example: A bank president should exercise judgment in deciding to whom the bank should make loans. She can, then, have a conflict of interest when deciding such questions even if she cannot have a conflict when deciding whether to embezzle or not.

There will be borderline cases. A relationship can be defined by tradition, rule, or express agreement. Such relationships are likely to be relatively well-defined. But relationships can also grow up more or less haphazardly. Much can be left unsaid and ill-defined. Such relationships, not the well-defined ones, are the ones likely to turn up near the border. If we allow "role" its full elasticity, we will allow for relationships in which it may be impossible to know whether the role requires judgment and so, impossible to say whether a situation involving that role constitutes a conflict of interest. Such inchoate relationships are, however, not common. Even most informal roles are not *that* informal.

The more common reason for doubt about whether a particular situation constitutes a conflict of interest is lack of information. Some of Margolis's business examples are of this sort. For example, he asks, "Is it a conflict of interest to recommend to one's own company a contract with another firm in which one holds substantial stock?"[9] The answer depends in part on whether the recommendation requires judgment. Many such recommendations may be so routine that making them could be left to any clerk. Deciding to make such recommendations, like deciding whether or not to embezzle, would involve no exercise of judgment and so, would not involve a conflict of interest. Margolis must tell us more about what is being decided before we can answer intelligently.

He must also tell us what is "proper" in the role. If it were not part of serving the company to forego serving oneself where one cannot serve both, an executive could not have a conflict of interest even when faced with deciding whether to recommend a contract disadvantageous to the company but beneficial to himself. The term "proper" is relatively well-defined for lawyers. The *Code* specifies that role in detail, amplifying what tradition leads us to expect anyway. For most roles, however, there is no such code and tradition is not so settled. Still, insofar as a role is defined at all, it justifies certain expectations just as surely as does being a lawyer. For our purposes, what is proper in a role is just what is ordinarily expected of persons in that role, those expectations themselves being justified by express agreement, ongoing practice, rule, or the like. Even so informal a role as looking after someone's bulls while the owner is away justifies certain expectations, for example, that I will act for your benefit while looking after your bulls. We may then identify what is proper in the role of recommending contracts by asking people who know about such things what they would expect of a person in such a role, what they generally rely on people in that role to be and do.

Because of the importance assigned "judgment," we need not be much concerned by the term "interest." "Interest" should be interpreted broadly to include all those influences, loyalties, concerns, emotions, or the like that can make (competent) judgment less reliable than it might otherwise be (without making it incompetent). Thus, even moral constraints, though not ordinarily considered mere interests, may be interests for the purposes of this analysis. Such constraints *may* be, because they too can reduce the reliability of someone's judgment in a particular role. For example, a conscience-stricken Machiavelli might have to refuse to advise his superior on a particular question (in part) because his conscience makes his judgment about how to proceed unreliable. He can no longer be trusted to tell his superior how not to be good. Moral constraints can create conflicts of interest. But, in general, they do not. They do not because in general we do not define roles to require judgments about whether or not to behave immorally and conflict of interest is always relative to judgment *within* a role.

We may now summarize these observations in the following fuller statement of the generalized analysis ("role" having its full elasticity):

II.   A person P_1 has a conflict of interest in role R if, and only if:

   a. P_1 occupies R;

   b.   R requires exercise of (competent) judgment with regard to certain questions Q;

   c.   A person's occupying R justifies another person relying on the occupant's judgment being exercised in the other's service with regard to Q;

   d.   Person P_2 is justified in relying on P_1's judgment in R with regard to Q (in part at least) because P_1 occupies R; and

   e. P_1 is (actually, latently, or potentially) subject to influences, loyalties, temptations, or other interests tending to make P_1's (competent) judgment in R with regard to Q less likely to benefit P_2 than P_1's occupying R justifies R_2 in expecting.

Conditions a–d define the relevant role. Condition e introduces the conflict (the parenthetical terms making it clear that even "potential conflicts of interest" are conflicts of interest).

The restatement is not yet perfect. For example, formulation II does not plainly include conflicts in which P_2 relies on P_1 but some P_3 benefits (as occurs, for example, when a bank administers a trust parent P_2 established for child P_3). Such imperfections are, however, minor enough for us to ignore them here. They do not seem likely to affect three important (and related) consequences to be drawn from this formulation of the generalized analysis.

First, under formulation II (as under the original lawyer's analysis), conflict of interest may continue even after full disclosure and consent of P_2. Whether it does or not will depend upon how the role is defined. *Not* P_2's *actual* expectations of P_1 but what P_2 is *justified* in expecting of P_1 because of the role P_1 occupies, is what determines whether a conflict exists. P_1 cannot change what *R* justifies P_2 in expecting simply by disclosing the conflict and getting consent (even though he can change P_2's actual expectations in that way). P_1 must actually change roles to escape the conflict. Consent after full disclosure might be a way of changing one role into another. That depends on the role itself. For lawyers, consent after full disclosure does not have that effect. But it might for roles which (unlike being-someone's-lawyer) are entirely defined by those party to it.

Second, formulation II does not expressly require that a conflict of interest be *avoidable*. It does not because some conflicts do not seem to be avoidable. A conflict can be upon us before we know what is happening. If, for example, a Senator's son applies for a job in her office, the Senator has a conflict of interest as soon as her son hands in the application (supposing the decision to hire would require some exercise of judgment). She does not have to do anything to have the conflict (though she would have to do something to end it). She need not even know that her son has applied. Her role as Senator is to pick the best person for the job; her duty as parent, to look after her son. Her being a parent makes her judgment as Senator unreliable for the question of whether to hire her son or someone else. For her even to consider his application is to act in a situation of actual conflict. It is, of course, always possible in retrospect to see how one might have prevented such a conflict. But, short of suicide, there does not seem to be any strategy for preventing all. Being born may be enough to guarantee some (potential) conflicts. Hence, there is no reason to require (as Margolis does) that all conflicts of interest be avoidable.

Third, formulation II does not expressly require that a conflict of interest be *escapable*. But escapability is probably implied. A conflict of interest is always a conflict relative to deciding certain questions. If we can always refuse to decide *those* questions, we can always escape the conflict. We cannot, of course, always escape deciding something. Not to decide is to decide (at least once we know that we are not deciding). But refusing to decide a question is not to decide precisely the same question. It is a "second-order" decision. Refusing to decide does not answer a question like whom the Senator should hire. Refusing to decide only answers a question like whether the Senator should make any hiring decisions at all while her son is an applicant. The second-order decision need not involve a conflict of interest just because the corresponding first-order decision would. Once the Senator recognizes the conflict, she knows all a *clerk* would need to know to decide that she should not decide whom to hire. The second-order question need not require judgment just because the corresponding first-order question does. Indeed, I have been unable to imagine a case in which conflict of interest cannot be escaped in this way (though I have been able to imagine cases in which such escape is perhaps too costly). The generalized analysis thus seems (partially) to confirm Margolis. Conflict of interest entails the possibility of divesting (even if not the possibility of avoiding).

But, it may seem, Margolis's chief example of mere "conflicting interests" is, under the generalized analysis, itself the inescapable conflict of interest I have been unable to imagine. Antigone is caught between two roles, her judgment in each role made unreliable by her duty in the other. Yet, she cannot escape either role. Here, it may seem, is a conflict of interest inescapable under the generalized analysis.

That may be how it seems, but in fact Antigone has no conflict of interest under our analysis any more than under Margolis's. Antigone is, it is true, caught between her duty to her brother and her duty to her city. But in this example neither duty requires judgment (though resolving the conflict between them does). Any clerk would know what Antigone should do as her brother's sister. She should bury his corpse. Any clerk would also know what she should do as citizen of Thebes. She should obey Creon and *not* bury the corpse. What is hard to know is what Antigone should do as a moral agent who is *both* her brother's sister *and* citizen of Thebes. The conflict of duty *is* inescapable, but it is not a conflict of interest under the generalized analysis. Resolving such conflicts is part of what moral agents are supposed to do in that role, not something compromising judgment in that role. Antigone is another illustration of how important focusing on judgment-in-a-role is to understanding conflict of interest.

III. CONCLUSION

I began this paper by describing Margolis's "Conflict of Interest and Conflicting Interests" as an "important paper." By now you may be wondering why I described in that way a paper I obviously consider seriously flawed. The reason makes a good conclusion.

Margolis's paper reveals that "business and professional ethics" is today a field which (for study of conflict of interest at least and no doubt for study of much else too) does not include legal ethics. Though Margolis uses some examples from legal ethics, his analysis owes nothing to that field. Apparently he did not think to read the relevant legal literature. His readers seem to have behaved exactly as he did. How else explain the silence with which so flawed a paper has been received in a field where the opportunity to criticize a respected writer is usually briskly seized by many? The collection in which the paper appeared has not gone unread.

Margolis's paper is important because it is the first in business and professional ethics (as actually constituted) to raise the theoretical problem of conflict of interest; important because the absence of subsequent alternatives to the Margolis analysis shows the theoretical weakness of business and professional ethics today; and important too because the existence of an alternative in (what is unfortunately only) the neighboring field of legal ethics shows a weakness as well in the way business and professional ethics is developing. There is a lesson here beyond that of how to analyze conflict of interest. The lesson is that those interested in problems of business and professional ethics should check the literature of legal ethics as part of their normal research procedure.[10] They may be surprised by what they find. Pleasantly surprised.

NOTES

1. Joseph Margolis, "Conflict of Interest and Conflicting Interests," in *Ethical Theory and Business*, ed. by Tom L. Beauchamp and Norman B. Bowie (Englewood Cliffs, NJ: Prentice-Hall, Inc., 1979), p. 361. I should like to thank my colleague Louis Andrade for calling my attention to this paper.

2. For a recent general discussion, see Geoffrey C. Hazard, Jr., *Ethics in the Practice of Law* (New Haven, CT: Yale University Press, 1978), especially Chapter 5. For a recent survey of the literature, see Robert H. Aronson, "Conflict of Interest," *Washington Law Review*, vol. 58 (1977), pp. 807–858.

3. American Bar Association, *Code of Professional Responsibility* (Chicago: National Center for Professional Responsibility, 1980), EC 5–1.

4. Ibid., EC 5–2.

5. Ibid., EC 5–3.

6. Margolis, p. 363.

7. See, for example, *Code*, DF 5–101(A), DR 5–104(A), or DR 5–105(A).

8. Ibid., DR 5–101(A) and DR 5–105(A).

9. Margolis, p. 365.

10. For someone who has learned this lesson, see Michael D. Bayles, *Professional Ethics* (Belmont, CA: Wadsworth Publishing Company, 1981), especially pp. 77–83 where he discusses conflict of interest in the professions under the heading "Loyalty."

27 Morality and Gift-Giving

Robert Almeder

A bribe is the offering of some good, service, or money to an appropriate person for the purpose of securing a privileged and favorable consideration (or purchase) of one's product or corporate project. Typically, but not necessarily, the person offering the bribe does so in secret and only when the person receiving the bribe antecedently agrees (either explicitly or implicitly) to accept the bribe under the conditions indicated by the briber. Understandably, the briber's business posture is enhanced by the successful bribe and it would not be otherwise enhanced, because, presumably, without the bribe the briber's product or project would not merit any special consideration as against the product or projects of the briber's competitors.[1]

For various reasons, few people in the business community are willing to defend the morality of the practice of bribery. Most people in the business community see the practice of bribery as one that, if adopted on a widescale basis, tends to undermine a free, competitive, and open economy by encouraging a lack of real competition for quality products. After all, where bribery is an acceptable practice, the briber (or the company with the biggest bribe) gains unfair advantage because the briber's product secures preferential treatment not based upon the merits or price of the product. Even at its best, the practice of bribery, *as a rule*, tends to undermine open competition along with the usual efficiencies and quality of goods characteristic of the open economy. Thus, what is basically wrong with bribery is that, *as a rule*, it strikes at the heart of capitalism by undermining a free and strenuously competitive economy. If capitalism is to survive as the best of economic systems, it can do so only where there is earnest and open competition.

The practice of bribery can also be faulted for the reason that the briber violates the golden rule because the briber, presumably, would not want his product discriminated against for reasons that had nothing to do with the quality of his product.

But what about the practice of giving gifts to persons with whom one is doing business? Is gift-giving of this sort a clear case of bribery? If it is, then for the reasons just mentioned it, like bribery, should be considered immoral. In other words, if one gives a gift in order to secure a business advantage that would not otherwise occur, and if in the typical case the person receiving the gift accepts it under the conditions indicated by the giver, then this act of gift-giving is in fact a bribe and should be considered a bribe. Many businessmen, however, do not see *all* gift-giving to one's clients as a clear case of bribery. They see nothing wrong with the practice of gift-giving if it is done under certain circumstances.

Those who favor some form of gift-giving in the marketplace do so because they think such a practice, unlike bribery, need not be an instance of deliberately intending to secure a decision that enhances one's business posture. A salesman, for example, may or may not intend his gift as a bribe. He may give a gift not for any special treatment, but only for fair treatment, or to insure equal treatment. He may even give the gift simply because in the years of doing business with someone he has become genuinely friendly with the person who just happens to be able to enhance the salesman's business posture and profit.

In response to this last line of reasoning, however, others are quick to note that what is wrong with bribery is not simply that those who offer bribes do so with the *intent* of securing special treatment, although certainly they do so. Rather, what is essentially wrong with bribery is that the practice has the effect of influencing the judgments of the bribed to provide special treatment not based on the merits or price of the product. This same effect can occur even when one merely offers a gift, that is, provides a service without intending or wishing that that service secure special treatment for the gift-giver. The person who receives the gift may, consciously or otherwise, be disposed predictably to favor the interests of the gift-giver. All that is needed to move a gift into the category of a bribe is that (a) the person receiving the gift be in a position to make a decision that enhances the assets of the giver and (b) the gift be of such a nontoken nature that it is reasonable to think that it may put the interests of the giver in a privileged status even when all else is equal.

As a result of these last considerations some corporations have in the past allowed gift-giving to their clients, or potential clients, only under the conditions that (a) the gift is not substantial enough to put the receiver into a conflict of interest position, and (b) the gift is given publicly and is not in any way a secret offering. Although these conditions seem sound in light of the reflections noted above, still we need to answer the question "Under what circumstances, if any, does an employee have a proportionate reason for running the risks involved in accepting gifts?" In answering this last question, Thomas Garrett urges that the basic question to be asked with regard to the practice of gift-giving is this: "Will this gift, entertainment or service cause any reasonable person to suspect my independence of judgment?"[2] Garrett goes on to urge that it should be clear that infrequent gifts of only a nominal cost, ten dollars or less, and small advertisement gifts will be acceptable by policy or law. On the other hand, practically any cash gift is liable to raise eyebrows and create a suspicion of bias.[3]

These same considerations would, presumably, apply with respect to entertainment. In other words, if the cost of entertainment is nominal, public, customary, and infrequent, there would be nothing morally wrong with the practice if it could not hamper the independence of the judgment of the person gifted or entertained. So, then, as Garrett would have it, if the gift is nominal, publicly given, and not intended to secure any special advantage, the practice of gift-giving would seem to be acceptable.

In spite of the sweet reasonableness of Garrett's conclusion, however, some people still think that even a nominal gift could, all else being equal, secure an advantage not merited in terms of quality or price of product. Even an annual gift of $10 (or its equivalent in goods or services) has the *potential* for securing an advantage for the giver, an advantage not merited by the quality or price of the product. Accordingly, even though Garrett's proposal seems quite sensible, any gift, depending on the nature of the receiver and the circumstances involved *could* have the effect of a bribe, even when the gift is nominal and public.

Given these last reasons, it would appear that the only safe moral position to adopt is the one that prohibits *all* gift-giving between corporate representatives and those with whom they would do business. In this latter regard, it is interesting to note that in a survey conducted by the Conference Board in 1964, most of the corporations surveyed were moving strongly in the direction of adopting policy statements prohibiting *all* gift-giving, even of the most nominal kind.[4] Only a few companies allowed, *officially*, small gifts provided the cost did not exceed $25 and did not occur more than three times annually. And, of course, some companies (perhaps too many) had perfectly ambiguous policy statements that provided no clear direction except to indicate that one should be "reasonable" and not do anything such that were it publicly disclosed it would embarrass the company.

In the end, the wisest policy to adopt would seem to be one of complete prohibition of any gift-giving between companies (and their representatives) and persons with whom companies do (or wish to do) business either directly or indirectly.

NOTES

1. Usually, but not necessarily, people are bribed not to do their job. We seldom talk about bribing someone to do his or her job rather than bribing them not to do their job. Still, it is possible to bribe somebody to do his or her job *faster* (thereby securing the briber a special advantage) than he might otherwise do it.

2. Thomas Garrett, *Business Ethics*, Appleton-Century Crofts, N.Y.: 1966, p. 78.

3. Ibid., p. 79.

4. *The Conference Board Record*, vol. 1, no. 12 (Dec. 1964), pp. 17–27.

28 The Phenomenon of International Bribery

Jack G. Kaikati

Improper payments by U.S. multinational companies to foreign officials have spread a darkening stain over the global reputation of American business. A Library of Congress study conducted in November 1975 reported that since January 1, 1974, American companies had publicly admitted making more than $300 million in illegal political payments or other forms of kickbacks.

The objectives of this article are four-fold. First, it provides a basic definition of bribery and contrasts it with other forms of payments. Second, it outlines the findings of at least three research studies that have been conducted since the advent of the current wave of questionable overseas payments. Third, it traces the growing list of federal agencies and congressional committees that have been investigating improper payments. Finally, it discusses in detail the national and international proposals and recommendations dealing with the ethical problem.

BASIC DEFINITION

The phenomenon of corporate bribery which is now agitating both the government and the corporate world is as old as sin itself. Although the patterns of bribery are essentially the same throughout the world, there exists a variety of regional epithets describing the phenomenon. Almost every country has a name for it—"la mordita" in Latin America, "baksheesh" in the Middle East, "bustarella" in Italy, "hai yo" or "hung pao" in Hong Kong, "dash" in some parts of Africa, "pot de vin" in France and

---

"schmiergelder" in Germany. Thus, no country has developed an immunity to bribery.

Although U.S. statutes and judicial interpretations vary, the legal essence of bribery is a payment voluntarily offered for the purpose of inducing a public official to do or omit doing something in violation of his lawful duty, or to exercise his official discretion in favor of the payor's request for a contract, concession or privilege on some basis other than merit. Many forms of payments now under attack do not constitute "bribery" under this definition.

First, there is a distinction between bribery and extortion.[1] The former type of payments are voluntarily offered by someone who seeks an unlawful advantage while the latter payments are extracted under genuine duress and coercion from an innocent victim seeking only the treatment to which he is lawfully entitled. For example, Gulf Oil's ex-chairman has explained to Senator Frank Church's Subcommittee on Multi-national Corporations that the payment of $4 million to help finance the reelection of President Chung Hee Park in South Korea was not so much a bribe as an extortion wrung from the company by threats against its $350 million investment in that country.

This author believes such extortion tactics may well jeopardize the existence of the company in the host country, and it is difficult to find a subject more important to the board's responsibilities than knowledge of such blackmail threats. The board may be compelled to take action which could easily involve both risk to the corporation and to the directors. Defining the best interests of the corporation and its shareholders may be difficult, but the board would seem obligated to face the issues and record its conclusions.

Second, there is a distinction, not always easily determined, between a "lubrication bribe" and a "whitemail bribe."[2] The former involves a relatively small sum of cash or other gift or service made by a businessman to a low-ranking government official in a country where such offerings are not prohibited. The purpose of these payments is to facilitate, expedite or express appreciation for normal, lawful performance of ministerial or procedural duties by the government official. The whitemail bribe, however, involves an elaborate system of concealing the use of large sums of corporate cash. These payments are invariably accompanied by false accounting, fictitious bookkeeping entries and bogus documentation. Based on the above two definitions, this author urges that "lubrication" payments should not be condemned since these payments are similar to the American and European customs of paying tips for prompt and efficient services. Lubrication payments should not be confused with bribing an official *not* to do his job.

Third, there is a distinction between bribe and agents' fees. A company contemplating business arrangements in a foreign country where it is not known may seek out an agent. Of course, a good agent's role is not restricted to bribing government officials. He can set up appointments between important government officials and company representatives, help the firm chart its investment strategy, advise it on how to shape its bid, as well as funnel back useful intelligence on government needs. It is next to impossible to determine how much of the agent's fee is a legitimate business expense and how much is passed on in bribes. Indeed, one well-known foreign commission agent now states that although he reported to the American company that he used certain sums to bribe a government official, in fact he kept the money for himself. Since there is no easy way to get the truth, this author believes company executives can treat the agent's fee as a tax-deductible business expense. In these circumstances, if bribes become public knowledge, company executives can categorically deny having ever knowingly authorized them.

It is clear that there are a wide variety of practices, differing in both degree and intent. Consequently, it is not easy to determine with certainty what constitutes a bribe, and gray areas of interpretation will always remain. The size, form and timing of payment, the adequacy of its disclosure as well as other pertinent facts must bear on the conclusion in a doubtful case.

Since the advent of the current wave of questionable or improper overseas payments, at least three research studies have been conducted. An examination of these studies reveals that large numbers of business executives believe that companies should pay bribes and kickbacks overseas if such practices are routine in the host country.

CONFERENCE BOARD STUDY

This research study surveyed seventy-three U.S. business leaders in the fall of 1975 to assess their policies and practices regarding unusual foreign payments.[3] Nearly half of the business leaders surveyed said that companies should make payoffs in countries where such practices are accepted. Three-quarters of the executives indicated that they had encountered demands from foreign officials or others for unusual payments, and 25% added that such demands were a problem for their industries as a whole.

The study also revealed that payoff pressures were more of a problem for certain types of companies than for others. The industries which seem most able to avoid payoff pressures are the consumer goods companies which do not deal with government agencies, and those best able to resist pressures are those with technology products or with especially strong market positions. Conversely, aerospace arms, whose customers often are governments, and pharmaceutical companies, often regulated by governments, are two industries which are subject to heavier than normal pressures for payoffs.

Payoff pressures are apparently heavier in certain parts of the world than others. The leading areas where U.S. companies encountered such pressures were Latin America and the Middle East, with the Far East, Africa and the developing countries not far behind.

Although the study was restricted to overseas payments, a few of the executives said that they believed there was no significant difference between U.S. business standards and those found in other countries. Moreover, 75% of the companies surveyed did not have written policy statements or guidelines on requests for unusual payments abroad.

The Conference Board report cautioned that while its survey of senior international executives represented a broad spectrum of companies across the nation, it should not be interpreted as being representative of all American companies. Nevertheless, the survey provided a rare indication of the extent of overseas bribery and of corporate attitudes toward foreign payoffs and bribery.

OPINION RESEARCH STUDY

The above startling results were confirmed by the Opinion Research Corporation study which was commissioned by Pitney-Bowes, Inc.[4] This study polled 531 top and middle managers on how they viewed the bribing of foreign officials by employees of U.S. corporations in attracting and retaining contracts. Although half of the business executives surveyed said that bribes should not be paid to foreign officials, 18% believed the latter should be paid if such practices were prevalent in the host country. Of those who condoned the practice, 47% indicated it was a cost of doing business in certain countries and 32% believed it was an established practice. In addition, 92% of the respondents did not believe legislation would effectively stop these practices. However, the executives believed that publicity would be effective in discouraging such bribery.

MARKETING MANAGEMENT STUDY

A third survey was conducted by the *Sales and Marketing Management* (SMM) magazine.[5] This study polled 146 members of SMM's Leadership Panel in April 1976 to assess their attitudes and practices regarding overseas and domestic bribery. Slightly more than 40% of the panel's members responded to the survey.

The results were startling. When quizzed whether they or someone else in their company had been asked to make payments either abroad or in the United States, 22% of the respondents confirmed the overseas requests and almost 50% confirmed domestic requests. However, the overwhelming majority of respondents indicated that they would disapprove such requests domestically. The majority of respondents believed that U.S. firms would be put a serious disadvantage should they be restricted from making such payments. In addition, though one-third of the respondents opposed governmental action to control overseas bribery, the majority believed that companies should attempt to agree voluntarily not to make such payments.

Currently, the Federal Trade Commission (FTC) and the Robinson-Patman Act prohibit commercial bribery in the United States on grounds of unfair methods of competition. Even though the SMM study revealed the existence of domestic commercial bribery, the FTC is reluctant to initiate a probe, claiming that it would duplicate other federal agency activities.

Although the fact of bribery has been admitted by some American multinational companies, the specifics in most cases remain ill defined. They remain obscure because law enforcement agencies in the United States have not yet completed their investigations. Yet some of the abuses detailed by the various investigations include illegal political contributions, huge payoffs made to foreign officials to gain sales or favorable treatment abroad, secret company slush funds, dummy foreign subsidiaries, numbered Swiss bank accounts and doctored corporate books. For example, the Securities and Exchange Commission (SEC) accused General Tire and Rubber Co. of a wide array of foreign and domestic payoffs, including some to get off the Arab boycott list.

SEC INVESTIGATIONS

The SEC has uncovered many bribery activities in following up domestic illegalities in the Watergate affair. Even though there is nothing in U.S. law that prohibits the payment of a bribe to a foreign official, there is a great deal of legislation that makes it a criminal offense for a company to disguise or omit such payments from its shareholders' accounts. More specifically, it is illegal for any corporation subject to the jurisdiction of the U.S. securities acts to fail to include and to describe accurately all payments, including bribes, payoffs, kickbacks, or other improper payments to foreign government officials, or any political contributions, in its various statements and periodic reports to the SEC and shareholders required by those acts. It is also illegal for any such corporation to finance such payments through secret slush funds or phony offshore corporate entities outside the normal system of financial accountability described by those acts.

Unfortunately, it cannot be said that the practice of making questionable payments abroad is confined to a few wayward companies. In early March 1976, the SEC was investigating eighty-four publicly held companies, whose 1974 revenues amounted to more than $200 billion. Forty-five of these companies were included in the *Fortune* 500 list of the largest enterprises in the United States.

More recently, the SEC introduced its "voluntary" program, which urges corporations to disclose illegal, improper or questionable payments abroad rather than be discovered by investigators. The SEC clearly held out the prospect that it might go easy on those that volunteered. A company had to pledge that it would not repeat the offending acts; and it had to undertake a thorough investigation of what had occurred. As a result, many companies have opened their books to complete reauditing of their financial returns over the last several years. Though this voluntary program applies only to companies listed on the American stock exchanges, there is reason to believe that this policy will have widespread effects and result in a general raising of ethical standards.

Prodded by the SEC, the New York Stock Exchange also is becoming a leader of the antibribery campaign. The NYSE has proposed that each listed company should be ordered to have an audit committee that is dominated by outside directors by the end of 1977. This would be a fierce deterrent to the use of bribery as a business practice. Under existing securities laws, members of audit committees who conceal improper payments risk going to jail for withholding material facts from shareholders.

IRS AUDITS

Escaping prosecution from the SEC does not mean the companies are free from prosecution by the IRS. According to the IRS, it is illegal for a U.S. corporation to deduct as an ordinary business expense on its U.S. income tax returns any improper payments to foreign government officials, whatever the label or justification, or any political contributions, whether lawful or not. Currently, the IRS is pushing a "large case audit" program against companies with more than $250 million in assets.

There is reason to believe that rulings by the SEC and IRS put American companies at a disadvantage in international competition. Both Britain and Germany, for example, allow companies to deduct on their tax returns at least some kind of payoffs abroad. But the IRS will not allow deduction of any payments abroad that would be illegal in the United States, even though they may be legal where they are paid. The SEC's disclosure requirements also make it difficult for U.S. companies to pay large bribes or kickbacks abroad.

JUSTICE, DEFENSE WARNINGS

The Departments of Justice and Defense also are warning companies that they are considering bribing charges outside the realms of breaking the tax or securities laws. The Antitrust Division of the Justice Department is likely to examine whether payments abroad by U.S. firms were used to block out other American companies or tie up a scarce commodity. The Department of Defense launched its own probe to ascertain the legitimacy of commissions paid to middlemen in negotiating the sale of military aircraft and hardware. The Defense Department also is reviewing its agreement with some two dozen companies to determine whether any may have charged Defense for "overhead expenses" under their contracts to provide some of the money they poured into political payoffs.

CONGRESSIONAL INQUIRIES

The Senate Foreign Relations Subcommittee was quick to hold public hearings on the leads developed by the SEC. Moreover, a parade of companies is being brought before the Senate Subcommittee on Multinational Corporations as well as the Senate Banking Committee. Testimonies before the committees have revealed specific cases of huge payoffs to foreign officials and concealed donations to foreign political parties, including the Italian Communists.

CABINET-LEVEL TASK FORCE

To the growing list of federal agencies and congressional committees investigating improper payments made overseas by American corporations, President Gerald Ford added his own blue-ribbon, cabinet-level panel. Its chairman is Secretary of Commerce Elliot Richardson. The panel will supervise the investigations going on at the SEC, the IRS and the Justice Department, as well as recommend what, if anything, can be done to stop such practices in the future.

LEGISLATIVE ACTION

Since the advent of the current wave of bribery scandals, there has been a growing outcry in Washington for a new law that would prohibit U.S. corporations from engaging in bribery and political payoffs abroad. Currently, there are at least four antibribery measures that have either been enacted or are being considered by Congress.

The Arms-Sales Measure

Congress has passed as arms-sales law compelling disclosure of consultant fees to the State Department and in some cases to law enforcement agencies and Congress. The law covers government-to-government sales as well as company-to-government transactions. Business representatives claim that the new law will adversely affect U.S. corporations because foreign firms can bribe at will. Where arms are not involved, a variety of measures have been proposed, and one has been included in the Tax Reform Act. Currently only two antibribery bills are under serious consideration: one is sponsored by the U.S. Senate, and another is from the Ford Administration.

Tax Reform Act

The Tax Reform Act requires that earnings equal to the bribe be repatriated and taxed by the United States. Previously, the law stipulated that such bribes were not deductible but it permitted deferral of tax on the money. The bribery provision was one of two related Senate proposals denying tax benefits for U.S. companies abroad. The other proposal would deny three foreign tax benefits to the U.S. companies that comply with the Arab boycott of Israel—the foreign tax credit, tax deferral on overseas earnings and DISC benefits for exports.[6]

Senate's Antibribery Bill

The Senate approved a bill outlawing bribery of foreign officials by U.S. companies. The bill, sponsored by Senate Banking Committee Chairman William Proxmire, would outlaw: (1) any payments to induce foreign officials to assist a company by not carrying out their duties, (2) payments to third parties when the U.S. company knows "or has reason to know" that the ultimate recipient will be a government official, and (3) payments to foreign political parties and candidates with the aim of influencing government business transactions. There is reason to believe that the wording is intended to exempt any foreign payments "extorted" from U.S. companies or the lubricating payments traditionally demanded by foreign government officials to speed up customs clearance, mail delivery and other routine government functions.

The Justice Department will enforce the legislation as it applies to unregistered companies by imposing criminal penalties of up to $10,000, two years in prison, or both. In addition, SEC-registered companies would be subject to the civil and criminal penalties already available to the commission under its existing authority. But Roderick Hills, SEC chairman, opposes such an enforcement role for the agency for two major reasons. First, during its forty-year history, the SEC has been concerned basically with adequate disclosure by corporations of information deemed important to investors. Second, it would be difficult for the SEC to judge whether foreign payments actually represented bribes.

In another action, the Senate rejected a payments disclosure proposal introduced by Senator Frank Church. The proposal would have required companies whose stock is registered with the SEC to tell the agency about any "contribution, payment, gift, commission or anything of value" disbursed abroad in connection with a sale. The SEC would have been required to keep these reports in a public file. The proposal also would have given a U.S. company the right to sue a bribe-paying domestic competitor for triple damages on grounds it lost foreign business because of the competitor's bribes.

The Administration's Bill

Secretary of Commerce Elliot Richardson, who headed the administration's task force on questionable corporate payments abroad, objected that the Senate's bill was unworkable. Enforcement of a criminal bar against foreign bribes would be very difficult, if not impossible. Witnesses and information might prove to be beyond the reach of U.S. courts, and foreign governments might refuse to cooperate on grounds of national sovereignty. Therefore, the Ford Administration presented its own anti-bribery bill.

The administration's bill would not outlaw payoffs to foreign officials. It would require U.S. corporations operating abroad to report to the Commerce Secretary both proper and improper payments, although it is intended the Secretary of Commerce would issue regulations exempting small payments and taxes. Reports of payments, including names of recipients, would be available earlier to the State and Justice Departments, the Internal Revenue Service, and the Securities and Exchange Commission, and could be made available earlier to foreign governments.

By confessing its misdeed, the U.S. corporation would gain immunity from prosecution at home. However, the administration's bill proposes a $100,000 civil penalty for failing to disclose payments or to keep certain records and up to $500,000 criminal fine for deliberately failing to disclose. Corporate officers convicted of deliberate violations could get up to three years in jail. In reality, the administration's bill suffers the weakness of expecting companies to report their own misdeeds, and the Senate's bill is probably unenforceable.

SELF-REGULATION

Some analysts acknowledge that bribery disclosure by the SEC and other government agencies, as well as corporate investigations triggered by those disclosures, have been accompanied by an increased demonstration of corporate self-regulation. Consequently, they argue that the government has done enough and that business, at least for now, should be left to reform itself. Indeed, the advent of the current wave of bribery scandals has led to an upsurge in self-regulatory activity on several levels.

National Code of Business Ethics

The idea of a national code of business ethics has drawn a number of supporters. W. Michael Blumenthal, chairman and president of Bendix Corp., proposed that a group of business executives devise such a national code of conduct. The code would correspond to the standards of other professional associations such as the American Medical Association, which sets minimal standards of behavior.

Reactions to drafting such a national code are mixed. Theologians and academic experts generally applaud the idea, but some sympathetic observers, including this author, wonder if many corporations are really ready to embrace a national code of ethics and make it stick. There is reason to believe that most executives will pay little attention to codes other than the ones companies formulate for themselves.

The idea of a national code of business ethics is not new, of course. For instance, the electrical equipment price-fixing scandals of the early 1960s triggered a barrage of criticism from the press and the public, and soon afterwards an ethics advisory council of top business leaders was set up under the Commerce Department. In 1962, the group presented a proposed code to President John F. Kennedy, but after his assassination, the Johnson Administration, seeking business support, let the code die.

Company Codes of Ethics

In more recent years, company codes have come into fashion, as they do after nearly every major business scandal. Responding to the current wave of corporate payoff scandals, dozens of major companies are issuing written rules governing corporate ethical questions, or are revising long-standing codes of conduct to cover new problems. Most of the codes being drafted now concentrate on two areas of current controversy: political contributions and overseas payments to increase sales.

The existing codes of conduct vary widely in form and content. They range from the terse, one-page "Statement of Business Principles" recently issued by Gulf's new chairman to the handsomely packaged, ten-page "Code of Worldwide Business Conduct" issued by Caterpillar Co. in late 1974. As one of the earliest comprehensive codes, the Caterpillar document has become a model of sorts for some of the companies currently drafting codes.

Codes of ethics require something more than the recent public relations announcements of companies rushing to "reemphasize long-standing policy." To develop effective codes of business ethics, companies should ascertain that the sales and profit goals can be attained by current ethical business practices. Unrealistic goals might induce subordinates to resort to under-the-table deals in order to attain the chief executive's targets. A study by the American Management Association of 3,000 executives showed that most felt they were under pressure to compromise their personal standards to meet company goals.[7] Pressure for results, as narrowly measured in money terms, has increased. As firms become larger, more decentralized, and under absentee ownership, performance is measured in numbers and not by broader or more humane criteria.

The real test of codes will come in their strenuous enforcement and prompt disciplinary action. Any code of ethical behavior is unlikely to be observed unless the chief executive declares that violators will be punished. When a company fails to take strict action, many employees may assume that unethical acts are accepted standards of corporate behavior. One strict disciplinary measure may include dismissal at any level, commensurate with the degree of transgression. For instance, except for a few spectacular resignations of top executives at companies such as Gulf Oil and Lockheed, very few executives involved in briberies have been fired, demoted or even transferred. Another control measure may require all responsible members of management to sign annual pledges that they have followed the rules in the company's ethics code.

Public Speeches by Executives

A number of business leaders, sensing rising public hostility and fearing that all companies could be tarred with the same brush if business merely closes ranks and shrugs off the subject, have begun to speak out for business to reform itself and raise its ethical standards. For example, Fred T. Allen, chairman and president of Pitney-Bowes, took a challenging position in his speech to the American Chamber of Commerce in Zurich, Switzerland.[8] He emphasized that corporate morality begins at the top and added, "those of us who have devoted our lives to the responsible growth and profitability of large corporations are, again, thought of—collectively—as little if any better than 'the robber barons' of an earlier era."

Trade Associations' Views

The International Trade Club of Chicago, the nation's largest professional association of international trade executives, recently issued a position paper condemning illegal and unethical conduct in international trade and investment. Since its founding in 1919, the club has encouraged international trade management on a high ethical plane; it repeated its policy because of current public attitudes triggered by revelations of alleged corrupt practices involving U.S. multinationals abroad. In addition to the above position paper, several other trade associations, including the U.S. Chamber of Commerce, have issued policy statements on business payments abroad.

INTERNATIONAL COOPERATION

No amount of U.S. regulation of companies subject to the jurisdiction of the SEC and the IRS can achieve a comprehensive long-run solution to the problem of transnational bribery. Consequently, some analysts believe that solutions to such problems can only be achieved through international cooperation. The United States has taken a number of initiatives that might lead to such cooperation.

OECD Guidelines

The Ministerial Conference of the Organization for Economic Cooperation and Development (OECD) recently adopted a document concerning rules for multinational corporations on issues ranging from bribery to restrictive business practices and disclosure of information. These voluntary guidelines are a product of more than a year's work by an OECD committee. The bribery section has been notably strengthened due to the insistence of the United States. Consequently, the guidelines call on multinational corporations not to render "any bribe or other improper benefit, direct or indirect, to any public servant" and to "abstain from any improper" political involvement. While this code of ethics does not possess statutory binding power or punitive rules, its significance lies in the fact that this is the first time that an international organization has worked out such guidelines for multinational corporations.

International Chamber Commission

The Paris-based International Chamber of Commerce, which represents multinational companies, has set up a commission headed by Lord Showcross, chairman of the City of London's panel on take-overs and mergers, to recommend guidelines for ethical business practices.

United Nations' Role

The United States proposed an international agreement at a meeting of the U.N. Center on Transnational Corporations in March 1976 in Lima, Peru. More specifically, the United States supplied the initiative for negotiations to curb bribery. It called for steps by governments to punish violators, to establish clear guidelines on the use of business agents, and to cooperate in exchanging information. Governments of developing nations seem anxious to sidestep the question, which they turned over to the U. N. Economic and Social Council for discussion as a separate issue.

STRINGENT AUDITING STANDARDS

According to official rules of the SEC and the American Institute of Certified Public Accountants (AICPA), an auditor is not required to disclose illegal political contributions or massive slush funds made by his client.[9] Consequently, when Price Waterhouse discovered that United Brands paid a bribe of $1.25 million to a Honduras official, the auditors did not require disclosure for fear of jeopardizing the company's operations in Latin America. As a matter of fact, when the auditors' decision was discussed with the SEC, the commission did not object.

AICPA Proposals

In light of this incident, the AICPA auditing standards executive committee has drafted guidelines governing auditors' conduct upon the discovery of illegal payments by a corporation during the course of an audit.[10] In addition to reiterating traditional auditing procedures, the proposed guidelines discuss the controversial questions of "materiality"—what is important enough to require disclosure or special provision in the financial statements. The guidelines direct auditors to consider not merely the dollar amount of an illegal payment but also "the related contingent monetary effects" such as fines, penalties and damages, and such "loss contingencies" as expropriation. The guidelines also indicate that if a substantial amount of business depends on paying a bribe, that risk might have to be disclosed.

The proposed guidelines stipulate that when an auditor comes across a "material" illegal act, he must promptly report it to a company official who can do something about it. If the illegal act then is not properly disclosed or accounted for, the auditor should give a qualified or adverse audit opinion, which presumably would bring the illegal act to light. When an auditor stumbles upon illegal acts that are "immaterial" financially, he should consider resigning if he fails to persuade the client company to take remedial action.

Overall, the proposed guidelines do not extend the traditional auditing doctrine very far. They explicitly state that the auditor is under no legal obligation to notify outside parties. The proposed guidelines rely on the company to reveal any "immaterial illegal act to the authorities or other outsiders."

Recent IRS Measures

The IRS decided to direct eleven questions on bribery, slush funds and overseas bank accounts to corporate managers when reviewing a company's tax return, hoping to get honest answers. As a check, the agency decided to put the same questions to the outside accounts who audit the company's books. However, accountants strongly opposed the idea of bringing auditors under the IRS investigatory umbrella. They were so infuriated that AICPA sent a delegation to Washington to protest to the IRS commissioner. Consequently, the IRS backed off on its new policy and accepted a compromise under which the accountants are to sign a letter stating that, to the best of their knowledge, belief and recollection, management's answers to the eleven questions are accurate.

Recent SEC Guidelines

After over a year of study, the Securities and Exchange Commission has put in writing its guidelines for disclosure of illegal or questionable corporate payments and practices. The report lists several factors which should be considered when deciding if disclosure is necessary, including the amount of payments, their legality and the awareness or participation of top management. Also important is whether accounting records were falsified and whether the questionable conduct has ceased.

When disclosure is appropriate, the SEC believes these matters should be discussed:

- the existence, amount, duration and purpose of payments
- the role of management
- tax consequences
- information as to lines of business to which the payments relate
- the company's intention to continue or terminate payments
- potential impact on the business of cessation of payments
- method of affecting the payments

To help curb questionable corporate conduct, the SEC proposes an amendment to the Securities Exchange Act of 1934, requiring registrants to maintain accurate accounting records and an adequate system to internal accounting controls, and making it unlawful to falsify records or give false information to an accountant.

Because of the current wave of bribery scandals, this author speculates that the U.S. government will introduce stringent antibribery regulations which go far beyond the actions of any other country, and that American firms will pursue at least six strategies in dealing with the overseas bribery issues.

Strategy 1.   Companies will continue to sell their products abroad without bribery because of their strong market positions, their advanced technology, and/or because their products are greatly in demand. Due to their unique positions, these firms will continue to resist payoff pressures.

Strategy 2.   Some companies will not be pressured to pay bribes abroad due to their low profiles and indistinct images. For example, Ingersoll-Rand Co. claims that it is relatively immune from direct solicitations of bribe-takers due to its low profile. However, this immunity may fade away in the long run as these corporations become more conspicuous.

Strategy 3.   Companies will continue to pay bribes to minor officials overseas whenever the practice is considered a normal way of conducting business. For example, Vetco Offshore Industries, Inc., adopted a corporate policy prohibiting payments to foreign officials in countries whose governments begin prosecuting the practice. However, in countries where "grease" is a normal practice, Vetco considers such payments legal, even if, in fact, illegal by law. More specifically, Vetco will continue its payments under three circumstances: where payments are widespread and an acceptable business practice; where reasonable alternatives do not exist; and where discontinuance of the payments might inhibit the conduct of Vetco's business.

Strategy 4.   As a result of the proposed antibribery regulations, some companies will cease paying bribes abroad even where it is acceptable practice. By ceasing to conform to payoff customs of host countries, these American companies complain that they will suffer a competitive disadvantage because foreign competitors in the same markets will continue to offer bribes. Consequently, the SEC and the U.S. Treasury Department are studying three alternatives to make foreign companies as clean as American ones:

- *Disclosure.* The 116 foreign companies listed on stock exchanges in the United States can, under securities laws, be required to disclose improper payments the same as domestic corporations are required to do. Thus far, a half-dozen companies have volunteered such reports. For example, Imperial Chemical Industries Ltd., a British concern, has disclosed "questionable" payments of $2.4 million since 1972 through mid-1976.
- *Retaliatory Trade Practices.* The President's existing powers can be used to discourage or prevent the import of products of foreign entities which have engaged in unfair competitive practices, or products of those countries which tolerate or encourage such conduct.
- *Federal Procurement Practices.* The federal government could boycott foreign companies that make improper payments while competing with American companies. The SEC notes that executive branch agencies have sufficient economic authority to reject, as against the public interest, bids and offers from such companies.

The SEC concedes that reliance on the disclosure rules has several limitations; obviously, only firms registered with the commission would be affected. The commission also admits that it has limited investigative and enforcement powers over transactions between foreign parties. The chief sanction against a foreign issuer of shares or bonds in the United States would probably be to suspend trading in its securities or rescind the securities' registration.

Consequently, trade reprisals as well as a blackball by the federal government on corrupt companies might be the most compelling means of discouraging bribery by foreign firms. Most major government procurement contracts contain a clause granting the comptroller-general direct access to the books and records of the contractor. This requirement is usually waived for foreign contracts, but the SEC suggests the President could direct government agencies to insist on inspection, thereby providing additional enforcement leverage.

Strategy 5.   Companies will avoid the antibribery regulations in the United States by exporting through their foreign subsidiaries in Western Europe where antibribery statutes are less stringent. For example, even though the German domestic antibribery regulations correspond to those in the United States, the Germans are far more tolerant of foreign bribery, which is deductible from income tax.

There is strong reason to believe that some American business abroad may be lost as a result of this strategy, and a reduction in foreign trade may have at least two serious economic consequences. First, the United States may lose a portion of its foreign exchange earnings which are badly needed to pay for the ever-increasing purchases of imported oil. Second, since many American jobs are related to international trade, unemployment may reach unnerving peaks.

Strategy 6.   The aerospace and defense-related industries could take advantage of the Webb-Pomerene Act which allows consortia of American exporters to enter joint bids in seeking foreign contracts. This would avoid the ironic and unethical use of commissions and kickbacks given to foreign buyers by one American company to beat out another American firm in a field where little if any real competition exists.

Corporate directors and officers are finding themselves in a vulnerable position as a result of the ongoing ballyhoo over questionable overseas payments. Though bribery is illegal and unethical in the United States, it is both customary and ethical in other countries. Consequently, American executives are being caught between the ethical standards of two cultures. American executives who pay bribes when local conditions seem to demand it can scarcely be accused of degrading the pure, since corporate payoffs are seen in many countries as venial sins, or even normal courtesies.[11] On the other hand, a few countries have implemented various antibribery measures. For example, foreign investors in Iran are confronted with a new anticorruption regulation that requires foreign companies to sign an affidavit testifying that no payoffs or kickbacks would be made to brokers or agents connected with a contract award.[12] Though this antibribery measure applies only to foreign investors in Iran, there is reason to believe that this policy will have widespread effects and result in a general raising of ethical standards if other countries follow Iran's footsteps.

NOTES

1. Joseph M. Waldman, "A Primer on Corruption," *Business Studies* (Spring 1973), p. 28.

2. Peter Nehemkis, "Business Payoffs Abroad: Rhetoric and Reality," *California Management Review* (Winter 1975), pp. 7 and 9.

3. James R. Basche, Jr., *Unusual Foreign Payments: A Survey of the Policies and Practices of U.S. Companies* (New York: The Conference Board Record, 1976).

4. *Executive Attitudes Toward Morality in Business* (Princeton, N.J.: Caravan Surveys, Opinion Research Corporation, July 1975); and Fred T. Allen, "Corporate Morality: Executive Responsibility," *Atlanta Economic Review* (May–June 1976), p. 9.

5. James D. Synder, "Bribery in Selling: The Scandal Comes Home," *Sales and Marketing Management* (May 10, 1976), pp. 35–38.

6. Jack G. Kaikati, "The Challenge of the Arab Boycott," *Sloan Management Review*, vol. 18, no. 2 (Winter 1977), pp. 83–100.

7. "After Watergate: Putting Business Ethics in Perspective," *Business Week* (September 15, 1973), p. 178.

8. Allen, "Corporate Morality."

9. "Are Auditors Required to Report Their Clients' Bribes?" *The CPA Journal* (September 1975), p. 59.

10. *Proposed Statement on Auditing Standards: Illegal Acts by Clients* (New York: The Auditing

Standards Executive Committee of the American Institute of Certified Public Accountants, April 30, 1976).

11. See, for example, Ronald Wraith and Edgar Simpkins, *Corruption in Developing Countries* (New York: W. W. Norton, 1964); and Victor T. LeVine, *Political Corruption: The Ghana Case* (Stanford, Calif.: Hoover Institute Press, 1975).

12. Jack G. Kaikati, "Doing Business in Iran: The Fastest Growing Import Market Between Europe and Japan," *Atlanta Economic Review* (September–October 1976), p. 19.

29 Ethics and the Foreign Corrupt Practices Act

Mark Pastin

Michael Hooker

Not long ago it was feared that as a fallout of Watergate, government officials would be hamstrung by artificially inflated moral standards. Recent events, however, suggest that the scapegoat of post-Watergate morality may have become American business rather than government officials.

One aspect of the recent attention paid to corporate morality is the controversy surrounding payments made by American corporations to foreign officials for the purpose of securing business abroad. Like any law or system of laws, the Foreign Corrupt Practices Act (FCPA), designed to control or eliminate such payments, should be grounded in morality, and should therefore be judged from an ethical perspective. Unfortunately, neither the law nor the question of its repeal has been adequately addressed from that perspective.

HISTORY OF THE FCPA

On December 20, 1977, President Carter signed into law S.305, the Foreign Corrupt Practices Act (FCPA), which makes it a crime for American corporations to offer or provide payments to officials of foreign governments for the purpose of obtaining or retaining business. The FCPA also establishes record keeping requirments for publicly held corporations to make it difficult to conceal political payments proscribed by the Act. Violators of the FCPA, both corporations and managers, face severe penalties. A company may be fined up to $1 million, while its officers who directly participated in violations of the Act or had reason to know of such violations, face up to

Reprinted from *Business Horizons*, vol. 23, no. 6 (December 1980), pp. 43–47. Copyright © 1980 by the Foundation for the School of Business at Indiana University. Used with permission.

five years in prison and/or $10,000 in fines. The Act also prohibits corporations from indemnifying fines imposed on their directors, officers, employees, or agents. The Act does not prohibit "grease" payments to foreign government employees whose duties are primarily ministerial or clerical, since such payments are sometimes required to persuade the recipients to perform their normal duties.

At the time of this writing, the precise consequences of the FCPA for American business are unclear, mainly because of confusion surrounding the government's enforcement intentions. Vigorous objections have been raised against the Act by corporate attorneys and recently by a few government officials. Among the latter is Frank A. Weil, former Assistant Secretary of Commerce, who has stated, "The questionable payments problem may turn out to be one of the most serious impediments to doing business in the rest of the world."[1]

The potentially severe economic impact of the FCPA was highlighted by the fall 1978 report of the Export Disincentives Task Force, which was created by the White House to recommend ways of improving our balance of trade. The Task Force identified the FCPA as contributing significantly to economic and political losses in the United States. Economic losses come from constricting the ability of American corporations to do business abroad, and political losses come from the creation of a holier-than-thou image.

The Task Force made three recommendations in regard to the FCPA:

- The Justice Department should issue guidelines on its enforcement policies and establish procedures by which corporations could get advance government reaction to anticipated payments to foreign officials.
- The FCPA should be amended to remove enforcement from the SEC, which now shares enforcement responsibility with the Department of Justice.
- The administration should periodically report to Congress and the public on export losses caused by the FCPA.

In response to the Task Force's report, the Justice Department, over SEC objections, drew up guidelines to enable corporations to check any proposed action possibly in violation of the FCPA. In response to such an inquiry, the Justice Department would inform the corporation of its enforcement intentions. The purpose of such an arrangement is in part to circumvent the intent of the law. As of this writing, the SEC appears to have been successful in blocking publication of the guidelines, although Justice recently reaffirmed its intention to publish guidelines. Being more responsive to political winds, Justice may be less inclined than the SEC to rigidly enforce the Act.

Particular concern has been expressed about the way in which bookkeeping requirements of the Act will be enforced by the SEC. The Act requires that company records will "accurately and fairly reflect the transactions and dispositions of the assets of the issuer." What is at question is the interpretation the SEC will give to the requirement and the degree of accuracy and detail it will demand. The SEC's post-Watergate behavior suggests that it will be rigid in requiring the disclosure of all information that bears on financial relationships between the company and any foreign or domestic public official. This level of accountability in record keeping, to which auditors and corporate attorneys have strongly objected, goes far beyond previous SEC requirements that records display only facts material to the financial position of the company.

Since the potential consequences of the FCPA for American businesses and business managers are very serious, it is important that the Act have a rationale capable of bearing close scrutiny. In looking at the foundation of the FCPA, it should be noted that its passage followed in the wake of intense newspaper coverage of the financial dealings of corporations. Such media attention was engendered by the dramatic disclosure of corporate slush funds during the Watergate hearings and by a voluntary disclosure program established shortly thereafter by the SEC. As a result of the SEC program, more than 400 corporations, including 117 of the Fortune 500, admitted to making more than $300 million in foreign political payments in less than ten years.

Throughout the period of media coverage leading up to passage of the FCPA, and especially during the hearings on the Act, there was in all public discussions of the issue a tone of righteous moral indignation at the idea of American companies making foreign political payments. Such payments were ubiquitously termed "bribes," although many of these could more accurately be called extortions, while others were more akin to brokers' fees or sales commissions.

American business can be faulted for its reluctance during this period to bring to public attention the fact that in a very large number of countries, payments to foreign officials are virtually required for doing business. Part of that reluctance, no doubt, comes from the awkwardly difficult position of attempting to excuse bribery or something closely resembling it. There is a popular abhorrence in this country of bribery directed at domestic government officials, and that abhorrence transfers itself to payments directed toward foreign officials as well.

Since its passage, the FCPA has been subjected to considerable critical analysis, and many practical arguments have been advanced in favor of its repeal.[2] However, there is always lurking in back of such analyses the uneasy feeling that no matter how strongly considerations of practicality and economics may count against this law, the fact remains that the law protects morality in forbidding bribery. For example, Gerald McLaughlin, professor of law at Fordham, has shown persuasively that where the legal system of a foreign country affords inadequate protection against the arbitrary exercise of power to the disadvantage of American corporations, payments to foreign officials may be required to provide a compensating mechanism against the use of such arbitrary power. McLaughlin observes, however, that "this does not mean that taking advantage of the compensating mechanism would necessarily make the payment moral."[3]

The FCPA, and questions regarding its enforcement or repeal, will not be addressed adequately until an effort has been made to come to terms with the Act's foundation in morality. While it may be very difficult, or even impossible, to legislate morality (that is, to change the moral character and sentiments of people by passing laws that regulate their behavior), the existing laws undoubtedly still reflect the moral beliefs we hold. Passage of the FCPA in Congress was eased by the simple connection most Congressmen made between bribery, seen as morally repugnant, and the Act, which is designed to prevent bribery.

Given the importance of the FCPA to American business and labor, it is imperative that attention be given to the question of whether there is adequate moral justification for the law.

ETHICAL ANALYSIS OF THE FCPA

The question we will address is not whether each payment prohibited by the FCPA is moral or immoral, but rather whether the FCPA, given all its consequences and ramifications, is itself moral. It is well known that morally sound laws and institutions may tolerate such immoral acts. The First Amendment's guarantee of freedom of speech allows individuals to utter racial slurs. And immoral laws and institutions may have some beneficial consequences, for example, segregationist legislation bringing deep-seated racism into the national limelight. But our concern is with the overall morality of the FCPA.

The ethical tradition has two distinct ways of assessing social institutions, including laws: *End-Point Assessment* and *Rule Assessment*. Since there is no consensus as to which approach is correct, we will apply both types of assessment to the FCPA.

The End-Point approach assesses a law in terms of its contribution to general social well-being. The ethical theory underlying End-Point Assessment is utilitarianism. According to utilitarianism, a law is morally sound if and only if the law promotes the well-being of those affected by the law to the greatest extent practically achievable. To satisfy the utilitarian principle, a law must promote the well-being of those affected by it at least as well as any alternative law that we might propose, and better than no law at all. A conclusive End-Point Assessment of a law requires specification of what constitutes the welfare of those affected by the law, which the liberal tradition generally sidesteps by identifying an individual's welfare with what he takes to be in his interests.

Considerations raised earlier in the paper suggest that the FCPA does not pass the End-Point test. The argument is not the too facile one that we could propose a better law. (Amendments to the FCPA are now being considered.[4]) The argument is that it may be better to have *no* such law than to have the FCPA. The main domestic consequences of the FCPA seem to include an adverse effect on the balance of payments, a loss of business and jobs, and another opportunity for the SEC and the Justice Department to compete. These negative effects must be weighed against possible gains in the conduct of American business within the United States. From the perspective of foreign countries in which American firms do business, the main consequence of the FCPA seems to be that certain officials now accept bribes and influence from non-American businesses. It is hard to see that who pays the bribes makes much difference to these nations.

Rule Assessment of the morality of laws is often favored by those who find that End-Point Assessment is too lax in supporting their moral codes. According to the

Rule Assessment approach: A law is morally sound if and only if the law accords with a code embodying correct ethical rules. This approach has no content until the rules are stated, and different rules will lead to different ethical assessments. Fortunately, what we have to say about Rule Assessment of the FCPA does not depend on the details of a particular ethical code.

Those who regard the FCPA as a worthwhile expression of morality, despite the adverse effects on American business and labor, clearly subscribe to a rule stating that it is unethical to bribe. Even if it is conceded that the payments proscribed by the FCPA warrant classification as bribes, citing a rule prohibiting bribery does not suffice to justify the FCPA.

Most of the rules in an ethical code are not *categorical* rules; they are *prima facie* rules. A categorical rule does not allow exceptions, whereas a prima facie rule does. The ethical rule that a person ought to keep promises is an example of a prima facie rule. If I promise to loan you a book on nuclear energy and later find out that you are a terrorist building a private atomic bomb, I am ethically obligated not to keep my promise. The rule that one ought to keep promises is "overridden" by the rule that one ought to prevent harm to others.

A rule prohibiting bribery is a prima facie rule. There are cases in which morality requires that a bribe be paid. If the only way to get essential medical care for a dying child is to bribe a doctor, morality requires one to bribe the doctor. So adopting an ethical code which includes a rule prohibiting the payment of bribes does not guarantee that a Rule Assessment of the FCPA will be favorable to it.

The fact that the FCPA imposes a cost on American business and labor weighs against the prima facie obligation not to bribe. If we suppose that American corporations have obligations, tantamount to promises, to promote the job security of their employees and the investments of shareholders, these obligations will also weigh against the obligation not to bribe. Again, if government legislative and enforcement bodies have an obligation to secure the welfare of American business and workers, the FCPA may force them to violate their public obligations.

The FCPA's moral status appears even more dubious if we note that many of the payments prohibited by the Act are neither bribes nor share features that make bribes morally reprehensible. Bribes are generally held to be malefic if they persuade one to act against his good judgment, and consequently purchase an inferior product. But the payments at issue in the FCPA are usually extorted *from the seller*. Further it is arguable that not paying the bribe is more likely to lead to purchase of an inferior product than paying the bribe. Finally, bribes paid to foreign officials may not involve deception when they accord with recognized local practices.

In conclusion, neither End-Point nor Rule Assessment uncovers a sound moral basis for the FCPA. It is shocking to find that a law prohibiting bribery has no clear moral basis, and may even be an immoral law. However, this is precisely what examination of the FCPA from a moral perspective reveals. This is symptomatic of the fact that moral conceptions which were appropriate to a simpler world are not adequate to the complex world in which contemporary business functions. Failure to appreciate this point often leads to righteous condemnation of business, when it should lead to careful reflection on one's own moral preconceptions.

NOTES

1. *National Journal*, June 3, 1978: 880.

2. David C. Gustman, "The Foreign Corrupt Practices Act of 1977," *The Journal of International Law and Economics*, Vol. 13, 1979: 367–401, and Walter S. Surrey, "The Foreign Corrupt Practices Act: Let the Punishment Fit the Crime," *Harvard International Law Journal*, Spring 1979: 203–303.

3. Gerald T. McLaughlin, "The Criminalization of Questionable Foreign Payments by Corporations," *Fordham Law Review*, Vol. 46: 1095.

4. "Foreign Bribery Law Amendments Drafted," *American Bar Association Journal*, February 1980: 135.

7

Changing Engineers and Engineering

INTRODUCTION

The selections in this chapter need no introduction. In the six preceding chapters we explored a variety of issues that call for tough moral, professional, and personal choices by engineers. In many of these readings the authors have offered suggestions for changes that might be made in engineering. It is now time to focus more extensively on proposals for change.

As we have learned more about the ethical issues in engineering, our attention has at times been drawn away from individual behavior to the systems that make engineering practice what it is today—that is, laws, professional organizations, corporations, our economic system, and so forth. Proposals for change have been wide ranging in targeting these different aspects of engineering. In a sense, they all aim at changing behavior, but they pick out different parts of the system as the lever for change—law, the education of engineers, professional codes, the role of professional societies, the corporate environment in which engineers work, and so on. It is important to remember that change does not have to be an either-or matter; that is, we do not have to pick just one of these levers for change. Although it is important to consider which approaches are most likely to make the most or best improvement in engineering, a many-pronged approach to change is plausible.

Along with the selections in this chapter you might want to go back and reread selections from previous chapters. In particular, it might be useful to reconsider Unger's model code of engineering ethics and Martin and Schinzinger's recommendation for a change in our conception of engineering.

The selections in this chapter focus on three different approaches to change in engineering: changing the behavior of individual engineers by changing law and the licensing process; strengthening the role of professional societies in supporting ethical engineers; and changing the way we teach engineering ethics. We begin with a piece by

Donald E. Wilson in which he is concerned with controlling the behavior of individual engineers. Wilson reviews the four standard means by which we now try to do this: civil law, criminal law, administrative law, and professional societies. He finds that these four social mechanisms for controlling the performance of engineers do not do a satisfactory job, and at the end of his piece he calls for an expansion of the licensing requirements for engineers. Wilson's discussion harks back to our earlier discussion of whistle-blowing and the need for more autonomy.

Wilson is critical of the role of professional societies in controlling the behavior of engineers, whereas Stephen H. Unger, whose ideas we have encountered in earlier selections, would like to see professional societies play a more significant role in promoting or facilitating ethical engineering. In this selection Unger mentions several measures that professional societies might take, such as censuring employers, publishing ratings of employers that indicate the extent to which they encourage ethical behavior, and giving awards to engineers who uphold ethical principles. Unger focuses specifically on the idea of professional societies playing a role by investigating cases in which engineers have adhered to high standards of professional conduct, but in doing so have jeopardized their careers because of the managerial response. He considers problems that might arise if professional societies were to investigate and then publish reports of cases in which employers behaved improperly. He argues that the problems that might arise for professional societies could be overcome.

Finally, Langdon Winner discusses recent attempts by American colleges and universities to teach ethics for scientists and engineers. Winner is particularly critical of the case study approach. He argues that the case study approach focuses too narrowly, thereby encouraging students to accept the "existing commitments, institutional patterns and power relationships" of the profession, instead of seizing the opportunity to instill in students the sense that they may "re-evaluate and reconstitute" the field. Winner calls for ethics courses that cultivate two crucial skills: political savvy and the capacity for political imagination.

30 Social Mechanisms for Controlling Engineers' Performance

Donald E. Wilson

This paper examines primary social mechanisms for controlling engineers' professional performance—civil law, criminal law, administrative law and peer review. It is the conclusion of the writer that these mechanisms are not effective (particularly in small and medium-size organizations) and that existing mechanisms should be improved or alternative means should be established.

This is interesting in light of the findings of the research and investigation conducted for the NSF funded project, "Engineering Ethics in Organizational Contexts." That project examined the mechanisms developed in several large organizations with proven records related to safety in manufacturing and product design. In the two diverse organizations examined, NASA and Monsanto, the studies indicate clearly that safety was achieved and that this was accomplished to a great extent by the high priority given to safety by management. The excellent safety records in both organizations were not accidental or providential, but were the result of careful planning toward a definite objective.

Undoubtedly, NASA has the most comprehensive safety program of the two due in large part to the catastrophic nature of any major failure and due to the advanced state of the art necessarily included in their designs. On the other hand, Monsanto is oriented to safety in the manufacturing process itself and reflects concern for the toxic nature of materials and environmental factors related to the production of exotic chemicals in large quantities.

It is evident from these studies that, notwithstanding the obvious differences in organization, strategy and purpose, effective control mechanisms to provide strong

From Albert Flores, ed., *Designing for Safety: Engineering Ethics in Organizational Contexts*, Proceedings of the "Workshop on Engineering Ethics: Designing for Safety," held May 24-26, 1982, at Rensselaer Polytechnic Institute, Troy, NY. Reprinted by permission of the editor.

safety programs are dependent upon a commitment by top management carried through at all levels of an organization with continuous re-enforcement and encouragement.

However, the funding, dedication and interest necessary to create effective mechanisms related to design safety, are not normally available in small and medium-size organizations nor in all large organizations.

Safety, from an engineering perspective, i.e., design safety, depends on responsible performance by engineers; and, responsibility, in a professional sense, implies that the engineer has the power, autonomy or professional independence to determine engineering solutions. Unfortunately, the engineering profession has fought a losing battle for professional independence. This struggle has been well documented by Edwin T. Layton, Jr. in "The Revolt of the Engineers" where he states: "One of the basic problems of American engineers is that the balance has tended to shift too far in the direction of business, and accommodation has taken place largely on terms laid down by employers. The professional independence of engineers has been drastically curtailed. The losers are not just engineers. The public would benefit greatly from the unbiased evaluations of technical matters that an independent profession could provide."

Whistle-blowing is a special case illustrating the need for effective social mechanisms for controlling engineers' conduct. All too often, engineers acquiesce to managers and others in their organization, regardless of their own opinions as to appropriate engineering technology.

Whistle-blowing is an heroic, albeit self-destructive response, when an engineer perceives it as a moral obligation.

Safe design also depends upon the competence of individual engineers and on the care exercised by those engineers in performing work. As we examine the four primary social mechanisms that have a direct influence on professional conduct, we will see that these mechanisms do not provide a satisfactory means to control individual conduct in the performance of engineering work. At the end of this paper, a suggestion is made concerning the development of one mechanism to partly overcome the deficiencies that have been identified.

THE CIVIL LAW

Civil Law, i.e., law relating to private rights and to remedies sought by civil action as contrasted with criminal proceedings, focuses on negligence as the primary area of interest in discussing sanctions and social mechanisms affecting engineers in the performance of professional services. "Negligent conduct may be either an act (which an engineer) should recognize as involving an unreasonable risk . . . or a failure to do an act which is necessary for the protection or assistance of another and which the (engineer) is under the duty to do" (2 Restatement of Torts 2d Section 284). Negligence may be from a lack of competence or a want of reasonable care. A professional person "is required to exercise the skill and knowledge normally possessed by members of that profession" (2 Restatement of Torts Section 299).

Damages (the sum of money awarded for an engineer's negligence) are for the purpose of punishment and to deter wrongful conduct as well as to give compensation or restitution for harm. There are circumstances, however, that make this form of sanction ineffective in many instances involving engineers. It should be readily apparent that the payment of damages by anyone other than the person who caused the harm, may do little more than compensate the injured party. As a sanction to influence future conduct, it may have little or no effect. Liability insurance payments certainly fall into this category. It is only when the liability insurance companies are adversely affected as an industry as a whole that increased premiums have a significant influence on the conduct of individuals.

This has happened to some extent in malpractice insurance for all professions and the exponential increase in malpractice insurance premiums over recent years has undoubtedly had some salutary effect on quality control and care in the performance of professional services. Engineers' professional liability insurance is based on the gross income of a firm and does not identify specific individuals as the insured, except in the case of an individual practitioner or small partnership. One of the largest insurers of engineers and architects has indicated that it is beginning to identify individuals, moving from firm to firm, who are the cause of repeated insurance claims. This is after-the-fact observation, and the insurance company is unable to prevent such individuals from going on to other firms and causing a repetition of the malpractice syndrome. Insurance companies are not able to blacklist incompetent or careless individuals to drive them out of the profession and in any event, this is not a proper role for them to perform.

The medical profession has become so conscious of the impact of malpractice insurance premiums that they have initiated legislation to limit the recovery from injured patients and to change the legal rules for the measurement of damages. One such rule affecting damages is known as the Collateral Source Rule. This rule prevents the reduction of the amount of damages recoverable by the amount of money or services the injured party has received from other sources. More specifically, workmen's compensation, medical and other insurance paid to the insured as a result of an injury may not be used to reduce the damages payable by a negligent party.

Another limiting aspect of civil sanctions for negligence is the "deep pocket" concept as practiced by attorneys. Unless there is a defendant with "deep pockets," i.e., able to pay the damages if they are awarded, there is no incentive to proceed with a lawsuit. One of the first questions asked is: Who can pay and how much? Between an individual engineer and a company with a positive balance sheet, insurance coverage, fixed and liquid assets, etc., it is no contest. Plaintiff's attorneys will choose the company every time. One might think that individual engineers also would be defendants, particularly if their signatures and seals are affixed to the negligent designs, but there seems to be a psychological factor at work that discourages plaintiffs from suing individuals. This factor derives from the sympathy that a jury might have for an individual defendant but are unlikely to have for an entity such as a large business enterprise.

If there is any element of doubt as to liability, a jury is more than likely to resolve the issue against a large company and for an injured person. If the defendant is an individual, the plaintiff may lose this advantage.

There are other elements of civil liability diluting the effect it might have as a sanction. Product liability is a relatively new civil law concept applying primarily to the manufacturing industry and was developed to overcome some of the legal difficulties with the concept of negligence. Contributory negligence is a defense to a claim of negligence, i.e., if both parties were negligent, then neither can recover from the other. Product liability avoids this problem, but it also virtually assures negligent employees that they will not be defendents in any malpractice lawsuits. Product liability is directed exclusively at the business entity and not at the culpable employee. The question asked in such cases is not "Was someone negligent?" but "Was there a defect in the product?"

Civil liability works most effectively as a sanction in relation to the independent practice of engineering by consultants. But even here, large consulting firms incorporate and, whether incorporated or not, large organizations of any kind act like corporations insofar as the decision-making process becomes bureaucratic.

THE CRIMINAL LAW

Criminal law differs from the civil law in many respects. While theoretically, criminal sanctions might appear more effective in obtaining proper conduct, in practice, with the constitutional safeguards of due process, strict interpretation of criminal statutes by courts, and jury sympathy for an individual who may have made a mistake, it is not a particularly good method to achieve a safe environment. Casual observations concerning the lack of enforcement of laws regulating motor vehicle operations and the public's general disregard for speed limits should give some appreciation of the difficulties.

The criminal law includes offenses for negligent conduct; however, the definition of negligence in criminal law involves higher standards of care, commonly referred to as gross negligence. This generally is treated as such a gross want of care and disregard for the rights of others as to justify a presumption of willful and wanton conduct. In the Pinto case, attempts to invoke criminal sanctions against the corporation proved unsuccessful. The criminal law centers on the state of mind of the actor. While it may be inferred from the circumstances, ignorance or mistake is a defense to a criminal charge and negates the intent (even for criminal negligence) required to establish a criminal offense. But the greatest weakness of criminal law as a sanction is the constant need for police enforcement. Our society prides itself on the limitation of police enforcement to traffic safety and violent or serious crimes.

Creating a safe environment has only relatively recently become of national concern with such legislation as the Occupational Safety and Health Act (OSHA) and the Consumer Product Safety Act, and the difficulties with enforcement of this type of statute are legion. Generally, OSHA violations are directed at construction contractors; however, in a case reported as the "stiffest construction penalties ever" by *Building Design and Construction* magazine (Dec., 1979), a total of $64,730 was assessed against five firms including the architect who was fined $5,050. This matter arose out of the construction of the Rosemont, Illinois, Stadium. The wood arch roof collapsed during construction and five persons died. The architect was cited for a willful violation penalty for permitting erection of the roof without a written erection procedure by a qualified person.

Another similar case was reported in *Civil Engineering*, July 1977. In this case, it was a Worcester, Massachusetts, bridge that collapsed during construction and killed three persons. The resident engineer in charge of the project for the Massachusetts Department of Public Works was indicted for manslaughter. After seven weeks of trial, including 52 prosecution witnesses, the court directed the jury to bring in a verdict of innocent. Interestingly, *Civil Engineering* categorized this, as follows: "The present situation can be described as an inverted triangle with the field engineer carrying the legal burden of the levels above him."

A companion article to the above pointed out that there is a special vulnerability for employed engineers in the public sector because of the concept of government immunity. Even with the gradual elimination of immunity for governmental agencies, there are limitations which apparently favor the inclusion of individual engineers as defendants together with the government. *Civil Engineering* cited a Transportation Research Board Report in this special case that advocated "Public acceptance of the fact that mistakes of judgment will be made in carrying out large public works programs and that the public, which benefits from these, should shoulder the social costs of protecting diligent public servants." In short, the criminal law is not an area conducive to achieving sanctions against professionals. In the few instances where it has been utilized, the results are inconclusive.

ADMINISTRATIVE LAW—PROFESSIONAL LICENSING

We have discussed the sanctions imposed by general civil law and criminal law and have found them wanting as an effective social mechanism for establishing personal engineering responsibility for unacceptable risks. Let us examine the Professional Licensing Laws to discover if they are a more positive approach for developing engineering responsibility.

The process of licensing, regulation and enforcement in the practice of engineering affects a relatively small percentage of the engineering profession. Approximately 300,000 engineers (NCEE Proceedings 1980) are licensed in the United States out of 1.5 million or more. Only licensed engineers come under the jurisdiction of the licensing boards; the large majority of engineers avoid licensing by reason of the many exemptions provided in the law. As will be evident from the following discussion, the licensing laws are not presently an effective means of controlling licensed engineers' conduct and have little or no direct effect on the great majority of unlicensed engineers.

The National Council of Engineering Examiners (NCEE) is an organization composed of the members of engineering licensing boards in all of the states and territories of the United States. The council has developed a model law that is fairly representative of the statutes currently adopted in the various states and jurisdictions with one very important exception known as the Industry Exemption. The Industry Exemption exempts industrial companies and their employees from the operation of the engineering licensing laws. This exemption may specifically enumerate manufacturing, mining, communications common carrier, and research and development companies (Pennsylvania Engineers Registration Law). Another exemption that is important, however, this one is recommended in the Model Law, exempts employees and subordinates of a licensed engineer (Section 23(c)).

One point should be made clear here, the engineering registration laws do not make a distinction between an individual engineer acting as a sole proprietor and an engineer acting as an employee. The law contemplates the exercise of engineering judgment as a separate and distinct activity solely within the control of the individual engineer who is in responsible charge of the work. Corporations are authorized by separate certificate to practice engineering provided that one or more of the corporate officers is designated by the corporation as being responsible for the engineering activities and decisions. The separate certificate further provides that all personnel who act in its behalf as professional engineers are registered (Section 22). There is a conflict between this requirement and the one mentioned earlier: the exemption for employees and subordinates. As interpreted in some states, one licensed individual can qualify a large corporation, such as Westinghouse, for all of the engineering services it performs in a particular state.

The enforcement activities of the licensing boards focuses on the revocation and suspension of the license rather than fines and imprisonment. The engineer who is in responsible charge of the engineering work is the individual held accountable for compliance with the law.

The term "responsible charge" is defined in the law to mean "direct control and personal supervision of engineering work" (Section 1(c)). Other terms used in the law tend to dilute the effect of this definition including such terms as "done by him or under his control," "registrant's complete direction and control" and "complete dominion and control." Note that the term "personal supervision" has not been used in these latter instances.

It is readily apparent that the legal concept of the practice of engineering by licensed individuals in responsible charge of the work becomes less and less appropriate as the complexity and scale of the engineering work increases. The Alaska pipeline or the Boeing 747 are examples where clearly no one person can be in responsible charge of the engineering work. It really does not take too great a degree of complexity, particularly where multiple disciplines of engineering are involved, before the concept of the engineer in responsible charge is lost. This is particularly true in industry where the design of the product is further complicated by the intricacies of the manufacturing process. High-rise buildings, sewage treatment plants and electric generating plants are other examples where the term "engineer in responsible charge" becomes meaningless. In today's complex technological society, it is doubtful that the term "engineer in responsible charge" is anything more than a pleasant concept which adds to one's ego when one says "I am an engineer." In this respect, it is much like the concept of the architect as the "Master Builder" who not only plans the project for sweeping aesthetic grandeur but tests the brick mortar with his fingers for proper consistency.

Particularly in large organizations, the concept of the engineer in responsible charge is by and large an illusion, and regulations for the control of the practice of engineering based on this concept cannot be effective.

Keeping this in mind, let us look at the ethical rules prescribed for engineers.

Section 19 of the Model Law is headed "Disciplinary Action—Revocation, Suspension or Reprimand." The Model Law incorporates by reference Rules of Professional Conduct (Rules). First and foremost in the Rules is Canon 1—*(Engineers) shall hold paramount the safety health and welfare of the public in the performance of their professional duties.* And, Rule 1a—*If their professional judgment is overruled under circumstances where the safety, health, property or welfare of the public are endangered, they shall notify their employer or client and such other authority as may be appropriate.* This is the rule that creates the moral dilemma in the whistle-blowing cases. The issues many times involve judgment where two people can differ. The situations always involve an organization with numerous individuals having varying degrees of responsibility on the project. In these situations, it is difficult to establish whether or not a particular individual has been overruled or whether a judgment has simply been made at a higher level in an organization. Questions immediately arise as to whom one gives notice to satisfy the ethical obligation to the employer, the client and/or other authority. And finally, if one satisfies one's moral obligation to notify, what protection is afforded to the individual from retributory action by management for disloyalty? At the very least, the individual is dependent upon favorable job performance evaluations in order to obtain salary increases and promotion, and there is always the possibility of termination on two weeks notice or transfer to the garbage detail. Is it any wonder that most engineers in large organizations equate whistle-blowing to Hobson's choice in the selection of four-footed transport? The whistle-blowers of this world should be and usually are considered Congressional Medal of Honor candidates in the corporate economic war.

The Model Law also provides for disciplinary action for gross negligence, incompetency or misconduct in the practice of engineering (Section 19(a)(2)). The number of licenses revoked for gross negligence is very small indeed. An inquiry to NCEE provided very little information as to documented cases. It is true, however, that NCEE does not have direct access to the records of state board disciplinary action and relies entirely upon voluntary disclosure by the Boards; but, still it is significant that the reported cases are so few. This writer, as a member of the Pennsylvania Engineers Registration Board and having been active with that board for more than 20 years, has never been made aware of a formal hearing by that board arising out of charges of gross negligence against an engineer. There have been several cases against surveyors, but they are not instructive as to the situation for engineers.

The lack of documented cases of revocation and suspension would appear to be a condemnation of the licensing boards for failure to enforce the registration laws; however, it is not the boards themselves that cause this anomaly. First, the boards do not go looking for engineers who have acted in a grossly negligent manner. Charges must be filed by someone. The engineering community is the most logical group to be charged with this duty, but it is not common for even gross engineering negligence to be readily apparent just by observation. Patients die irrespective of the quality of medical services. Someone must lose in a lawsuit regardless of the quality of legal services. Buildings may fall down or lose their windows, as in the Hancock Building in Boston, without a clear understanding of why it happened or whether it could have been prevented. Most malpractice claims are highly technical and require the expenditure of large sums just to analyze the problem.

It is extremely unlikely that an engineer on the street can look at a failure and diagnose gross negligence. Engineers within the designer's organization may have the technical information to make such a determination, but they are restrained because of the civil damages that might be imposed against their company. Engineers in the owner's organization may be able to make such determinations, but again they will be more interested in indemnification than in future protection of the public. If they bring charges against an individual engineer for gross negligence, which is more difficult to prove than simple negligence, and lose that case, it could have adverse effect on their claim for indemnification against the engineering company. And so it goes, no one has a clear mandate to press for revocation or suspension of the license of a grossly negligent engineer.

As indicated earlier, the licensing laws apply to only a small percentage of engineers because of the numerous exemptions under the law. Charges of gross negligence cannot even be processed by an engineering board against an unlicensed engineer.

Finally, engineering boards are underfunded and operate on the unwritten policy that their primary objective is to protect the public through the licensing process and not through policing the practice of engineering. With the exemptions available, the poorly defined areas of enforcement and the lack of administrative support, the boards have not taken an aggressive position on enforcement of the law with respect to incompetency and gross negligence.

Without redirection in the law and proper funding, it is probably unrealistic to expect effective control of engineers' conduct by engineering boards.

There are only a few recorded cases dealing with engineering boards' determination on the issues of gross negligence and incompetence. Reviewing some of the cases will give a better understanding as to what constitutes gross negligence warranting revocation or suspension of an engineering license. Also, it is evident from these cases that the engineering boards can invoke sanctions against licensed engineers for gross negligence and incompetence notwithstanding the fact that this mechanism is infrequently utilized.

In the case of Vivian v. Examining Board of Architects, Professional Engineers, Designers and Land Surveyors, 213 NW 2d 359 (1974), a complaint was filed against a registered professional engineer alleging gross negligence and incompetence in designing and supervising the construction of a building that collapsed.

The board, after a hearing, found that Vivian prepared the plans and was responsible for supervising construction of the building and that the collapse was due to deficiencies in the design and construction of the building. The board determined that the design deficiency consisted of failure to design a truss to support a "reasonable live load" and that this constituted incompetency. The board also determined that the failure to correct the design prior to construction constituted gross negligence in the practice of engineering. The board thereupon ordered that the engineer's certificate of registration be revoked and that an application for reissuance of the engineer's license not be considered prior to six months from the date of revocation.

The board's decision was appealed to the Supreme Court of Wisconsin. The Supreme Court's decision in this case recites two significant points concerning the definition of gross negligence and incompetence. First, "the determination of whether the failure to properly design or supervise the construction of the roof supporting truss was or was not gross negligence is a matter for the board to determine. . . ." Here, the court recognized that the Board must act like a jury in determining matters of fact and that the Court cannot substitute its judgment on such matters. However, one caveat that caused a reversal in this case was that the board's decision must be supported by substantial evidence.

The second point was the court's denial of any implication that it is only continued or repeated acts that can constitute incompetency or negligence in any situation.

The judicial history of the term "gross negligence" in other contexts such as automobile accident cases was deemed not applicable to professional gross negligence. The language in these other cases is taken as implying a course of conduct "so reckless or in wanton disregard of the rights and safety of others as to evince a willingness to cause injury or damage." When applied to professional negligence, it is simply one of degree and "distinguishes between gross or grave acts of negligence as compared to less serious or more ordinary acts of negligence."

In another case, Shapiro v. Board of Regents of the University of the State of New York 286 NYS 2d 1001 (1968), the Supreme Court confirmed a determination by the Board of Regents to suspend the license of a professional engineer for six months for gross negligence, incompetency, misconduct and unprofessional conduct relative to testing of mechanical ventilating system in a newly constructed apartment building.

The engineer was hired to perform the testing to establish compliance with building department rules. The building consisted of six floors plus a basement and mechanical ventilation was required under the rules on all floors and in the basement. The architect's plans furnished to the engineer did not show the basement and did not indicate any ventilation requirements for the basement. The engineer, after performing tests, certified that the ventilation requirements of the building department rules were satisfied. Approximately one year later, the building owner had another engineer inspect the premises. It was then discovered that the vertical ventilating shaft, which extended from the basement through the six floors of the building, was cut off by a concrete slab at the first floor level making it impossible to provide mechanical ventilation to the basement. The board found numerous defects throughout the building ventilating system in addition to the concrete slab which cut the basement out of the system. Shafts, ducts and registers functioned deficiently because of dirt and debris attributed to the original construction of the building. There were areas that had no registers, there was a duct behind a register which was not connected to the shaft and there were ducts which terminated in cabinets that were constructed over the registers.

The engineer stated that he visited the premises and examined the architectural plan "superficially, that's all." He said he relied entirely upon the judgment of his two sons. One son was in training and the other son had been licensed as an engineer a few months prior to this work. Also, this was the first multi-story dwelling building that the engineer had experience with. The architect's plan furnished to the engineer was marked Sheet 7 of 12, but the engineer made no attempt to determine whether the basement was included in the ventilation design. The engineer stated that the architect's plan was ambiguous as to this matter. Finally, when the engineer was advised that his certification was in error and that serious defects existed in the building ventilation system, he made no effort to notify the city building department as to the erroneous certification.

The Supreme Court held that there was substantial evidence to support the charges of gross negligence, incompetence and misconduct in the practice of engineering and unprofessional conduct in failing to exercise due regard for the safety of life or health of the public who may be affected by the engineer's professional work.

ENR News reported June 18, 1981 that the agency that oversees professionals in the State of Florida is proposing disciplinary action against two engineers responsible for the design of the Harbor Cay condominium in Cocoa Beach. Eleven construction workers were killed and 23 others injured when the concrete roof slab, which was in process of being poured, collapsed triggering the progressive collapse of the lower floors of this five-story building. A subsequent review of project documents by a consulting engineer for the Department of Professional Regulation labeled the design "seriously deficient" and the contract documents "inadequate."

The deficiency identified in the design indicated that under full loading of the building (this would include the dead load weight of the building members, live or movable loads and exterior loading for wind), the punching shear (vertical stress in the slab at the face of the building columns) would have exceeded allowable stress by as much as 469 percent. The consulting engineer is reported to have said that the building would have collapsed under dead load alone.

The article goes on to indicate that the consulting engineer found no evidence that the design engineers had ever checked their design for punching shear at the columns "typically the most vulnerable aspect of a flat plate," the "strong likelihood" that load imposed during construction would exceed design loads, "Equivalent Frame" effects, slenderness of columns or slab deflections. Other errors cited in the design included failure to take into account the weight of the building's exterior masonry walls or columns in designing the foundations, errors in calculations of lateral sway, floor slab live loads, roof loads and column sizes and in the design of some reinforcing steel. Wind calculations were based on columns 8″ by 24″ in area; however, columns were actually 10″ by 18″ or 10″ × 12.″

Apparently, there was no checking of the design computations or at least only a cursory review. The Cocoa Beach city engineer indicated that the plans "were fairly complex" and stated, "In this case, I skimmed through the calculations and felt that the engineer had taken an adequate approach to the design, so I accepted the calculations as signed and sealed by a professional engineer."

As is the case in most serious failures of this kind, there are allegations of major deficiencies on the part of other parties involved in the project. The floor slabs were designed eight inches thick, but were only constructed seven and one-half inches thick. Developers in the area were charged with price gouging for design services and of trying to adapt one thorough design to other sites without proper design analysis. This latter charge, of course, does not appear relevant in the specific situation. And governmental agencies, whether from understaffing or lack of competent staff, are unable to provide competent review of building design.

The above cases illustrate that engineering boards, with proper procedures and safeguards and subject to court review, can administer the practice of engineering and can exercise some control over engineering conduct; however, this mechanism is not presently being utilized to any great extent (witness the very few instances that have been recorded).

PROFESSIONAL SOCIETIES

The last area we can examine for sanctions influencing engineering conduct is within the engineering societies. John Kultgen from the University of Missouri in an unpublished paper "Evaluating Codes of Professional Ethics," lists as one of the attributes of a profession that it is an occupation whose performance is organized and regulated by the group itself through an association with a formal code of ethics.

Kultgen also states that the utility of engineering codes of ethics are limited because they provide no ranking principles or, at most, vague and incomplete ones.

The National Society of Professional Engineers has attempted to overcome this problem by formal interpretation of their code on a case by case basis. It has published written opinions of its Board of Ethical Review, dating from 1958. The Board of Ethical Review considers actual facts and circumstances as submitted by state societies and others without the use of actual names of persons or firms. The purpose is stated to be educational rather than punitive or disciplinary.

A review of the most recent published volume of opinions by NSPE in Volume IV 1976 reveals the following areas of concern. From a total of 57 cases, 20 or 35% relate to advertising; 19 or 33% to relations between engineers and engineering fees; 8 or 14% to conflict of interest; 7 or 12% to government employment and political contributions; and 2 or 3% to misconduct. The two cases dealing with misconduct involved a criminal offense of theft in the first degree in one instance and plagiarism in the other instance. No cases related to gross negligence or incompetence are discussed. It is, of course, possible that gross negligence and incompetence do not present issues needing analysis for educational purposes. However, the paucity of cases presented to registration boards for disciplinary action seems to indicate that the state registration boards and the societies are reluctant, unable or unwilling to address this issue.

An inquiry concerning a recent report in the July 1981 issue of *Engineering News* by ASCE covering 72 ethics cases handled since 1972 indicated that none of these cases involved gross negligence or incompetence. Since the registration boards have legal authority to deal with gross negligence and incompetence but nevertheless do so only infrequently, it is very unlikely that a professional society would be effective in this area of professional conduct.

Peer review procedures have been suggested by professional societies to review plans and specifications before the project goes into construction, but this type of peer review has not been successful. Checking for peer review purposes is a laborious process and adds considerably to the cost. Normal design contemplates quality control procedures that include detailed checking within an organization. Also, much engineering work is for sophisticated engineering departments of government and industry and, to varying degrees, they check the work of consulting firms. To date, peer review of design prior to construction has proven to be much too burdensome.

Peer review after a problem surfaces has been utilized in at least one instance to the mutual satisfaction of client and engineer, not for the purpose of disciplinary action or punishment but simply for indemnification of the client for losses occasioned by negligent (as distinguished from gross negligent) work. The Pennsylvania Department of Transportation, PennDOT, has established a procedure for review of an engineer's work by a group consisting of three department engineers and three outside consulting engineers, all of whom are expected to be knowledgeable in the specific discipline of engineering out of which the allegations of negligence arise. The procedure is not binding on either party. As a result of the peer review, the charges are dropped, a settlement is negotiated or the case is taken to binding arbitration. Most of these cases are settled or dropped as a result of the peer review procedure.

The recent case of Mardirosian v. The American Institute of Architects (AIA), *474 F Supp. 628* (1979) illustrates the hazards faced by professional societies in connection with the imposition of sanctions for unethical conduct. The case was filed in the United States District Court for the District of Columbia by an architect who had been suspended from membership in the AIA for violating its ethical standards. The architect challenged the validity of the ethics standards alleging unreasonable restraint of trade in violation of the Sherman Anti-Trust Act. The District Court granted the architect's motion for summary judgment as to liability. The amount of damages including punitive (triple) damages [was] to be established by jury trial. In late 1981, an offer by AIA to pay Mardirosian $700,000 damages was accepted and the case was settled. In addition, AIA had expended approximately $500,000 in legal expenses.

Mardirosian was hired by the government to review the work of another design architect whose contract included the alteration and refurbishing of historic Union Station, Washington, D.C., and new facilities for a National Visitor Center, passenger station and parking structure. The design architect's contract contained a provision for termination at the convenience of the "Owners." After the design was completed on the Visitor's Center and in the same month in which construction bids were received, the design architect's services on that project were terminated and Mardirosian was requested to undertake the remaining architectural services. The design architect continued under his contract as to the passenger station and the parking facility.

Mardirosian was charged with supplanting the design architect as to subsequent architectural services on the Visitor's Center in violation of AIA Standard 9: "An architect shall not attempt to obtain, offer to undertake or accept a commission for which the architect knows another legally qualified individual or firm has been selected or employed, until the architect has evidence that the latter's agreement has been terminated and the architect gives the latter written notice that the architect is so doing."

The AIA's National Judicial Board, after lengthy proceedings, issued a report on the charges against Mardirosian. They concluded that he was guilty of violating the ethical standards and recommended his membership in AIA be terminated. Mardirosian appealed to the AIA Executive Committee which modified the penalty to a one-year suspension of his AIA membership.

As a direct result of this case, the AIA in June 1980 voted to make compliance with its ethical standards voluntary rather than mandatory. *ENR News* described this action as throwing out the "bath water, baby and all."

The Mardirosian case illustrates the greatest detriment to utilizing the peer review process in controlling engineers conduct. The societies are exposed to suit by the engineer they attempt to discipline, not only for violation of the antitrust act and other legal challenges to the code of ethics, but also for defamation and tortious interference. Based on this case, it is unlikely that the professional societies will ever be able to develop a strong internal system to deter and punish gross negligence or to ferret out incompetence in the professions.

SUMMARY

We have examined four different social mechanisms intended to influence conduct in the performance of engineering work; however, as presently utilized, none of these mechanisms appears to be an effective means to control the conduct of individual engineers in large organizations where the majority of engineers work. In an ideal situation typified by NASA and Monsanto, an internal organization is developed to thoroughly review design safety matters. In such an organization, it is unlikely that an engineer would need to resort to whistle-blowing to correct unsafe designs; and, likewise, it is unlikely that incompetence or gross negligence in engineering design would go undetected for very long. The problem remains as to what can be done to assure the public that proper engineering safeguards are maintained in the design of products, structures and systems intended for sale to or use by the public. Whistle-blowing and gross negligence or incompetence appear to be opposite sides of the same coin. In one case, it is the individual engineer who wants to act ethically, responsibly and professionally; and, in the other case, it is an individual engineer who either does not want to or cannot perform to the standards of the profession. A solution addressed to both matters may be the ideal way to resolve the problem of providing adequate safeguards for design safety. One way is to select the system most likely to be able to provide these safeguards, overcome the deficiencies presently existing in that system and, hopefully, implement the necessary changes to make that system operate effectively.

The system that appears most likely to be effective in this regard is the one discussed under Administrative Law utilizing the machinery of the licensing boards. Some of the deficiencies presently existing can be categorized as follows:

1. Licensing laws presently apply only to licensed engineers; approximately one out of five engineers is licensed. Licensing specifically exempts large categories of practicing engineers.
2. Funding is presently insufficient for effective policing.
3. Licensing is performed on a part-time basis by professional engineers with minimum administrative support.
4. Licensing is performed on a state-by-state basis.
5. Engineering encompasses hundreds of specialties and disciplines.

It seems obvious that the jurisdiction of the registration boards must be expanded to cover all practicing engineers. Many attempts have been made to eliminate the industry exemption but such attempts have been unsuccessful. The manufacturing industry particularly has been fearful that top management will lose control if their employed engineers are independent and not subject to final determinations made by the business managers. The thinking of such representatives of industry is reflected in the often repeated statement by Charles E. Wilson many years ago: "What is good for General Motors is good for the Country." Our society has become much too complex and its impact on our environment has gone beyond the point where excesses can be absorbed without harm. Disposal of toxic waste, for that matter even non-toxic waste and pollution of all kinds, are having a serious, deleterious effect on our living conditions. Engineers cannot turn a blind eye to these matters because management wants to reduce the production costs in order to be competitive.

To avoid opposition from industry, it would be advisable to initiate a voluntary program offering benefits to engineers and at the same time bringing them within the gambit of policing and enforcement. A suggestion in this regard is to amend the licensing laws to provide certification for engineers immediately upon graduation from college. Registration for signing and sealing final engineering plans could still follow the same course as before, and industry could retain its exemption; but, the engineers in industry would become subject to disciplinary procedures for violation of Professional Rules of Conduct. This change in the registration laws would then tie in with the current legislative drive to protect whistle-blowers from retaliatory action by their employer. Michigan presently has such a law, and other states are considering similar protection for employees. The courts are beginning to recognize a right of the employee to be protected from unjust firing by an employer.

The registration boards with increased jurisdiction then would have to be reorganized to handle their greater responsibilities. Additional funding would undoubtedly be needed, and greater participation by all engineers would probably be warranted to develop proper peer review in connection with the enforcement functions. A major criticism of professions today is that they do not police themselves. Through amendment of the licensing laws and restructuring of our licensing boards as indicated above, this matter may be correctable.

31 Would Helping Ethical Professionals Get Professional Societies into Trouble?

Stephen H. Unger

INTRODUCTION

We have seen in recent years numerous cases of harm being caused to individuals and to society as a whole through badly implemented technology. The Chernobyl, Challenger, and Bhopal disasters come to mind immediately, but there have also been many lesser instances involving such matters as releases of toxic chemicals into the environment and defects in the design of automobiles.

A common factor in such cases is that the problems were known in advance to some individuals, usually to engineers in the organizations involved. It is also often the case that these people called attention to the problems and their possible consequences, but that their warnings were ignored. Engineers who persist in efforts to get such problems corrected despite negative reactions from their managers are often punished. Hence, as in the case of the Challenger episode, the engineers frequently stop short of going over the heads of management when their professional judgments are arbitrarily overridden.

In certain types of cases, there are laws to protect those who act to correct hazardous situations, but these are, at present, rather limited in effectiveness, as well as in scope. (The Morton Thiokol engineers, for example, would not have been covered.) It would be very helpful to broaden and strengthen these laws, and efforts along those lines are now being made.

It has been suggested that it would be very appropriate for engineering societies to play an active role in these matters by backing up engineers who, when seeking to adhere to high standards of professional conduct, find their careers jeopardized by managerial actions. The model pointed to here is that of the American Association of University Professors (AAUP), which has for more than half a century been an effective force in safeguarding academic freedom for university professors.

Among the ideas proposed for implementation by the societies are the following:

1. Carefully investigating specific cases and publishing reports, where justified, that show how an employer has acted improperly toward an engineer in cases of the type referred to above. (Central to the AAUP approach.)
2. Explicitly censuring the employer in such cases, and calling the matter to the attention of the profession in general. (Also part of the AAUP procedure.)
3. Publishing ratings of employers indicating the extent to which they encourage ethical behavior on the part of their engineering employees.
4. Establishing legal defense funds to help ethical engineers who find it necessary to resort to the courts.
5. Giving awards to engineers who uphold ethical principles in situations where this places their careers in jeopardy.

The IEEE has already established machinery for implementing items 1 and 5. However, the mechanism related to item 1 has been fully exercised in only one case. There are several explanations for the fact that the IEEE (and perhaps other engineering societies) has not taken a strong position on the matter of supporting ethical engineers.

Since a portion of IEEE's membership consists of upper-level managers and owners of businesses, there is some feeling that it would be divisive to have the IEEE appear to take sides in disputes between members. Rather than analyze this position in detail, I will simply point out here that, as is understood by many managers who are IEEE members, measures to encourage ethical behavior by engineers and to discourage improper behavior by managers serve the interests of good managers as well as the interests of ethical engineers and of society as a whole. This is because the existence of such measures has the effect of alleviating pressure on honorable managers to cut corners to keep up with less scrupulous competitors. It also helps them resist efforts by *their* managers to get them to do things that they feel are improper.

Other explanations of the lack of vigorous action by engineering societies are concerned with costs that may be incurred in the process. These include direct expenses, such as the need for added staff and legal services; the possibility of being faced with extraordinary legal costs in defending against lawsuits brought by companies and individuals in conflict with the engineers being defended; the possibility of losing such suits and, thereby, being required to pay large sums in compensatory or even punitive damages; and the possibility of losing the support of employers of engineers. In the following sections, the reality of these dangers is assessed, and means for minimizing them are proposed.

LAWSUITS

There are two basic parts to this problem. First, to what extent is it likely that a society involved in defending the engineer's rights to practice ethically might be found guilty of unjustifiably causing significant financial losses to individuals or corporations? If it can be shown that the answer to this question is that such an event is, or can be made to be, extremely unlikely, then at least the threat of having to pay huge amounts in damages could be dismissed. But the matter does not end there. The second part of the problem is the extent to which suits might be filed against the society that, even if unsuccessful, would still be costly to defend against. An organization could conceivably be bankrupted by lawyers' fees and other costs entailed in fighting off attacks by vengeful employers. Both of these issues are addressed below.

HOW TO AVOID LOSING

The processes for defending ethical engineers can gain respect and become effective only if they are, and are perceived to be, executed in a careful manner, with strict attention to accuracy and fair play. Their objectives must also be, and be perceived as, the raising of the moral level of the practice of engineering. They cannot be effectively used to further the selfish interests of the members of any group.

If, for example, reports are published based on investigations that misrepresent facts, or that do not fully explore pertinent arguments in support of the management position, then engineers reading these reports will soon learn that they cannot be trusted, and, hence, that it would not be sensible to take them into account when considering job offers. If the support machinery is used to pursue selfish economic interests of society members, then it will be considered as only another weapon in economic warfare, to be attacked or defended according to one's own economic interests. (I do not mean to imply here that there is no proper place for organized efforts by engineers to increase their incomes. The rights and wrongs of such efforts should be considered in the same way as corresponding efforts of other groups, such as physicians, nurses, or airline pilots. But any mechanisms for promoting economic interests should be kept separate from those intended to promote engineering ethics.)

It happens that the same characteristics that make support efforts effective, principally truth and fairness, also serve to protect these efforts against successful litigation. There are two components to this protection. First, in American courts, truth is an absolute defense against charges of libel or slander, or causing actionable damage in the marketplace. (This is *not* the case in many other countries, including some democracies such as Great Britain.) Hence, if the reports published by the support committees are free of factual errors, then there is no basis for successful damage suits. Nor is a report summarizing, in a factual manner, the responses of engineers to a questionnaire pertaining to the way their employers deal with dissenting professional opinions a very good target for a lawsuit.

But, human enterprises being what they are, is it really possible, even with the best will, to guarantee that, over a long period of time, with many reports being issued, that absolutely *no* factual errors will creep in? The question answers itself. Perfection, while a worthy goal, is not a wholly attainable one. Mistakes *will* be made. Not surprisingly, this fact is taken into account by our legal system. As a second line of defense, if it can be shown that an error, even a damaging one, occurred despite sincere, *diligent* efforts to be accurate, and if the thrust of the enterprise in which this error was made was one operating on behalf of a good cause, then the likelihood of being found at fault is very small.

What is needed then is a carefully designed set of procedures to guard against error, incorporating a variety of mechanisms for cross-checking the essential ingredients of the report. (While great care should be taken to make the reports completely accurate, obviously some errors are of little consequence, while others might be of a critical nature.) In this respect, we can draw upon the experience of the AAUP for an extremely powerful tool that they have used to ensure both accuracy and fairness.

After doing the best they can to ascertain all of the relevant facts and arguments, the AAUP investigators submit drafts of their reports to all of the parties concerned for their review and comments. Thus, if there are significant errors or omissions, these can be corrected by the parties concerned. Where there may be disagreement as to the validity of certain statements in the report, it is revised to include the opposing views, perhaps with some arguments supporting one or the other, so that the reader can decide for himself. If, at some later date, it is argued (say, in a courtroom) that some crucial misrepresentation of the situation is embodied in the published report, a powerful defense is available; namely, that the parties concerned all had the opportunity to call attention to the error(s) prior to publication. A clear case can be made that the publishers were *not* negligent in their effort to get at the truth.

One might still argue, that, even with all these efforts, one cannot rely upon people to carry out such procedures perfectly, and that, as a result of such imperfections, including the imperfect implementation of the law in real courtrooms, an engineering society would eventually suffer a crushing defeat. Fortunately, we can again draw upon the experience of the AAUP, this time not for a specific technique, but rather for experimental evidence as to the validity of the above-outlined procedure for avoiding courtroom losses. The bottom line here is that, after over half a century of publications that pull no punches in assigning fault for improper treatment of faculty members, the association has never been successfully sued for damages.

Is this an artifact due to the milieu in which the AAUP operates? Is it because colleges and universities are administered by softhearted, gentle people who would not wish to become involved in such sordid activities as libel suits? I can almost hear the laughter of fellow university employees. But let us turn to a very different realm for further evidence leading to the same result.

Consumers Union (CU) has been evaluating consumer products and publishing detailed critical and comparative reports ranking specific commercial products for about 50 years. Each month, perhaps, a hundred different brand names are mentioned. Clearly, being ranked low in the list of competitive brands or, worse yet, being listed as "not acceptable" can have significant effects on sales of an item. This, of course, would mean real, possibly very large, losses in income for the firms involved. Now we are in what everyone would have to admit is the "real" world. The basis for

CU's evaluations are laboratory tests and judgments by panels of experts or, sometimes, by panels of just ordinary users of the product being evaluated.

CU makes every effort to be accurate and fair, but, given the scale on which they operate, it would be impossible to avoid all kinds of errors, ranging from mistakes in the reading of instruments to editorial errors in their publication. Often subjective judgments are being made by the panels. Certainly, if there were ever a natural battlefield for lawyers to wage warfare in, this is it. Obviously CU must maintain a vast legal establishment to keep them from being destroyed by enraged manufacturers of such items as "not acceptable" toilet tissues. Even when defended by the best legal talent, one would expect the CU would periodically suffer major defeats and have to pay huge amounts in damages.

Not so. While lawsuits against CU are occasionally filed, they seldom cause much trouble. Only *once* did they lose, and in this instance the judgment against them was for less than $16,000—and even *this* decision was overturned on appeal. Most of the time spent by CU in court is in the role of *plaintiff* against companies who try to use its ratings in their advertising.

What is the explanation for this record? Here we encounter another aspect of our legal system that is also very pertinent to the topic of defending ethical engineers. As does the AAUP, CU makes every reasonable effort to be fair and accurate. They make a practice of correcting errors when they find them or when others call attention to them. (They do *not*, however, submit reports to manufacturers for comment prior to publication—this would be too unwieldy a practice in their case.) But the courts recognize that CU is not furthering the selfish ends of any group—unless we define "consumers" (which, of course, all of us are) as such a group. They are considered as promoting the welfare of the public. Hence, when they make an honest mistake, they are not penalized in the same way that other types of organizations would be. For example, a sensational commercial magazine that publishes a colorful story written to attract attention and promote sales had better be extremely careful not to malign anyone with incorrect statements. Should a damaging story be found to contain any significant errors of fact, even if they were not grossly negligent in checking out the statements, they would be vulnerable to major libel suits.

But even if defeat in the courtroom is unlikely, what about the danger of winning a series of victories so costly as to lead to financial ruin? Indeed, a legal maxim is that "anyone can sue anybody over anything." Thus, an angry individual or corporation might file a suit even if there is little chance of victory, simply to punish the organization that exposed some instance of wrongdoing. The fact is that such vengeance suits have, in fact, *not* been filed against either AAUP (it has been sued only once—unsuccessfully) or CU. Some explanations for this, which apply very directly to the case of engineering societies, follow.

REVENGE CAN BE BITTER

Let us now imagine that an IEEE committee, operating in a careful and fair manner, has published a report supporting an engineer and showing the employer of that engineer in a bad light. Suppose, to be more specific, that the issue involved a protest against inadequate testing of some safety-related product. Outraged by the fact that their shoddy practices have been publicly exposed, the company president decides that no amount of stockholders' money is too great to spend in an attempt to entangle the IEEE in a costly lawsuit, even though the company's lawyers have indicated that the chances of victory are nil (for reasons along lines discussed in the previous section). Ignoring their advice, he files suit against the IEEE for $20 million in damages. What happens next?

Before the case even comes to trial, the IEEE attorneys initiate pretrial discovery proceedings. They subpoena all of the company's files having to do with the testing of not only the product directly involved in the case, but of all other related products. They call as witnesses in the proceedings (to testify under oath) all of the managers, engineers, and company officials involved in these processes. In the course of this operation, they turn up not only a wealth of evidence corroborating further the original claims made by the engineer (previously they were able to establish only that his technical position was "plausible"), but also discover hard evidence of a number of other parallel cases of slipshod practices, in some cases, violating state safety codes.

By the time the trial begins, the press and TV news departments, previously indifferent to the fate of a "mere" engineer, are closely following developments as horror stories concerning the company's products begin to take shape. At this point, the chairman of the board begins to see the handwriting on the wall and the president of the firm decides that perhaps he is not spending enough time with his family—he tenders his resignation. The new president orders the suit dropped—but now the matter cannot be ended that easily, as IEEE attorneys file a motion against the company, demanding compensation and punitive damages for their having misused the court system by bringing to it a case obviously without merit. Charges are also filed against the company's attorneys for having participated in this activity.

Thus, as illustrated in this hypothetical case, an organization has a great deal to lose by resorting to the courts in a situation where they are basically in the wrong. The damage that they might have suffered as a result of the publication of a critical report by a professional society, or by an unfavorable rating by such a society with respect to the disregard of their engineers' professional rights, may be greatly amplified by the uncovering of additional evidence concerning previously known cases, the existence of other, previously *unknown* instances of similar, or even quite different abuses of either engineering employees or of the public welfare. There will almost certainly be a great deal of publicity about all of these matters. In additions, they may wind up paying court costs and legal fees for *both* sides, as well as punitive damages. I suggest that these are the sort of considerations that account for the fact that CU and the AAUP have not been impeded by harassing litigation. If properly organized, there seems to be no reason why ethics support operations carried out by engineering societies would not enjoy similar success in avoiding legal entanglements.

LOSING EMPLOYER SUPPORT

At present, engineering societies receive significant backing from those who employ engineers. Some employers pay society dues for their engineers, the great bulk of advertising revenue from society publications comes from the same organizations, and employers often encourage engineers to attend professional society meetings on company time, with all expenses paid. In addition, many engineers carry out society business on company time, often using office services while doing so. Thus, if employers of engineers were suddenly to terminate all forms of support for engineering societies, the latter would certainly feel the pinch. How likely is it that, by instituting strong ethics support measures, a society might provoke such a response?

As in the case of kamikaze lawsuits, it is not hard to show that any organization adopting such a tactic would be damaging itself far more than it could possibly damage a society. To begin with, one should ask why organizations, particularly those whose purpose it is to make money for the owners, are *now* supporting engineering societies to the extent suggested above. The short answer is that they do so because they themselves profit from this.

In the most general sense, organizations that employ engineers clearly benefit from progress in technology, and that, in essence, is the reason for the existence of professional engineering societies. Through such activities as the publishing of technical journals, the organizing of technical meetings and exhibits, and participation in standards committees, engineering societies play a major role in the development and promulgation of new and old technology. Hence, it is little wonder that users of technology are anxious to support them.

On a more detailed level, organizations benefit directly from each type of support mentioned here. They advertise their products in the publications read by those who make the decisions about purchasing them. If they are interested in having their engineers apply the latest technology to their products, it is clear that encouraging them to be active in engineering society technical activities would be clearly beneficial.

On the other hand, if any organization decided to stop sending its engineers to technical meetings and to terminate other forms of support for society membership, they would be handicapping themselves in the engineering job market. An organization that acquired a reputation for being hostile to engineering societies on the grounds of the latter's support for ethical engineers would thereby incur resentment on the part of many in the profession. This ill will could easily be translated into a loss of sales when engineers must make choices among products that do not differ much in price or performance.

The support supplied by employers stems from self-interest, and it is not likely to be withdrawn as a result of temper tantrums that would have serious consequences to the all-important bottom line.

CONCLUSIONS

Providing strong support for the ethical practice of engineering is a very worthwhile and appropriate endeavor for engineering societies. As in the case of most significant activities, there are indeed risks invovled. It is quite possible to bungle the job and get the society involved in various kinds of trouble. But the degree of competence necessary to avoid trouble is by no means out of the range of those who run engineering societies.

If you are interested in doing something that may have legal implications, do *not* ask a lawyer if it is legally safe. The answer is bound to be that this activity is fraught with hazards. This would apply if what you wished to do was as simple as buying a house. What you must do is to ask the lawyer *how* to do what you wish in a manner that minimizes legal risks. Some general principles for minimizing the risks of ethics support have already been pointed out. An additional point is made below, and, doubtless, a good lawyer would be of great value in making sure that the detailed procedures were both efficacious and minimally dangerous from a legal standpoint.

In order to emphasize that they are not merely acting in the interest of their own members, the AAUP defends the academic freedom of *all* professors, whether or not they are members of the association. Engineering societies should do likewise. (This *is* done in the case of the IEEE SSIT Award for Outstanding Service in the Public Interest, but it is *not* now done by the IEEE Member Conduct Committee.)

Ethics support should be carried out prudently, but vigorously, by engineering societies. In particular, when threatened with lawsuits, they should make it known in advance that bluffs will be called and that the full resources of the law will be utilized.

The time is ripe for action in this area. It is up to engineers, standing together in their professional societies, to see to it that they are no longer subjected to agonizing choices between sacrificing either conscience or career.

FOR FURTHER BACKGROUND

MARTIN, M. W., and R. SCHINZINGER. 1983. *Ethics in Engineering*. New York: McGraw-Hill.
UNGER, S.H. 1982. *Controlling Technology: Ethics and the Responsible Engineer*. New York: Holt, Rinehart & Winston.

32 Engineering Ethics and Political Imagination

Langdon Winner

Recent attempts by American colleges and universities to teach ethics for scientists and engineers deserve strong praise. They represent a shift away from the idea that questions about ethics and morality are best left to humanists or to elder statesmen of science, a recognition that such matters ought to be an important part of education in the technical professions. One can hope that through these efforts a new generation of men and women will obtain a firm grounding in the ethical aspects of their vocations early enough to make a difference.

Despite these admirable aims, however, the approach often used to teach ethics to scientists and engineers leaves much to be desired. In the way the topic is usually presented, personal responsibilities are situated in extremely limited contexts and ethical choices made to seem something like extraordinary, unwelcome intrusions within a person's normal working life. Rather than lead students to evaluate the most basic, most practical features of their career choices—the kinds of work they select and the social conditions in which that work is done—courses on professional ethics tend to focus upon relatively rare, narrowly bounded crises portrayed against on otherwise happy background of business as usual.[1]

One way in which college courses avoid the difficult, underlying questions that technology-oriented professions involve is to focus upon case studies of particular ethical dilemmas. This can seem to be nothing more than a useful attempt to transcend mere abstractions and to provide contexts for issues by locating them in the "real world" of practice.[2] Unfortunately, what such moves often do is to bracket the realities of daily work in favor of hypothetical situations that are comforting because they are so

---

Reprinted from *Broad and Narrow Interpretations of Philosophy of Technology*, ed. P. Durbin; *Philosophy and Technology*, vol. 7 (Dordrecht: Kluwer, 1990), with permission from the publisher.

remote. Cartoons of concreteness become the abstractions at hand. Hence, the tone of such pedagogical case studies is often something like the following.

"You are an engineer working for a defense contractor helping to assemble [the] latest version of the cruise missile. One day you discover that the paint used on the shell of the missile is emitting toxic fumes that may be dangerous to people working in the assembly plant. The project is behind schedule and your boss has made it clear that it must be completed within deadline. Should you blow the whistle on the toxic fumes or keep silent thereby avoiding risk to your job and career?"

I have exaggerated, but not by very much. So-called ethics case studies usually point students toward specific troubling incidents within what are assumed to be otherwise harmonious patterns in ongoing institutions. The patterns themselves, however, are not identified as anything problematic. Indeed, it is a property of the "case study" approach to education in business, law, and engineering that the contexts that underlie particular cases are never themselves called into question. By failing to analyze and criticize these contexts, case studies tend to legitimate and reinforce the status quo. Thus, the decision to work for a defense contractor building thermonuclear weapons can well go unnoticed as an ethical issue at all. A student may learn how to deal with the moral dilemmas, perhaps even ones that involve great personal courage. But missing from the inquiry are some important dimensions of the lives of technical professionals.

POWER AND THE "GOOD SLOT"

A story from my own experience with engineering students will help illustrate the point I am making. While it is only one incident, it reflects situations I've encountered all too often.

Several years ago I taught a course on the history of technology, co-teaching it with a professor of aeronautical engineering. We had reached the part of the term in which we studied the founding of the modern engineering professions and engineering education. That history is, of course, one in which the engineering schools and large corporations work closely together to tailor an engineering curriculum suited to the immediate needs of the corporations.[3] After the class had gone over the facts in the readings, my colleague turned to the group of about thirty science and engineering undergraduates and asked a question that I would probably never have had the nerve to raise.

"Well," he said, "how does it feel to be on a conveyor belt being turned out into slots?"

There was a long embarrassing pause. Finally, one of the students, a fellow who'd been very quiet most of the term, raised his hand and answered.

"I don't want to be put into any slot," he said confidently. Then he thought for a moment and added, "I want to find . . . . a good slot!"

The classroom filled with laughter; seldom is a point so eloquently made.

But the story does not end there. During the ensuing months I got to know this fellow fairly well. We took long walks by the Charles River and talked about his life and the choices he faced. It turned out that he was, in a pattern fairly typical of engineering undergraduates, the son of a machinist and had gone to college to fulfill his working class family's dream of upward social mobility. He talked about his major, electrical engineering, and expressed his qualms about some of the uses being made of computers these days and of his desire to use his skills for something socially beneficial.

Since I always encourage students to think about the social and ethical dimensions of their work, I thought to myself: "Good. Here's someone I've really reached."

About a year later during the summer break I ran into the fellow walking across campus and asked how he was doing.

"Very well," he replied, "I've got a great job."

"Where is it?" I inquired.

"The Draper Lab," he said.

"Oh. What do they have you doing?" I asked.

"Computer programming," he said and went on to explain that it was programming of an especially intricate, challenging kind.

"And what are the programs used for?" I probed.

"Guidance systems," he replied.

My next question was obvious. "And what do these guidance systems guide?"

"Intercontinental ballistic missiles," he allowed with an uncomfortable smile spreading across his face.

"Bruce, you're building bombs, aren't you? Tell me, on the basis of your own personal commitments, how you can justify that."

He went on to list the kind of deals today's small time Fausts tend to make with today's big time Mephistopheles: the problems were challenging in a purely technical sense, "cutting edge" stuff. The recognition by senior colleagues was gratifying, especially for someone who'd never had much recognition. And, of course, you just couldn't beat the money they were paying.

I told him of my disappointment at what he was doing and silently pondered my contempt for a system that would lure a fine young fellow like himself into the company of those who build the instruments of war and death.

"I guess you've found your *good slot*," I groaned, and we went our separate ways.

There is, in my view, a tendency in our engineering professions as presently constituted not to see the kind of work they do as involved with serious moral questions. Convinced that technology is merely neutral, persuaded that somehow the important questions will be raised by somebody else, many engineers seem almost proud of their inability or unwillingness to talk about ethical concerns. They are, by-and-large, more than ready to become the passive tools of whichever corporation or bureaucracy makes the highest bid.

Students do not enter our colleges saying to themselves: "Oh, how I wish I could learn to build hydrogen bombs. If only I could learn the techniques of producing environmental carcinogens. Teach me the methods that will help an automobile firm decide whether or not it is cost-effective to replace gasoline tanks that explode on impact." No, they do not enter engineering school affirming goals like these. But what do they end up doing when they leave and look for a job?

The condition I am describing is not, I want to emphasize, one that characterizes the engineering profession alone. In other prominent vocations of our age we see similar circumstances in which people no longer see themselves as self-conscious moral agents and citizens of a free society, but rather as subjects of large corporate bodies that, while extending organizational control, gradually eliminate the individual's need to think.

From this point of view, one element notably missing from the education of technical professionals is any critical encounter with a person's relationship to power. Indeed, the phenomenon of power and one's involvement in it is perhaps the best kept secret in modern education generally. Courses and whole curricula simply assume that certain people and institutions hold power; such people have the jobs and define the possibilities for a working life in engineering. Hence, a lecture or problem set in a science or engineering course may begin with the words: "Assume you're working for a defense contractor. . . ." "Assume you're employed by a large corporation. . . ." Such contextualizing statements assume that a student need not ask such prior questions as: Is this the way it ought to be? Is that the proper setting for the practice of my hard-earned knowledge and skill? How might it be otherwise?

The tacit premise of the case study approach to professional ethics is that as one enters a profession, one simply embraces the existing commitments, institutional patterns, and power relationships the profession contains. There is no understanding that as one ponders joining the enterprise, one also has an opportunity to re-evaluate or even reconstitute that field. Only after the newcomer's basic compliance has been secured is he or she assumed ready for the bracing ethical challenges that lie ahead.

A SENSE OF VOCATION

The failure of engineering ethics courses to explore the phenomenon of power reveals another significant lack: exploration of the question of vocation, one's calling in a moral sense.[4] It is reasonable to expect that as a person contemplates committing several decades to a profession, some basic issues ought to be addressed. What are the fundamental ends of a life invested in this line of work? What is the purpose of developing my knowledge and skill in this direction in the first place? Who ought to control the most basic definitions of what my vocation entails? Our educational institutions now shortchange students by avoiding such issues, neglecting focused study of the moral and political groundwork of professional life.

Courses on engineering ethics tend to focus upon issues of right and wrong in personal conduct—extremely important matters indeed. But beginning with Aristotle, philosophers have noticed that there is a logical juncture where ethics finds its limits and politics begins. That turning point comes when we move beyond questions of individual conduct to consider the nature of human collectivities and our membership in them. This calls upon us to ponder the quality of life in political society and what membership in it means for us, not merely as individual actors but as participants in a community.

In my own teaching of engineers and scientists I find some who are actually prepared to act heroically at the level of individual ethics, but who have no sense whatsoever [of] what their work means in an organizational or political sense. It comes as a surprise, for example, for students to learn that engineering projects tend to reflect some economic or social interests and not others. They learn next to nothing about the history of their fields, about who works for whom and how that came to be. These are, once again, well-kept secrets. By the time one gets to be a graduating senior, all he or she may want to know is: Where are those nice people with all the high-paying jobs?

The lack of an ability among engineers and other technical professionals to engage in political reflection is by now much more than a small failure in education; it threatens to become a great tragedy. We live in an age of scientific technology. Many of the most significant ways in which old forms of power are reproduced and new ones created are reflected in the technologies we use. To a great extent the possibilities of social and political life in the twentieth century are defined by technological opportunities and constraints. Whether we are to have a good society or a bad one is powerfully influenced by the technologies we develop and put to use. For that reason the role of engineers and technical professionals is crucial. Such persons are intimately involved in maintaining key social patterns and in inventing new ones as well. In that work they become, in effect, unelected delegates and representatives of the rest of us, charged with the work of building basic structures of our social and political future. If it turns out that they lack vision, lack the ability to make choices that express not only knowledge but also personal strength born of wisdom, our society is headed for trouble.

From this vantage point what is needed is less the study of pre-packaged ethical dilemmas than the cultivation of two crucial skills: political savvy and the capacity for political imagination. At some point in their education engineering students need to examine critically the historical origins of their own chosen profession. They need to understand how their branch of engineering was first organized, by whom and for what reason. They need to examine the kinds of social and economic interests their field represented at the beginning as well as the ones it expresses now. And they need to understand who controls the choice of projects and why.

Casual observers might suppose that learning to become savvy about the social realities of the world students are entering would be a standard part of a good engineering education. In fact, it is almost never explicitly addressed. What students receive instead is a kind of hidden curriculum, a set of unstated assumptions, expectations, and role models which provide a subtle but thorough enculturation. Its underlying text is: Don't ask questions; just find your place in the established hierarchy and obey orders.

There are many ways in which political savvy of this kind might be nurtured and even tested. In my own courses, for example, I have sometimes used the following quiz.

Read carefully Lewis Mumford's chapter on "The Nucleation of Power" in *The Pentagon of Power*[5] and answer the following questions:

1. Do you consider Mumford's description valid or not?
2. Will you in all likelihood join "The Power Complex"?
3. Explain why.

Of course, achieving political savvy alone is not sufficient; it may leave a person aware but cynical, thus accomplishing more harm than good. For that reason there is a need to nurture something more—political imagination, the ability to envision the contributions of one's work to society as a whole, to the quality of public life. Within the plans, methods, models, and prototypes an engineer produces are the blueprints of our social future. This is true whether these products have to do with water projects, highways, industrial machines, electronic components, or energy systems. As part of mastering the fundamentals in their fields, engineers and other technical professionals ought to be encouraged to ask: Can we imagine technologies that enhance democratic participation and social equality? Can we innovate in ways that help enlarge human freedom rather than curtail it? How can planning for technological change include a concern for the public good as distinct from narrowly defined economic interests?

An ability to investigate questions like these ought to be part of the intellectual tool chest that engineers carry with them when they leave the university. While there is no established curriculum that imparts such skill, many of the disciplines in the humanities and social sciences have important resources to offer, resources that at present remain largely untapped. In political philosophy, for example, it is possible to build bridges to the study of engineering by showing ways in which political philosophers are to some extent designers. From Plato to Rousseau to John Rawls, political theory has involved an attempt to translate the ideals of the good society into workable institutional structures. Those who met at the Philadelphia convention of 1787, for example, sought to invent a political machine, the Constitution, that would generate beneficial results generation after generation. To some extent, therefore, political theory and engineering share a common project—making things that will endure. It might even be argued that they share some of the same criteria of evaluation: a concern for the appropriate furnishings of the good life.[6]

Whatever specific fields in the humanities may be chosen to illuminate such questions, however, it is crucially important to allow our students to become competent not only as scientific and technical problem-solvers (the only need currently recognized by the academy and business), but as dreamers and visionaries as well.[7] Drawing upon materials in their own fields, they should be encouraged to imagine the best possible uses to which their intelligence and know-how might be put. Engineers and technical professionals are the unacknowledged legislators of our technological age. Choices that affirm the public good or trample it often rest in their hands. If they overlook this critical role and responsibility, they will also acquiesce in yielding power to agents whose ends are increasingly distant from humanity's best.

OURS IS NOT TO REASON WHY?

Much of the vocation of engineering is legitimately, admirably involved with questions of "how?"—how to solve problems, how to achieve particular results within physical and economic constraints, how to get things done. Such concerns are and will always be central to an engineer's daily activity. Providing students the wherewithal to grapple effectively with "how" questions is bound to remain the heart of engineering education. But in a world of rapidly advancing technology, issues about "how" are often less important than ones that concern "why?" Our society has increasingly powerful means at its disposal and a great many expediencies that seem to justify applying these means all over the planet as rapidly as possible. But typically missing from our deliberations about new technical means are deeply grounded reasons to guide our choices.

Yes, it is possible to build the next intriguing generations of space-based offensive and so-called defensive weapons. But why? In the face of pressing human needs in other domains, why invest our scarce resources in things designed only to destroy? Before going further, it is crucial that we examine the underlying rationale that governs policy. Perhaps that pause for reflection would suggest alternatives other than blindly continuing the arms race.

Yes, it now appears possible to renovate the genetic structure of life forms on the planet. But why? In what sense are such projects needed? What ends or purposes are to be served? Before going ahead, one needs to explore the reasons. And, yes, it is possible to build any number of nearly or totally automated systems of production. But why? Which ends will be furthered? Who stands to benefit and who to lose? Before we engineer systems of this kind we need to be clear about the grounds that justify our projects.

As one examines such topics, the question of "why" can be reformulated in a number of useful, challenging ways. One can ask: For the sake of what deeply meaningful ends are our technologies well-suited or ill-suited? In response to what central human needs are our techniques and instruments developed and applied? On the basis of what fundamental orienting principles do our technology-based practices and institutions find their uses and their limits? In selecting a particular engineering project, what kind of world do we affirm and seek to create?

There are bound to be strong disagreements in our answers to any of these questions. Indeed, it is no easy matter to set about clarifying the basic notions that ought to guide the development and use of our technical means. People have widely different understandings about the meaning and proper application of terms like freedom, justice, security, human rights, well-being, public good, and other key concepts. But it is crucial that such ideas be continually discussed and debated throughout our deliberations about key technological choices. If we do not do this, ideas about "how" begin to comprise the whole of our thinking. Indeed, as Jacques Ellul has argued, it appears to be the destiny of modern thought to replace any living concern about human ends with sterile discussion about instrumentality and efficiency.[8]

A stunning example of this tendency was the Star Wars debate of the early 1980s. President Reagan announced the Strategic Defense Initiative in March 1983, proclaiming its noble goal for the United States, that of "rendering nuclear weapons impotent and obsolete." From that moment forward most of the debate, for and against, focused on the question: Will it work? Will the technologies function as planned? In the heated debates that followed, people seized upon the instrumental issues—issues about "how"—as if they were the truly essential ones.[9] Looking back on this period of history, it is interesting that S.D.I. was offered at a time in which there was, for a while, intense public questioning around the world of the very ends of defense policy, questioning expressed in the Nuclear Freeze movement and in widespread discussion of Jonathan Schell's book, *The Fate of the Earth*.[10] Reagan's move was a clever one. Once again it got people back to talking about gadgetry and instrumental concerns and far away from thinking about fundamental purposes and the relationship between ends and technical means.[11]

This unwillingness to explore the basic reasoning behind our policies accounts for much of the absurdity that passes for informed discourse about technological choices nowadays. Thus, there is much attention to "cost/benefit" analysis, but without the slightest regard for the ultimate foundations of our judgments of benefit and cost. Similarly, one finds people nodding in confident agreement about "efficiency" without pausing to consider what is being maximized and for what reason; that is, what defines our numerators and denominators and on what grounds? Or one hears a great deal of praise for "progress' which seems to assume that one is progressing along a particular path, but never is the path or its destination specified. Similarly, there are anguished cries for increased national "competitiveness" with no attempt to justify the desirability of the things at stake in the competition.[12]

In all discussions of ambitious proposals for technological change, inevitably the most revealing and embarrassing question one can ask is simply, "Why?" What one discovers in a great many cases is that the answers have somehow been ignored, forgotten or even suppressed. That is why any program of engineering education that does not equip students insistently to inquire into the basic purposes of their work is simply an affront to reason. Any technical analysis that asks "how?" without first considering "why?" is bound to be vapid.

With some ingenuity, the "why" could well be included in difficult technical courses, not just humanities electives set aside in a separate, easily forgotten corner of the curriculum. For example, one useful strategy in doing cost/benefit analysis is to begin by listing costs and benefits and, before plowing on, simply reverse the labels over the two columns to see how things look. Analyses by transportation engineers during the 1950s counted "increased traffic flow" as a benefit, something that communities affected by highway planning would later count as a significant cost. To approach cost/benefit analysis by reversing labels always causes a great commotion and you seldom get asked back, but it can add some life to the otherwise rigid, routinized processes of technocratic thinking.

ENGINEER AS CITIZEN

In sum, the great need at present is for our professionals to take a mindful, critical stance with respect to their own work. This requires, first of all, that a person scrutinize the projects in his/her field and the consequences of those projects within the context of a continuing dialogue about our culture's most cherished ideals and principles. It implies, secondly, that scientific and technical professionals must locate and, when necessary, actively create public roles in which one's understanding of important conditions can become a focus of new thinking, debate, and action for the public as a whole. Ethical responsibility now involves more than leading a decent, honest, truthful life, as important as such lives certainly remain. And it involves something much more than making wise choices when such choices suddenly, unexpectedly present themselves. Our moral obligations must now include a willingness to engage others in the difficult work of defining the crucial choices that confront technological society and how to confront them intelligently.

The first requirement, therefore, might be called the responsibility of dialogue; the second, the responsibility of citizenship. Both of these were, of course, well understood by the ancient Greeks. Our task is that of bringing these practices to life for the era of high technology. It is obvious that these are not responsibilities, in fact, that are widely cultivated or practiced. At present, engineering students are encouraged to become careerist and self-interested in ways that exclude dialogue altogether. Their university degrees could well carry not only the title "Bachelor of Science," but also "Certified Uncommitted."

Nevertheless, considerable hope can be found in a single fact: it does not require many people to turn things around. Even one voice speaking at the right moment and in the right area can make all the difference. The contribution of Rachel Carson in the early 1960s was an instance of this kind.[13] At first widely denounced by much of the community of scientists and chemical engineers, Carson's message foreshadowed an international environmental awakening and a gradual move away from the use of destructive chemicals in agriculture.[14] A similar sense of ethical commitment was evident in the petition drive by many scientists and engineers of the mid-1980s, pledging not to work on any part of Reagan's Strategic Defense Initiative. Organizations such as "Physicians for Social Responsibility," "Computer Professionals for Social Responsibility," "The Union of Concerned Scientists," and other groups have set out to raise public consciousness about important public policy issues in their fields. A number of computer scientists in the United States and Europe, for example, have begun devoting their attention to ways in which new information systems might protect freedom rather than undermine it.[15]

Examples like these suggest what I understand to be the genuine promise of the exercise of responsibility among scientific and technical professionals: a gradual re-orientation of patterns of research, development, and application of emerging and already existing technologies to accord with our civilization's higher principles. It is "progress" conceived in this manner, rather than melodramatic rehearsals for "whistle-blowing," that offers the real challenge for engineering ethics in our time.

Those who acknowledge the two kinds of responsibility I have mentioned, those of dialogue and citizenship, face an unsettling paradox. On the one hand it is clear that, properly speaking, a person can be responsible only for his or her own decisions, actions, and their consequences. At the same time, there is an important sense in which each person is now responsible for nothing less than the future of humanity itself. Confronted with that paradox and the burdens it carries, many people are inclined to flee into the security of their private lives and the satisfactions of narrowly defined competence, areas where they feel they have at least some safety and control. That impulse, more than any other cause, is what renders technical professionals morally impotent, ready to be manipulated by whatever enticements that large corporations have at their disposal. Any effort to define and teach engineering ethics which does not produce a vital, practical, and continuing involvement in public life must be counted not just a failure, but a betrayal as well.

NOTES

1. See, for example, Stephen H. Unger, *Controlling Technology: Ethics and the Responsible Engineer* (New York: Holt, Rinehart and Winston, 1982).

2. For a defense of this method see C. Roland Christensen, et al., *Teaching and the Case Method* (Boston: Harvard Business School Press, 1987).

3. David F. Noble, *America by Design: Science, Technology and the Rise of Corporate Capitalism* (New York: Alfred Knopf, 1977).

4. Max Weber explores a similar issue in "Science as a Vocation," in H. H. Gerth and C. Wright Mills, eds., *From Max Weber* (New York: Oxford University Press, 1946).

5. Lewis Mumford, *The Myth of the Machine: The Pentagon of Power* (New York: Harcourt Brace Jovanovich, 1970), Ch. 9.

6. I discuss this topic in "Techne and Politeia," in *The Whale and the Reactor* (Chicago: University of Chicago Press, 1986), Ch. 3.

7. An early, but overly optimistic, attempt to portray computer scientists in this light can be found in Robert Boguslaw, *The New Utopians: A Study of Systems Design and Social Change* (Englewood Cliffs, N.J.: Prentice-Hall, 1965).

8. Jacques Ellul, *The Technological Society*, translated from the French by John Wilkinson (New York: Alfred Knopf, 1965).

9. An exception is John Tirman, ed., *Empty Promise: The Growing Case Against Star Wars* (Boston: Beacon Press, 1986).

10. Jonathan Schell, *The Fate of the Earth* (New York: Alfred Knopf, 1982).

11. An excellent discussion of Reagan's rhetoric here is Janice Hocker Rushing, "Ronald Reagan's 'Star Wars' Address: Mythic Containment of Technical Reasoning," *Quarterly Journal of Speech*, 72 (1986), pp. 415–33.

12. See Martin Kenneth Starr, ed., *Global Competitiveness: Getting the U.S. Back on Track* (New York: W. W. Norton, 1988).

13. Rachel Carson, *Silent Spring* (Boston: Houghton Mifflin, 1962).

14. Keith Schneider, "Science Academy Says Chemicals Do Not Necessarily Increase Crops," *New York Times*, September 8, 1989, p. 1.

15. I discuss such attempts in "Political Ergonomics: Technological Design and the Quality of Public Life," *Wissenschaftszentrum Discussion Papers*, IIUG dp 87–7 (Berlin: Wissenschaftszentrum Berlin, 1987).

Index